Land Deed Genealogy of Davidson County Tennessee

1783-1792
Volume 1

By

Helen C. & Timothy R. Marsh

Southern Historical Press, Inc.
Greenville, South Carolina

Copyright 1992
By: Southern Historical Press, Inc.

All rights reserved. No part of this publication may be
reproduced, stored in a retrieval system or transmitted
in any form or by any means without the
prior permission of the publisher.

SOUTHERN HISTORICAL PRESS, INC.
PO BOX 1267
Greenville, SC   29601

ISBN #0-89308-461-1

Printed in the United States of America

INTRODUCTION

This book is an extended abstract of the Land Deeds of Davidson County, Tennessee from the beginning of the county in 1783 through 1792, presenting a true copy of the deeds as originally recorded in the Clerk's Office in Nashville, Tennessee. Microfilm copies are on file in the Tennessee State Library and Archives in Nashville.

Old Davidson County established before' statehood encompassed a large area of middle Tennessee that included Bedford, Cheatham, Davidson, Marshall, Maury, Rutherford, part of Robertson, Sumner and Williamson. The rest of the territory was included in the Indian Lands until the signing of the Dearborn Treaty in 1806.

Helen C. and Timothy R. Marsh
Shelbyville, Tennessee
1991

EARLY MIDDLE TENNESSEE

NORTH CAROLINA MILITARY RESERVATION
1789

CONGRESSIONAL RESERVATION
April 18, 1806

Adams
Orlinda
Millsale
Youngville
Portland
Providence

Royal
Cedar Hill
Cross Plains
Den Grove
Fountain Head
Westmoreland
Siloam

ROBERTSON
Kinneys
Springfield
Calista
New Deal
Highland Academy
Rock Bridge
Euka

Stroudville
White House
SUMNER
South Tunnel
Bethpage

Sandy Springs
Cottontown
Castalian Springs

Coopertown
Greenbrier
Willard
Temple
TRO

Thomasville
Pleasant View
Ridgetop
Castalian Springs
Hartsville

Chapmansboro
Millersville
Gallatin

Sycamore
Joelton
Goodlettsville
Saundersville
Hendersonville
Laguardo
Centr

Ashland City
Whites Creek
Lickton
Old Hickory
Bellwoo

CHEATHAM
DAVIDSON
Green Hill
Martha
Lebanon

Pelway
Hermitage
Mt. Juliet
Leeville

NASHVILLE
DONELSON
WILSON

Kingston Springs
Belle Meade
Gladeville
Shop Sp

Pegram
Oak Hill
Fourth Mill
Cherry Valley

Craggie Hope
Antioch
Jurena

Bellevue
Forest Hills

Pasque
Linton
Brentwood
La Vergne

Fairview
Smyrna
1973
Cainsville

DAVIDSON COUNTY DEEDS FROM THE REGISTER'S OFFICE
GENERAL RECORDS
VOL. A

Page   1 - JONATHAN GUISE - of Davidson County, North Carolina - Made 5 Sept 1784
        Made between Christopher Guise and his wife Marget Guise of one part and
·Jonathan Guise of same place of other part, a tract of land in Florida about twenty miles
northeast from the Natchez Old Fort. Land bounded by John Stuart, Elizabeth Augusta
Carigul (or Caregal), and George Patrice, William Featherson, and James Day. Containing
706 acres containing all houses, barnes, buildings &c. Made 2 September 1784. Proven by
Thomas Molloy on 4 Oct 1784. Andrew Ewing, C.D.C. & D.R.

Page   3 - JOHN ARMSTRONG
        We, Samuel Barton, Thomas Molloy and James Shaw, directors and trustees of
the town of Nashville, State of North Carolina, sold to John Armstrong of Nashville Lot No.
61 (or 69?) and erect one well framed square log, brick or stone house. This 16 Aug 1784.
Proven 8 April 1785. Andrew Ewing, C.D.C. & D.R.

Page   3 - GEORGE DOUGHERTY
        We, Samuel Barton, Thomas Molloy and James Shaw, directors and trustees of
the town of Nashville, NC, sold George Dougherty the Lot No. 26 in the town of Nashville,
to erect, build on said lot a well framed square log, brick or stone house with a brick or
stone chimney. This 16, Aug 1784. Proven 8 April 1785.

Page   4 - MARTIN ARMSTRONG
        We, Samuel Barton, Thomas Molloy and James Shaw, directors and trustees of
the town of Nashville, NC, sold unto said Armstrong Lot No. 45 in town of Nashville, to
erect a well framed square log, brick or stone house with a brick or stone chimney. This 16
Aug 1784. Proven April 8, 1785.

Page   4 - WILLIAM CRUTCHER
        We, Samuel Barton, Thomas Molloy and James Shaw and Isaac Linsey, directors
and trustees of the town of Nashville, NC, sold to William Crutcher Lot No. 19, to build
one well frames square log, brick or stone house with a brick or stone chimney. This 26 ?,
1784. Proven 8 April 1785.

Page   5 - LARDNER CLARK - of North Carolina, No. 248
        By an Act of the General Assembly for the relief of the Officers and Soldiers

of the Continental Line, in consideration of the bravery and zeal of Robert Martin, granted unto Lardner Clark, assignee of said Robert Martin, a tract of land containing 428 acres in Davidson County on the waters of Stones River adjoining Col. James Armstrong's Military Claim of 7200 acres and Stones River, also Kenedy's west line. This 17 March 1786. Surveyed June 13, 1785 by virtue of a Military Warrant No. 1029. March 9, 1785.

Page   5 - LARDNER CLARK - North Carolina - No. 92

By an Act for the relief of the Officers and Soldiers of the Continental Line, in consideration of the bravery and zeal of Thomas Jones, a private in the said line, granted unto Lardner Clark, assignee of said Thomas Jones, a tract of land containing 228 acres in Davidson County on both sides of a branch of the west fork of Harpeth. Military Warrant No. 1232. 21 May 1785.

Page   6 - LARDNER CLARK- North Carolina - No. 205

By an Act for the relief of the Officers and Soldiers of the Continental Line, in   consideration of the bravery and zeal of William Farmer, a private in the said line, granted unto Lardner Clark and Wicoff, assignees of William Farmer, a tract of land containing 228 acres in Davidson County on the north side of Cumberland River and adjoining lands of Samuel Mason and at the river bank. 22 April 1785.

Page   7 - MEMUCAN HUNT - North Carolina - No. 731

By an Act for the relief of the Officers and Soldiers of the Continental Line, in consideration of the bravery and zeal of Jonathan Glase, a sorporal in the said line, granted unto Memucan Hunt, assignee of Samuel Glase of said Jonathan Glase, a tract of land containing 1000 acres in Davidson County on the west fork of Harpeth River bordering lands of General Tatum. December 6, 1784.

Page   8 - MARTIN ARMSTRONG

Indenture made 25 March 1785 between Captain David Hays of Davidson County, NC of one part and Col. Martin Armstrong of same place of other part, a lot in the town of Nashville, Lot No. 37 on the east side fronting the public lots, past Mr. James Sanders' line and the French Lick, being of a part of a lot of land formerly granted by the Commissioners, to wit, Samuel Barton, Thomas Molloy and James Shaw to Obediah Terrell by deed dated 26 July 1784 and afterwards granted by said Terrell to said Hays, dated 25 March 1785. 5 April 1785.

Page   9 - LARDNER CLARK

We, Samuel Barton, Thomas Molloy, James Shaw and Isaac Linsey, directors and trustees of the town of Nashville, NC, sold unto Lardner Clark the Lot No. 62 in Nashville, to erect and build a well framed square lof, brick of stone house with a brick or stone chimney. 8 April 1785.

Page   9 - MARTIN ARMSTRONG

This 24 March 1785, made between Lardner Clark, merchant in town of Nashville, of one part and Martin Armstrong of other part. Said Lardner Clark sold unto Martin Armstrong one half of a lot of one acre of land in town of Nashville known to be on

2

the east side nearest the public building and being part of No. 7 formerly granted by Samuel Barton, Thomas Molloy and other Commissioners, by deed dated 6 July 1784. 8 April 1785.

Page   10 - WILLIAM BLOUNT
        We, Samuel Barton, Thomas Molloy and James Shaw, directors and trustees of the town of Nashville, sold unto William Blount Lot No. 56 in Nashville, to erect and build a well framed square lof, brick or stone house with a brick or stone chimney. This 16 Aug 1784. 8 April 1785.

Page   10 - WILLIAM LYTLE
        We, Samuel Barton, Thomas Molloy and James Shaw, directors and trustees of the town of Nashville, sold Lot No. 37 to William Lytle, shall within three years after date of conveyance, build and erect and finish on said lot one well framed square log, brick or stone house with a brick or stone chimney. This 16 Aug 1784. 8 April 1785.

Page   11 - JAMES ROBINSON
        We, Samuel Barton, Thomas Molloy and James Shaw, directors and trustees of town of Nashville, conveyed unto James Robinson Lot No. 24 and within three years of daye of coveyance, build a well framed square log, brick or stone house with brick or stone chimney. This 15 Aug 1784. 8 April 1785.

Page   11 - SAMUEL MARTIN
        We, Samuel Barton, Thomas Molloy and James Shaw, directors and trustees of town of Nashville, conveyed unto Samuel Martin Lot No. 43 in Nashville and within three years of date of conveyance build a well framed square log, brick or stone house with brick or stone chimney. This 16 Aug 1784. 8 April 1785.

Page   12 - JULIUS SANDERS
        We, Samuel Barton, Thomas Molloy and Jamws Shaw conveyed unto Julius Sanders Lot No. 75 in town of Nashville and within three years of date of conveyance erect and build a well framed square log, brick or stone house with brick or stone chimney. This 26 July 1784. 8 April 1785.

Page   12 - JULIUS SANDERS
        We, Samuel Barton, Thomas Molloy and James Shaw conveyed unto Julius Sanders Lot No. 44 in town of Nashville and within three years of date of conveyance, erect and build a well framed square log, brick or stone house with brick of stone chimney. This 26 July 1784. 8 April 1785.

Page   13 - JAMES ROBERTSON
We, Samuel Barton, THomas Molloy and James Shaw, directors and trustees of the town of Nashville, conveyed unto James Robertson Lot No. 9 in Nashville and within three years of Conveyance to erect and finish a well framed square log, brick or stone house with a brick or stone chimney. This 15 Aug 1784. 8 April 1785.

Page   13 - LARDNER CLARK
        We, Samuel Barton, THomas Molloy and James Shaw, conveyed unto Lardner

Clark Lot No. 11 in Nashville and within three years build and finish a well framed square log, brick or stone house with brick or stone chimney. This 6 July 1784. 8 April 1785.

Page 14 - JAMES HOGGATT - Deed of Lease

Indenture made 1 March 1785 between Daniel Oglesby of one part and James Hoggatt of other part, sold unto James Hoggatt all that tract of land lying in South Carolina and District of Ninety Six which was surveyed for Mary King, lying on a small river running into Broad River formerly called "Collins River" now "Enoree River" and containing about 350 acres. 4 April 1785.

Page 15 - DEED OF RELEASE

Indenture made 2 (blank) 1785 between Daniel Oglesby of one part and James Hoggatt of other part, conveyed unto James Hoggatt all that tract of land lying in State of Carolina and District of Ninety Six which was surveyed for Mary King, on a small river running into Broad River, formerly called Collins River, now Enoree River and containing 350 acres.

Page 16 - JOHN RICE

This indenture made 8 July 1785 between George Flynn of one part and John Rice of other part. Flynn sold unto John Rice one Lot No. 42 of one acre of land in town of Nashville and he shall within three years of this date and after 26 July last, erect, build and finish on said lot one well framed square log, brick or stone house with brick or stone chimney. July 8, 1785.

Page 16 - WILLIAM MECKLIN

We, Samuel Barton, Thomas Molloy and James Shaw, directors and trustees of Nashville, conveyed unto William Mecklin Lot No. 55 and shall within three years of this date, build a well framed square log, brick or stone house with brick or stone chimney. This 15 Aug 1785. July 8, 1785.

Page 17 - JAMES BOSLEY

This indenture made 6 July 1785 between William Mecklin of Davidson County, NC of one part and James Bosley of same place. William Mecklin conveyed unto James Bosley a certain lot of an acre of land in the town of Nashville known by No. 55 being the lot formerly granted to William Mecklin by the Commissioners of said town by deed dated 15 Aug 1784. July 8, 1785.

Page 17 - James Shaw

We, Samuel Barton, THomas Molloy and James Shaw, directors and trustees of town of Nashville, conveyed unto James Shaw Lot No. 22 in Nashville and within three years of date of conveyence build a well framed square log, brick or stone house with a brick or stone chimney. This 30 July 1784. 8 July 1785.

Page 17 - WILLIAM HAMILTON

(2nd page) We, Samuel Barton, Thomas Molloy and James Shaw, directors and trustees of town of Nashville, conveyed unto William Hamilton Lot No. 63 in Nashville and within three years build a well framed square log, brick or stone house with brick or stone chimney.

4

Page 17 - JOHN RICE

(2nd page) I, Thomas Fletcher of Davidson County, NC, grantee of Samuel Barton, Thomas Molloy and James Shaw, directors and trustees of the town of Nashville, conveyed unto John Rice Lot No. 30 in town of Nashville and shall within three years of date of conveyance from 30 July last past erect, build and finish on said lot one well framed square log, brick or stone house with a brick or stone chimney. This 30 June 1785. 8 July 1785.

Page 18 - JAMES BOSLEY

This indenture made 5 July 1785 between Joseph Ramsey of Davidson County, NC of one part and James Bosley of same place pf other part. Joseph Ramsey sold unto James Bosley a certain lot of one acre of land in Nashville known as Lot No. 63.

This indenture made 6 July 1785 between Joseph Ramsey of one part and James Bosley of other part. Joseph Ramsey sold unto James Bosley a certain lot of one acre of land in Nashville and known as Lot No. 63, being the lot formerly granted to William Hamilton by deed dated 30 July 1784. 8 July 1785.

Page 19 - JAMES BOSLEY

This indenture made 5 July 1785 between George Nevill of Davidson County, NC of one part and James Bosley of same place of other part. George Nevill conveyed unto James Bosley a certain lot of one acre of land in the town of Nashville and known as Lot No. 82.

This indenture made 6 July 1785 between George Nevill and James Bosley for a certain lot of one acre of land in the town of Nashville and known by Lot No. 82, being the lot formerly granted to George Nevill by the Commissioners of said town by deed dated 16 Aug 1784. July 8, 1785.

Page 20 - JONATHAN DRAKE

We, Samuel Barton, Thomas Molloy, James Shaw and Isaac Linsey, directors and trustees of the town of Nashville, grant unto Jonathan Drake Lot No. 8 in town of Nashville and shall from three years of date of conveyance erect, build and finish a well framed square log, brick or stone house with a brick or stone chimney. This 30 July 1784. July 8, 1785.

Page 20 - JAMES SHAW

We, Samuel Barton, Thomas Molloy, James Shaw and Isaac Linsey, directors and trustees of the town of Nashville, grant unto James Shaw Lot No. 51 in town of Nashville and shall within three years from date of conveyance erect, build and finish a well square log, brick or stone house with a brick or stone chimney. This 30 July 1784. July 8, 1785.

Page 21 - GEORGE NEVILLE

We, Samuel Barton, Thomas Molloy and James Shaw, directors and trustees of town of Nashville, conveyed unto George Neville Lot No. 87 in Nashville and shall within three years from date of conveyance erect, build and finish a well framed square log, brick or stone house with a brick or stone chimney. This 16 May 1784. July 8, 1785.

Page 21 - ABEDNEGO LLEWALLEN

We, Samuel Barton, Thomas Molloy, James Shaw and Isaac Linsey conveyed unto Abednego Llewallen Lot No. 23 in Nashville and shall within three years of date of conveyance erect, build and finish a well framed square log, brick or stone house with a brick or stone chimney. This 9 July 1784. July 8, 1785.

Page   22 - JAMES MAULDIN

We, Samuel Barton, Thomas Molloy and James Shaw, directors and trustees of town of Nashville, conveyed unto James Mauldin Lot No. 17 in Nashville and shall within three years from date of conveyance erect, build and finish a well framed square log, brick or stone house with a brick or stone chimney. This 6 Aug 1784. July 8, 1785.

Page   22 - SAMUEL BARTON

We, Samuel Barton, THomas Molloy, James Shaw and Isaac Linsey conveyed unto Samuel Barton Lot No. 73 in Nashville and shall within three years of date of conveyance erect, build and finish a well framed square log, brick or stone house with brick or stone chimney. This 30 July 1784. July 8, 1785.

Page   23 - ANTHONY CRUTCHER

We, Samuel Barton, Thomas Molloy, James Shaw and Isaac Linsey conveyed unto Anthony Crutcher Lot No. 31 in Nashville and shall within three years of date of conveyance erect, build and finish a well framed square log, brick or stone house with brick or stone chimney. This 26 July 1784. July 8, 1785.

Page   23 - DAVID LOONEY

We, Samuel Barton, Thomas Molloy and James Shaw, directors and trustees of Nashville, conveyed unto David Looney Lot No. 33 in Nashville and shall within three years of date of conveyance erect, build and finish a well framed square log, brick or stone house with brick or stone chimney. This 16 Aug 1784. July 8, 1785.

Page   24 - LANDON CARTER

We, Samuel Barton, Thomas Molloy, James Shaw and Isaac Linsey, conveyed unto Landon Carter Lot No. 76 in Nashville and shall erect, build and finish a well framed square lof, brick or stone house with brick or stone chimney within three years of date of conveyance. This 16 Aug 1784. July 8, 1785.

Page   24 - ROBERT THOMPSON

We, Samuel Barton, Thomas Molloy, James Shaw and Isaac Linsey, conveyed unto Robert Thompson Lot No. 77 in Nashville and shall within three years erect, build and finish a well framed square log, brick or stone house with brick or stone chimney. This 30 July 1784. July 8, 1785.

Page   25 - WILLIAM CAGE

We, Samuel Barton, Thomas Molloy, James Shaw and Isaac Linsey, conveyed unto William Cage Lot No. 40 in Nashville and shall within three years from date of conveyance erect, build and finish a well framed square log, brick or stone house with brick or stone chimney.. This 16 July 1784. July 8, 1785.

Page   25 - ANDREW LUCAS

We, Samuel Barton, Thomas Molloy, James Shaw and Isaac Linsey conveyed unto Andrew Lucas Lot No. 34 in Nashville and shall within three years of date of conveyance erect, build and finish a well framed square log, brick or stone house with brick or stone chimney. This 30 July 1784. July 8, 1785.

Page   26 - JAMES THOMPSON

We, Samuel Barton, Thomas Molloy, James Shaw and Isaac Linsey conveyed unto James Thompson Lot No. 48 in Nashville and shall within three years from date of conveyance erect, build and finish a well framed square log, brick or stone house with brick or stone chimney. This 13 July 1784. July 8, 1785.

Page   26 - THOMAS FLETCHER

We, Samuel Barton, Thomas Molloy and James Shaw conveyed unto Thomas Fletcher Lot No. 30 in Nashville and shall within three years from date of conveyance erect, build and finish a well framed square log, brick or stone house with brick or stone chimney. This 6 April 1785. April 7, 1785.

Page   27 - ANDREW EWING

We, Samuel Barton, Thomas Molloy, James Shaw and Isaac Linsey conveyed unto Andrew Ewing Lot No. 18 in Nashville and shall within three years of date of conveyance erect, build and finish a well framed square log, brick or stone house with brick or stone chimney. This 30 July 1784. July 8, 1785.

Page   27 - JAMES TODD

We, Samuel Barton, Thomas Molloy, James Shaw and Isaac Linsey conveyed unto James Todd Lot No. 60 in Nashville and shall within three years of date of conveyance erect, build and finish a well framed square log, brick or stone house with brick or stone chimney. This 26 July 1784. Oct 5, 1785.

Page   28 - JAMES BOSLEY

This indenture made 5 July 1785 between Samuel Martin of Davidson County, NC of one part and James Bosley of other part, conveyed unto said Bosley a certain lot of one acre in Nashville and known by Lot No. 43.
This indenture made 6 July 1785 between Samuel Martin of one part and James Bosley of other part, for a certain lot of one acre of land in town of Nashville known by No. 43 being said lot formerly granted to (blank) by Commissioners by deed dated 16 Aug (blank). July 8, 1785.

Page   29 - JOHN BOYD

We, Samuel Barton, Thomas Molloy and James Shaw conveyed unto John Boyd of Nashville Lot No. 1 in town of Nashville and shall within three years of date of conveyance erect, build and finish a well framed square log, brick or stone house with brick or stone chimney. This 16 Aug 1784. Oct 5, 1785.

Page   29 - JOHN BOYD

We, Samuel Barton, Thomas Molloy and Jamws Shaw conveyed unto John Boyd of Nashville, NC a Lot No. 12 in town of Nashville and shall within three years of date of conveyance erect, build and finish a well framed square log, brick or stone house with brick or stone chimney. This 16 Aug 1784. Oct 5, 1785.

Page   30 - JOHN BOYD

We, Samuel Barton, Thomas Molloy and James Shaw conveyed unto John Boyd of Nashville Lot No. 13 in Nashville and shall within three years from date of conveyance erect, build and finish a well framed square log, brick or stone house with brick or stone chimney. This 16 Aug 1784. Oct 5, 1785.

Page   30 - JOHN BOYD

This indenture made 3 Oct 1785 between James Todd of Davidson County of one part and John Boyd of same place of other part. Said Todd sold unto John Boyd one lot of an acre of land in Nashville known as Lot No. 60. Said lot granted to James Todd dated 26 July 1784. Oct 5, 1785.

Page   31 - THOMAS MARTIN

This indenture made 7 Sept 1785 between Andrew Lucas of Davidson County of one part and Thomas Martin of same place of other part. Said Lucas sold unto Thomas Martin a lot of one acre of land in Nashville and known as Lot No. 34. Said lot was granted to Andrew Lucas dated 30 July 1784. 5 Oct 1785.

Page   31 - ROBERT HAYS

This indenture made 6 Jan 1785 between Captain Anthony Crutcher of Davidson County of one part and Captain Robert Hays of same place of other part. Captain Crutcher sold unto Captain Robert Hays one half of a lot of one acre of land in Nashville and known by Lot No. 8. Oct 6, 1785.

Page   32 - ALEXANDER McENTIRE

We, Samuel Barton, Thomas Molloy, James Shaw and Isaac Linsey, directors and trustees of town of Nashville, conveyed unto Alexander McEntire Lot No. 65 in Nashville and shall within three years of date of conveyance erect, build and finish a well framed square log, brick or stone house with brick or stone chimney. This 26 July 1784. Oct 6, 1785.

Page   33 - GEORGE FLYN

We, Samuel Barton, Thomas Molloy, James Shaw and Isaac Linsey conveyed unto George Flyn Lot No. 42 in Nashville and shall within three years of date of conveyance erect, build and finish a well framed square log, brick or stone house with brick or stone chimney. This 26 July 1784. Oct 5, 1785.

Page   33 - RUSSELL GOWER

We, Samuel Barton, Thomas Molloy, James Shaw and Isaac Linsey conveyed unto Russell Gower Lot No. 30 in Nashville and shall within three years of date of conveyance erect, build and finish a well framed square log, brick or stone house with brick or stone chimney. This 26 July 1784. Oct 5, 1785.

Page   34 - THOMAS MOLLOY

We, Samuel Barton, Thomas Molloy, James Shaw and Isaac Linsey conveyed unto Thomas Molloy Lot No. 21 in Nashville and within three years of date of conveyance erect, build and finish a well framed square log, brick and stone house and brick   or stone chimney. This 30 July 1784. 4 Oct 1785.

Page   34 - JOHN McFARLAND

We, Samuel Barton, Thomas Molloy, James Shaw and Isaac Linsey conveyed unto John McFarland Lot No. 78 in Nashville and shall within three years of date of conveyence erect, build and finish a well framed square log, brick or stone house and brick or stone chimney. This 16 Aug 1784. Oct 4, 1785.

Page   35 - JOHN BOYD

This indenture made 17 Sept 1785 between Julius Sanders of Davidson County of one part and John Boyd of same place of other part. Julius Sanders conveyed unto John Boyd one lot of an acre of land in Nashville and known as Lot No. 44. Said lot being granted to Julius Sanders dated by deed July 26, 1784. Oct 5, 1785.

Page   35 - PETER CAFFREY

We, Samuel Barton, Thomas Molloy and James Shaw conveyed unto Peter Caffrey Lot No. 35 in Nashville and shall within three years of date of conveyance erect, build and finish a well framed square log, brick or stone house with brick or stone chimney. This 16 Aug 1784. Oct 5, 1785.

Page   36 - BARKLEY WILLIAM POLLOCK

This indenture made 5 Oct 1785 between Ebenezer Titus of Davidson County of one part and Barkley William Pollock of same place. Said Titus conveyed unto Barkley William Pollock a certain lot of one acre of land in Nashville known as Lot No. 5, being the lot formerly granted to Jacob Castleman by deed dated 26 July 1784. Oct 5, 1785.

Page   37 - BENJAMIN PETTIT

We, Samuel Barton, Thoomas Molloy and James Shaw conveyed unto Benjamin Pettit Lot No. 29 in Nashville and shall within three years of date of conveyance erect, build and finish a well framed square log, brick or stone house with brick or stone chimney. This Aug 16, 1784. Oct 5, 1785.

Page   37 - B. WILLIAM POLLOCK

This indenture made 4 Oct 1785 between Ebenezer Titus of Davidson COunty and Barkley William Pollock of same place of other part. Ebenezer Titus conveyed unto Barkley William Pollock a certain lot of one acre of land in Nashville known as Lot No. 4, being formerly granted to Levi Hand by deed dated July 26, 1784. Oct 5, 1785.

Page   38 - JAMES THOMPSON

This indenture made 29 July 1785 between Robert Thompson of Davidson County of one part and James Thompson of same place of other part, conveyed unto James Thompson one lot of an acre of land in Nashville and known as Lot No. 77 and being the lot granted to Robert Thompson by deed dated July 30, 1784. Oct 5, 1785.

Page   38 - JAMES TROWSDALL - NC - No. 1

James Trowsdall was conveyed a tract of land containing 640 acres in Davidson County. Adjoining lands of Tilman Dixon and Thomas Spencer. Wit: Alex Martin, Esq., our Governor &c at Newbern the 4 Dec 1784. Surveyed for Hugh Magary April 24, 1784. Entered Dec 31, 1783.

Page   39 - JAMES RAY - NC - No. 3

For ten pounds per one hundred acres, granted to James Ray a tract of land containing 640 acres in Davidson County, adjoining a branch of west fork of Mill Creek, lands of said Ray and Daniel Hogan. Wit: Alexander Martin, Esq., our Governor &c Nov 10, 1784. Surveyed for said Ray 28 April 1784 by James Mulherin in consequence of a warrant granted by Samuel Barton, Entry Taker for said county No. 39, entered Dec 31, 1783.

Page   40 - JAMES MENESS

We, Samuel Barton, Thomas Molloy and James Shaw conveyed unto James Meness Lot No. 32 in Nashville and shall within three years of date of conveyance erect, build and finish a well framed square log, brick or stone house with brick or stone chimney. This 16 Aug 1784. April 7, 1786.

Page   40 - OLIVE SHAW (female)

This indenture made 3 Oct 1785 between Lardner Clark of Davidson County, Esq., of one part and Olive Shaw of same place of other part, a lot or parcel of land known as Lot No. 46 in Nashville. Which lot or parcel of land was by deed of conveyance, dated July 26, 1784 granted and conveyed by the directors and trustees of town of Lardner Clark, deed dated July 26, 1784. April 7, 1786.

Page   41 - LARDNER CLARK

This indenture made 22 Aug 1785 between Olive Shaw of Davidson County of one part and Lardner Clark of same place of other part, conveyed unto Olive Shaw all that lot or parcel of land known by Lot No. 10 in Nashville. Said lot by deed dated July 26, 1784 granted and conveyed by the directors and trustees of said Olive Shaw. Oct 7, 1786.

Page   42 - JOHN BOYD

This indenture made 4 March 1786 between Benjamin Castleman of Davidson County of one part and John Boyd of same place of other part, conveyed unto John Boyd a lot of an acre of land in Nashville and known as Lot No. 3, formerly granted by deed dated July 26, 2784. April 5, 1786.

Page   43 - ARCHIBALD LYTLE - NC

By an Act for the relief of the Office and Soldiers for the Continental Line, in consideration for the bravery and zeal of Archibald Lytle, Esq., Lieutenant Colonel Commander in the Continental line, granted unto Archibald Lytle a tract of land containing 7200 acres in Davidson County on the west fork of Stones River. Also on Lytles Creek and Stones River. 5 Jan 1786. Entered 29 Mar 1785 and surveyed by Robert Hayes. Military Warrant No. 1.

Page   44 - ENSEBIUS BUSHNELL

This indenture made 30 June 1786 between Lardner Clark of one part and Ensebius Bushnell of other part, both of Davidson County, NC. For $18.00 by E. Bushnell was conveyed a certain lot of one acre of land in Nashville and known as Lot No. 28, formerly granted to James Bisswell dated July 26, 1784. July 5, 1786.

Page   44 - SAMUEL JONES - NC - No. 12

By an Act for the relief of the Officers and Soldiers of the Continental Line, in consideration of the bravery and zeal of Samuel Jones, a Captain in the Continental line, was granted a tract of land containing 3840 acres in Davidson County on Spring and Cedar Creeks on south side of Cumberland River. Registered in Register's office. Wit: Richard Caswell, Esq., our Governor &c at Kinston, 14 March 1786. Surveyed Oct 13, 1784 by Joseph Brook by virtue of a Military Warrant No. 176. Entered July 9, 1784.

Page   45 - JOHN CRADDOCK - NC - Onslow County

This indenture made 22 Feb 1786 between Captain Samuel Jones, late of Captain in the Continental Line of this state of one part and Captain John Craddock of same place of other part, conveyed unto John Craddock a parcel or tract of land containing 3200 acres, lying and being within the State of North Carolina and within bounds of the lands reserved by an Act of Assembly of said State for the Officers and Soldiers of the Continental Line and surveyed for Captain Samuel Jones. This July 15, 1786 by oaths of Thomas Evens. Wit: William Slade and John McCollough.

Page   46 - JAMES MOORE - Davidson County, NC

This indenture made 20 May 1786 between John Craddock, late Captain in the Continental Army of the Continental Line of this State of one part and James Moore of Davidson County, NC of other part, Patent dated 14 March 1786 did grant unto Captain Samuel Jones a tract of land containing 3840 acres in Davidson County, deed dated Feb 22, 1786, sold unto John Craddock 3200 acres being part of 3840 acres. The 3200 being on south side of Cumberland River on Spring and Cedar Creeks. July 5, 1786 by oaths of John Rice and Thomas Molloy.

Page   46 - JOHN BOYD

This indenture made 18 May 1786 between Andrew Ewing of Davidson County of one part and John Boyd of same place of other part, conveyed unto John Boyd one lot of an acre of land in town of Nashville, known as Lot No. 18 formerly granted by the Commissioners of Nashville to said Ewing by deed dated July 30, 1784. July 4, 1786.

Page   47 - LEWIS & HICKMAN

This indenture made 1 Sept 1786 between Barkley William Pollock of Davidson County of one part and James Martin Lewis and Edwin Hickman of same place of other part, conveyed unto Lewis and Hickman all that parcel or piece of land in town of Nashville and known by Lot No. 5. Deed proved by Moses Shelby. Oct 5, 1786.

Page   48 - WILLIAM MOORE

We, Samuel Barton, Thomas Molloy, James Shaw and Isaac Linsey conveyed unto William Moore Lot No. 54 in Nashville and shall within three years from date of conveyance erect, build and finish a well framed square log, brick or stone house with brick or stone chimney. This 30 July 1784. Oct 5, 1786.

Page 48 - JOHN BOYD

This indenture made 29 Sept 1786 between William Moore of one part and John Boyd of other part, both of Davidson County, conveyed unto William Moore Lot No. 54 in town of Nashville. Proven by oath of Esquire Grant Oct 5, 1786.

Page 49 - JOHN FOREMAN

We, Samuel Barton, Thomas Molloy, James Shaw and Isaac Linsey conveyed unto John Foreman Lot No. 36 in Nashville and shall within three years of date of conveyance erect, build and finish a well framed square log, brick or stone house with brick or stone chimney. This 30 July 1784. Oct 4, 1786.

Page 49 - JAMES SANDERS

We, Samuel Barton, Thomas Molloy and James Shaw conveyed unto James Sanders Lot No. 47 in Nashville and shall within three years of date of conveyance erect, build and finish a well framed square log, brick or stone house with brick or stone chimney. This 16 Aug 1784. Oct 5, 1786.

Page 50 - ROBERT THOMPSON - NC - No. 3

By an Act for the relief of the Officers and Soldiers of the Continental Line, in consideration of the services of Col. Martin Armstrong, surveyor of the lands, granted unto Robert Thompson, assignee of said Armstrong, a tract of land containing 100 acres in Davidson County on waters of John Fletcher's Lick Creek adjoining lands of James Thompson. This Feb 16, 1786. Surveyed by Robert Weakley 12 May 1785. Entered Mar 5, 1785.

Page 51 - JOHN FORDE - NC - No. 10

By an Act for the relief of the Officers and Soldiers of the Continental Line, in consideration of the service of Col Martin Armstrong, surveyor of lands, granted unto John Forde, assignee of said Armstrong, a tract of land containing 640 acres in Davidson County on north side of Cumnerland River and on the head of Thomas' Creek, adjoining Nowlan's Preemption. This Feb 16, 1786. Surveyed by Robert Nelson July 15, 1785. Entered March 29, 1785. No. 142.

Page 51 - JAMES ROBERTSON - NC - No. 2

By an Act for the relief of the Officers and Soldiers of the Continental Line, in consideration of the service of Col. Martin Armstrong, granted unto James Robertson, assignee of said Armstrong, a tract of land containing 100 acres of land in Davidson County in the bend of the Cumberland River above the mouth of Richland Creek adjoining other lands of said Robertson. This Feb 16, 1786. Surveyed by Henry Rutherford. Entered July 5, 1785. No. 1092.

Page 52 - JAMES ROBERTSON - NC - No. 13

By an Act for the relief of the Officers and Soldiers of the Continental Line, in consideration of the service of Col. Martin Armstrong, granted unto James Robertson a assignee of said Armstrong, granted unto said Robertson a tract of land containing 150 acres in Davidson County on south side of Cumberland River a small distance below the mouth of Whites Creek. This 16 Feb 1786. Surveyed by Henry Rutherford and entered May 9, 1785, No. 986.

Page   53 - JOHN RICHARDSON - NC - No. 172
By an Act for the relief of the Officers and Soldiers of the Continental Line, in consideration of the bravery and zeal of John Richardson, a private in the said line, granted unto said John Robertson a tract of land containing 274 acres in Davidson County on the waters of Browns Creek adjoining Samuel Barton's and Francis Armstrong's Preemptions. This Mar 7, 1786. Surveyed by Thomas Molloy Feb 17, 1785. Entered July 9, 1784. Warrant No. 391.

Page   54 - WILLIAM SEXTON - NC - No. 171
By an Act for the relief of the Officers and Soldiers of the Continental Line, in consideration of the bravery and zeal of William Sexton, a private in the said line, granted unto said Sexton a tract of land containing 640 acres of land in Davidson County on the south side of Cumberland River and on the waters of Cedar Lick Creek. This 7 Mar 1786. Surveyed by James Mulherin July 27, 1785 by virtue of a Military Warrant No. 826. Entered July 24, 1784.

Page   54 - JOHN JENNINGS - NC - No. 114
By an Act for the relief of the Officers and Soldiers of the Continental Line, in consideration of the bravery and zeal of John Jennings, a private in the said line, conveyed unto John Jennings a tract of land containing 365 acres in Davidson County on south side of Cumberland River on Spencers Creek adjoining John Kanes' corner. This 7 Mar 1786. Surveyed by James Mulherin Nov 12, 1785 by virtue of a Military Warrant No. 825. Entered Aug 9, 1785.

Page   55 - THOMAS SAWYER - NC - No. 255
By an Act for the relief of the Officers and Soldiers of the Continental Line, in consideration of the bravery and zeal of Thomas Sawyer, a private in the said line, granted unto said Sawyer a tract of land containing 274 acres in Davidson County on south side of Cumberland River joining Russell Gower's lands. This 7 Mar 1786. Surveyed by Thomas Molloy by virtue of a Warrant No. 827. Entered June 30, 1785.

Page   56 - ELISHA DAVIS - NC - No. 108
By an Act for the relief of the Officers and Soldiers of the Continental Line, in consideration of the bravert and zeal of Banjamin Easeman, a private in the said line, granted unto Elisha Davis, assignee of said Easeman, a tract of land containing 274 acres in Davidson Countyon south side of Cumberland River and on waters of Spencers Creek joining Thomas Spencer's corner. This 7 Mar 1786. Surveyed by James Mulherin Nov 11, 1786 by virtue of a Military Warrant No. 825. Entered Aug 9, 1785.

Page   57 - MARMADUKE SCOTT - NC - No. 130
By an Act for the relief of the Officers and Soldiers of the Continental Line, in consideration of the bravery and zeal of William Thomas, a private in the said line,

granted unto Marmaduke Scott, assignee of William Thomas, a tract of land containing 640 acres in Davidson County on both sides on the east fork of Yellow Creek and south side of Cumberland River. This 14 Mar 1786. Surveyed by Jos. Brock 4 April 1785 by virtue of a Warrant No. 416. Entered 11 Dec 1784.

Page   57 - SILAS LINTOR - NC - No. 196
        By an Act for the relief of the Officers and Soldiers of the Continental Line, in consideration of the bravery and zeal of Silas Lintor, a private in the said line, granted a tract of land containing 640 acres in Davidson County on south side of Cumberland River above the mouth of Spencers Creek and adjoining Thomas Spencer's survey. This 7 Mar 1786. Surveyed by James Mulherin Nov 11, 1786 by virtue of a Military Warrant No. 829. Entered Aug 9, 1786.

Page   58 - WILLIAM MABANE - NC - No. 13
        By an Act for the relief of the Officers and Soldiers of the Continental Line, in consideration of the bravery and zeal of Robert Mabane, a Lieut Col. Commandant in said line, granted unto William Mabane, heir of said Robert Mabane, a tract of land containing 7210 acres in Davidson County on both sides of the west fork of Big Harpeth River joining Major Abson Tatone's north and south boundary of his 5000 acre survey. This 4 Mar 1786. Surveyed by John Donnaldson 7 May 1785 by virtue of a Military Warrant No. 162. Entered Feb 7, 1784.

Page   59 - FRANCIS CHILD - NC - No. 77
        By an Act for the relief of the Officers and Soldiers of the Continental Line, in consideration of the bravery and zeal of Francis Child, a captain in the said line, granted unto Francis Child a tract of land containing 3840 acres in Davidson County on the (blank) Cain Fork, the waters of Cumberland River beginning a small distance from a large spring. This 14 Mar 1786. Surveyed by William Dobbins Mar 23, 1785 by virtue of a Military Warrant No. 3??(illegible). Entered July 9, 1784.

Page   60 - JONATHAN DRAKE - NC - No. 210
        By an Act for the relief of the Officers and Soldiers of the Continental Line, in consideration of the bravery and zeal of William Leaton, a private in the said line, granted unto Jonathan Drake, assignee of said Leaton, a tract of land containing 640 acres in Davidson County on north side of Cumberland and south side of Whites Creek and joining Fred Stump's corner on the river bank, and John Drake's land. This 17 Mar 1786. Surveyed by Henry Rutherford Dec 2, 1784 by virtue of a Military Warrant No. 608. Entered July 13, 1784.

Page   60 - JONATHAN DRAKE - NC - No. 180
        By an Act for the relief of the Officers and Soldiers of the Continental Line, in consideration of the bravery and zeal of James Christian, a private in the said line, granted unto Jonathan Drake, assignee of said James Christian, a tract of land containing 640 acres in Davidson County. Beginning on the banks of Cumberland River, the lower corner of Isaac Butler's survey of 228 acres. This 7 Mar 1786. Surveyed by James Mulherin by virtue of a Military Warrant No. 143. Entered Feb 7, 1784.

Page   61 - JESSEE STEAD - NC - No. 82

By an Act for the relief of the Officers and Soldiers of the Continental Line, in consideration of the bravery and zeal of Jessee Stead, a Lieutenant in the said line, was granted a tract of land containing 2560 acres in Davidson County on the waters of the main fork of Harpeth River on a large branch known by the name of Leipers Fork. Beginning about half a mile above Leiper's Spring. This 14 Mar 1786. Surveyed by B.W. Pollock by virtue of a Military Warrant No. 53. Entered Oct (blank).

Page   62 - LAZARUS FLORON - NC - No. 7

By an Act for the relief of the Officers and Soldiers of the Continental Line, in consideration of the bravery and zeal of Lazarus Floron, a pricate in the said line, granted unto said Floron a tract of land containing 274 acres in Davidson County on Little Harpeth, joining James Crockett's land and Andrew Crockett's Preemption. This 16 Feb 1786. Surveyed by John Buchanan May 4, 1785 by virtue of a Military Warrant No. 988. Entered Oct 29, 1784.

Page   63 - WILLIAM ARMSTRONG - NC - No. 25

By an Act for the relief of the Officers and Soldiers of the Continental Line, in consideration of the bravery and zeal of William Armstrong, a captain in the said line, granted a tract of land containing 3840 acres in Davidson County on the south side of Cumberland River before the first bluff below the second island below Red River. This 14 Mar 1786. Surveyed by Ed Harris July 21, 1785 by virtue of a Military Warrant No. 62. Entered Nov 30, 1784.

Page   64 - RICHARD FLOWRON - NC - No. 9

By an Act for the relief of the Officers and Soldiers of the Continental Line, granted unto Richard Flowron, a private in the said line, granted a tract of land containing 274 acres of land in Davidson County on the south side of Cumberland River near the little south road adjoining Robert Roseberry's Preemption, John Cockrill's line, and Peter Turney's line. This 16 Feb 1786. Surveyed by Thomas Molloy Apr 11, 1785 by virtue of a Military Warrant No. 989. Entered July 27, 1784.

Page   64 - JOHN SAPPINGTON

This indenture made 10 Oct 1786 between Col. James Robertson of Davidson County, NC of one part and John Sappington of same place of other part. James Robertson sold unto John Sappington the one half of the Lot No. 24 in Nashville. It is not the intention of said Col. Robertson that the indenture should interfer with Captain Julius Sander's large dwelling house which is supposed to be on the half lot. This April 5, 1786.

Page   65 - JOHN SAPPINGTON

I, James Bosley of Davidson County, sold unto Doctor John Sappington of same place, all that tract of land in Davidson County. Beginning on the south bank of Cumberland River, John Boyd's north west corner, and containing 200 acres. This 24 Mar 1787. 5 April 1787.

Page   66 - MATHIAS YOCUM

This indenture made 7 Sept 1786 between Thomas Denton and his wife Sarah

15

Denton of the County of Mercer of one part and Mathias Yocum of same place of other part, sold unto Mathias Yocum a certain tract or parcel of land containing 320 acres on the middle fork of Red River in Davidson County. Proven by David Kay, Esq., April 5, 1787 also likewise William Moore.

Page   67 - JOHN BOYD
        This indenture made 6 Mar 1787 between James Bosley of Davidson County of one part and John Boyd of Nashville of other part, said Bosley sold unto John Boyd a tract of land containing 43 acres on the south side of Cumberland River. Beginning at Doctor Sappington's east corner on the bank of the river. April 5, 1787.

Page   68 - THOMAS MOLLOY
        This indenture made 15 Dec 1786 between Thomas Callendar of New Hanover County, town of Wilmington, State of North Carolina of one part and Julius Sanders and Thomas Molloy of Davidson County of other part, sold unto said Sanders and Molloy a tract of land containing 384 acres in Davidson County on the north side of Cumberland River, it being part of a tract of 3840 acres granted to said Callender by the State of North Carolina for his services as Captain in the Continental Line of State of North Carolina by grant dated Mar 14, 1786 and No. 49. This 21 Dec 1786 before Anthony Bledsoe a witness. John Williams, Judge, S.C.L.D. This 6 April 1787.

Page   69 -JAMES LENEAR
        This indenture made 3 April 1787 between James Robertson of one part and James Lenear, both of Davidson County, sold unto James Lenear one equal undivided half part of a lot of ground in town of Nashville and known as Lot No. 9, it being that part of said lot that joins Lardner Clark. Acknowledged April 5, 1787.

Page   70 - CHRISTIAN CRIPPS
        James Bosley of Davidson County, NC, sold unto Christian Cripps of same place, all that tract of land lying in the (blank). Beginning on the bank of Cumberland River, northeast corner of George Freeland's grant right, and to Sandy Hollow. Containing 25 acres. This 21 Mar 1787. April 5, 1787.

Page   71 - LENEAR & CRUTCHER
        This indenture made 15 Dec 1786 between Eusebius Bushnell of one part and Antony Crutcher and James Lenear of other part, both of Davidson County, sold unto Crutcher and Lenear a lot in Nashville, of one acre of land and known as Lot No. 28, being the lot formerly granted to James Bisnell (Biswell ?) by the Commissioners and dated 26 July 1784. Proven by Lewis Forde and Anthony Foster. 3 April 1787.

Page   72 - THOMAS WHITE
        This indenture made 3 April 1787 between Samuel Barton of Davidson County of one part and Thomas White of same place of other part, sold unto Thomas White one lot of an acre of land in Nashville and known as Lot No. 23, formerly granted to said Barton by Thomas Molloy, James Shaw and said Barton, directors and trustees of the town of Nashville, dated 30 July 1784. April 3, 1787.

Page   73 - TAITT & EDGAR

This indenture made 16 Jan 1787. Sold unto Taitt & Edgar one half of Lot. No. 25 of one half acre of land in town of Nashville. April. 3, 1787.

Page   73 - SAMUEL FELIN

This indenture made 3 April 1787 between Russell Gower of Davidson County of one part and Samuel Felin of same place of other part, sold unto Samuel Felin one lot of an acre of land in Nashville and known as Lot No. 34, formerly granted by Samuel Barton, Thomas Molloy and James Shaw, directors and trustees for the town of Nashville, to Andrew Lucas by deed dated July 30, 1784 and said Lucas conveyed to Thomas Martin by deed dated Sept 7, 1785 and by said Martin to said Gower by deed dated Feb 20, 1786. April 1787.

Page   74 - JAMES LENEAR

This indenture made 27 Jan 1787 between Julius Sanders of Davidson County of one part and James Lenear of same place of other part, sold unto James Lenear all that part of the Lot No. 25 joining the one half sold by said Sanders to William Taitt, also one Lot No. 75 and one Lot No. 72 in Davidson County, which lots was by deed of conveyance dated July 30, 1784, granted and conveyed by the directors and trustees of town of Nashville. April 1787.

Page   74 - JOHN STERN SINGLETARY

This indenture made 15 Mar 1787 between James Donnally of Davidson County of one part and John Stern Singletary of same place of other part, sold unto John Stern Singletary one lot of an acre of land in town of Nashville, known by Lot No. 49, formerly granted to Thomas Fletcher by Samuel Barton, Thomas Molloy and James Shaw by deed dated 26 July 1784 and afterwards by said Fletcher to said Donnally by deed dated 4 Jan 1785. 4 April 1787.

Page   75 - ROBERT KAN - NC - No. 6

By an Act for relief of the Officers and Soldiers of the Continental Line, in consideration of the service of Col. Martin Armstrong, surveyor of the lands, granted unto Robert Kan, assignee of said Armstrong, a tract of land containing 228 acres in Davidson County on Sulphur Lick Creek of Red River and on west boundary of said Kan's other claim. This 16 Feb 1786. Surveyed by Robert Nelson 13 June 1785. 16 Jan 1785.

Page   76 - JOHN CAMPBELL - NC - No. 86

By an Act for the relief of the Officers and Soldiers of the Continental Line, in consideration of the bravery and zeal of John Campbell, a Lieutenant in the said line, granted unto John Campbell a tract of land containing 2560 acres in Davidson County on the south side of Cumberland River on the west fork of Lick Creek. This 14 Mar 1786. Surveyed 21 July 1785 by Edward Harris by virtue of a Military Warrant No. 41. Located Nov 30, 1784.

Page   76 - ISAAC PENNINGTON - NC - No. 236

By an Act for the relief of the Officers and Soldiers of the Continental Line, in consideration of the bravery and zeal of Nicholas Tyner, a private in the said line, granted unto Isaac Pennington, assignee of Nicholas Tyner a tract of land containing 266 acres in Davidson County on Red River. Beginning at the upper end of the first bottom below James McFaddins on the north side of the river and runs to the barrens. This 14 Mar 1786 to which grant is as marked the name Richard Caswell. Surveyed by Robert Nelson 7 Feb 1785 by virtue of a Military Warrant No. 707. Entered 14 Feb 1784.

Page   77 - WILLIAM BUXTON - NC - No. 111
        By an Act for the relief of the Officers and Soldiers of the Continental Line, in consideration of the bravery and zeal of William Teer, a private in the said line, granted unto William Buxton, assignee of said Teer, a tract of land containing 640 acres in Davidson County on the south side of Cumberland River on the east side of Yellow Creek, adjoining the south east corner of William Thomas' 640 acres. This 7 Mar 1786. Surveyed by Joseph Brock by virtue of a Military Warrant No. 652. Entered Dec 11, 1784.

Page   78 - ANDREW BREAKY - NC - No. 289
        By an Act for the relief of the Officers and Soldiers of the Continental Line, in consideration of the bravery and zeal of Gardner Maye, a corporal in the said line, granted unto Andrew Breaky, assignee of Gardner Maye, a tract of land containing 428 acres in Davidson County on Gilkisons Creek a branch of the Sulphur Fork. This 3 May 1787. Surveyed for James Morgan, Esq., by Robert Weakley 12 Aug 1785 by virtue of a Military Warrant No. 1324. Entered Apr 25, 1785. May 1, 1787.

Page   79 - ANDREW BREAKY - NC - No. 291
        By an Act for the relief of the Officers and Soldiers of the Continental Line, in consideration of the bravery and zeal of John Cherry, a private in the said line, granted unto Andrew Breaky, assignee of John Cherry, a tract of land containing 640 acres in Davidson County on the south side of Red River and on the north side of Cumberland River, adjoining the southeast corner of Col. Martin Armstrong's survey of 640 acres. This 3 May 1787. Surveyed for James Glasgow, Esq., by Robert Nelson 22 Apr 1785 by virtue of a Military Warrant No. 1156. Entered Jan 10, 1785.

Page   80 - ANDREW BREAKY - NC - No. 290
        By an Act for the relief of the Officers and Soldiers of the Continental Line, in consideration of the bravery and zeal of Joel Ballard, a private in the said line, granted unto Andrew Breaky, assignee of Joel Ballard, a tract of land containing 640 acres in Davidson County on the south side of Red River about seven miles from the mouth, adjoining corner of Joseph Brock and Rev. Adam Boyd. This 3 May 1786. Surveyed for James Glasgow by Robert Nelson by virtue of a Military Warrant No. 448 and entered Jan 10, 1785.

Page   80 - ANDREW BREAKY
        By an Act for the relief of the Officers and Soldiers of the Continental Line, in consideration for the bravery and zeal of John Smith, a private in the said line, granted unto Andrew Breaky, assignee of John Smith, a tract of land containing 640 acres in Davidson Countyon the waters of Sulphur Fork. This 1 May 1787. To which grant was marked the name Richard Caswell, Esq. Surveyed for James Glasgow, Esq. by Robert Weakley 13 Aug 1785 by virtue of a Military Warrant No. 1115. Entered Apr 25, 1785.

Grant marked dated May 1, 1785 for said Glasgow to said Breaky.

Page   81 - LARDNER CLARK
We, Samuel Barton, Thomas Molloy, James Shaw and Isaac Linsey, directors and trustees of town of Nashville, granted unto Lardner Clark Lot No. 7 in Nashville and shall within three years of date of conveyance erect, build and finish a square log, brick or stone house with brick or stone chimney. This _?_ July 1784. July 3, 1787.

Page   82 - JAMES HOGGATT
I, James Bosley of Davidson County sold unto James Hoggatt of same place all that tract of land in Davidson County, adjoining James Ireson's south corner, Crockett's north west corner, Robertson's line, and McGavock's line. Containing 640 acres. This 17 May 1787. July 3, 1787.

Page   82 - JAMES BOSLEY - NC - No. (blank)
By an Act for the relief of the Officers and Soldiers of the Continental Line, in consideration of the services of Col. Martin Armstrong, surveyor of the lands, granted unto James Bosley, assignee of Col. Martin Armstrong, a tract of land containing 34 acres in Davidson County on the south side of Cumberland River, joining the northern corner of George Freeland's Guard Right. This 16 Feb 1786. Surveyed for James Bosley 18 June 1785. Entered Apr 11, 1785.

Page   83 - JAMES BOSLEY - NC - No. 6
By an Act for the relief of the Officers and Soldiers of the Continental Line, in consideration of the bravery and zeal of Federick Rigsby, a private in the said line, granted unto James Bosley, assignee of Federick Rigsby, a tract of land containing 275 acres in Davidson County on the south side of Cumberland River adjoining said Bosley's Preemption No. 14. This 16 Feb 178?. Surveyed Mar 13, 1785 by Thomas Molloy by virtue of a Military Warrant No. (illeg). Entered July 8, 1784.

Page   84 - JAMES BOSLEY - NC - No. 5
By an Act for the relief of the Officers and Soldiers of the Continental Line, in consideration of the services of Col. Martin Armstrong, surveyor of the lands, granted unto James Bosley, assignee of said Armstrong, a tract of land containing 107 acres in Davidson County adjoining John Cockrill and Peter Turney's Preemptions and on the waters of French Lick branch, bordering southeast corner of Bosley's Guard Right, Peter Turney's line and John Cockrill's line. This 16 Feb 1786. Surveyed for James Bosley 30 Apr 1785. Entered Apr 15, 1785.

Page   84 - JAMES BOSLEY - NC - No. 7
By an Act for the relief of the Officers and Soldiers of the Continental Line, in consideration of the service of Col. Martin Armstrong, surveyor of the lands, granted unto James Bosley, assignee of said Armstrong, a tract of land containing 139 acres in Davidson County on south side of Cumberland River joining the upper line of said Bosley's Preemption No. 43. This 16 Feb 1786. Surveyed by Thomas Molloy 12 May 1785. Entered Mar 26, 1785.

Page   85 - JAMES BOSLEY - NC - No. 4

By an Act for the relief of the Officers and Soldiers of the Continental Line, in consideration for the service of COl. Martin Armstrong, a surveyor of the lands, granted unto James Bosley, assignee of said Armstrong, a tract of land containing 21 acres in Davidson County on south side of Cumberland River near Stones Lick, joining Peter Turney's northwest corner, Robertson's line, and Bosley's line. This 16 Feb 1786. Surveyed by Thomas Molloy 17 June 1785. Entered 11 Apr 1785 by No. 846.

Page   85 - JAMES BOSLEY - NC - No. 9

By an Act for the relief of the Officers and Soldiers of the Continental Line, in consideration of the service of Col. Martin Armstrong, surveyor of the lands, granted unto James Bosley, assignee of said Armstrong, a tract of land containing 103 acres in Davidson County near the Stone Lick joining and between the lines of said Bosley's Preemption and Guard Right. Bordering Elijah Robertson. This 16 Feb 1786. Surveyed May 30, 1785 by Thomas Molloy. Entered Mar 31, 1785.

Page   86 - RICHARD THOMAS

This indenture made 27 Jan 1787 between Willoughby Williams of Dobbs County, North Carolina of one part and Richard Thomas of Orange County, North Carolina of other part, sold unto Richard Thomas a tract of land containing 640 acres in Davidson County on the east side of Blooming Grove joining the east boundary of John Mackey's Preemption. Which land said Williams obtained by patent dated 24 Jan 1787 as assignee of William Martin,a private Soldier of the Continental Line of North Carolina. This Feb 1, 1787. Proven by Mathias Handy, witness.

Page   86 - RICHARD THOMAS

This indenture made 7 Jan 1787 between Col James Glasgow of Dobbs County, North Carolina of one part and Richard Thomas of Orange County, North Carolina of other part. Said Glasgow sold unto said Richard Thomas a tract of land containing 640 acres in Davidson County, on the Wartrace Creek, a branch of the Sulphur Fork of Red River. Beginning about half mile above Kerrs Trace. Which land said Glasgow obtained by Patent dated 24 Jan 1787 as assignee of Nathan Nelson who was heir of William Nelson, deceased, a private soldier in the Continental Line of North Carolina. This Feb 1, 1787.

Page   87 - RICHARD THOMAS

This indenture made 27 Jan 1787 between Col. James Glasgow of Dobbs County, North Carolina of one part and Richard Thomas of Orange County, North Carolina of other part, sold unto Richard Thomas a tract of land containing 228 acres in Davidson County on the north side of Cumberland River joining Nicholas Conrod's claim and Carter Williams line. Which land said Glasgow obtained by patent dated Jan 24, 1787 as assignee of Thomas Martin, a private soldier of the Continental line of North Carolina. This Feb 1, 1787. Samuel Spencer, J.S.C.D.E.

Page   87 - RICHARD THOMAS

(2nd page) This indenture made 27 July 1787 between Col. James Glasgow of Dobbs County, North Carolina of one part and Richard Thomas of Orange County, North Carolina of other part, sold unto Richard Thomas a tract of land of 640 acres in Davidson County on

20

south side of Red River, on both sides of Buzzard Creek, a branch of Red River, adjoining a west corner of Henry Martin. Which land said Glasgow obtained by patent dated Jan 24, 1787, as assignee of Thomas Aims, a private soldier in the Continental Line of North Carolina. This Feb 1, 1787. The above transferred to Andrew McBroom, 1787.

Page   88 - RICHARD THOMAS
        This indenture made 27 Jan 1787 between Willoughby Williams of Dobbs County, North Carolina of one part and Richard Thomas of Orange County, North Carolina of other part, sold unto Richard Thomas a tract of land containing 640 acres in Davidson County on both sides of Buzzard Creek on the south side of Red River. Beginning about three quarters of a mile above a spring and tree marked E.E. Which land Willoughby Williams obtained by patent dated Jan 24, 1787, as assignee of Henry Martin, a private soldier in the Continental Line of North Carolina. This Feb 1, 1787. Test: Andrew Ewing, D.S. The above transferred to David Gibson, 1787.

Page   88 - WILLOUGHBY WILLIAMS - NC - No. 270
        By an Act for the relief of the Officers and Soldiers of the Continental Line, in consideration of the bravery and zeal of Henry Martin, a private in the said line, granted unto Willoughby Williams, assignee of Henry Martin, a tract of land containing 640 acres in Davidson County on both sides of Buzzard Creek on the south side of Red River. Beginning about three quarters of a mile above a spring and tree marked E.E. This 24 Jan 1787. Surveyed by Robert Nelson Nov 24, 1787 by virtue of a Military Warrant No. 394. Entered 19 Mar 1785.

Page   89 - COL. JAMES GLASGOW - NC - No. 271
        By an Act for the relief of the Officers and Soldiers of the Continental Line, in consideration of the bravery and zeal of Thomas Aims, a private in the said line, granted unto Col. James Glasgow, assignee of said Thomas Aims, a tract of land containing 640 acres in Davidson County on south side of Red River, on both sides of Buzzard Creek of Red River, joining survey of Henry Martin. This 24 Jan 1787. Surveyed by Robert Nelson 24 Nov 1785 by virtue of a Military Warrant No. 1154. Entered 19 Mar 1785.

Page   89 - COL. JAMES GLASGOW - NC - No. 272
        By an Act for the relief of the Officers and Soldiers of the Continental line, in consideration of the bravery and zeal of William Nelson, deceased, a private in the said line, granted unto James Glasgow, assignee of Nathan Nelson heir of said William Nelson, a tract of land containing 640 acres in Davidson County on the War trace a branch of Sulphus Fork of Red River. Beginning about half mile above Kerrs Trace. This 24 Jan 1787. Surveyed by Robert Nelson Nov 25, 1785 by virtue of a Military Warrant No. 1313. Entered Mar 5, 1785.

Page   90 - COL. JAMES GLASGOW - NC - No. 273
        By an Act for the relief of the Officers and Soldiers of the Continental Line, in consideration of the bravery and zeal of Thomas Martin, a private in the said line, granted unto Col. James Glasgow, assignee of Thomas Martin, a tract of land containing 228 acres in Davidson County on north side of Cumberland River joining Nicholas Conrod's claim, and Carter Williams' line. This Jan 24, 1787. Surveyed by Robert Nelson Mar 9,

1786 by virtue of a Military Warrant No. 1132. Entered Aug 10, 1785.

Page   90 - WILLOUGHBY WILLIAMS - NC - No. 269

By an Act for the relief of the Officers and Soldiers of the Continental Line, in consideration of the bravery and zeal of William Martin, a private in sale line, granted unto Willoughby Williams, assignee of William Martin, a tract of land containing 640 acres in Davidson County on east side of Blooming Grove joining the east boundary of (illegible) Mackey's Preemption. This Jan 24, 1787. Surveyed by Robert Nelson by virtue of a Military Warrant No. 1212. Entered Dec 6, 1785.

Page   91 - RICHARD THOMAS - NC - No. 133

By an Act for the relief of the Officers and Soldiers of the Continental Line, in consideration of the bravery and zeal of Richard Thomas, a private in the said line, granted unto Richard Thomas a tract of land of 228 acres in Davidson County on Parsons Creek, a branch of Red River, that empties in on the south side opposite to Rentfro's Old Station and on the west boundary of Captain Linton. This Mar 14, 1786. Surveyed by Robert Nelson 10 Feb 1785 by virtue of a Military Warrant No. 79?. Entered July 26, 1784.

Page   91 - JAMES ROBERTSON - NC - No. 182

By an Act for the relief of the Officers and Soldiers of the Continental Line, in consideration of the bravery and zeal of Richard Davis, a private in the said line, granted unto James Robertson, assignee of Richard Davis, a tract of land of 274 acres in Davidson County on south side of Cumberland River above the mouth of Richland Creek adjoining other lands of said Robertson. This 7 Mar 1786. Surveyed by Henry Rutherford 20 Oct 1785 by virtue of a Military Warrant No. 29. Entered July 4, 1895.

Page   92 - JAMES ROBERTSON - NC - No. 191

By an Act for the relief of the Officers and Soldiers of the Continental Line, in consideration of the bravery and zeal of Job Pendergrass, a private in the said line, granted unto James Robertson, assignee of Job Pendergrass, a tract of land containing 274 acres in Davidson County on the waters of Big Harpeth River. Beginning at the south side of a 640 acre survey of said Robertson. This 7 Mar 1786. Surveyed 21 Nov 1784 by B. Wm. Pollock, D.S., by virtue of a Military Warrant No. 76. Entered Dec 18, 1784.

Page   92 - JAMES ROBERTSON - NC - No. 214

By an Act for the relief of the Officers and Soldiers of the Continental Line, in consideration of the bravery and zeal of Jacob White, a private in the said line, granted unto James Robertson, assignee of Jacob White, a tract of land containing 274 acres in Davidson County lying on the (illegible) of Cumberland River above the mouth of Richland Creek, joining other lands of said Robertson. This 7 Mar 1786. Surveyed Sept 23, 1785 by Henry Rutherford, D.S., by virtue of a Military Warrant No. 275. Entered June 25, 1785.

Page   93 - JAMES ROBERTSON - NC - No. 209

By an Act for the relief of the Officers and Soldiers of the Continental Line, in consideration of the bravery and zeal of James Deal, a private in said line, granted unto James Robertson, assignee of James Deal, a tract of land containing 274 acres in Davidson County, in the bend of Cumberland River above the mouth of Richland Creek adjoining other lands of said Robertson. This 7 Mar 1786. Surveyed by Henry Rutherford Oct 5, 1785 by virtue of a Military Warrant No. 756. Entered July 4, 1785.

Page   93 - JAMES ROBERTSON - NC - No. 176
        By an Act for the relief of the Officers and Soldiers of the Continental Line, in consideration of the bravery and zeal of Samuel Smith, a corporal in the said line, granted unto James Robertson, assignee of Samuel Smith, a tract of land containing 428 acres in Davidson County on the east side of the West Fork of Harpeth River joining southern boundary of Samuel Moore's Preemption. This 7 Mar 1786. Surveyed 20 Jan 1786 by Thomas Molloy, D.S., by virtue of a Military Warrant No. 169. Entered July ?, 1784.

Page   94 - JOSHUA HOWARD - NC - No. 115
        By an Act for the relief of the Officers and Soldiers of the Continental Line, in consideration of the bravery and zeal of Caleb Merchant, a private in the said line, granted unto Joshua Howard, assignee of Caleb Merchant, a tract of land containing 274 acres in Davidson County on both sides of Whites Creek and Hentons Creek. This 7 Mar 1786. Surveyed for James Robertson 13 July 1784 by Joseph Brock, D.S., by virtue of a Military Warrant No. 833. Located July 8, 1784.

Page   94 -JOHN WILLIAMS - NC - No. 207
        By an Act for the relief of the Officers and Soldiers of the Continental Line, in consideration of the bravery and zeal of George Wallis, fife major in the said line, granted unto John Williams, assignee of George Wallis, a tract of land containing 857 acres in Davidson County on the middle fork of Goose Creek. This 7 Mar 1786. Surveyed by James Sanders 16 Mar 1785 by virtue of a Military Warrant No. 306. Located Jan 26, 1785.

Page   95 - LARDNER CLARK - NC - No. 168
        By an Act for the relief of the Officers and Soldiers of the Continental Line, in consideration of the bravery and zeal of Thomas Siskon, a private in the said line, granted unto Lardner Clark, assignee of Thomas Siskon, a tract of land containing 640 acres in Davidson County in the forks of Mill Creek, adjoining the southeast corner to James Wilson, northeast corner of John Tucker's Preemption, and Peter Catron's east boundary. This 7 Mar 1786. Surveyed by John Buchanan Mar 11, 1785, D.S., by virtue of a Military Warrant No. 816. Located July 8, 1784.

Page   95 - THOMAS TAYLOR - NC - No. 136
        By an Act for the relief of the Officers and Soldiers of the Continental Line, in consideration of the bravery and zeal of Jessee Cole, a private in the said line, granted unto Thomas Taylor, assignee of Jesse Cole, a tract of land containing 640 acres in Davidson County on the east side of the west fork of Harpeth River, joining Joseph Brock and James Robertson. This 14 Mar 1786. Surveyed 21 May 1785 by Joseph Brock, D.S., by virtue of a Military Warrant No. (illegible). Located Jan 24, 1785.

Page   96 - JOHN BUCHANAN - NC - No. 135
        By an Act for the relief of the Officers and Soldiers of the Continental Line, in consideration for the bravery and zeal of Thomas Thompson, a private in the said line, granted unto John Buchanan, assignee of Thomas Thompson, a tract of land containing 640

acres in Davidson County on the waters of Mill Creek, joining lands of John Tucker, Jason Thompson and Lardner Clark's Preemption. This 14 Mar 1786. Surveyed July 20, 1785 by John Buchanan by virtue of a Military Warrant No. 817. Located Apr 19, 1785.

Page   96 - SUTHERLIN MAYFIELD - NC - No. 103
(2nd page) By an Act for the relief of the Officers and Soldiers of the Continental Line, in consideration of the bravery and zeal of Joseph Copeland, a private in said line, granted unto Sutherlin Mayfield, assignee of Joseph Copeland, a tract of land containing 640 acres in Davidson County on Mill Creek. Beginning at the Big Hurricane, then to his survey as assignee of Anthony Crutcher, and then crossing Mill Creek. This Mar 7, 1786. Surveyed July 6, 1785 by John Buchanan, D.S., by virtue of a Military Warrant No. 783. Located Mar 17, 1785.

Page   97 - SUTHERLIN MAYFIELD - NC - No. 242
By an Act for the relief of the Officers and Soldiers of the Continental Line, in consideration of the bravery and zeal of Robert Morrison, a private in the said line, granted unto Sutherlin Mayfield, assignee of Robert Morrison, a tract of land containing 640 acres in Davidson County on the east fork of Mill Creek waters, adjoining the Big Hurricane, and crossing Indian Camp Creek. This 7 Mar 1786. Surveyed Apr 14, 1785 by John Buchanan, D.S., by virtue of a Military Warrant No. 641. Located July 24, 1785.

Page   97 - JASON THOMPSON - NC - No. 212
By an Act for the relief of the Officers and Soldiers of the Continental Line, in consideration of the bravery and zeal of Alexander Ramage, a private of the said line, granted unto Jason Thompson, assignee of Alexander Ramage, a tract of land containing 640 acres in Davidson County on waters of Mill Creek, joining John Tucker's land and John Cockrill's land. This 7 Mar 1786. Surveyed Mar ?, 1785 by John Buchanan, D.S., by virtue of a Military Warrant No. 815. Located July 8, 1785.

Page   98 - JAMES FERGUS - NC - No. 75
By an Act for the relief of the Officers and Soldiers of the Continental Line, in consideration of the bravery and zeal of James Fergus, a surgeon in the said line, granted unto James Fergus a tract of land containing 4800 acres in Davidson County on waters of Mill Creek and Big Harpeth, adjoining William Collinsworth's Preemption, Ebenezer Titus and William Nevels' line, and William Simpson's Preemption. This 14 Mar 1787. Surveyed Feb 20, 1785 by John Buchanan, D.S., by virtue of a Military Warrant No. (blank). Located (blank).

Page   98 - CURTIS IVEY - NC - No. 45
By an Act for the relief of the Officers and Soldiers of the Continental Line, in consideration of the bravery and zeal of Curtis Ivey, a Lieutenant in the said line, granted unto Curtis Ivey a tract of land containing 2560 acres in Davidson County on both sides of Harpeth River, adjoining James Robertson's 640 acre survey. This Mar 14, 1787. Surveyed Nov 23, 1785 by B. William Pollock, D.S., by virtue of a Military Warrant No. 177. Located Aug 16, 1784.

Page   99 - THOMAS JAMES

This indenture made 3 Oct 1787 between Jonathan Drake and his wife Lucy Drake of Davidson County of one part and Thomas James of same place of other part, granted unto Thomas James a tract of land containing 640 acres in Davidson County on north side of Cumberland River and on the south side of Whites Creek, adjoining lands of Federick Stump and John Drake. Which land Jonathan Drake obtained by patent dated Mar 17, 1786 as assignee of William Leaton, a private soldier in the Continental Line. Oct 3, 1787.

Page   99 - THE HEIRS OF MARK ROBERTSON

I, Jonathan Drake and Lucy Drake of Davidson County, NC, in consequence of a bragain heretofore made with Mark Robertson, lately deceased, and for and inconsideration of one hundred pounds currency, granted and sold unto the heirs of Mark Robertson their heirs and assignees a certain tract of land containing 640 acres in Davidson County on the bank of Cumberland River and joining Isaac Butler's survey of 228 acres. Which land Jonathan Drake obtained by a patent dated Mar 7, 1786 as assignee of James Christian, a private in the Continental Line. This Oct 3, 1786. Oct 3, 1787.

Page   100 - PHILEMON THOMAS

This indenture made 9 June 1787 between Richard Thomas of Orange County, North Carolina of one part and Philemon Thomas of Fayette County, Virginia of other part. Richard Thomas sold unto Philemon Thomas a tract of land containing 228 acres in Davidson County, NC on Parsons Creek, a branch of Red River, that empties in on the south side opposite Rentfro's Old Station and on the west boundary of Captain William Linton's. Which land Richard Thomas obtained by patent dated 14 Mar 1786 for his service in the Continental Army as a private soldier. Proven by Andrew Ewing, Sen. Oct 1, 1787.

Page   100 - PHILEMON THOMAS

(2nd page)   This indenture made 9 June 1787 between Richard Thomas of Orange County, NC of one part and Philemon Thomas of Fayette County, VA of other part.   Richard Thomas sold unto Philemon Thomas a tract of land containing 228 acres in Davidson County on the north side of Cumberland River joining Nicholas Coonrod's claim and to Carter Williams' line. Which land Richard Thomas obtained of Col. James Glasgow by conveyance dated 27 Jan 1787 who obtained the same by patent dated 24 Jan 1787 as assignee of Thomas Martin, a private soldier in the Continental Line in NC. Proven Oct 1, 1787 by Andrew Ewing.

Page   101 - PHILEMON THOMAS

This indenture made 9 June 1787 between Richard Thomas of Orange County, NC of one part and Philemon Thomas of Fayette County, VA of other part.   Richard Thomas sold unto Philemon Thomas a tract of land containing 640 acres in Davidson County on the War Trace Creek, a branch of the Sulphur Fork of Red River. Beginning about half a mile above Kerr's Trace. Which land Richard Thomas obtained from Col. James Glasgow by conveyance dated Jan 27, 1787 and said Glasgow obtained the same by patent dated 24 Jan 1787 as assignee of Nathan Nelson who was heir of William Nelson, deceased, a private soldier in the Continental Line of NC. Proven Oct 1, 1787 by Andrew Ewing. The one half of the above conveyed to Charles Arrington (see page 319).

Page   101 - PHILEMON THOMAS

This indenture made 9 June 1787 between Richard Thomas of Orange County, NC, of one part and Philemon Thomas of Fayette County, VA of other part. Richard Thomas sold unto Philemon Thomas a tract of land containing 640 acres in Davidson County on east side of Blooming Grove joining the east boundary of John Mackey's Preemption. Which land Richard Thomas obtained of Willoughby Williams by conveyance dated 27 Jan 1787 and said Williams obtained the same by patent dated Jan 24, 1787 as assignee of William Martin, a private soldier in the Continental Line of NC. Proven Oct 1, 1787.

Page   102 - JOHN BELL

I, James Bosley of Davidson County sold unto John Bell of same place a tract of land in Davidson County adjoining Captain Anthony Crutcher and McGavock's line. Containing 75 acres. This 26 Mar 1787. Proven Oct 3, 1787.

Page   102 - LARDNER CLARK

This indenture made 7 July 1787 between James Wood of Davidson County of one part and Lardner Clark of same place of other part.John Wood sold unto Lardner Clark a tract lot of land known in town of Nashville as Lot No. 69. Which lot was by deed dated July 30, 1784 conveyed to said Wood by the Trustees of the town of Nashville. Proven Oct 3, 1787.

Page   103 - WILLIAM DOBBINS

This indenture made 20 Sept 1787 between James Allen of North Carolina of one part and William Dobbins of Davidson County, NC of other part. James Allen sold unto William Dobbins a tract or lot of ground in town of Nashville and known as Lot No. 6. Which lot was conveyed by William Mulherin to Lardner Clark and from said Clark to said Allen. Which deed of conveyance was by Daniel Rowan, attorney for said Allen. Oct 2, 1787.

Page   103 - JOHN DONALDSON - NC - No. 137

(2nd page) By an Act for the relief of the Officers and Soldiers of the Continental Line, in consideration for the bravery and zeal of Joseph Ryal, a private in the said line, conveyed unto John Donaldson, assignee of Joseph Ryal, a tract of land containing 640 acres in Davidson County on the west side of Big Harpeth River, on the west side of James McGavock's Preemption, adjoining McGavock'sline and Manifee's line. This 14 Mar 1786. Surveyed by John Donaldson, D.S. by virtue of a Military Warrant No. 1074.

Page   104 - ROBERT WEAKLEY - NC - No. 341 - Reg. Dec 3, 1787

By an Act for the relief of the Officers and Soldiers of the Continental Line, in consideration of the bravery and zeal of James Mallobey, a private in the said line, granted unto Robert Weakley, assignee of said James Mallobey, a tract of land containing 640 acres in Davidson County on the north side of Cumberland River, on the north waters of Sycamore Creek on a branch running from Turnbulls horse stump and borders John Nichols' line. This Sept 4, 1787. Surveyed Jule 11, 1786 by said Weakley, D.S. by virtue of a Military Warrant No. 3282. Located April 5, 1785. Griffith Dickson and John Ca(illegible), chain carriers.

26

Page   104 - ROBERT WEAKLEY - NC - No. 4

By an Act for the relief of the Officers and Soldiers of the Continental Line, in consideration of the services of Col. Martin Armstrong, surveyor of lands, granted him a tract of land containing 200 acres in Davidson County on both sides of Red River. Beginning on the south bank of Red River near Thomas Kilgore's corner. This Sept 4, 1787. Surveyed Dec 3, 1785 by Robert Weakley, D.S. for himself by virtue of a Service Right. Located Sept 21, 1785. Moses Williams and James Gilkison, C.C.

Page   105 - ROBERT WEAKLEY - NC - No. 343 - Reg. Dec 4, 1787

By an Act for the relief of the Officers and Soldiers of the Continental Line, in consideration of the bravery and zeal of John Crawford, a private in the said line, granted unto Robert Weakley, assignee of John Crawford, a tract of land containing 640 acres in Davidson County on the west side of Sycamore Creek and on the east side of Spring Creek, a branch that runs into the same, including a spring. This 4 Sept 1787. Surveyed Mar 24, 1786 by Robert Weakley, D.S. for himself by virtue of a Military Warrant No. 1753. Located Dec 20, 1785. Josiah Ramsey and Mark Noble, C.C.

Page   105 - ROBERT WEAKLEY - NC - No. 343 - Reg. Dec 4, 1787

By an Act for the relief of the Officers and Soldiers of the Continental Line, in consideration of the bravery and zeal of John Crawford, a private in the said line, granted unto Robert Weakley, assignee of John Crawford, a tract of land containing 640 acres in Davidson County on west side of Sycamore Creek and on east side of Spring Creek on a branch that runs into the same, including a spring. This 4 ? , 1787. Surveyed ∴ Mar 24, 1786 by Robert Weakley, D.S. for himself by virtue of a Military Warrant No. 1753. Located Dec 20, 1785. Josiah Ramsey and Mark Noble, Entry and chain carriers.

Page   105 - ROBERT WEAKLEY - NC - No. 342 - Reg. Dec 4, 1787

By an Act for the relief of the Officers and Soldiers of the Continental Line, in consideration of the bravery and zeal of Amos Raynor, a private in the said line, granted unto Robert Weakley, assignee of the heirs of said Amos Raynor, a tract of land containing 640 acres in Davidson County on north side of Cumberland River, on the north waters of Sycamore Creek in Turnsbull's horse stump and a large spring at said stump. This 4 Sept 1787. Surveyed June 10, 1786 by Robert Weakley, D.S. for himself by virtue of a Military Warrant No. 2578. Located Jan 18, 1786. Griffith Dickson and John Ca(illegible), C.C.

Page   106 - ROBERT WEAKLEY - NC - No. 338 - Reg. Dec 4, 1787

By an Act for the relief of the Officers and Soldiers of the Continental Line, granted unto Robert Weakley, assignee of the heirs of Jonas Sharp, a tract of land containing 640 acres in Davidson County on the north side of Cumberland River and on the north waters of Sycamore Creek between the mouth of Ramseys Spring branch and Spring Creek, joining John Nichols nertheast corner of a 1000 acre survey and borders Weakley's line of a survey No. 1753. This 4 Sept 1787. Surveyed Oct 21, 1786 by Robert Weakley, D.S. for himself by virtue of a Military Warrant No. 2580. Located June 3, 1786. Griffith Dickson and Willis Hicks, Sen., C.C.

Page   106 - WILLIAM TAITTE - NC - No. 340 - Reg. Dec 4, 1786

By an Act for the relief of the Officers and Soldiers of the Continental Line,

in consideration of the bravery and zeal of Joshua Searchwell, a private in said line, granted unto William Taitt, assignee of Joshua Searchwell, a tract of land containing 640 acres in Davidson County on the west branch of Half (illegible). Beginning at Reading Blount's south east corner, then to James Turrentine's line, and to Elijah Robertson's line. This 4 Sept 1787. Surveyed Feb 5, 1787 for William Taitt by Robert Weakley, D.S. by virtue of a Military Warrant No. 2234. Located April 5, 1785. Jonathan Drake and Joseph (illegible), C.C.

Page 107 - JOSIAH RAMSEY - NC - No. 3 - Reg. Dec 5, 1787

By an Act for the relief of the Officers and Soldiers of the Continental Line, in consideration of the services of Col. Martin Armstrong, surveyor of lands, granted unto Josiah Ramsey, assignee of said Armstrong, a tract of land containing 200 acres in Davidson County on Sycamore Creek below the mouth of Ramseys Fork. This 4 Sept 1787. Surveyed May 7, 1786 for Josiah Ramsey by Robert Weakley, D.S., inconsequence of a Service Right of said Armstrong. Located Feb 4, 1786. Mark Noble and Josiah Ramsey, C.C.

Page 108 MARK NOBLES - NC - No. 6 - Reg. Dec 5, 1787

By an Act for the relief of the Officers and Soldiers in the Continental Line, in consideration of the services of Col. Martin Armstrong, surveyor of lands, granted unto Mark Nobles, assignee of said Armstrong, a tract of land containing 200 acres in Davidson County on the north side of Sycamore Creek on the first branch above Ramseys Fork. This 4 Sept 1787. Surveyed for Mark Nobles Jan 27, 1786 in consequence of a Service Right of said Armstrong. Located 6 Aug 1785. Surveyed by Robert Weakley. Josiah Ramsey and Mark Nobles, C.C.

Page 108 - JAMES DONNALLY - NC - No. 339 - Reg. Dec 5, 1787
(2nd page)   By an Act for the relief of the Officers and Soldiers of the Continental Line, in consideration of the bravery and zeal of Isaac Howard, a private in the said line, granted unto James Donnally, assignee of said Howard, a tract of land containing 274 acres in Davidson County on the clear branch of Richland Creek, Beginning at James Thompson's corner. This 4 Sept 1787. Surveyed by David Steele, D.S. for James Donnally by virtue of a Military Warrant No. 550. Located June 21, 1785. Robert Thomas and John Thompson, C.C.

Page 109 - WILLIAM POE - Reg. Dec 21, 1787

This indenture made 10 Sept 1787 between Andrew Breaky of Davidson County of one part and William Poe of Baltimore town, Baltimore County, Maryland, hatter, of other part. Andrew Breaky sold unto William Poe all those two tracts of land in Davidson County containing 640 acres each and grants of patents No. 290 and No. 291 from said State of North Carolina to said Brady. Patent No. 290 is on the south side of Red River about seven miles from the mouth, and borders Joseph Brooks and the Rev. Adam Boyd. Patent No. 291 is on the south side of Red River and north side of Cumberland and borders southeast corner of Col. Martin Armstrong's survey of 640 acres. Wit: James Adcock.

Page 110 - State of Maryland
        Baltimore County
        This 10 Sept 1787 - Andrew Breaky deeded unto William Poe and heirs

28

forever. Acknowledged by Lyde Goodwin and Isaac U. Bibbler. Received and recorded 8 Oct 1787 in Baltimore, Maryland. William Gibson, Clerk.

Page   110 - WILLIAM GUBBINS - NC - No. 344 - Reg. Dec 21, 1787
        By an Act for the relief of the Officers and Soldiers of the Continental Line, in consideration of the bravery and zeal of Henry Dickson, a private in the said line, granted unto William Gubbins, assignee of the heirs of Henry Dickson, a tract of land containing 640 acres in Davidson County on the south side of Sulphur Fork of Red River adjoining south line of William Gilkison and Benjamin Harden's corner. This Sept 4, 1787. To which grant was surveyed for William Gubbins Apr 10, 1786 by Robert Weakley, D.S. by virtue of a Military Warrant No. 1802. Located 10 Oct 1785. Moses Williams and James Gilkison, C.C.

Page   111 - JAMES HOLLINS (HOLLIS) - NC - No. 185 - Reg. Jan 15, 1788
        By an Act for the relief of the Officers and Soldiers of the Continental Line, in consideration for the bravery and zeal of Arthur Pew, a private in the said line, granted unto James Hollis, assignee of David Pew, heir of Auther Pew, a tract of land containing 640 acres in Davidson County on a branch of Halfpoan Creek, adjoining Joseph Ramsey and James Turner's lands. This 7 Mar 1786. Surveyed for James Hollis 17 June 1785 by Ed Harris, D.S. by virtue of a Military Warrant No. 728. Located July 22, 178?.

Page   111 - EDWARD COX - NC - No. 74 - Reg. Feb 17, 1788
        By an Act for the relief of the Officers and Soldiers of the Continental Line, in consideration of the services of Edward Cox, one of the Guards to the Commissioners, granted unto Edward Cox a tract of land containing 640 acres in Davidson County on the east branch of Mill Creek, adjoining Ebenezer Titus. This Oct 8, 1787. Surveyed 4 Mar 1785 by John Buchanan, D.S. Location entered into the Preemption Office Jan 7, 178?. Warrant No. 151. Thomas Cox and John Robertson, C.C.

Page   112 - THOMAS COX - NC - No. 43 - Reg. Feb 19, 1788
        By an Act for the relief of the Officers and Soldiers of the Continental Line, in consideration of the services of Thomas Cox, one of the Commission Guard, granted unto Thomas Cox a tract of land containing 320 acres in Davidson County adjoining his Service Right of 640 acres on the upper side. Surveyed Mar 9, 1785 for said Cox by B. William Pollock, D.S. Jonathan Robertson and Benjamin Watkins, C.C. in consequence of a Warrant No. 151. Located and entered Jan 17, 1784 in the Preemption Office this Oct 8, 1787.

Page   112 - THOMAS COX - NC - No. 81 - Reg. Feb 19, 1788
        By an Act for the relief of the Officers and Soldiers in the Continental Line, in consideration of the services of Thomas Cox, one of the Guards to the Commissioners, granted unto Thomas Cox a tract of land containing 640 acres in Davidson County adjoining Samuel Willson's Preemption in the main west fork of Stones River. Surveyed for Thomas Cox Mar 12, 1785 by B. William Pollock, D.S. Benjamin Watkins and Jonath Robertson, C.C. in consequence of a Warrant No. 149. Located and entered 16 Jan 1784. Oct 8, 1787.

Page   112 - ROBERT HEATON - NC - No. 42 - Reg. Feb 19, 1788
        By an Act for the relief of the Officers and Soldiers of the Continental Line,

29

in consideration of the services of Robert Heaton, one of the Commission Guards &c, granted unto Robert Heaton a tract of land containing320 acres in Davidson County on Red River. Beginning on Buzzard Creek. Surveyed for said Heaton May 20, 1785 by James Sanders, D.S. Benjamin Condry and Joshua Hollis in consequence of a Warrant No. 143. Located and entered Mar 10, 1784. Oct 8, 1787.

Page   113 - JOHN ELLIOTT - NC - No. 40 - Reg. Feb 24, 1788
By an Act for the relief of the Officers and Soldiers of the Continental Line, in consideration of the services of John Elliott, one of the Guards to the Commissioners, granted unto John Elliott a tract of land containing 640 acres in Davidson County. Surveyed for said Elliott Dec 8, 1784 by James Sanders, D.S. Joseph Motherall and Uriah Anderson, C.C. in consequence of a Warrant No. 159. Located and entered Jan 17, 1784. 8 Oct 1787.

Page   113 - ZACHARIAH STULL - NC - No. 47 - Reg. Feb 20, 1788
For ten pounds per one hundred acres paid by Zachariah Stull, granted unto said Stull a tract of land containing 640 acres in Davidson County on the old trace below his spring adjoining James McGavock's line. Surveyed for said Stull May 19, 1784 by James Sanders, D.S. Joseph Hannah and Isaac Shoat, C.C. Located and entered Jan 28, 1784. Apr 17, 1786.

Page   113 - SAMUEL MOORE - NC - No. 168 - Reg. Feb 20, 1788
(2nd page)   For 10 lbs per 100 acres paid by Samuel Moore, granted unto said Moore a tract of land containing 640 acres in Davidson County. Beginning at the bank of river at the mouth of a spring. Surveyed Dec 14, 1784 by David McGavock, D.S. in consequence of a Warrant No. 38, located nad entered Mar 30, 1784. April 17, 1786.

Page   114   SAMUEL MOORE - NC - No. 106 - Reg. Feb 20, 1788
For 10 lbs per 100 acres paid by Samuel Moore was granted a tract of land containing 640 acres in Davidson County on the west side of Harpeth River about three miles above fork adjoining a military survey of James Robertson. Surveyed by Samuel Moore Jan 22, 1785, D.S. William Stuart and Thomas Edmiston, C.C. in consequence of a Warrant No. 631. Located and Entered Dec 8, 1784. April 17, 1786.

Page   114 - JAMES THOMPSON - NC - No. 132 - Reg. Feb 20, 1788
For 10 lbs per 100 acres paid by James Thompson, was granted a tract of land in Davidson County adjoining a dividing ridge between Fletchers Lick and Richland Creek. Surveyed for said Thompson May 7, 1784 by Thomas Molloy, D.S. Robert Thompson and William Hamilton, C.C. in consequence of a Warrant No. 104. Located and entered Jan 15, 1784. Apr 17, 1786.

Page   114 - JOHN JOHNSTON - NC - No. 102 - Reg. Feb 20, 1788
For 10 lbs per 100 acres paid by John Johnston, granted a tract of land in Davidson County, containing 640 acres on the waters of Dry Creek. Beginning at the forks of Heatons Road. Surveyed for John Johnston July 24, 1784 by James Sanders and William Johnston and John Elliott, C.C. in consequence of a Warrant No. 314. Located and entered Feb 27, 1784. Apr 17, 1786.

Page   115 - JOHN EVANS - NC - No. 49 - Reg. Feb 21, 1788

For 10 lbs per 100 acres paid by John Evans was granted a tract of land containing 640 acres in Davidson County on the north side of Cumberland and on both sides of Evans Spring branch, adjoining Ephraim McLane's Warrant No. 5, heirs of Edward Carvin's Spring branch, crossing the road from Gaspers Station to Nashville, and thence a conditional line with Ephraim McLane's survey No. 6. Surveyed for said Evans 10 Aug 1784 by James Mulherin, D.S. George McLane and John Johnston, C.C. in consequence of a Warrant No. 202. Located and entered Jan 29, 1784. April 17, 1786.

Page   115 - JAMES SCOTT - NC - No. 48 - Reg. Feb 21, 1788

For 10 lbs per 100 acres paid by James Scott, heir of Samuel Scott, was granted a tract of land containing 640 acres in Davidson County. Surveyed for James Scott Mar 29, 1785 by B. William Pollock, D.S. James Kerr and William (illegible), C.C. in consequence of a Warrant No. 51. Located and entered Jan 2, 1784. April 17, 1786.

Page   115 - JOHN DRAKE - NC - No. 91 - Reg. Feb 21, 1788

(2nd page)   For 10 lbs per 100 acres paid by John Drake was granted a tract of land containing 640 acres in Davidson County on the north side of Cumberland River, on Whites Creek, adjoining a conditional line with David Rounsevall and crossing Whites Creek, and Jacob Shively's line. Surveyed for said Drake April 13, 1784 by James Mulherin, D.S. Benjamin Drake and Fed. Stump, C.C. in consequence of a Warrant No. 63. Located and entered Jan 6, 1784. April 17, 1786.

Page   116 - BENJAMIN DRAKE - NC - No. 58 - Reg. Feb 21, 1788

By an Act for the relief of the Officers and Soldiers of the Continental Line, in consideration of the services of Benjamin Drake, one of the Guards to the Commissioners, granted unto said Drake a tract of land containing 320 acres in Davidson County on the north side of Cumberland River on the waters of Whites Creek. Beginning at corner of his own Preemption, a double ash in Amos Heaton's line. Surveyed for said Drake Aug 15, 1785 by Anthony Bledsoe, D.S. Jonathan Drake and John Drake, C.C. in consequence of a Warrant No. (blank). Located and entered in the Preemption Office (date not given). 8 Oct 1787.

Page   116 - BENJAMIN DRAKE - NC - No. 169 - Reg. Feb 21, 1788

For 10 lbs per 100 acres paid by Benjamin Drake a tract of land containing 640 acres in Davidson County, on the north side of Cumberland River, on Whites Creek, adjoining Amos Heaton's Preemption and on bank of Heatons Creek. Surveyed for said Drake April 12, 1784 by James Mulherin, D.S. Ezekiel Smith and Robert Heaton, C.C. in consequence of a Warrant No. 64. Located and entered Jan 6, 1784 in Preemption Office. April 17, 1786.

Page   116- JAMES BRYAN - NC - No. 439 - Reg. Feb 21, 1788

By an Act for the relief of the Officers and Soldiers of the Continental Line, in consideration of the bravery and zeal of James Elliott, a private in the said line, granted unto James Bryan, assignee of said Elliott, a tract of land containing 274 acres in Davidson County on the south side of Cumberland River and on Mill Creek. Beginning at the mouth of Mill Creek, lower side and running down Cumberland River, and Col. Joseph Martin's upper corner, also by John Rice and to a conditional line with James Mulherin. Surveyed for said Bryant Mar 25, 1786 by James Mulherin, D.S. James Bryant and George Neville, C.C. in consequence of a Warrant No. 453. Located July 2, 1784.

Page   117 - JONATHAN DRAKE - NC - No. 39 - Reg. Feb 21, 1788
By an Act for the relief of the Officers and Soldiers of the Continental Line, in consideration of the services of John Drake, one of the hunters for the Guards to the Commissioners, granted unto Jonathan Drake, assignee of said John Drake, a tract of land containing 640 acres in Davidson County on the south side of Cumberland River and waters of Little Harpeth adjoining Benjamin Reed's west boundary. Surveyed for said Drake Apr 29, 1785 by James Mulherin, D.S. Jonathan Drake and Joseph Crabtree, C.C. in consequence of a Warrant No. 264. Located and entered Feb 10, 1784. Oct 8, 1787.

Page   117 - JONATHAN DRAKE - NC - No. 107 - Reg. Feb 21, 1788
For 10 lbs per 100 acres paid by Jonathan Drake granted unto said Drake a tract of land containing 640 acres in Davidson County on south side of Cumberland River and waters of Mill Creek and Browns Creek, adjoining corner of William Simpson's Preemption, as assignee of Benjamin Drake. Surveyed for said Drake Apr 21, 1784 by James Mulherin, D.S. William Ellis and Samuel Barton, C.C. in consequence of a Warrant No. 34. Located and entered Dec 30, 1783. Apr 17, 1786.

Page   117 - SAMUEL BARTON - NC - No. 121 - Reg. Feb 21, 1788
(2nd page)   For 10 lbs per 100 acres paid by Samuel Barton, granted unto Samuel Barton a tract of land containing 640 acres in Davidson County on west fork of Browns Creek and joining line of said Barton and David Mitchel and crossing the west fork of Browns Creek. Surveyed for said Barton by Thomas Molloy, D.S. Francis Armstrong and Nicholas Baker, C.C. Apr 17, 1786.

Page   118 - SAMUEL BARTON - NC - No. 60 - Reg. Feb 22, 1788
For 10 lbs per 100 acres paid by Samuel Barton, was granted a tract of land containing 640 acres in Davidson County on the head of Browns Creek adjoining the heirs of Nicholas Gentry's south line, the heirs of David Maxell's west line, and Andrew Boyd's line. Surveyed for said Barton Feb 12, 1785 by John Buchanan, D.S. William Simson and Samuel McMurry, C.C. in consequence of a Warrant No. 646. Located and entered Jan 5, 1785. 17 Apr 1786.

Page   118 - AMOS HEATON - NC - No. 82 - Reg. Feb 22, 1788
For 10 lbs per 100 acres paid by Amos Heaton, a tract of land containing 640 acres in Davidson County on the north side of Cumberland River, on the west waters of Whites Creek, adjoining Heatons Lake, Benjamin Drake's Guard Right, and Heatons Lick Creek. Surveyed for said Heaton Aug 16, 1785 by A. Bledsoe, D.S. Robert Heaton and Enoch Heaton, C.C. in consequence of a Warrant No. (blank). Located and entered at the Preemption Office. Apr 17, 1786.

Page   118 - DANIEL DUNCAN - NC - No. 193 - Reg. Feb 22, 1788
For 10 labs per 100 acres paid by Daniel Duncan, a tract of land containing

32

640 acres in Davidson County. Borders James Thompson, a conditional line formerly made between Samuel Morton and William Fletcher, crossing the west fork of Richland Creek, and Isaac Johnston's line. Surveyed for said Duncan May 8, 1784 by Thomas Molloy, D.S. Isaac Johnston and Jonathan Drake, C.C. in consequence of a Warrant No. 122. Located and entered Jan 15, 1784. Apr 17, 1786.

Page   119 - ISAAC JOHNSTON - NC - No. 13 - Reg. Feb 22, 1788
        For 10 lbs per 100 acres paid by Isaac Johnston, a tract of land containing 640 acres in Davidson County crossing Richland Creek, near the dividing ridge of Richland Creek and Fletcher Lick Creek. Surveyed for said Johnston Apr 23, 1784 by Thomas Molloy, D.S. Jacob Mills and Patrick McClary, C.C. in consequence of a Warrant No. 3. Located and entered Dec 26, 1783. April 1786.

Page   119 - ISAAC JOHNSTON - NC - No. 66 - Reg. Feb 22, 1788
        By an Act for the relief of the Officers and Soldiers of the Continental Line, in consideration of the services of Isaac Johnston, one of the Guards to the Commissioners, granted a tract of land to said Johnston containing 190 acres in Davidson County adjoining Johnston's tract No. 3, a conditional line between said Johnston and John Dunam, Richland Creek, and Johnston's tract No. 76. Surveyed for said Johnston Apr 24, 1784 by Thomas Molloy, D.S. Jacob Mills and Patrick McClary, C.C. in consequence of a Warrant No. 4. Located and entered Dec 26, 1783. Oct 8, 1787.

Page   119 - JOHN DUNAM - NC - No. 77 - Reg. Feb 22, 1788
        For 10 lbs per 100 acres paid by John Dunam, a tract of land containing 640 acres in Davidson County. Beginning near east fork of Richland Creek, joining Isaac Johnston and Francis Hodges' lines. Surveyed for said Dunam Oct 26, 1784 by Thomas Molloy, D.S. Elijah Robertson and Joseph Dunam, C.C. in consequence of a Warrant No. 269. Located and entered Feb 11, 1784. Apr 17, 1786.

Page   120 - ISAAC JOHNSTON - NC - No. 37 - Reg. Feb 22, 1788
        For 10 lbs per 100 acres paid by Isaac Johnston, a tract of land containing 640 acres in Davidson County, bounded by lands of Isaac Johnston's tract No. 3, and west of Richland Creek. Surveyed for said Johnston Apr 24, 178? by Thomas Molloy, D.S. Daniel Dunam and Patrick McClary, C.C. in consequence of a Warrant No. 76. Located and entered Jan 10, 1784. Apr 17, 1786.

Page   120 - JOHN RICE - NC - No. 5 - Reg. Feb 22, 1788
        By an Act for the relief of the Officers and Soldiers of the Continental Line, in consideration of the services of John Porter, one of the Guards to the Commissioners, granted unto John Rice, assignee of said Porter, a tract of land containing 320 acres in Davidson County about three miles below the mouth of Red River on the north side of Cumberland River joining the upper side of a Preemption in the name Barnard Tatum. Surveyed for said Rice Sept 29, 178? by B. William Pollard, D.S. Shepperd McFaddin and William Fletcher, C.C. in consequence of a Warrant No. 181. Jan 26, 1784. Oct 8, 1787.

Page   120 - JOHN RICE - NC - No. 25 - Reg. Feb 23, 1788
        By an Act for the relief of the Officers and Soldiers of the Continental Line,

in consideration of the services of William Porter, one of the Guards to the Commissioners, granted unto John Rice, assignee of said William Porter, a tract of land containing 320 acres in Davidson County in the forks of Red River and Cumberland River about east of said fork eight or ten miles. Beginning above the head of a spring that empties into Red River marked on a white oak tree E.B., bordering George Neville's line. Surveyed for said Rice June 26, 1786 by Robert Nelson, D.S. Harrison Parsons and John Lockart, C.C. in consequence of a Warrant No. 102. Located and entered Feb 22, 1784. Oct 8, 1787.

Page   121 - JOSHUA HADLEY - NC - No. 69 - Reg. Feb 23, 1788
          By an Act for the relief of the Officers and Soldiers of the Continental Line, in consideration of the bravery and zeal of Joshua Hadley, one of the Captains in the said line, granted unto Joshua Hadley a tract of land containing 3840 acres in Davidson County adjoining George Dougharty's line and to Joseph Blythe's corner. Surveyed for Joshua Hadley Mar 26, 1785 by Robert Hayes, D.S. James Robertson and Charles Crayton, C.C. in consequence of a Warrant No. 59. Located and entered Dec 22, 1783. Mar 14, 1786.

Page   121 - JOSHUA HADLEY - NC - No. 436 - Reg. Feb 23, 1788
          By an Act for the relief of the Officers and Soldiers in the Continental Line, in consideration of the bravery and zeal of Dempsey Gardner, a private in the said line, granted unto Joshua Hadley, assignee of said Dempsey Gardner, a tract of land containing 274 acres in Davidson County on the north side of Cumberland River about two miles above Roaring River. Surveyed for said Hadley Mar 14, 1787 by Edwin Hickman, D.S. Jacob My(illegible) and William Mulherin, C.C. in consequence of a Warrant No. 459. Located and entered Mar 7, 1787. Sept 15, 1787.

Page   121 - JESSEE REED - NC - No. 563 - Reg. Feb 23, 1788
(2nd page)   By an Act for the relief of the Officers and Soldiers of the Continental Line, in consideration of the bravery and zeal of Elisha Bezell, a private in the said line, granted unto Jessee Reed, assignee of said Elisha Bezell, a tract of land containing 640 acres on the south side of Big Barren River on one of the main forks of Big Barren. Surveyed for Jesse Reed Dec 6, 1786 by Thomas Hickman, D.S. James Douglass and James Bratchy, C.C. in consequence of a Warrant No. 2003. Located and entered Nov 24, 1786. Sept 15, 1787.

Page   122 - JESSE REED - NC - No. 432 - Reg. Feb 23, 1788
By an Act for the relief of the Officers and Soldiers of the Continental Line, in consideration of the bravery and zeal of George Dilway, a private in the said line, granted unto said Jesse Reed, assignee of George Dilway a tract of land containing 274 acres in Davidson County on south side of Big Bullrun the fourth creek that the Virginia line crosses to the east of Red River. Surveyed for said Reed Dec 10, 1786 by Thomas Hickman, D.S. James Douglass and James Bradley, C.C. Located and entered Dec 10, 1786. Sept 15, 1787.

Page   122 - JESSE REED - NC - No. 507 - Reg. Feb 23, 1788
          By an Act for the relief of the Officers and Soldiers of the Continental Line, in consideration of the bravery and zeal of Ahab Thompson, a private in the said line, granted unto said Jesse Reed, assignee of Ahab Thompson, a tract of land containing 640 acres in Davidson County on south side of Big Barren River on a creek known by the name

34

of Long Creek of Barren. Beginning on the Virginia line running to the creek. Surveyed for said Reed Dec 6, 1786 by Thomas Hickman, D.S. James Douglass and James Bradley, C.C. in consequence of a Warrant No. 3504. Located Nov 24, 1786. Sept 15, 1787.

Page   122 - DANIEL FLANRY - NC - No. 3 - Reg. Feb 23, 1788
By an Act for the relief of the Officers and Soldiers of the Continental Line, in consideration of the services of William Fork, one of the Guards to the Commissioners, granted unto Daniel Flanry, assignee to William Fork, a tract of land containing 320 acres in Davidson County lying on Red River. Surveyed for said Flanry Jan 9, 1786 by Henry Bradford, D.S. John Bourland and Lewis Barker, C.C. in consequence of a Warrant No. 419. Located and entered Apr 24, 1784. Oct 8, 1787.

Page   123 - EBENEZER TITUS - NC - No. 61 - Reg. Feb 25, 1788
By an Act for the relief of the Officers and Soldiers of the Continental Line, in consideration of the services of Ebenezer Titus, one of the Guards to the Commissioners, granted unto Ebenezer Titus a tract of land containing 320 acres in Davidson County on a branch of the Dry Creek on the north side of Cumberland River. Beginning at John Johnston's corner. Surveyed for said Titus July 29, 1784 by James Sanders, D.S. Morris Shean and George Frazer, C.C. in consequence of a Warrant No. 36. Located and entered Dec 30, 1785. Oct 8, 1787.

Page   123 - EBENEZER TITUS - NC - No. 21 - Reg. Feb 25, 1788
By an Acy for the relief of the Officers and Soldiers of the Continental Line, in consideration of the services of Ebenezer Titus, one of the Guards to the Commissioners, granted unto Ebenezer Titus a tract of land containing 320 acres in Davidson County lying on the north side of Little Harpeth River. Beginning at William Collinsworth's south east corner and crossing Little Harpeth River. Surveyed for said Titus Feb 25, 1785 by John Buchanan, D.S. William Marshall and Samuel McMurry, C.C. in consequence of a Warrant No. 689. Entered Feb 22, 1785. Oct 8, 1787.

Page   123 - JAMES MEANS - NC - No. 62 - Reg. Feb 25, 1788
(2nd page)   By an Act for the relief of the Officers and Soldiers, in consideration of the service of James Means, one of the Guards to the Commissioners, granted unto James Means a tract of land containing 320 acres in Davidson County. Bordering David Shannon's Preemption and east branch of Whites Creek. Surveyed for James Means June 19, 1784. John Shannon and David Shannon, C.C. in consequence of a Warrant No. 317. Located and entered Feb 28, 1784. Oct 8, 1787.

Page   124 - EBENEZER TITUS - NC - No. 110 - Reg. Feb 25, 1788
For 10 lbs per 100 acres paid by Ebenezer Titus, granted unto Ebenezer Titus a tract of land containing 640 acres in Davidson County on the east branch of Whites Creek. Beginning on a conditional line between said Titus and William G(illegible). Surveyed for said Titus Apr 20, 1784 by John Buchanan, D.S. Richard Sh(illegible) and Samuel Buchanan, C.C. in consequence of a Warrant No. 127. Located and entered Jan 15, 1784. Apr 17, 1786.

Page   124 - DANIEL FRAZER - NC - No. 15 - Reg. Feb 25, 1788

For 10 lbs per 100 acres paid by Daniel Frazer, granted unto Daniel Frazer a tract of land containing 640 acres in Davidson County on the north side of Cumberland River and on both sides of Dry Creek, adjoining John Johnston, Thomas Kilgore, John Blackamore, and James Hanady.   Surveyed for Daniel Frazer Oct 26, 1784 by James Sanders, D.S. John Frazer and William Frazer, C.C. in consequence of a Warrant No. 608. Apr 17, 1786.

Page   124 - GEORGE FREELAND - NC - No. 40 - Reg. Feb 25, 1788

For 10 lbs per 100 acres paid by George Freeland a tract of land containing 640 acres in Davidson County. Beginning on the land laid off for the French Lick eighty poles from the Cumberland River, and on a conditional line made between James Robertson, Benjamin Logan and George Freeland. Surveyed for said Freeland Mar 1, 1785 by Thomas Molloy, D.S. in consequence of a Warrant No. 85. Located and entered Jan 13, 1784. Apr 17, 1786.

Page   125 - GEORGE FREELAND - NC - No. 82 - Reg. Feb 25, 1788

By an Act for the relief of the Officers and Soldiers of the Continental Line, in consideration of the service of George Freeland, one of the Guards to the Commissioners, reanted unto George Freeland a tract of land containing 320 acres in Davidson County. Beginning at the bank of the Cumberland River the northeast corner of the land laid off for the French Lick and borders George Freeland's Preemption. Surveyed for said Freeland Mar 14, 1785 by Thomas Molloy, D.S. in consequence of a Warrant No. (blank). Located and entered Jan 13, 1784. Oct 8, 1787.

Page   125 - DANIEL FRAZER - NC - No. 104 - Reg. Feb 25, 1788

For 10 lbs per 100 acres paid by Daniel Frazer a tract of land containing 640 acres in Davidson County on Whites Creek. Beginning at James Hollans north boundary and John Crow's line. Surveyed for said Frazer May 18, 1785 by James Sanders, D.S. John Frazer and William Loggins, C.C. in consequence of a Warrant No. 390. Located and entered Apr 5, 1784. Apr 17, 1786.

Page   125 - JOHN CROW - NC - No. 122 - Reg. Feb 26, 1788
(2nd page)   For 10 lbs per 100 acres paid by John Crow, a tract of land containing 640 acres in Davidson County on the waters of Whites Creek, on north side of Cumberland River. Surveyed for said Crow Dec 15, 1784 by James Sanders, D.S. David and Jos. Shannon, C.C. in consequence of a Warrant No. 319. Located and entered Feb 28, 1784. Apr 17, 1786.

Page   126 - WILLIAM MARSHALL - NC - No. 45 - Reg. Feb 26, 1788

By an Act for the relief of the Officers and Soldiers of the Continental Line, in consideration of the service of William Marshall, one of the Guards to the Commissioners, granted unto William Marshall a tract of land containing 320 acres in Davidson County on the waters of Big Harpeth. Adjoining lands of Laurence Stephens, crossing a branch of Big Harpeth, and John McMurry's land. Surveyed for William Marshall Feb 21, 1785 by John Buchanan, D.S. Samuel McHenry and William Simpson, C.C. in consequence of a Warrant No. 192. Located and entered Jan 27, 1784. 8 Oct 1787.

Page   126 - DAVID SHANNON - NC - No. 30 - Reg. Feb 26, 1788

For 10 lbs per 100 acres paid by David Shannon, granted unto said Shannon a tract of land containing 640 acres in Davidson County on the north branch of Whites Creek. Beginning above the head of his speing. Surveyed for said Shannon June 18, 1784 by James Sanders, D.S. John Shannon and James Mean, C.C. in consequence of a Warrant No. 320. Located and entered Feb 28, 1784. Apr 17, 1786.

Page   126 - NATHAN McCLURE - NC - No. 10 - Reg. Feb 26, 1788

By an Act for the relief of the Officers and Soldiers of the Continental Line, in consideration of the service of Nathan McClure, one of the Guards to the Commissioners, granted unto Nathan McClure a tract of land containing 320 acres in Davidson County on Whites Creek. Surveyed for said McClure Aug 4, 1784 by James Sanders, D.S. James Means and Abraham Price, C.C. in consequence of a Warrant No. 376. Located and entered Mar 30, 1784. Oct 8, 1787.

Page   127 - ELIJAH ROBERTSON - NC - No. 597 - Reg. Feb 26, 1788

By an Act for the relief of the Officers and Soldiers of the Continental Line, in consideration of the bravery and zeal of Amos Thomas, a private in the said line, granted unto Elijah Robertson, assignee of Amos Thomas, a tract of land containing 640 acres in Davidson County on the north side of Cumberland River, on the north branch of Sycamore Creek on the lower road that leads from Nashville to Red River, adjoining lands of Henry Rutherford and Reading Blount. Surveyed for said Robertson June 3, 1786 by Robert Weakley, D.S. Jonathan Drake and John Drake, C.C. in consequence of a Warrant No. 1832. Located and entered Mar 1, 1786. Sept 15, 1787.

Page   127 - ELIJAH ROBERTSON - NC - No. 488 - Reg. Feb 26, 1788

By an Act for the relief of the Officers and Soldiers of the Continental Line, in consideration for the bravery and zeal of Thomas Morgan, a private in the said line, granted unto Elijah Robertson, assignee of said Thomas Morgan, a tract of land containing 640 acres in Davidson County, on the north side of Cumberland River, on the head branches of the second small creek that runs into said river above McFarlin's cabin. Adjoining lands of Readen Blount. Surveyed for said Robertson July 6, 1786 by Robert Weakley, D.S. James Hollis and Jonathan Drake, C.C. in consequence of a Warrant No. 2209. Located and entered Apr 5, 1786.

Page   127 - THOMAS THOMPSON - NC - No. 687 - Reg. Feb 26, 1788

By an Act for the relief of the Officers and Soldiers of the Continental Line, in consideration of the bravery and zeal of William Thomas, a private in the said line, granted unto Thomas Thompson, assignee of William Thomas, a tract of land containing 640 acres in Davidson County on the west fork of Jones Creek. Beginning at a white oak on the Chickasaw Trace being Robert Capers beginning corner. Surveyed for said Thompson Oct 12, 1787 by John Buchanan, D.S. Jason Thompson and J. Thomas, C.C. in consequence of a Warrant No. 818. Located Jan 21, 1786.

Page   128 - SAMUEL BUCCHANAN - NC - No. 323 - Reg. Feb 26, 1788

By an Act for the relief of the Officers and Soldiers of the Continental Line,

in consideration of the bravery and zeal of Anthony Charter, a private in the said line, granted unto Samuel Bucchanan, assignee of Anthony Charter, a tract of land containing 640 acres in Davidson County adjoining west bank of Spring Creek, and Robert Marley's south boundary. Surveyed for said Bucchanan May 1, 1786 by John Buchanan, D.S. Cornelius Rudd and Samuel Buchanan, C.C. in consequence of a Warrant No. 1755. Located Jan 21, 1786. Aug 1, 1787.

Page   128 - SAMUEL BUCCHANAN - NC - No. 324 - Reg. Feb 26, 1788
By an Act for the relief of the Officers and Soldiers in the Continental Line, in consideration of the bravery and zeal of Col. Martin Armstrong, surveyor of the lands, granted unto Samuel Bucchanan, assignee of said Armstrong, a tract of land containing 400 acres in Davidson County on the west waters of Stones River. Adjoining lands of Cirnelius Rudd. Surveyed for said Bucchanan Apr 5, 1786 by John Bucchanan, D.S. Cornelius Rudd and William Mulherin, C.C. by virtue of the aforesaid Right. Located Dec 5, 1785. Aug 1, 1787.

Page   128 - JOHN FORDE - NC - No. 591 - Reg. Feb 27, 1788
(2nd page)   By an Act for the relief of the Officers and Soldiers of the Continental Line, in consideration of the bravery and zeal of James Hagins, a private in the said line, granted unto John Forde, assignee of said Hagins, a tract of land containing 640 acres in Davidson County, on the south side of Cumberland River about four miles above the Virginia line. Surveyed for said Forde Dec 17, 1785 by Robert Hays, D.S. James Taton and Patrick Dillen, C.C. in consequence of a Warrant No. 898. Located July 19, 1785. Sept 15, 1787.

Page   129 - JOHN COCKRILL - NC - No. 148 - Reg. Feb 27, 1788
For 10 lbs per 100 acres paid by John Cockrill, granted unto said Cockrill a tract of land containing 640 acres in Davidson County. Beginning at an ash marked R about 120 poles southeast of Nealey's Spring, and crossing a fork of the French Lick branch twice. Surveyed for said Cockrill Apr 26, 1784 by Thomas Molloy, D.S. Mark Robertson and William Meelin, C.C. in consequence of a Warrant No. 13. Entry dated Dec 26, 1783. Apr 17, 1786.

Page   129 - JOHN COCKRILL - NC - No. 171 - Reg. Feb 27, 1788
For 10 lbs per 100 acres paid by John Cockrill, granted unto said Cockrill a tract of land containing 640 acres in Davidson County on the waters of the east fork of Mill Creek, adjoining James Foster's Preemption, crossing Foster's spring branch, and crossing a branch of Mill Creek. Surveyed for said Cockrill June 19, 1784 by John Buchanan, D.S. James Collins and Thomas Russell, C.C. in consequence of a Warrant No. 83. Entered Jan 12, 1784. Apr 17, 1786.

Page   129 - JOHN COCKRILL - NC - No. 149 - Reg. Feb 27, 1788
For 10 lbs per 100 acres paid by John Cockrill, granted unto said Cockrill a tract of land containing 640 acres in Davidson County on the head of some south branches of Little Harpeth adjoining lands of William Collinsworth and John Crockett. Surveyed for said Cockrill Oct 28, 1784 by JOhn Buchanan, D.S. Andrew Crockett and James Collins, C.C. in consequence of a Warrant No. 113. Entered Jan 15, 1784. Apr 15, 1786.

Page   130 - JOHN WALKER - NC - No. 12 - Reg. Feb 27, 1788
                For 10 lbs per 100 acres paid by John Walker, granted unto said Walker a
tract of land containing 640 acres in Davidson County on the head of Gibsons Creek
adjoining James Scott's Preemption. Surveyed for John Walker Dec ?, 1783 by B. William
Pollock, D.S. in consequence of a Warrant No. 265. Located and entered Feb 10, 1784. Apr
17, 1786.

Page   130 - WILLIAM SIMPSON - NC - No. 69 - Reg. Feb 27, 1788
                For 10 lbs per 100 acres paid by William Simpson, granted unto said Simpson
a tract of land containing 640 acres in Davidson County on the head of Little Harpeth
adjoining William Nevel's Preemption and crossing Little Harpeth.   Surveyed for said
Simpson Feb 15, 1785 by John Buchanan, D.S. Samuel Barton and William Marshall, C.C. in
consequence of a Warrant No. 30. Located and entered Dec 30, 1783. Apr 17, 1786.

Page   130 - WILLIAM SIMPSON - NC - No. 174 - Reg. Feb 27, 1788
                For 10 lbs per 100 acres paid by William Simpson, granted unto said Simpson
a tract of land containing 640 acres in Davidson County on the waters of Mill Creek
adjoining Jonathan Drake. Surveyed for said Simpson Apr 21, 1784 by James Mulherin, D.S.
James Ray and William Marshall, C.C. in consequence of a Warrant No. 31. Located and
entered Dec 30, 1783. Apr 17, 1786.

Page   131 - WILLIAM GALLASPY - NC - No. 36 - Reg. Feb 27, 1788
                For 10 lbs per 100 acres paid by William Gallaspy, granted unto said Gallaspy
a tract of land containing 640 acres in Davidson County adjoining James McGavock's land.
Surveyed for said Gallaspy Nov 10, 1784 by D. McGavock, D.S. in consequence of a Warrant
No. 68. Entered Jan 8, 1784. Apr 17, 1786.

Page   131 - WILLIAM GALLASPY - NC - No. 62 - Reg. Feb 27, 1788
                For 10 lbs per 100 acres paid by William Gallaspy, granted unto said Gallaspy
a tract of land containing 640 acres in Davidson County on Thompsons Creek adjoining
William Bowen's Preemption. Surveyed for said Gallaspy June 17, 1785 by John Buchanan,
D.S.   William Bowen and James Henson, C.C. in consequence of a Warrant No. 224.
Entered Jan 31, 1784. Apr 17, 1786.

Page   131 - JAMES McGAVOCK - NC - No. 20 - Reg. Feb 28, 1788
(2nd page)   By an Act for the relief of the Officers and Soldiers of the Continental Line
and in consideration of the services of James McGavock, one of the Commissioner's Guard,
granted unto James McGavock a tract of land containing 640 acres in Davidson County
south of the river. Surveyed for said McGavock Nov 9, 1784 by David McGavock, D.S.
Warrant No. 67. Located and entered Jan 8, 1784. Oct 8, 1787.

Page   132 - WILLIAM COLLINSWORTH - NC - No. 72 - Reg. Feb 28, 1788
                By an Act for the relief of the Officers and Soldiers of the Continental Line,
in consideration of the service of William Collinsworth, one of the Guards to the
Commissioners, granted unto said Collinsworth a tract of land containing 640 acres in
Davidson Countyon a north branch of Little Harpeth adjoining James Leeper, John
Henderson, the heirs of James Mayfield, and Thomas Denton.   Surveyed for said

39

Collinsworth May 26, 1785 by John Buchanan, D.S. William Collinsworth and George Leeper, C.C. in consequence of a Warrant No. 410. Located and entered Apr 19, 1784. Oct 8, 1787.

Page   132 - WILLIAM COLLINSWORTH - NC - No. 43 - Reg. Feb 28, 1788
            For 10 lbs per 100 acres paid by William Collinsworth, granted unto said Collinsworth a tract of land containing 640 acres in Davidson County on Little Harpeth River. Line crosses Cockrill's spring branch. Surveyed for said Collinsworth Oct 27, 1784 by John Buchanan, D.S. Jonas Manifee and James Ingram, C.C. in consequence of a Warrant No. 315. Located and entered Feb 28, 1784. Apr 17, 1786.

Page   132 - DANIEL HOW - NC - No. 128 - Reg. Feb 28, 1788
            For 10 lbs per 100 acres paid by Daniel How, granted unto said How a tract of land containing 640 acres in Davidson County on the north side of Big Harpeth River adjoining William Marshall and crossing a branch of Big Harpeth. Surveyed for said How Feb 24, 1785 by John Buchanan, D.S. William Simpson and Samuel McMurry, C.C. in consequence of a Warrant No. 364. Located and entered Mar 18, 1784. Apr 17, 1786.

Page   133 - WILLIAM NEWELL - NC - No. 138 - Reg. FEB 28, 1788
            For 10 lbs per 100 acres paid by William Newell, granted unto said Newell a tract of land containing 640 acres of land in Davidson County on the head of Little Harpeth. Surveyed for said Newell Feb 17, 1785 by John Buchanan, D.S. William Simpson and William Marshall, C.C. in consequence of a Warrant No. 481. Located and entered June 9, 1784. Apr 17, 1786.

Page   133 - ANDREW EWING - NC - No. 156 - Reg. Feb 28, 1788
            For 10 lbs per 100 acres paid by Andrew Ewing, granted unto said Ewing a tract of land containing 640 acres in Davidson County on the west fork of Mill Creek. Beginning about half mile below his spring and bordering Simpson's line. Surveyed for said Ewing Sept 7, 1784 by James Mulherin, D.S. Dan. Hogan and John Tucker, C.C. in consequence of a Warrant No. 129. Located and entered Jan 10, 1784. Apr 17, 1786.

Page   133 - GREEN HILL - NC - No. 184 - Reg. Feb 29, 1788
            By an Act for the relief of the Officers and Soldiers of the Continental Line, in consideration of the bravery and zeal of John McCoy, a private in the said line, granted unto Green Hill, assignee of John McCoy, a tract of land containing 640 acres in Davidson County on the north side of Tennessee River, one mile and a half below the mouth of Dyers Creek. Surveyed for said Hill Oct 5, 1785 by William Murry, D.S. John Dyer and Thomas Sturgen, C.C. Grant signed by Richard Caswell Mar 7, 1786. Located July 4, 1785.

Page   134 - GREEN HILL - NC - No. 166 - Reg. Feb 29, 1788
            By an Act for the relief of the Officers and Soldiers of the Continental Line, in consideration of the bravery and zeal of Randolph Humphries, a private in the said line, granted unto said Green Hill, assignee of said Randolph Humphries, a tract of land containing 640 acres in Davidson County on the waters of Little Harpeth and Mill Creek and adjoining William Collinsworth and Thomas Denton. Surveyed for said Hill Aug 6, 1785. by

John Buchanan, D.S. William Mor(illegible) and Ephraim McLane, C.C. in consequence of a Warrant No. 811. Located June 2, 1785. Mar 7, 1786.

Page   134 - GREEN HILL - NC - No. 152 - Ret. Feb 29, 1788
        By an Act for the relief of the Officers and Soldiers of the Continental Line, in consideration of the bravery and zeal of John Henry, a private in the said line, granted unto Green Hill, assignee of John Henry, a tract of land containing 640 acres in Davidson County on the north side of Tennessee River, adjoining Sugron Alexander's corner. Surveyed for Green Hill Aug 23, 1785 by William Murry, D.S. James Ireson(?) and Obediah Roberts, C.C. in consequence of a Warrant No. 1071. Located 7 May 1785. Mar 7, 1786.

Page   134 - GREEN HILL - NC - No. 208 - Reg. Feb 29, 1788
        By an Act for the relief of the Officers and Soldiers of the Continental Line, in consideration of the bravery and zeal of David Driskill, a private in the said line, granted unto Green Hill a tract of land consisting 274 acres in Davidson County on the north side of Cumberland River, adjoining Ephraim McLane, John Evans, and John Thomas. Warrant No. 1057. Located Aug 7, 1784, surveyed June 24, 1785 by Ephraim McLane. Grant signed by Caswell Mar 7, 1786.

Page   135 - GREEN HILL - NC - No. 181 - Reg. Feb 29, 1788
        By an Act for the relief of the Officers and Soldiers of the Continental Line, in consideration of the bravery and zeal of Andrew Randall, a sergeant in the said line, granted unto Green Hill, assignee of said Randall, a tract of land consisting of 1000 acres in Davidson County on the south side of Duck River. Beginning below Captain Fannin's Corner. Surveyed for Green Hill July 20, 1785 by William Murry, D.S. James Ireson and James Johnston, C.C. in consequence of a Warrant No 425. Located May 17, 1785. Mar 7, 1786.

Page   135 - RICHARD FENNER - NC - No. 277 - Reg. Feb 29, 1788
        By an Act for the relief of the Officers and Soldiers of the Continental Line, in consideration of the bravery and zeal of John Benson, a private in the said line, granted unto Richard Fenner a tract of land containing 640 acres in Davidson County on south side of Cumberland River below the mouth of Tolleys Creek. Surveyed for Richard Fenner Mar 17, 1786 by Mulherin, D.S. Henry Howdyshall and Jeremiah York, C.C. by virtue of a Military Warrant No. 2171. Located Sept 3, 1785. Mar 27, 1787.

Page   136 - GREEN HILL - NC - No. 299 - Reg. Mar 1, 1788
        By an Act for the relief of the Soldiers and Soldiers of the Continental Line, in consideration of the bravery and zeal of William Walter, a private in the said line, granted unto Green Hill, assignee of said William Walter, a tract of land containing 640 acres in Davidson County on the waters of Stones Creek on the Big Hurricane Creek. Beginning northeast corner near Elizabeth Readen's line. Surveyed for Green Hill Aug 6, 1785 by John Buchanan, D.S. Ephraim McLane and William Morrow, C.C. in consequence of a Military Warrant No. 1067. Located June 2, 1785. Mar 7, 1786.

Page   136 - RICHARD FENNER - NC - No. 276 - Reg. Mar 1, 1788
        By an Act for the relief of the Officers and Soldiers of the Continental Line,

granted unto Richard Fenner, assignee of said Fenner, a tract of land containing 640 acres in Davidson County on the south side of Cumberland River and on Collins River. Beginning at a southwest corner to a tract of 640 acres of James C. Montflorence, and of the heirs of Thomas Syms. Surveyed for Richard Fenner (blank), 1786 by James Mulherin, D.S. Henry Howdyshall and Jeremiah York, C.C. by virtue of a Military Warrant No. 2076. Located Feb 23, 1786. Mar 22, 1787.

Page   136 - RICHARD FENNER - NC - No. 278 - Reg Mar 1, 1788
        By an Act for the relief of the Officers and Soldiers of the Continental Line, in consideration of the bravery and zeal of Randal Green, a private in the said line, granted unto Richard Fenner, assignee of Randal Green, assignee of said Green, a tract of land containing 640 acres in Davidson County on the southside of Cumberland River and waters of Collins River, adjoining the heirs of Jacob Griffin's tract. Surveyed for Richard Fenner June 20, 1786 by James Mulherin, D.S. Henry Howdyshall and Jeremiah York, C.C. in consequence of a Military Warrant No. 2096. located Feb 25, 1786. Mar 22, 1787.

Page   136 - JAMES COLE MONTFLORENCE - NC - No. 287 - Reg. Mar 1, 1788
        By an Act for the relief of the Officers and Soldiers of the Continental Line, in consideration of the bravery and zeal of Robert Hutchens, a private in the said line, granted unto James Cole Montflorence, assignee of Robert Hutchens, a tract of land containing 640 acres in Davidson County on the south side of Cumberland River. Beginning on the south bank of said river opposite the upper end of the first timbered island below the mouth of Thompsons Creek. Surveyed for James Cole Montflorence Mar 3, 1786 by James Mulherin, D.S. Henry Howdyshall and Jeremiah York, C.C. in consequence of a Military Warrant No. 2033. Located Sept 23, 1786. Mar 22, 1787.

Page   137 - JAMES COLE MONTFLORENCE - NC - No. 279 - Reg. Mar 1, 1788
        By an Act for the relief of the Officers and Soldiers of the Continental Line, in consideration of the bravery and zeal of Daniel Monhouse, a private in the said line, granted unto James Cole Montflorence, assignee of heirs of said Monhouse, a tract of land containing 640 acres in Davidson County on the north side of Cumberland River. Beginng on the banks of said river opposite the mouth of Thompsons Creek. Surveyed for James Cole Montflorence Mar 13, 1786 by James Mulherin, D.S. Henry Howdyshall and Jeremiah York, C.C. in consequence of a Military Warrant No. 2044. Located Feb 25, 1786. Mar 22, 1787.

Page   137 - JAMES COLE MONTFLORENCE - NC - No. 280 - Reg. Mar 1, 1788
        By an Act for the relief of the Officers and Soldiers of the Continental Line, in consideration of the bravery and zeal of Thomas Sims, a private in the said line, granted unto James Cole Montflorence, assignee of heirs of said Sims, a tract of land containing 640 acres in Davidson County crossing Collins River. Surveyed for said Montflorence Mar 25, 1786 by James Mulherin, D.S. Henry Howdyshall and Jeremiah York, C.C. in consequence of a Military Warrant No. 2057. Located Feb 25, 1786. Mar 22, 1787.

Page   137 - JAMES COLE MONTFLORENCE - NC - No. 285 - Reg. Mar 1, 1788
        By an Act for the relief of the Officers and Soldiers of the Continental Line, in consideration of the bravery and zeal of William Lawson, a private in the said line,

granted unto James Cole Montflorence, assignee of the heirs of William Lawson, a tract of land containing 640 acres in Davidson County on the north side of Cumberland River. Surveyed for said Montflorence Mar 13, 1786 by James Mulherin, D.S. Henry Howdyshall and Jeremiah York, C.C. in consequence of a Military Warrant No. 2054. Located Feb 24, 1786. Mar 22, 1787.

Page   138 - JAMES COLE MONTFLORENCE - NC - No. 284 - Reg. Mar 1, 1788
        By an Act for the relief of the Officers and Soldiers of the Continental Line, in consideration for the bravery and zeal of John Nelson, a private on the said line, granted unto James Cole Montflorence, assignee of John Nelson's heirs, a tract of land containing 640 acres in Davidson County on the south side of Cumberland River and waters of Collins River, adjoining his tract as assignee of Sims. Surveyed for said Montflorence June 20, 1786 by James Mulherin, D.S. Henry Howdyshall and Jeremiah York, C.C. in consequence of a Military Warrant No. 2062. Located Feb 25, 1786. Mar 22, 1787.

Page   138 - JAMES COLE MONTFLORENCE - NC - No. 281 - Reg. Mar 1, 1788
        By an Act for the relief of the Officers and Soldiers of the Continental Line, in consideration of the bravery and zeal of Joseph Hawkins, a private in the said line, granted unto James Cole Montflorence, assignee of the heirs of Joseph Hawkins, a tract of land containing 640 acres in Davidson County on the south side of Cumberland River and on Collins River, adjoining a corner of said Montflorence, assignee of the heirs of Thomas Sims' tract and crossing Collins River. Surveyed for said Montflorence (blank) 1786 by James Mulherin, D.S. Henry Howdyshall and Jeremiah York, C.C. in consequence of a Military Warrant No. 2098. Located 25 Feb 1786. Mar 22, 1787.

Page   138 - JAMES COLE MONTFLORENCE - NC - No. 282 - Reg. Mar 1, 1788
(2nd page)   By an Act for the relief of the Officers and Soldiers of the Continental Line, in consideration of the bravery and zeal of Timothy Mars, a private in the said line, granted unto James Cole Montflorence, assignee of the heirs of Timothy Mars, a tract of land containing 640 acres in Davidson County on south side of Cumberland River and on the waters of Collins River. Surveyed for said Montflorence June 20, 1786 by James Mulherin, D.S. Henry Howdyshall and Jeremiah York, C.C. in consequence of a Warrant No. 2094. Located Feb 25, 1786. Mar 22, 1787.

Page   139 - JAMES COLE MONTFLORENCE - NC - No. 286 - Reg. Mar 1, 1788
        By an Act for the relief of the Officers and Soldiers of the Continental Line, in consideration of the bravery and zeal of William Nowell, a private in the said line, granted unto said Montflorence, assignee of the heirs of William Nowell, a tract of land containing 640 acres in Davidson County on the south side of Cumberland River and on Collins River. Surveyed for said Montflorence June 20, 1786 by James Mulherin, D.S. Henry Howdyshall and Jeremiah York, C.C. in consequence of a Warrant No. 2097. Located Feb 25,, 1786. Mar 22, 1787.

Page   139 - JAMES COLE MONTFLORENCE - NC - No. 213 - Reg. Mar 1, 1788
        By an Act for the relief of the Officers and Soldiers of the Continental Line, in consideration of the bravery and zeal of John Polk, a sergeant in the said line, granted

unto James Cole Montflorence, assignee of the heirs of John Polk, a tract of land containing 1000 acres in Davidson County adjoining a survey of 1600 acres which lies on one of the head branches of Cedar Creek and includes two small licks on the north side of Cumberland River, and a buffalo road. Surveyed for said Montflorence Apr 23, 1786 by Robert Ewing, D.S. Edward Jones and Edmond Jennings, C.C. Warrant No. 2149. Located Jan 23, 1786. Mar 22, 1787.

Page   139 - JOHN DONNALDSON, SEN. - NC - No. 115 - Reg. Mar 3, 1788
        For 10 lbs per 100 acres paid by John Donnaldson, Sen., granted unto John Donnaldson a tract of land containing 640 acres in Davidson County on branches of Big Harpeth River and on north side of James McGavock's Preemption. Beginning on the little south road, and to Anthony Sharp's line. Surveyed for said Donnaldson, Sen., Apr 12, 1785 by John Donnaldson, D.S. William Marshall and William Pursell, C.C. in consequence of a Warrant No. 282. Located Feb 14, 1784. Apr 17, 1786.

Page   140 - LARDNER CLARK - NC - No. 15 - Reg. Mar 3, 1788
        By an Act for the relief of the Officers and Soldiers of the Continental Line, in consideration of the bravery and zeal of Col. Martin Armstrong, surveyor of the lands, granted unto Lardner Clark, assignee of said Armstrong, a tract of land containing 640 acres in Davidson County on the south side of Cumberland River adjoining corner of Joseph Davis' Preemption, and the banks of Cumberland River. Surveyed for said Clark Apr 1, 1785 by Joseph Brock, D.S. Ephraim Drake and James Ireson, C.C. in consequence of a Service Right No. 498. Located Dec 10, 1784. Oct 8, 1787.

Page   140 - WICOFF & CLARK - NC - No. 593 - Reg. Mar 3, 1788
        By an Act for the relief of the Officers and Soldiers of the Continental Line, in consideration of the bravery and zeal of Charles Burk, a private in the said line, granted unto Wicoff and Clark, assignees of said Burk, a tract of land containing 640 acres in Davidson County on the north side of Cumberland River above Blooming Grove, joining the north boundary of John Shelby's claim, east boundary of Hamilton's Preemption. Beginning at John Hamilton's north east corner, Shelby's line and Robert Nelson's corner. Surveyed for Wicoff and Clark Mar 10, 1786 by Robert Nelson, D.S. George Bell and William Bell, C.C. in consequence of a Military Warrant No. 1947. Located Nov 28, 1785. Sept 15, 1787.

Page   140 - WILLIAM WICOFF & LARDNER CLARK - NC - No. 523 - Reg. Mar 3, 1788
        By an Act for the relief of the Officers and Soldiers of the Continental Line, in consideration of the bravery and zeal of James Roper, a private in the said line, granted unto William Wicoff and Lardner Clark, assignees of said James Roper, a tract of land containing 274 acres in Davidson County on the waters of North Cross Creek adjoining Thomas Sharp and Jessee Maxey's west boundary. Surveyed for said Wicoff and Clark Mar 15, 1786 by Thomas Molloy, D.S. William Hamilton and Edward McDonald, C.C. in consequence of a Warrant No. 2267. Located Dec 8, 1785. Sept 15, 1787.

Page   141 - WICOFF & CLARK - NC - No. 524 - Reg. Mar 3, 1788
        By an Act for the relief of the Officers and Soldiers of the Continental Line, in consideration of the bravery and zeal of Marmaduke Hedgpeth, a private in the said line,

granted unto William Wicoff and Lardner Clark, assignees of said Hedgpeth, a tract of land containing 274 acres in Davidson County on the south side of Cumberland River about one mile and a half above the mouth of Harpeth, adjoining Jesse Harrison's corner. Surveyed for Wicoff and Clark Mar 12, 1786 by Thomas Molloy, D.S. William Harrington and Edward McDonald, C.C. in consequence of a Military Warrant No. 1953. Located Dec 6, 1785. Sept 15, 1787.

Page   141 - LARDNER CLARK - NC - No. 585 - Reg. Mar 3, 1788
          By an Act for the relief of the Officers and Soldiers of the Continental Line, in consideration of the bravery and zeal of Andrew Faddis, a private in the said line, granted unto Lardner Clark, assignee of said Faddis, a tract of land containing 640 acres in Davidson County on the first small creek on the north side of Cumberland River below John Rice's Preemption. Surveyed for Lardner Clark Mar 7, 1786 by Robert Nelson, D.S. George Bell and Hugh Bell, C.C. in consequence of a Military Warrant No. 1190. Located Apr 7, 1785. Sept 15, 1788.

Page   141 - LARDNER CLARK - NC - No. 4 - Reg. Mar 3, 1788
(2nd page)   By an Act for the relief of the Officers and Soldiers of the Continental Line, in consideration of the services of Col. Martin Armstrong, surveyor of lands, granted unto Lardner Clark, assignee of said Armstrong, a tract of land containing 560 acres in Davidson County on Indian Camp Creek, adjoining Samuel McMurry's land. Surveyed for Lardner Clark by John Buchanan, D.S. Samuel McMurry and James Mulherin, C.C. in consequence of a Service Right No. 937. Located Apr 31, 1785. Oct 8, 1787.

Page   142 - LARDNER CLARK - NC - No. 127 - Reg. Mar 3, 1788
          For 10 lbs per 100 acres paid by Lardner Clark granted unto said Clark a tract of land containing 640 acres in Davidson County adjoining Green Hill's west boundary, crossing a ford of Hurricane Creek. Surveyed for said Clark June 1, 1785 by John Buchanan, D.S. Ephraim McLane and William Morrow, C.C. Located and entered July 6, 1784. Apr 17, 1786.

Page   142 - WICOFF & CLARK - NC - No. 652 - Reg. Mar 3, 1788
          By an Act for the relief of the Officers and Soldiers of the Continental Line, in consideration of the bravery and zeal of Joseph Gross, a private in the said line, granted unto Wicoff and Clark, assignees of said Gross, a tract of land containing 640 acres in Davidson County on the south boundary of Capt. Fawn's survey on Elk River. Surveyed for Wicoff and Clark June 1786 by Robert Nelson, D.S. in consequence of a Military Warrant No. 2186. Located (blank) 1786. Dec 8, 1787.

Page   142 - LARDNER CLARK - NC - No. 648 - Reg. Mar 3, 1788
          By an Act for the relief of the Officers and Soldiers of the Continental Line, in consideration for the bravery and zeal of Mordica Holman, a private in the said line, granted unto Lardner Clark, assignee of Mordica Holman, a tract of land containing 640 acres in Davidson County on waters of Hurricane Creek a branch of Stones Creek, adjoining Capt. James Bradley's line and Henry Oharrow's line. Surveyed for said Clark Feb 1, 1786 by John Buchanan, D.S. Samuel McMurry and James Mulherin, C.C. in consequence of a Warrant No. 1661. Located Sept 9, 1785. Dec 8, 1787.

Page   143 - WILLIAM DONNALDSON - NC - No. 140 - Reg. Mar 4, 1788
          For 10 lbs per 100 acres paid by William Donnaldson, granted unto said
Donnaldson a tract of land containing 640 acres of land in Davidson County on a branch of
Big Harpeth River adjoining John Donaldson.   Beginning on William Marshall's line.
Surveyed for said Donnaldson Apr 12, 1785 by John Donnaldson, D.S.   William Purnel and
William Marshall, C.C. in consequence of a Warrant No. 286. Located and entered Feb 14,
1785. Signed by Richard Caswell Apr 17, 1786.

Page   143 - JOHN DONNALDSON, JR. - NC - No. 114 - Reg. Mar 4, 1788
          For 10 lbs per 100 acres paid by John Donnaldson, Jun. a tract of land
containing 3640 acres in Davidson County on Big Harpeth. Surveyed for said Donaldson Apr
9, 1785 by John Donnaldson, D.S. Jonathan Robertson and Joseph Neal, C.C. in consequence
of a Warrant No. 290. Located and entered Feb 16, 1784. Apr 17, 1786.

Page   143 - WILLIAM PURNELL - NC - No. 123 - Reg. Mar 4, 1788
          For 10 lbs per 100 acres paid by William Purnell, granted unto William
Purnell a tract of land containing 640 acres in Davidson Countyon the south side of Big
Harpeth River. Surveyed for said Purnell Apr 9, 1785 by John Donaldson, D.S.   William
Gallaspy and William Donaldson, C.C. in consequence of a Warrant No. 323. Located and
entered Mar 1, 1784. Apr 17, 1786.

Page   144 - TURNER WILLIAMS - NC - No. 4 - Reg. Mar 4, 1788
          By an Act for the relief of the Officers and Soldiers of the Continental Line,
in consideration of the service of Turner Williams, one of the Guards to the Commissioners,
granted unto said Williams a tract of land containing 320 acres in Davidson County on the
north side of Cumberland River adjoining Daniel Williams' Preemption.   Surveyed for said
Williams Jan 14, 1786 by James Mulherin, D.S.   William Overall and John Rice, C.C. in
consequence of a Warrant No. 22. Located and entered Dec 29, 1783. Oct 8, 1787.

Page   144 - JOHN BROWN - NC - No. 133 - Reg. Mar 4, 1788
          For 10 lbs per 100 acres paid by John Brown, granted unto John Brown a
tract of land containing 640 acres in Davidson County on south side of Cumberland River
and waters of the west fork of Mill Creek, adjoining William Overall's north boundary,
Samuel Walker's Preemption, John Henderson's Preemption, and James Ray's Preemption.
Surveyed for said Brown Feb 10, 1785 by James Mulherin, D.S.   Daniel Hogan and Sutherlin
Mayfield, C.C. in consequence of a Warrant No. 202(252?). Located and entered Feb 7,
1784. Apr 17, 1786.

Page   145 - ROBERT MOORE - NC - No. 68 - Reg. Mar 4, 1788
          For 10 lbs per 100 acres paid by Robert Moore, granted unto said Moore a
tract of land containing 640 acres in Davidson County, joining Josiah Ramsey's line.
Surveyed for said Moore Dec 11, 1784 by David McGavock, D.S. in consequence of a
Warrant No. 379. Located and entered Mar 30, 1784. Apr 17, 1787.

Page   145 - JOHN CAFFREY - NC - No. 142 - Reg. Mar 4, 1788
          For 10 lbs per 100 acres paid by John Caffrey, granted unto said Caffrey a

tract of land containing 640 acres in Davidson Countyon both sides of Stones Creek a branch of Stones River and about three miles above Stones River. Surveyed for said Caffrey Apr 4, 1785 by John Buchanan, D.S. Hugh Henry and William Donaldson, C.C. in consequence of a Warrant No. 284. Located and entered Feb 14, 1784. Apr 17, 1786.

Page   145 - JAMES MAYFIELD - NC - No. 101 - Reg. Mar 4, 1788
    For 10 lbs per 100 acres paid by James Mayfield, granted unto James Mayfield a tract of land containing 640 acres in Davidson County on the head of the west fork of Mill Creek. Beginning at Thomas Denton's north boundary, and William Overall's line, crossing a branch of the west fork of Mill Creek, John Henderson's line. Surveyed for James Mayfield Mar 3, 1785 by John Buchanan, D.S. in consequence of a Warrant No. 245. Located and entered Jan 6, 1784.

Page   146 - PATRICK McCUTCHEN - NC - No. 130 - Reg. Mar 4, 1788
    For 10 lbs per 100 acres paid by Patrick McCutchen, granted unto Patrick McCutchen a tract of land containing 640 acres in Davidson County on the north side of Harpeth River at the mouth of Arringtons Creek. Surveyed for Patrick McCutchen Feb 24, 1785 by Samuel Moore, D.S. in consequence of a Warrant No. 260. Located and entered Feb 9, 1784. Apr 17, 1786.

Page   146 - SAMUEL McCUTCHEN - NC - No. 7, Reg. Mar 4, 1788
    By an Act for the relief of the Officers and Soldiers of the Continental Line, in consideration of the services of Samuel McCutchen, one of the Commission Guards &c, granted unto said McCutchen a tract of land containing 320 acres in Davidson County on Little Harpeth River. Surveyed for said McCutchen Feb 6, 1786 by Samuel McCutchen, D.S. in consequence of a Warrant No. 261. Located and entered Feb 9, 1784. Oct 8, 1787.

Page   146 - THOMAS DAVIS - NC - No. 151 - Reg. Mar 4, 1788
    For 10 lbs per 100 acres paid by Thomas Davis, granted unto Thomas Davis a tract of land containing 640 acres in Davidson County on the south side of Cumberland River. Beginning near the mouth of a small branch opposite to the middle of the first islandbelow the mouth of Red River, on the bank of Cumberland River crossing Davis Creek and several branches of said creek. Surveyed for Thomas Davis Aug 18, 1784 by James Mulherin, D.S. in consequence of a Warrant No. 458. Located and entered May 24, 1784. Apr 17, 1786.

Page   147 - GEORGE NEVILLE - NC - No. 15 - Reg. Mar 5, 1788
    By an Act for the relief of the Officers and Soldiers of the Continental Line, in consideration of the service of Ransom Day, one of the Commission Guards, granted unto George Neville, assignee of Ransom Day, a tract of land containing 320 acres in Davidson County on the south side of Cumberland River and on Mill Creek.Beginning on the east side of the creek about one hundred yards above the old trail leading to Stones River, adjoining west side of Ebenezer Titus' Preemption, crossing a branch of Mill Creek. Surveyed for said Neville July 5, 1784 by James Mulherin, D.S. in consequence of a Warrant No. 117. Located and entered Jan 15, 1784.

Page   147 - JOHN HENDERSON - NC - No. 78 - Reg. Mar 5, 1788

For 10 lbs per 100 acres paid by John Henderson, granted unto said Henderson a tract of land containing 640 acres in Davidson County on the south side of Cumberland River and on both sides of the south road, adjoining the south road and crossing the south road and his spring branch, and another branch of Little Harpeth. Surveyed for said Henderson Dec 15, 1784 by James Mulherin, D.S. in consequence of a Warrant No. 346. Located and entered Mar 10, 1784. Apr 17, 1786.

Page   147 - FAULKNER ELLIOTT & ISAAC PETERSON - NC - No. 27 - Reg. Mar 5, 1788

By an Act for the relief of the Officers and Soldiers on the Continental Line, in consideration of the service of William Davidson, a corporal on the said line, granted unto Faulkner Elliott and Isaac Peterson, assignees of said Davidson, a tract of land containing 480 acres in Davidson County on the north side of Red River. Surveyed for said Elliott and Peterson Sept 22, 1785 by Robert Nelson, D.S. in consequence of a Warrant No. 334. Located and entered Mar 8, 1784. Oct 8, 1787.

Page   148 - JOSIAH RAMSEY - NC - No. 22 - Reg. Mar 5, 1788

For 10 lbs per 100 acres paid by Josiah Ramsey, granted unto said Ramsey a tract of land containing 640 acres in Davidson County. Beginning at the head of a hollow south east corner to Author McAdoe's land. Surveyed for said Ramsey Dec 4, 1784 by David McGavock, D.S. in consequence of a Warrant No. 225. Located and entered Jan 31, 1784. Apr 17, 1786.

Page   148 - CHARLES THOMPSON - NC - No. 56 - Reg. Mar 5, 1788

For 10 lbs per 100 acres paid by Charles Thompson, granted unto Charles Thompson a tract of land containing 640 acres in Davidson County on the north side of Cumberland River on Richland Creek, a branch of Red River, and crossing Milners Creek. Surveyed for said Thompson Aug 7, 1784 by James Sanders, D.S. in consequence of a Warrant No. 350. Located and entered Mar 11, 1784. Apr 17, 1786.

Page   148 - JESSEE MAXEY - NC - No. 13 - Reg. Mar 5, 1788

By an Act for the relief of the Officers and Soldiers of the Continental Line, inconsideration of the services of Jessee Maxey, one of the Commission Guards, granted unto said   Maxey a tract of land containing 640 acres in Davidson County adjoining William Thompson's south line. Surveyed for said Maxey Oct 31, 1785 by Thomas Molloy, D.S. in consequence of a Warrant No. 659. Located and entered Jan 10, 1785. Oct 8, 1787.

Page   149 - ADAM HAMPTON - NC - No. 12 - Reg. Mar 5, 1788

By an Act for the relief of the Officers and Soldiers of the Continental Line, in consideration of the services of Adam Hampton, one of the Commission Guards &c, granted unto said Hampton a tract of land containing 320 acres in Davidson County on the Sulphus Fork of Red River. Surveyed for said Hampton Feb 26, 1785 by Sqr. Grant, D.S. in consequence of a Warrant No. 230. Located and entered Feb 2, 1784. Oct 8, 1787.

Page   149 - JAMES BOSLEY - NC - No. 6 - Reg. Mar 5, 1788

By an Act for the relief of the Officers and Soldiers of the Continental Line, in consideration of the services of Russell Gower, one of the Commission Guards, granted unto James Bosley a tract of land containing 320 acres in Davidson County, adjoining James Robertson's Preemption, Peter Turney's line, and Mark Robertson's line. Surveyed for said James Bosley Mar 31, 1785 by Thomas Molloy, D.S. in consequence of a Warrant No. 8. Located and entered Dec 26, 1783. Oct 8, 1787.

Page   149 - PETER TURNEY - NC - No. 65 - Reg. Mar 5, 1788
        For 10 lbs per 100 acres paid by Peter Turney, granted unto said Turney a tract of land containing 640 acres in Davidson County, adjoining Isaac Johnston, a conditional line between said Turney and Mark Robertson, near Stone Lick, and Francis Hodge's line. Which grant was dated Apr 17, 1786. Entry No. 178. Jan 26, 1784.

Page   150 - SAMUEL WALKER - NC - No. 44 - Reg. Mar 5, 1788
        For 10 lbs per 100 acres paid by Samuel Walker, granted unto said Walker a tract of land containing 640 acres in Davidson Countyon the west fork of Mill Creek, joining William Overall's line, and John Brown. Surveyed for said Walker Mar 1, 1785 by John Buchanan, D.S. in consequence of a Warrant No. 239. Located and entered Feb 5, 1784. Apr 17, 1786.

Page   150 - MORRIS SHEAN - NC - No. 57 - Reg. Mar 5, 1788
        For 10 lbs per 100 acres paid by Morris Shean, granted unto said Shean a tract of land containing 640 acres in Davidson County on the forks of Gasper Creekadjoining Simson Kuykendall, Gasper Mansker's line. Surveyed for Morris Shean Dec 13, 1784 by James Sanders, D.S. in consequence of a Warrant No. 291. Located and entered Feb 16, 1784. Apr 1786.

Page   150 - SOLOMON WHITE - NC - No. 134 - Reg. Mar 5, 1788
        For 10 lbs per 100 acres paid by Solomon White, granted unto said White a tract of land containing 640 acres in Davidson County on Red River. Surveyed for said White Sept 1, 1784 by James Sanders, D.S. in consequence of a Warrant No. 69. Located and entered Jan 8, 1784. Apr 17, 1786.

Page   151 - THOMAS McFARLAND - NC - No. 17 - Reg. Mar 6, 1788
        By an Act for the relief of the Officers and Soldiers of the Continental Line, in consideration of the services of Thomas McFarland, one of the Commission Guards, granted unto said McFarland a tract of land containing 320 acres in Davidson County on the north side of Cumberland River on both sides of McFarlands Creek. Surveyed for Thomas McFarland Aug 9, 1784 in consequence of a Warrant No. 504. Located and entered July 1, 1784. Oct 8, 1787.

Page   151 - LARDNER CLARK - NC - No. 22 - Reg. Mar 6, 1788
        By an Act for the relief of the Officers and Soldiers of the Continental Line, in consideration of the services of Col. Martin Armstrong, surveyor of lands, granted unto Lardner Clark, assignee of said Armstrong, a tract of land containing 96 acres in Davidson County on the west fork of Mill Creek, adjoining Lardner Clark's Preemption, assignee of James Wilson, thence to John Foreman's north east corner, then to Peter Catron's line. Surveyed for said Clark Aug 25, 1785 by John Buchanan, D.S. in consequence of a Warrant No. 993. Located and entered May 16, 1785. Oct 8, 1787.

Page   151 - LARDNER CLARK - NC - No. 57 - Reg. Mar 6, 1788

By an Act for the relief of the Officers and Soldiers of the Continental Line, in consideration of the services of Lardner Clark, one of the Guards to the Commissioners, granted unto said Clark a tract of land containing 320 acres in Davidson County on the east fork of Mill Creek. Surveyed for said Clark Mar 12, 1786 by John Buchanan D.S. in consequence of a Warrant No. 81. Located and entered Jan 12, 1784. Oct 8, 1787.

Page   152 - LARDNER CLARK - NC - No. 89 - Reg. Mar 7, 1788

For 10 lbs per 100 acres paid by Lardner Clarkgranted unto said Clark a tract of land containing 640 acres in Davidson County, crossing Mill Creek at Ebenezer Titus' southwest corner. Surveyed for said Clark May 11, 1784 by John Buchanan, D.S. in consequence of a Warrant No. 77. Located and entered Jan 10, 1784. Apr 17, 1786.

Page   152 - LARDNER CLARK - NC - No. 26 - Reg. Mar 7, 1788

By an Act for the relief of the Officers and Soldiers of the Continental Line, in consideration of the services of Col. Martin Armstrong, surveyor of lands, granted unto Lardner Clark, assignee of said Armstrong, a tract of land containing 200 acres in Davidson Countyon south side of Cumberland River in the big bend below the mouth of Stones River, adjoining the banks of Cumberland River, Col. Armstrong's tract. Surveyed for said Clark Aug 15, 1785 by James Mulherin, D.S. in consequence of a Warrant No. 1387. Located Sept 19, 1785. Dec 8, 1787.

Page   152 - WILLIAM GUBBINS - NC - No. 599 - Reg. Mar 7, 1788

By an Act for the relief of the Officers and Soldiers of the Continental Line, in consideration of the bravery and zeal of Thomas Green, a private on the said line, granted unto William Gubbins, assignee of said Green, a tract of land containing 640 acres in Davidson County on the north side of Cumberland River on the west side of Blooming Grove, adjoining John Hamilton, John Shelby's line. Surveyed for William Gubbins Mar 30, 1786 by Robert Nelson, D.S. in consequence of a Military Warrant No. 1758. Located Dec 6, 1785. Sept 15, 1787.

Page   153 - ROBERT BRANKS - NC - No. 14 - Reg. Mar 7, 1788

By an Act for the relief of the Officers and Soldiers of the Continental Line, in consideration of the services of Henry Hollins, one of the Guards to the Commissioners, granted unto Robert Branks, assignee of said Hollis, a tract of land containing 320 acres in Davidson County on the south side of Cumberland Riverand on the west side of Stones River. Surveyed for said Branks Jan 4, 1785 by James Mulherin, D.S. in consequence of a Warrant No. 508. Located and entered July 5, 1784. Oct 8, 1787.

Page   153 - DAVID ROUNSEVALL - NC - No. 11 - Reg. Mar 7, 1788

For 10 lbs per 100 acres paid by David Rounsevall, granted unto David Rounsevall a tract of land containing 640 acres in Davidson County on Whites Creek, joining Benjamin Drake's Preemption, Reddick Stump's line. Surveyed for said Rounsevall Nov 11, 1784 by James Sanders, D.S. in consequence of a Warrant No. 348. Located and entered Mar 11, 1784. Apr 17, 1786.

Page   153 - EVAN SHELBY - NC - No. 510 - Reg. Mar 7, 1788
By an Act for the relief of the Officers and Soldiers of the Continental Line, in consideration of the bravery and zeal of John Hedgpeth, a private in the said line, granted unto Evan Shelby, assignee of John Hedgpeth, a tract of land containing 640 acres in Davidson Countyon the north side of Cumberland River. Surveyed for said Shelby by Robert Hays, D.S. in consequence of a Warrant No. 1662. Located and entered Aug 2, 1785. Sept 15, 1787.

Page   154 - HEADON WELLS - NC - No. 124 - Reg. Mar 7, 1788
For 10 lbs per 100 acres paid by Headon Wells, granted unto Headon Wells,a tract of land containing 640 acres in Davidson County. Surveyed for said Wells Dec 10, 1784 by David McGavock, D.S. in consequence of a Warrant No. 172. Located and entered Jan 24, 1784. Apr 17, 1786.

Page   154 - JOHN FOREMAN - NC - No. 46 - Reg. Mar 7, 1788
For 10 lbs per 100 acres paid by John Foreman, granted unto said Foreman a tract of land containing 640 acres in Davidson County, joining Jonathan Drake's land, James Manion's line, crossing a small branch of Mill Creek, and Drakes Spring branch. Surveyed for said Foreman by John Bucchanan, D.S. in consequence of a Warrant No. 310. Located and entered Feb 20, 1784. April 1786.

Page   154 - GEORGE FRANCISCO & THOMAS FLETCHER - NC - No. 52
Reg. Mar 7, 1788
For 10 lbs per 100 acres paid by George Francisco and Thomas Fletcher, granted unto said Francisco and Fletcher a tract of land in Davidson County, on Red River, crossing Richland Creek. Surveyed for said Francisco and Fletcher Aug 31, 1784 by James Sanders, D.S. in consequence of a Warrant No. 456. Located and entered May 20, 1784. Apr 17, 1786.

Page   155 - WILLIAM EDMISTON - NC - No. 46 - Reg. Mar 8, 1788
In consideration of the services of William Edmiston, one of the Guards to the Commissioners for laying off the lands for the Officers and Soldiers of the Continental Line, granted unto William Edmiston a tract of land containing 320 acres in Davidson County on both sides of Arrington Creek, adjoining John Williams' land. Surveyed for William Edmiston Feb 1, 1785 by Samuel Moore, D.S. in consequence of a Warrant No. 190. Located and entered Jan 28, 1784. Oct 8, 1787.

Page   155 - JOHN SHELBY, Junior - NC - No. (blank) - Reg. Mar 8, 1788
By an Act for the relief of the Officers and Soldiers of the Continental Line, in consideration of the service of John Shelby, surveyor of the lands, granted unto John Shelby a tract of land containing 2500 acres in Davidson County. Beginning at a bluff above the mouth of the first big creek below the mouth of Red River running to Cumberland River. Surveyed for John Shelby Aug 4, 1785 by Robert Nelson, D.S. in consequence of a Warrant No. 166. Located and entered Jan 24, 1784. Oct 8, 1787.

Page   155 - NATHANIEL HOLLY - NC - No. 11 - Reg. Mar 8, 1788
By an Act for the relief of the Officers and Soldiers of the Continental Line,

51

in consideration of the services of David Shelby, one of the Commission Guards, granted unto Nathaniel Holly, assignee of David Shelby, a tract of land containing 320 acres in Davidson County on the waters of Sulphur Fork about one mile west from a clay lick, adjoining Hugh Henry's line. Surveyed for Nathaniel Holly Feb 2, 1785 by Sq. Grant in consequence of a Warrant No. 506. Located and entered July 2, 1784. Oct 8, 1787.

Page   156 - WILLIAM MITCHEL - NC - No. 16 - Reg. Mar 8, 1788
        For 10 lbs per 100 acres paid by William Mitchel, granted unto said Mitchel a tract of land containing 640 acres in Davidson County on the banks of the east fork of Whites Creek, adjoining William Loggins' line. Surveyed for William Mitchel May 19, 1785 by James Sanders, D.S. in consequence of a Warrant No. 246 dated Feb 6, 1784. Apr 17, 1786.

Page   156 - WILLIAM LOGGINS - NC - No. 144 - Reg. Mar 8, 1788
        For 10 lbs per 100 acres paid by William Loggins, granted unto William Loggins a tract of land containing 640 acres in Davidson County onm the east fork of Whites Creek, adjoining David Rounsevall's line, Fedrick Stump's line, and William Mitchel's line. Surveyed for William Loggins Nov 12, 1784 by James Sanders, D.S. in consequence of a Warrant No. 616. Located and entered Nov 10, 1784. Apr 17, 1786.

Page   156 - JOHN TUCKER - NC - No. 54 - Reg. Mar 8, 1788
        For 10 lbs per 100 acres paid by John Tucker, granted unto John Tucker a tract of land containing 640 acres in Davidson County between the forks of Mill Creek. Beginning at a small branch of the east fork of Mill Creek, to Cockrill's corner. Surveyed for said John Tucker Aug 26, 1784 in consequence of a Warrant No. 155. Located and entered Jan 17, 1784. Apr 17, 1786.

Page   157 - PHILIP WALKER - NC - No. 136 - Reg. Mar 8, 1788
        For 10 lbs per 100 acres paid by Philip Walker, granted unto Philip Walker a tract of land containing 640 acres in Davidson County, adjoining the north west corner of James Scott's Preemption, John Walker's Preemption. Surveyed for Philip Walker Mar 30, 1785 by Barkley William Pollock, D.S. in consequence of a Warrant No. 579. Located and entered Aug 14, 1784. Apr 17, 1786.

Page   157 - DANIEL WILLIAMS - NC - No. 125 - Reg. Mar 8, 1788
        For 10 lbs per 100 acres paid by Daniel Williams, granted unto Daniel Williams a tract of land containing 640 acres in Davidson County on the north side of Cumberland River. Beginning at the side of the path that leads from Williams Station to Overall's. Surveyed for Daniel Williams Mar 1, 1784 by James Mulherin, D.S. in consequence of a Warrant No. 82. Located and entered Jan 12, 1784. Apr 17, 1786.

Page   157 - WILLIAM STUART - NC - No. 169 - Reg. Mar 8, 1788
        For 10 lbs per 100 acres paid by William Stuart, granted unto said Stuart a tract of land containing 640 acres in Davidson County on the east side of Stones River and south of the public land which includes Stones Lick. Beginning at the line of the public survey, thence to the top of cliff at the bank of Stones River, to the north east bank at the Buffalo Ford. Surveyed for said William Stuart. Signed Apr 17, 1786.

Page   158 - ROBERT GIVENS - NC - No. 64 - Reg. Mar 8, 1788
For 10 lbs per 100 acres paid by Robert Givens, granted unto said Givens a tract of land containing 640 acres in Davidson County on both sides Station Fork of Red River, joining a ridge on William Starr's line and to a tree in the barrens. Surveyed for said Givens July 23, 1788 by Daniel Smith in consequence of a Warrant No. 566. Located and entered Aug 7, 1784. Apr 17, 1786.

Page   158 - SAMUEL HAYBERT - NC - No. 116 - Reg. Mar 10, 1788
For 10 lbs per 100 acres paid by Samuel Haybert, granted unto said Haybert a tract of land containing 640 acres in Davidson County on both sides of Big Harpeth River, adjoining John Wilson's line. Surveyed for said Haybert Feb 17, 1785 by Samuel Moore, D.S. in consequence of a Warrant No. 680. Located and entered Feb 12, 1785. Apr 17, 1786.

Page   158 - SAMUEL BUCCHANAN - NC - No. 78 - Reg. Mar 10, 1788
By an Act for the relief of the Officers and Soldiers of the Continental Line, in consideration of the services of Samuel Bucchanan, one of the Commission Guards, granted unto said Bucchanan a tract of land containing 320 acres in Davidson County on the head of Whites branch and joining Ebenezer Titus' line. Surveyed for Samuel Bucchanan Apr 21, 1784 by John Bucchanan, D.S. in consequence of a Warrant No. 74. Located and entered Jan 10, 1784. Oct 8, 1787.

Page   159 - JOHN McMURRY - NC - No. 50 - Reg. Mar 10, 1788
By an Act for the relief of the Officer and Soldiers of the Continental Line, in consideration of the service of John McMurry, one of the Commission Guards, granted unto said McMurry a tract of land containing 320 acres in Davidson County on the south side of Big Harpeth River. Surveyed for said McMurry Feb 22, 1785 by John Bucchanan, D.S. in consequence of a Warrant No. 690. Located and entered Feb 26, 1785. Oct 8, 1787.

Page   159 - MOSES SHELBY - NC - No. 67 - Reg. Mar 10, 1788
By an Act for the relief of the Officers and Soldiers of the Continental Line, in consideration of the service of Moses Shelby, one of the Commission Guards, granted unto said Shelby a tract of land containing 1200 acres in Davidson County, crossing Stuarts Creek on west side. Surveyed for said Shelby June 9, 1785 by John Bucchanan, D.S. in consequence of a Warrant No. 242. Located and entered Feb 6, 1784. Oct 8, 1787.

Page   159 - ARTHUR McADOE - NC - No. 45 - Reg. Mar 10, 1788
For 10 lbs per 100 acres paid by Arthur McAdoe, granted unto said McAdoe a tract of land containing 640 acres in Davidson County, joining Headon Wells' land. Surveyed for said McAdoe Dec 11, 1784 by D. McGavock in consequence of a Warrant No. 244. Located and entered Feb 6, 1784. Apr 17, 1786.

Page   160 - EVAN SHELBY - NC - No. 44 - Reg. Mar 10, 1788
By an Act for the relief of the Officers and Soldiers of the Continental Line, in consideration of the services of Evan Shelby, one of the Commission Guards, granted unto said Shelby a tract of land containing 1200 acres in Davidson Countyon Stewarts Creek, adjoining Moses Shelby's line. Surveyed for said Shelby June 9, 1783 by John Bucchanan, D.S. in consequence of a Warrant No. 241. Located and entered Feb 6, 1784. Oct 8, 1787.

Page   160 - WILLIAM CARVIN - NC - No. 129 - Reg. Mar 10, 1788

For 10 lbs per 100 acres paid by Edward Carvin, granted unto William Carvin, heir of Edward Carvin, a tract of land containing 640 acres in Davidson County on the north side of Cumberland River and joining John Evans' corner, and John Bucchanan south line. Surveyed for William Carvin Aug 11, 1784 by James Mulherin, D.S. in consequence of a Warrant No. 427. Located and entered May 5, 1784. Apr 17, 1786.

Page   160 - SAMUEL WILSON - NC - No. 39 - Reg. Mar 10, 1788

For 10 lbs per 100 acres paid by Samuel Willson, granted unto said Wilson a tract of land containing 640 acres in Davidson County. Beginning at the bank of Stones River, crossing Sinking Creek. Surveyed for said Wilson Jan 22, 1785 by John Buchanan, D.S. in consequence of a Warrant No. 29. Located and entered Dec 29, 1783. Apr 1786.

Page   161 - PHILIP CATRON - NC - No. 14 - Reg. Mar 10, 1788

For 10 lbs per 100 acres paid by Philip Catron, granted unto said Catron a tract of land containing 640 acres in Davidson County on east waters of of the west fork of Mill Creek, adjoining John Tucker's line, Andrew Ewing's line, and Samuel Barton's line. Surveyed for said Catron Feb 10, 1785 by John Bucchanan, D.S. in consequence of a Warrant No. 584. Located and entered Aug 18, 1784. Apr 17, 1786.

Page   161 - FRANCIS ARMSTRONG - NC - No. 18 - Reg. Mar 10, 1788

For 10 lbs per 100 acres paid by Francis Armstrong, granted unto said Armstrong a tract of land containing 640 acres in Davidson County. Beginning on the north west fork of Richland Creek, adjoining Samuel Barton's line, crossing the west forks of Browns Creek. Surveyed for said Armstrong June 25, 1784 by Thomas Molloy, D.S. in consequence of a Warrant No. 164. Located and entered Jan 21, 1784. Apr 17, 1786.

Page   161 - WILLIAM GOWEN - NC - No. 20 - Reg. Mar 11, 1788

For 10 lbs per 100 acres paid by William Gowen, granted unto said Gowen a tract of land containing 640 acres in Davidson County on the east branches of Mill Creek, adjoining Ebenezer Titus' lands. Surveyed for said Gowen Mar 16, 1785 by John Buchanan, D.S. in consequence of a Warrant No. 116. Located and entered Jan 15, 1784. Apr 17, 1786.

Page   162 - JOHN MULHERIN - NC - No. 5 - Reg. Mar 11, 1788

For 10 lbs per 100 acres paid by John Mulherin, granted unto said Mulherin a tract of land containing 640 acres in Davidson County on Overalls Creek, adjoining William Overall's Preemption. Surveyed for said Mulherin Jan 20, 1785 by John Buchanan, D.S. in consequence of a Warrant No. 11. Located and entered Dec 26, 1783. Apr 17, 1786.

Page   162 - JAMES McFADDIN - NC - No. (blank) - Reg. Mar 11, 1788

By an Act for the relief of the Officers and Soldiers in the Continental Line, in consideration of the services of James McFaddin, one of the Commission Guards, granted unto said McFaddin a tract of land containing 320 acres in Davidson County on Red River. Surveyed for said McFaddin Sept 2, 1784 by James Sanders, D.S. in consequence of a Warrant No. 403. Located and entered Apr 10, 1784. Oct 8, 1787.

Page   162 - SAMUEL VERNOR - NC - No. 31 - Reg. Mar 11, 1788

By an Act for the relief of the Officers and Soldiers of the Continental Line, in consideration of the services of James Hollis, one of the hunters in the Commission Guards &c, granted unto Samuel Vernor, assignee of said Hollis, a tract of land containing 640 acres in Davidson County on the waters of Whites Creek joining the Preemption of James Hollis on the east. Surveyed for said Vernor Mar 29, 1895 by B. William Pollock, D.S. in consequence of a Warrant No. 432. Located and entered May 10, 1784. Oct 8, 1787.

Page   163 - HEADON WELLS - NC - No. 676 - Reg. Mar 11, 1788

By an Act for the relief of the Officers and Soldiers of the Continental Line, in consideration of the bravery and zeal of John Jeffers, a private in the said line, granted unto said Headon Wells, assignee of said Jeffers, a tract of land containing 224 acres in Davidson County on the north side of Cumberland River. Surveyed for said Wells Sept 6, 1787 by William Crutcher, D.S. in consequence of a Military Warrant No. 321. Located and entered July 16, 1784. Dec 8, 1787.

Page   163 - SAMUEL MARTIN - NC - No. 612 - Reg. Mar 11, 1788

By an Act for the relief of the Officers and Soldiers of the Continental Line, in consideration of the bravery and zeal of Abraham Jenkins, a private in the said line, granted unto Samuel Martin, assignee of said Jenkins, a tract of land containing 350 acres in Davidson County on the south side of Cumberland River at the mouth of a branch four or five miles below the mouth of Red River. Surveyed for said Martin Apr 20, 1786 by Robert Nelson, D.S. in consequence of a Warrant No. 414. Located and entered Aug 16, 1784. Sept 12, 1787.

Page   163 - JOHN HARRIS - NC - No. 26 - Reg. Mar 11, 1788

By an Act for the relief of the Officers and Soldiers of the Continental Line, in consideration of the services of John Harris, one of the Commission Guards, granted unto John Harris a tract of land containing 320 acres in Davidson County. Beginning at the mouth of the West Fork. Surveyed for John Harris Feb 25, 1785 by Robert Wilson, D.S. in consequence of a Warrant No. 372. Located and entered Mar 27, 1784. Oct 8, 1787.

Page   164 - THOMAS KILGORE - NC - No. 38 - Reg. Mar 11, 1788

For 10 lbs per 100 acres of land paid by Thomas Kilgore, granted unto Thomas Kilgore a tract of land containing 640 acres in Davidson Countyon a branch of Dry Creek near the line of the Public Survey and Gasper Manskers' line. Surveyed for said Kilgore July 20, 1784 by James Sanders, D.S. in consequence of a Warrant No. 187. Located and entered Jan 26, 1784. Apr 17, 1786.

Page   164 - ANDREW THOMPSON - NC - No. 70 - Reg. Mar 11, 1788

For 10 lbs per 100 acres paid by Andrew Thompson, granted unto said THompson a tract of land containing 640 acres in Davidson County on the Sulphur Fork of Red River. Surveyed for said Thompson Sept 3, 1784 by James Sanders, D.S. in consequence of a Warrant No. 351. Located and entered Mar 11, 1784. Apr 17, 1786.

Page   164 - SAMUEL McMURRY - NC - No. 23 - Reg. Mar 11, 1788

By an Act for the relief of the Officers and Soldiers of the Continental Line, in consideration of the services of Samuel McMurry, one of the Commission Guards, granted unto said McMurry a tract of land containing 320 acres in Davidson County, crossing Indian Camp Creek, Martin Armstrong's line, and to James Bradley. Surveyed for said McMurry June 22, 1785 by John Buchanan, D.S. in consequence of a Warrant No. 713. Located and enteredApr 25, 1785. Oct 8, 1787.

Page   165 - JACOB PENNINGTON - NC - No. 30 - Mar 12, 1788

By an Act for the relief of the Officers and Soldiers of the Continental Line, in consideration of the services of Francis Ballard, one of the Commission Guards, granted unto Jacob Pennington, assignee of said Ballard, a tract of land containing 320 acres in Davidson County on Spring Creek a branch of the West Fork of Red River. Surveyed for Jacob Pennington Mar 5, 1786 by Robert Nelson, D.S. in consequence of a Warrant No. 224. Located and entered Feb 2, 1784. Oct 8, 1787.

Page   165 - JOHN FOREMAN - NC - No. 85 - Reg. Mar 12, 1788

For 10 lbs per 100 acres paid by John Foreman, granted unto John Foreman a tract of land containing 640 acres in Davidson County crossing Mill Creek. Surveyed for John Foreman July 28, 1784 by John Bucchanan, D.S. in consequence of a Warrant No. 309. Located and entered Feb 20, 1784. Apr 17, 1786.

Page   165 - WILLIAM GRAHAM - NC - No. 6 - Reg. Mar 12, 1788

For 10 lbs per 100 acres paid by William Graham, granted unto William Graham a tract of land containing 640 acres in Davidson County on the Sulphur Fork of Red River. Joining Adam Hampton's line. Surveyed for said Graham Aug 12, 1784 by James Sanders, D.S. in consequence of a Warrant No. 102. Located and entered Jan 14, 1784. Apr 17, 1784.

Page   166 - JOHN BOWEN - NC - No. 65 - Reg. Mar 12, 1788

By an Act for the relief of the Officers and Soldiers of the Continental Line, in consideration of the services of Moses Bowen, one of the Commission Guards, granted unto John Bowen, heir of said Moses Bowen, a tract of land containing 320 acres in Davidson County on Stuarts Creek a branch of Stones River. Surveyed for said Bowen Apr 13, 1785 by Robert Russell, D.S. in consequence of a Warrant No. 326. Located and entered Mar 20, 1784. Oct 8, 1787.

Page   166 - JOHN HENDERSON - NC - No. 63 - Reg. Mar 12, 1788

By an Act for the relief of the Officers and Soldiers of the Continental line, in consideration of the services of John Henderson, granted unto said Henderson a tract of land containing 320 acres in Davidson Countyon Little Harpeth. Surveyed for said Henderson Dec 15, 1784 by James Mulherin, D.S. in consequence of a Warrant No. 345. Located and entered Mar 10, 1784. Oct 8, 1787.

Page   166 - JERROTT MANIFEE - NC - No. 120 - Reg. Mar 12, 1788

For 10 lbs per 100 acres paid by Jerrott Manifee, granted unto said Manifee a tract of land containing 640 acres in Davidson County on both sides of Big Harpeth.

Beginning at the south west of the spring and crossing Five Mile Creek, crossing Big Harpeth. Surveyed for said Manifee Feb 25, 1785 by John Bucchanan, D.S. in consequence of a Warrant No. 482. Located June 9, 1784. Apr 17, 1786.

Page   167 - WILLIAM OVERALL - NC - No. 166 - Reg. Mar 12, 1788
            For 10 lbs per 100 acres paid by William Overall, granted unto said Overall a tract of land containing 640 acres in Davidson County on Overalls Creek. Surveyed for William Overall Jan 20, 1785 by John Bucchanan, D.S. in consequence of a Warrant No. 131. Located and entered Jan 15, 1784. Apr 17, 1786.

Page   167 - WILLIAM OVERALL - NC - No. 146 - Reg. Mar 12, 1788
            For 10 lbs per 100 acres paid by William Overall, granted unto William Overall a tract of land containing 640 acres in Davidson County on a branch of Overall Spring Branch about four hundred yards below the spring and branch of the west fork of Mill Creek. Surveyed for said Overall Aug 16, 1784 by John Bucchanan, D.S. in consequence of a Warrant No. 130. Located and entered Jan 15, 1784. Apr 17, 1786.

Page   167 - WILLIAM STEAM - NC - No. 9 - Reg. Mar 12, 1788
            For 10 lbs per 100 acres paid by William Steam, granted unto William Steam a tract of land containing 640 acres in Davidson County on Red River, adjoining Thomas Kilgore's corner. Surveyed for William Steam May 25, 1785 by James Sanders, D.S. in consequence of a Warrant No. 118. Located and entered Jan 15, 1784. Apr 17, 1786.

Page   168 - JOSIAH RAMSEY - NC - No. 79 - Reg. Mar 12, 1788
            By an Act for the relief of the Officers and Soldiers of the Continental Line, in consideration of the services of Josiah Ramsey, one of the Commission Guards, granted unto Josiah Ramsey a tract of land containing 640 acres in Davidson County on the waters of Half Pone Creek a branch running into the Cumberland River on the southside. Surveyed for said Josiah Ramsey Dec 8, 1784 by McGavock, D.S. in consequence of a Warrant No. 226. Located and entered Jan 31, 1784. Oct 8, 1787.

Page   168 - JAMES BYRNS - NC - No. 53 - Reg. Mar 12, 1788
            By an Act for the relief of the Officers and Soldiers of the Continental Line, in consideration of the services of James Byrns, one of the Commission guard, granted unto James Byrns a tract of land containing 320 acres of land in Davidson County on a branch of the left hand fork of Kaspers Creek, adjoining Kasper Mansker's line. Surveyed for James Byrns Dec 14, 1784 by James Sanders, D.S. in consequence of a Warrant No. 55. Located and entered Jan 5, 1784. Oct 8, 1787.

Page   168 - ADAM HAMPTON - NC - No. 32 - Reg. Mar 13, 1788
            By an Act for the relief of the Officers and Soldiers of the Continental Line, in consideration of the services of Adam Hampton, one of the Commission Guards, granted unto Adam Hampton a tract of land containing 320 acres in Davidson Countyon the Sulphur Fork of Red River. Adjoining William Graham's line. Surveyed for Adam Hampton Aug 13, 1784 by James Sanders, D.S. in consequence of a Warrant No. 231. Located and entered Feb 2, 1784. Oct 8, 1787.

Page   169 - JOHN STEWART - NC - No. 49 - Reg. Mar 13, 1788
          By an Act for the relief of the Officers and Soldiers of the Continental Line,
in consideration of the services of Mathew Kincannon, one of the Guards to the
Commissioners, granted unto John Stewart, assignee of Mathew Kincannon, a tract of land
containing 640 acres in Davidson County on the south side of Sulphur Fork of Red River on
Milners Creek. Joining lands of Charles Thompson and Ralph Fleming. Surveyed for said
Stewart Sept 15, 1785 by Robert Nelson, D.S. in consequence of a Warrant No. 137.
Located and entered Jan 16, 1784. Oct 8, 1787.

Page   169 - THOMAS McMURRY - NC - No. 9 - Reg. Mar 13, 1788
          By an Act for the relief of the Officers and Soldiers of the Continental Line,
in consideration of the services of Thomas McMurry, one of the Guards to the
Commissioners, granted unto Thomas McMurry a tract of land containing 320 acres in
Davidson County on the south side of Cumberland River adjoining a tract formerly claimed
by Benjamin Pettit. Surveyed for said McMurry Aug 15, 1785 by James Mulherin, D.S. in
consequence of a Warrant No. 328. Located and entered Mar 3, 1784. Oct 8, 1787.

Page   169 - JESSEE THOMAS - NC - No. 76 - Reg. Mar 13, 1788
          By an Act for the relief of the Officers and Soldiers of the Continental Line,
in consideration for the services of Jesse Thomas, one of the Guards to the Commissioners,
granted unto Jesse Thomas a tract of land containing 320 acres in Davidson County on a
small creek on the north side of Big harpeth River. Beginning on the Davidson County line
the place where the Commissioners first began to run it. Surveyed for said Thomas Feb 20,
1784 by Daniel Smith in consequence of a Warrant No. 271. Located Feb 12, 1784. Oct 8,
1787.

Page   170 - JESSE MAXELL - NC - No. 164 - Reg. Mar 13, 1788
          For 10 lbs per 100 acres paid by Jesse Maxwell, granted unto Jesse Maxwell a
tract of land containing 562 acres in Davidson County on the waters of the west fork of
Mill Creek, adjoining lands of William Simpson, the heirs of David Maxell, Thomas
Hardiman, Daniel Hogan, and Andrew Ewing. Surveyed for said Maxell Jan 26, 1785 by
James Mulherin, D.S. in consequence of a Warrant No. 257. Located and entered Feb 9,
1784. Apr 17, 1787.

Page   170 - THOMAS DUNOHO - NC - No. 73 - Reg. Mar 17, 1788
          By an Act for the relief of the Officers and Soldiers of the Continental Line,
in consideration of the bravery and zeal of Thomas Dunoho, a major in the said line,
granted unto Thomas Dunoho a tract of land containing 4800 acres in Davidson County
on the north side of Cumberland River and on Goose Creek. Beginning at the river at
Phifer's and joining Charles Dixon's line, and Turney's line. Surveyed for said Dunoho Feb
22, 1785 by James Sanders, D.S. in consequence of a Military Warrant No. 194. Located
July 8, 1784. Mar 14, 1786.

Page   170 - LARDNER CLARK - NC - No. 641 - Reg. Mar 17, 1788
          By an Act for the relief of the Officers and Soldiers of the Continental Line,
in consideration of the services of Henry Fetner, granted unto Lardner Clark, assignee of
George Fetner, heir of the said Fetner, a tract of land containing 1000 acres in Davidson

County on Biggwells salteen joining an entry of John Henrys at his north east corner. Grant dated Nov 15, 1787.

Page   171 - LARDNER CLARK - NC - No. 642 - Reg. Mar 17, 1788
By an Act for the relief of the Officers and Soldiers of the Continental Line, in consideration of the bravery and zeal of Charles Lewis, a private in the said line, granted unto Lardner Clark, assignee of Charles Lewis, a tract of land containing 640 acres in Davidson County on the waters of Sallien (?) on Clarks Creek, adjoining survey of Robert Hays. Date of Grant Nov 15, 1787.

Page   171 - LARDNER CLARK - NC - No. 643 - Reg. Mar 17, 1788
By an Act for the relief of the Officers and Soldiers of the Continental Line, in consideration of the bravery and zeal of Samuel Styrow, a private in the said line, granted unto Lardner Clark, assignee of said Styrow, a tract of land containing 640 acres in Davidson County on the Sallien, adjoining Hays line. The grant dated Nov 15, 1787.

Page   171 - MARK ROBERTSON - NC - No. 24 - Reg. Mar 24, 1788
By an Act for the relief of the Officers and Soldiers of the Continental Line, in consideration of the services of Mark Robertson, a sergeant in the Commissioners Guard, granted unto Mark Robertson a tract of land containing 640 acres in Davidson County on the south side of Cumberland River on the waters of Spencers Creek adjoining Robertson's spring and improvement. Surveyed for Mark RobertsonDec 12, 1786 by B. William Pollock in consequence of a Warrant No. 15. Located and entered Dec 29, 1783. Oct 8, 1787.

Page   172 - GEORGE BELL - NC - No. 19 - Reg. Mar 24, 1788
For 10 lbs per 100 acres paid by George Bell, granted unto George Bell a tract of land containing 640 acres in Davidson County. Surveyed for said Bell Sept 22, 1784 by James Sanders, D.S. in consequence of a Warrant No. 404. Located and entered May 10, 1784. Apr 17, 1786.

Page   172 - JAMES ESPEY - NC - No. 145 - Reg. Mar 24, 1788
For 10 lbs per 100 acres paid by James Espey, granted unto said Espey a tract of land containing 640 acres in Davidson County on the north side of Cumberland River. Beginning about two hundred yards below Sinking Spring and joins Daniel Williams' line. Surveyed for said Espey May 15, 1784 by James Mulherin, D.S. in consequence of a Warrant No. 144. Located and entered Jan 16, 1784. Apr 17, 1786.

Page   172 - JAMES ESPEY - NC - No. 100 - Reg. Mar 24, 1788
For 10 lbs per 100 acres paid by James Espey, granted unto said Espey a tract of land containing 640 acres in Davidson County on the north side of Cumberland River on both sides of Espeys branch. Surveyed for said Espey Feb 11, 1785 by Daniel Smith in consequence of a Warrant No. 145. Located and entered Jan 16, 1784. Apr 17, 1786.

Page   173 - THOMAS EDMISTON - NC - No. 131 - Reg. Mar 29, 1788
For 10 lbs per 100 acres paid by Thomas Edmiston, granted unto said Edmiston a tract of land containing 640 acres in Davidson County on   the north side of

Harpeth River about one mile and a half above the fork. Surveyed for said Edmiston Feb 18, 1785 by Samuel Moore, D.S. in consequence of a Warrant No. 188. Located and entered Jan 26, 1784. Apr 17, 1786.

Page   173 - JOHN WILSON - NC - No. 95 - Reg. Mar 29, 1788
        For 10 lbs per 100 acres paid by John Wilson, granted unto said Wilson a tract of land containing 640 acres in Davidson County on Big Harpeth River about three quarters of a mile above the mouth of Arrington Creek, adjoining William Edmiston, Wilsons Creek, Samuel Haybird's line. Surveyed for said Wilson Feb 5, 1785 by Samuel Moore, D.S. in consequence of a Warrant No. 336. Located and entered Mar 10, 1784. Dated Apr 17, 1786.

Page   173 - EPHRAIM McLEAN - NC - No. 18 - Reg. Mar 29, 1788
        By an Act for the relief of the Officers and Soldiers of the Continental Line, in consideration of the services of Daniel Dunam, one of the Commission Guards, granted unto said McLean a tract of land containing 320 acres in Davidson County on the north side of Cumberland River adjoining John Evans' Preemption. Surveyed for said McLean Aug 9, 1784 by James Mulherin, D.S. Warrant No. 5. Located Dec 26, 1783. Oct 8, 1787.

Page   174 - EPHRAIM McLEAN - NC - No. 16 - Reg. Mar 29, 1788
        By an Act for the relief of the Officers and Soldiers of the Continental Line, in consideration of the services of Ephraim McLean, one of the Commission Guards, granted unto said McLean a tract of land containing 320 acres in Davidson County on the north side of Cumberland, adjoining John Evans' Preemption. Surveyed for said McLean Aug 9, 1784 by James Mulherin, D.S. in consequence of a Warrant No. 6. Located and entered Dec 26, 1783. Oct 8, 1787.

Page 174 - JOHN RAINS - NC - No. 96 - Reg. Mar 31, 1788
        For 10 lbs per 100 acres paid by John Rains, granted unto John Rains a tract of land containing 640 acres in Davidson County on south side of Cumberland River and upon Browns Creek, adjoining Roger Topp. Surveyed for said Rains May 18, 1784 by James Mulherin, D.S. in consequence of a Warrant No. 201. Located and entered Jan 29, 1784. Apr 17, 1786.

Page   174 - JOHN THOMAS - NC - No. 103 - Reg. Mar 31, 1788
        For 10 lbs per 100 acres paid by John Thomas, granted unto said Thomas a tract of land containing 640 acres in Davidson County on the north side of Cumberland River, adjoining corner of James Espey, William Overall. Surveyed for said Thomas Nov 9, 1784 in consequence of a Warrant No. 292. Located and entered Feb 16, 1784. Apr 17, 1786.

Page   175 -WILLIAM MAN - April 8, 1788
        This indenture made 26 Mar between William Man of Lincoln County, State of Kentucky of one part and James Lenier of Davidson County, NC of other part. James Lenier sold unto William Man all that tract of land containing 640 acres in Davidson County on Brush Creek, adjoining Person's line, and to Hudson's corner. Signed and sealed Apr 7, 1788.

Page   175 - ANTHONY SHARP - NC - No. 36 - Reg. Apr 9, 1788
By an Act for the relief of the Officers and Soldiers of the Continental Line, in consideration of the beavery and zeal of Anthony Sharp, a captain in the said line, granted unto Anthony Sharp a tract of land containing 3840 acres in Davidson County on Big Harpeth River, adjoining William Gallaspie's corner, Alex. Ewing's 640 acres. Surveyed for said Sharp Apr 7, 1785 by B. William Pollock, D.S. in consequence of a Military Warrant No. 52. Located Feb 4, 1784. Mar 14, 1786.

Page   176 - JOHN SAPPINGTON - Apr 15, 1788
This indenture made 8 April 1788 between George Neville of Davidson County, NC of one part and John Sappington of same place of other part. George Neville sold unto John Sappington a tract of land containing 320 acres in Davidson County on the south side of Cumberland River and on Mill Creek on east side of the creek about one hundred yards above the Old Trace leading to Stones River, adjoining Ebenezer Titus' Preemption. Deeded Apr 10, 1788.

Page   176 - JOHN SAPPINGTON - April 15, 1788
This indenture made 9 Apr 1788 between John Forde of Davidson County, NC of one part and John Sappington of same place of other part. John Forde sold unto John Sappington a tract of land containing 640 acres in Davidson Countyon the south side of Cumberland River about four miles above the Virginia line. Deed signed Apr 10, 1788.

Page   177 - HENRY LENIER - April 15, 1788
This indenture made 3 Dec 1787 between James Lenier of Davidson County, NC of one part and Henry Lenear of same place of other part. James Lenear sold unto Henry Lenear all that part of Lot No. 25 lying joining the half sold by Julius Sanders to William Tate with all the houses, battery and every improvement thereunto belonging which is now on the Lot No. 25 also one Lot No. 75 and one Lot No. 72, lying and being in the town of Nashville. Said Lots was by deed dated 6 July and 13 July 1784 granted by the directors and trustees of town of Nashville to said Julius Sanders. Which deed of conveyance was acknowledged to Henry Lenear by James Lenear and his wife Sarah Lenier April 7, 1788.

Page   177 - EPHRAIM McLANE - April 16, 1788
This indenture made 25 Dec 1787 between Green Hall of Franklin County, NC of one part and Ephraim McLane of Davidson County, NC of other part. Green Hall sold unto Ephraim McLane all that tract or parcel of land lying and being in Davidson County on the north side of the Cumberland River, containing 274 acres. Adjoining John Evans' line, John Thomas' line, and McLane's line. Proven by William Stokes April 7, 1788.

Page   178 - PLEASANT LOCKART - April 16, 1788
This indenture made 20 Feb 1788 between John Marney of Davidson County of one part and Pleasant Lockart of same place of other part. John Marney sold unto Pleasant Lockart a tract of land containing 120 acres in Davidson County on both sides of Whites Creek. Adjoining lands of Robert Weakley, William Stumps. It being part of a tract of 274 acres of land granted to Joshua Howard, assignee of Caleb Merchant by the State of North Carolina for said Merchants service as a private in the Continental Line, dated Mar 7, 1786.

No. 115 with the appurtenances lying and being in Davidson County. Proven April 9, 1788.

Page   179 - THOMAS and GEORGE BLACKAMORE - April 16, 1788
        This indenture made 21 Feb 1788 between John Marney of one part and Thomas and George Blackamore of other part, all of Davidson County, NC. John Marney sold unto Thomas and George Blackamore a tract or parcel of land containing 227 acres in Davidson County on both sides of Whites and Heatons Creeks. Adjoining Heaton's and Drakes' Preemption on the bank of Heatons Creek. A tract granted to Caleb Merchant for his services as a private in the Continental Line and No. 115 bearing date of 20 March 1786. Proven April 7, 1788.

Page   179 - ROBERT NELSON - April 16, 1788
        This indenture made 15 Sept 1786 between William Polk, John Montgomery and Anthony Crutcher of one part and Robert Nelson of other part, all of Davidson County, NC. Said Polk, Montgomery and Crutcher sold unto Robert Nelson a piece or lot of ground in the town of Clarksville, known in the plan of the town by Lot No. 56, containing half an acre. Proven April 9, 1788 by Robert Weakley and Robert Hays.

Page   180 - ROBERT WEAKLEY - April 16, 1788
        This indenture made 15 Sept 1786 between William Polk, John Montgomery and A. Crutcher of one part and Robert Weskley of other part, all of Davidson County. Said Polk, Montgomery and Crutcher sold unto Robert Weakley a piece or lot of ground in the town of Clarksville and known as Lot No. 20 containing half an acre. Proven Apr 9, 1788 by Robert Nelson and Robert Hays.

Page   180 - DANIEL JAMES - Apr 16, 1788
        We, Samuel Barton, Thomas Molloy, James Shaw and Isaac Linsey, directors and trustees of the town of Nashville, conveyed unto Daniel James a Lot No. 68 in town of Nashville. Proven Apr 9, 1788

Page   181 - JOHN COCKRILL - April 16, 1788
        This indenture made 29 Dec 1788 between James Lenear of Davidson County of one part and John Cockrill of same place of other part. James Lenear conveyed unto John Cockrill a tract of land containing 640 acres in Davidson County lying on the south east of Nicholas Coonrod's survey. Adjoining Coonrod's corner and Fenner's line. Proven April 9, 1788 by Andrew Ewing, C.D.C. & D.R.

Page   181 - SAMUEL SHANNON - NC - Apr 16, 1788
        This indenture made 7 April 1788 between David Shannon and Jane Shannon of Davidson County of one part and Samuel Shannon of same place of other part. Said David and Jane Shannon conveyed unto Samuel Shannon a certain tract of land containing 200 acres in Davidson Countyon the north waters of Whites Creek, joining David Shannon's Preemptions. It being part of the preemption granted to the said David Shannon by patent dated April 17, 1786. Proven April 7, 1788.

Page   182 - JAMES ROSS - April 17, 1788
        This indenture made 6 Sept 1787 between John Campbell of Guilford County,

62

of one part and James Ross of Davidson County of other part. John Campbell conveyed unto James Ross all that piece or parcel of land in Davidson County on the south side of Cumberland River on the west fork of Lick Creek, containing 2560 acres of land, being a tract of land granted to the said John Campbell by State of North Carolina bearing date Mar 14, 1786. Proven by Thomas Blair and John Carnahan Apr 8, 1788.

Page   182 - ELIJAH HAMILTON - April 17, 1788
        This indenture made 7 Apr 1788 between Pleasant Lockett of Davidson County of one part and Elijah Hamilton of same place of other part. Pleasant Lockett conveyed unto Elijah Hamilton a certain tract or parcel of land in Davidson County on the west side of Whites Creek, containing 87½ acres, adjoining William Stuarts east boundary, Robert Weakley's north west corner. Land being part of a tract of land granted by State of North Carolina to Joshua Howard grant dated Mar 17, 1786, No. 115. April 9, 1788.

Page   183 - JAMES McGAVOCK - Apr 17, 1788
        This indenture made 27 Feb 1788 between George Freeland and his wife Mary Freeland of Davidson County of one part and James McGavock of Montgomery County, Virginia, of other part. George Freeland and wife Mary Freeland conveyed unto James McGavock a tract of land containing 640 acres in Davidson County. Beginning at a line of the land laid off for the French Lick eighty poles from the Cumberland River. On a conditional line made between James Robertson, Benjamin Logan and George Freeland. Proven by John Sappington and Daniel James Apr 9, 1788.

Page   184 - JAMES McGAVOCK - April 17, 1788
        This indenture made 27 Feb 1788 between George Freeland and his wife Mary Freeland of Davidson County of one part and James McGavock of Montgomery County, Virginia of other part. George and Mary Freeland conveyed unto James McGavock a tract of land in Davidson County containing 320 acres on the bank of Cumberland River the north east corner laid off for the French Lick. Adjoining George Freeland's Preemption. Which land said Freeland obtained by patent dated Oct 8, 1787. Proven by Daniel James and John Sappington April 9, 1788.

Page   184 - JONATHAN DRAKE - April 17, 1788
        This indenture made 7 April 1788 between Benjamin Drake and Susannah Drake his wife of Davidson County of one part and Jonathan Drake of same place of other part. Benjamin and Susannah Drake conveyed unto Jonathan Drake a tract of land containing 340 acres in Davidson County on the waters of Whites Creek. Beginning on east side of Whites Creek a corner of Benjamin Drake's Preemption, to Amos Heaton's line, to banks of Heatons Creek. Land being part of a 640 acres granted unto Benjamin Drake by patent dated April 17, 1786. April 9, 1788.

Page   185 - JOSEPH MARTIN - April 17, 1788
        This indenture made 7 April 1788 between William Loggins and his wife Nancy Loggins of Davidson County of one part and Joseph Martin of same place of other part. William and Nancy Loggins conveyed unto Joseph Martin a tract of land containing 320 acres in Davidson County on the east fork of Whites Creek, adjoining David Rounsevall's line, crosses Whites Creek, and Loggin's corner. Proven by John Harlin April 9, 1788.

Page   186 - EZEKIEL SMITH - April 17, 1788

This indenture made 10 Apr 1788 between John Drake and Elizabeth his wife of Davidson County of one part and Ezekiel Smith of same place of other place. John and Elizabeth Drake conveyed unto Ezekiel Smith a tract of land containing 300 acres in Davidson County on the waters of Whites Creek, adjoining lands of Thomas James. Land being a part of 640 acres granted unto said Drake by patent dated Apr 17, 1786. Proven Apr 10, 1788.

Page   186 - JOHN DONNALDSON - April 19, 1788

This indenture made 29 Mar 1788 between Thomas Kilgore of Sumner County, NC of one part and William Donnaldson of same place of other part. Thomas Kilgore conveyed unto said John Donnaldson a tract of land containing 320 acres in Davidson County on a north branch of Dry Creek, adjoining lands of Gasper and Thomas Kilgore. Proven by John Donaldson and Robert Cartwright April 8, 1788.

Page   187 - ROBERT CARTWRIGHT - April 19, 1788

This indenture made 9 Mar 1788 between Thomas Kilgore of Sumner County, NC of one part and Robert Cartwright of Davidson County of other part. Thomas Kilgore conveyed unto Robert Cartwright a tract of land containing 320 acres in Davidson County and on a north branch of Dry Creek, adjoining lands of Gasper Mansker, the Preemption of Thomas Kilgore. Proven by John Donnaldson and James McCarroll April 8, 1788.

Page   187 - JOSEPH DAVIDSON

This indenture made 7 April 1788 between Thomas McFarland and Margret McFarland his wife of Davidson County of one part and Joseph Davidson of same place of other part. Thomas McFarland and Margret McFarland conveyed unto Joseph Davidson a tract of land containing 320 acres in Davidson County on the north side of Cumberland on both sides of McFarlin's Creek. Proven April 7, 1788.

Page   188 - JONATHAN LOOMAS - NC - No. 59 - Reg. April 21, 1788

By an Act for the relief of the Officers and Soldiers of the Continental Line, in consideration of the services of Jonathan Loomas, a doctor in the said line, granted unto said Loomas a tract of land containing 3942 acres in Davidson County on Cedar Creek on south side of Cumberland River. 14 Mar 1786.

Page   189 - PETER BACOTE - NC - No. 46 - Reg. April 21, 1788

By an Act for the relief of the Officers and Soldiers of the Continental Line, in consideration of the bravery and zeal of Peter Bacote, a a captain in the said line, granted unto Peter Bacote a tract of land containing 3840 acres in Davidson County on north side of Duck River, adjoining Elijah Moore's corner. Mar 14, 1786.

Page   189 - SAMUEL ASHE - NC - No. 66 - April 21, 1788

By an Act for the relief of the Officers and Soldiers of the Continental Line, in consideration of the bravery and zeal of Samuel Ashe, a lieutenant in the said line, granted a tract of land containing 2560 acres in Davidson County on Wolf Creek the waters of Cane Fork. Mar 14, 1788.

Page   190 - JOHN BAPTIST ASHE - NC - No. 257 - Reg. Apr 21, 1788
        By an Act for the relief of the Officers and Soldiers of the Continental Line,
in consideration of the bravery and zeal of John Baptist Ashe, a lieutenant in the said line,
granted unto said John Baptist Ashe a tract of land containing 4450 acres in Davidson
County on north side of Tennessee River on Ashe Creek. Adjoining below the mouth of the
creek Alexander Brevard's upper corner and to Joseph Brevard's corner. Mar 14, 1786.

Page   190 - JOHN GRAY BLOUNT - NC - No. 412 - Reg. Apr 21, 1788
        By an Act for the relief of the Officers and Soldiers of the Continental Line,
in consideration of the bravery and zeal of John Patten, a colonel in the said line, granted
unto John Gray Blount, assignee of said John Patten, a tract of land containing 7200 acres
in Davidson County on the east fork of the third big creek above Stones River, and on the
south side of Cumberland River. Sept 15, 1787.

Page   190 - JOHN GRAY BLOUNT & THOMAS BLOUNT - NC - No. 19 - Reg. Apr 21,
        1788
        By an Act for the relief of the Officers and Soldiers of the Continental Line,
in consideration of the bravery and zeal of William Capps, a private in the said line,
granted unto John Gray Blount and Thomas Blount, assignees of William Capps, atract of
land containing 640 acres in Davidson County on the east side of Tennessee River below
Mark Creek. Beginning on the bank at the mouth of said creek, William Blount's corner.

Page   191 - JOHN GRAY BLOUNT - NC - No. 412 - Reg. Apr 22, 1788
        By an Act for the relief of the Officers and Soldiers of the Continental Line,
in consideration of the bravery and zeal of James Lenier, an ensign in the said line, granted
unto John Gray Blount, assignee of said James Lenier, a tract of land containing 2560 acres
in Davidson County on the waters of Harpeth River, adjoining Mabane's corner. Dated Mar
14, 1786.

Page   191 - JOHN GRAY BLOUNT - NC - No. 16 - Reg. Apr 22, 1788
        By an Act for the relief of the Officers and Soldiers of the Continental Line,
in consideration of the bravery and zeal of Thomas (illegible), a private in the said line,
granted unto John Gray Blount a tract of land containing 274 acres in Davidson County on
Big Harpeth River. Beginning at Daniel McMahan's corner, on Anthony Sharp's north
boundary. Mar 14, 1786.

Page   191 - READING BLOUNT - NC - No. 14 - Apr 22, 1788
        By an Act for the relief of the Officers and Soldiers of the Continental Line,
in consideration of the bravery and zeal of Reading Blount, a major in the said line, granted
unto Reading Blount a tract of land containing 4800 acres in Davidson County on the waters
of Stones River between the east and west forks. Mar 10, 1786.

Page   192 - WILLIAM BLOUNT - NC - No. 17 - Reg. Apr 22, 1788
        By an Act for the relief of the Officers and Soldiers of the Continental Line,
in consideration of the Robert Ralston, a captain in the said line, granted unto William
Blount, assignee of said Robert Ralston, a tract of land containing 1097 acres in Davidson
County on the waters of Harpeth River, crossing Mabane's line. Mar 14, 1786.

Page   192 - WILLIAM BLOUNTS - NC - No. 15 - Reg. Apr 22, 1788
By an Act for the relief of the Officers and Soldiers of the Continental Line,
in consideration of the bravery and zeal of Isaac Ralston, a lieutenant in the said line,
granted unto William Blount, assignee of said Isaac Ralston, a tract of land containing 1240
acres in Davidson County on the north side of Tennessee River on Marks Creek, adjoining
John Gray Blount's corner, on river bank of Alexander Brevard's corner. Mar 14, 1786.

Page 192 - JAMES THACKSTON - NC - No. 40 - Reg. Apr 22, 1788
By an Act for the relief of the Officers and Soldiers of the Continental Line,
in consideration of the bravery and zeal of James Thackston, a lieutenant colonel in the
said line, granted unto James Thackston a tract of land containing 4352 acres in Davidson
County on the head branches of the west fork of Big Harpeth River and adjoining Col.
William Mabane. Surveyed for said James Thackston Mar 2, 1785 by John Donaldson, D.S.
in consequence of a Military Warrant No. 208. Located and entered Dec 6, 1784. Mar 14,
1786.

Page   193 - JOHN ALISON - NC - No. 384 - Reg. Apr 22, 1788
By an Act for the relief of the Officers and Soldiers of the Continental Line,
in consideration of the bravery and zeal of Francis Willis, a private in the said line, granted
unto John Alison, assignee of Francis Willis, a tract of land containing 228 acres in
Davidson County lying on the north side of his claim No. 1090. Surveyed for said John
Allison Nov 14, 1785 by Robert Nelson, D.S. in consequence of a Military Warrant No. 1091.
Located Apr 7, 1785. Sept 15, 1787.

Page   193 - JOHN ALLISON - NC - No. 395 - Reg. Apr 22, 1788
By an Act for the relief of the Officers and Soldiers of the Continental Line,
in consideration of the bravery and zeal of William Fanon, a private in the said line,
granted unto John Allison, assignee of William Fanon, a tract of land containing 228 acres
in Davidson County on the north side of Cumberland River on the middle fork of the first
big creek below the mouth of Red River. Surveyed for John Allison Nov 14, 1785 by Robert
Nelson, D.S. in consequence of a Military Warrant No. 1090. Located and entered Apr 8,
1785. Sept 15, 1787.

Page   193 - DAVID PHILLIPS - NC - No. 588 - Reg. Apr 22, 1788
By an Act for the relief of the Officers and Soldiers of the Continental Line,
in consideration of the beavery and zeal of David Phillips, a private in the said line, granted
unto David Philips a tract of land containing 228 acres in Davidson County on the south side
of Big Harpeth River, adjoining John Patten's corner. Warrant No. 15. Located Oct 28,
1783. Grant dated Sept 15, 1787.

Page   194 - JAMES ROBERTSON - NC - No. 580 - Reg. Apr 22, 1788
By an Act for the relief of the Officers and Soldiers of the Continental Line,
in consideration of the bravery and zeal of James Marr, a private in the said line, granted
unto James Robertson, assignee of James Marr, a tract of land containing 335 acres in
Davidson County on the south side of Cumberland River. Surveyed for James Robertson Mar
23, 1786 by John Donaldson, D.S. in consequence of a Military Warrant No. 750. Located
July 10, 1784. Oct 8, 1787.

Page   194 - JAMES ROBERTSON - NC - No. 38 - Reg. Apr 22, 1788

By an Act for the relief of the Officers and Soldiers of the Continental Line, in consideration of the service of James Robertson, one of the Guards, granted unto James Robertson a tract of land containing 2000 acres in Davidson County. Beginning at the mouth of a small Glade branch on Richland Creek. Surveyed for said James Robertson Oct 12, 1784 by Thomas Molloy, D.S. in consideration of a Warrant No. 9. Located Dec 26, 1784. Oct 8, 1787.

Page   194 - JAMES ROBERTSON - NC - No. 60 - Reg. Apr 22, 1788

By an Act for the relief of the Officers and Soldiers of the Continental Line, in consideration of the service of John Shelby, one of the Commission Guards, granted unto James Robertson, assignee of John Shelby, a tract of land containing 320 acres in Davidson County above the mouth of Richland River adjoining the land of said Robertson. Surveyed for James Robertson July 1, 1785 by Henry Rutherford in consequence of a Warrant No. 12. Located Dec 26, 1783. Oct 8, 1787.

Page   195 - JAMES ROBERTSON - NC - No. 73 - Reg. Apr 23, 1788

For 10 lbs per 100 acres paid by James Robertson, granted unto said Robertson a tract of land containing 640 acres in Davidson County. Beginning about half a mile below an improvement made by Russell Gower on the bank of Cumberland River. Surveyed for said Robertson Oct 11, 1784 by Thomas Molloy, D.S. in consequence of a Warrant No. 10. Located Dec 26, 1783. Apr 17, 1786.

Page   195 - BENJAMIN LOGAN - NC - No. 162 - Reg. Apr 23, 1788

For 10 lbs per 100 acres paid by Benjamin Logan, granted unto said Benjamin Logan a tract of land containing 640 acres in Davidson County on the south side of Cumberland River. Beginning at Charles Robertson's corner. Surveyed for said Benjamin Logan Apr 11, 1785 by James Mulherin, D.S. Warrant No. 88. Located Jan 14, 1784. Apr 17, 1786.

Page   196 - RICHARD WILLIAM CASWELL - NC - No. 620 - Reg. Apr 23, 1788

By an Act for the relief of the Officers and Soldiers of the Continental Line, in consideration of the bravery and zeal of John Husler, a private in the said line, granted unto Richard William Caswell, heir of William Caswell, assignee of John Husler, a tract of land containing 640 acres in Davidson County on the north side of Joseph Brock's entry of 100 acres opposite to James McFarlin's tract on the Sulphur Fork of Red River. Adjoining Phil Alston's line, Charles Thompson's corner. Surveyed for Richard William Caswell Oct 17, 1785 by Robert Nelson, D.S. in consequence of a Military Warrant No. 483. Located Apr 25, 1785. Sept 15, 1787.

Page   196 - RICHARD WILLIAM CASWELL - NC - No. 619 - Reg. Apr 23, 1788

By an Act for the relief of the Officers and Soldiers of the Continental Line, in consideration of the bravery and zeal of David Wilcocks, a private in the said line, granted unto Richard William Caswell, heir of William Caswell, assignee of David Wilcocks, a tract of land containing 640 acres in Davidson County on the north boundary of his other servey No. 483 on the waters of the Sulphur Fork of Red River. Surveyed for said Caswell Oct 7, 1785 by Robert Nelson, D.S. in consequence of a Military Warrant No. 497. Located

Apr 25, 1785. Sept 15, 1787.

Page   196 - MELONE MULLIN - NC - No. 418 - Reg. Apr 23, 1788

By an Act for the relief of the Officers and Soldiers of the Continental Line, in consideration of the bravery and zeal of Melone Mullin, a private in the said line, granted a tract of land containing 228 acres in Davidson County on the south side of Big Harpeth River. Surveyed for said Mullin Jan 17, 1786 by Robert Nelson, D.S. in consequence of a Military Warrant No. 131. Located Oct 17, 1783. Sept 15, 1787.

Page   197 - JOHN POTTER - NC - No. 587 - Reg. Apr 23, 1788

By an Act for the relief of the Officers and Soldiers of the Continental Line, in consideration of the bravery and zeal of John Potter, a private in the said line, granted a tract of land containing 228 acres in Davidson County on south side of Big Harpeth River, adjoining Melone Mullin's corner. Surveyed for John Potter Jan 17, 1786 by Robert Nelson, D.S. in consequence of Military Warrant No. 14. Located Oct 17, 1783. Sept 15, 1787.

Page   197 - BENJAMIN PETTIT - NC - No. 75 - Reg. Apr 23, 1788

By an Act for the relief of the Officers and Soldiers of the Continental Line, in consideration of the services of Benjamin Pettit, one of the Commission Guards, granted a tract of land containing 640 acres in Davidson County on Whites Creek. Beginning at Jacob Stump's line. Surveyed for Benjamin Pettit July 10, 1784 by James Sanders, D.S. in consequence of a Warrant No. 75. Located Jan 10, 1784. Oct 8, 1787.

Page   198 - GASPER MANSKER - NC - No. 33 - Reg. Apr 23, 1788

By an Act for the relief of the Officers and Soldiers of the Continental Line, in consideration of the services of Gasper Mansker, one of the Guards to the Commissioners, granted unto Gasper Mansker a tract of land containing 640 acres in Davidson County on the left hand fork of Gasper's Creek, adjoining John Shannon's line and James Burns' line. Surveyed for Mansker Dec 14, 1784 by James Sanders, D.S. in consequence of a Warrant No. 89. Located Jan 14, 1784. Oct 8, 1787.

Page   198 - GASPER MANSKER - NC - No. 36 - Reg. Apr 23, 1788

By an Act for the relief of the Officers and Soldiers of the Continental Line, in consideration of the services of Gasper Mansker, one of the Commissioners Guard, granted a tract of land containing 640 acres in Davidson County on Gasper's Creek. Beginning at the corner of the Public Survey at Gasper's Lick. Surveyed for said Mansker May 31, 1784 by James Sanders, D.S. in consequence of a Warrant No. 54. Located Jan 5, 1784. Oct 8, 1787.

Page   198 - THOMAS BERRY - NC - No. 640 - Reg. Apr 23, 1788

By an Act for the relief of the Officers and Soldiers of the Continental Line, in consideration of the bravery and zeal of Azariah Massey, a private in the said line, granted unto Thomas Berry, assignee of Azariah Massey, a tract of land containing 640 acres in Davidson County on a small creek that empties into Tennessee River on the north side of said river known by the name of Indian Creek. Surveyed for Thomas Berry April 1, 1786 by Isaac Roberts, D.S. in consequence of a Military Warrant No. 1112. located Dec 23, 1785. Nov 15, 1787.

Page   199 - THOMAS BERRY - NC - No. 639 - Reg. Apr 23, 1788
By an Act for the relief of the Officers and Soldiers of the Continental Line, in consideration of the bravery and zeal of William Morgan, a private in the said line, granted unto Thomas Berry, assignee of William Morgan, a tract of land containing 274 acres in Davidson County on a small creek that emptied into the Tennessee River known by the name of Indian Creek. Surveyed for Thomas Berry Jan 8, 1786 by Isaac Roberts, D.S. in consequence of a Warrant No. 1398. Located Dec 23, 1785. Nov 15, 1787.

Page   199 - THOMAS BERRY - NC - No. 547 - Reg. Apr 23, 1788
By an Act for the relief of the Officers and Soldiers of the Continental Line, in consideration of the bravery and zeal of Thomas Berry, a private in the said line, granted unto said Berry 429 acres in Davidson County on the north fork of main Harpeth about one mile and a half above where the west fork and main Harpeth meet.   Adjoining lands of Thomas Edmondson's entry. Surveyed for said Berry Dec 28, 1785 by Isaac Roberts, D.S. in consequence of a Military Warrant No. 711. Located Feb 23, 1785. Sept 15, 1787.

Page   200 - THOMAS BERRY - NC - No. 638 - Reg. Apr 24, 1788
By an Act for the relief of the Officers and Soldiers of the Continental Line, in consideration of the bravery and zeal of John Conner, a private in the said line, granted unto Thomas Berry, assignee of John Conner, a tract of land containing 274 acres in Davidson County on a small creek that empties into the north side of Tennessee River known by the name of Indian Creek. Joining Thomas Berry's entry No. 1398. Surveyed for Thomas Berry Jan 20, 1786 by Isaac Roberts, D.S. in consequence of a Military Warrant No. 1397. Located Dec 23, 1785. Nov 16, 1787.

Page   200 - ROBERT NELSON - NC - No. 11 - Reg. Apr 24, 1788
By an Act for the relief of the Officers and Soldiers of the Continental Line, in consideration of the services of Col. Martin Armstrong, surveyor of lands, granted unto Robert Nelson, assignee of said Armstrong, a tract of land containing 60 acres in Davidson County on the north side of Cumberland River on the east boundary of the land said Nelson got of Captain John Forde on the west of Bucchanan's and Swanson's Preemptions. Surveyed for said Nelson Oct 22, 1785 by said Nelson, D.S. in consequence of a Warrant No. 1154. Located July 20, 1785. Oct 8, 1787.

Page   200 - ROBERT NELSON - NC - No. 397 - Reg. Apr 24, 1788
By an Act for the relief of the Officers and Soldiers of the Continental Line, in consideration of the bravery and zeal of William Orange, a private in the said line, granted unto Robert Nelson, assignee of William Orange, a tract of land containing 640 acres in Davidson County of the north side of Cumberland River joining Joseph Fleming's survey on a small creek that empties into the river at McFarlin's cabin.   Surveyed for Robert Nelson June 25, 1786 by said Nelson, D.S. in consequence of a Military Warrant No. 2056. Located Mar 21, 1786. Sept 15, 1787.

Page   201 - ROBERT NELSON - NC - No. 373 - Reg. Apr 24, 1788
By an Act for the relief of the Officers and Soldiers of the Continental Line, in consideration of the bravery and zeal of Josiah Stedham, a private in the said line, granted unto Robert Nelson, assignee of Josiah Stedham, a tract of land containing 640

acres in Davidson County on the Sulphur Fork of Red River about one mile from the mouth. Adjoining William Purnel's corner, Cantrell's line, and to Prence's line. Surveyed for Robert Nelson Sept 26, 1786 by said Nelson in consequence of a Warrant No. 2543. Located May 12, 1786. Sept 15, 1787.

Page   201 - ROBERT NELSON - NC - No. 12 - Reg. Apr 24, 1788
          By an Act for the relief of the Officers and Soldiers of the Continental Line, in consideration of the services of Col. Martin Armstrong, surveyor of lands, granted unto Robert Nelson, assignee of said Armstrong, a tract of land containing 200 acres in Davidson County on the north side of Cumberland River between Stump's Guard Right and the mouth of Whites Creek. Surveyed for Robert Nelson June 20, 1785 by said Robert Nelson, D.S. in consequence of a Warrant No. 554. Located Jan 3, 1785. Oct 8, 1787.

Page   202 - ROBERT NELSON - NC - No. 376 - Reg. Apr 24, 1788
          By an Act for the relief of the Officers and Soldiers of the Continental Line, in consideration of the bravery and zeal of Christopher Taw, a private in the said line, granted unto Robert Nelson, assignee of Christopher Taw, a tract of land containing 640 acres in Davidson County on the north boundary of Topp's claim on Red River about three or four miles from Clarksville, adjoining Forkner Elliott's line. Surveyed for Robert Nelson by himself June 27, 1786 in consequence of a Military Warrant No. 3119. Located Jan 10, 1786. Sept 15, 1787.

Page   202 - ROBERT NELSON - NC - No. 13 - Reg. Apr 24, 1788
          By an Act for the relief of the Officers and Soldiers of the Continental line, in consideration of the services of Col. Martin Armstrong, surveyor of lands, granted unto Robert Nelson, assignee of said Armstrong, a tract of land containing 100 acres in Davidson County on Calebs Creek on the east of Samuel Henry's survey. Surveyed for Robert Nelson by himself Sept 30, 1785 in consequence of a Warrant No. 1068. Located Jan 30, 1785. Oct 8, 1787.

Page   202 - ROBERT NELSON - NC - No. 396 - Reg. Apr 24, 1788
          By an Act for the relief of the Officers and Soldiers of the Continental Line, in consideration of the bravery and zeal of John Man, a private in the said line, granted unto Robert Nelson, assignee of said John Man, a tract of land containing 640 acres in Davidson County on the north side of Cumberland River about three miles from Clarksville. Surveyed for said nelson Apr 25, 1786 in consequence of a Military Warrant No. 730. located July 22, 1785. Sept 15, 1787.

Page   203 - ROBERT NELSON - NC - No. 386 - Reg. Apr 24, 1788
          By an Act for the relief of the Officers and Soldiers of the Continental Line, in consideration of the bravery and zeal of George Shader, a sergeant in the said line, granted unto Robert Nelson, assignee of George Shader, a tract of land containing 1000 acres in Davidson County on Big Harpeth joining Governor Martin's north boundary and to John Nelson's line. Surveyed for Robert Nelson by himself June 25, 1786 in consequence of a Military Warrant No. 1886. Located Mar 22, 1786. Sept 15, 1787.

Page   203 - ROBERT NELSON - NC - No. 29 - Reg. Apr 24, 1788
By an Act for the relief of the Officers and Soldiers of the Continental Line, in consideration of the services of William Moore, one of the Guards to the Commissioners, granted unto Robert Nelson, assignee of William Moore, a tract of land containing 320 acres in Davidson County on the north side of Cumberland River about a mile from Clarksville. Adjoining Col. Martin Armstrong's corner and Mason's line. Surveyed for Robert Nelson by himself Dec 15, 1785 in consequence of a Warrant No. 757. Located Aug 16, 1785. Oct 8, 1787.

Page   203 - ROBERT NELSON - NC - No. 10 - Reg. Apr 24, 1788
By an Act for the relief of the Officers and Soldiers of the Continental Line, in consideration of the services of Col. Martin Armstrong, surveyor of lands, granted unto Robert Nelson, assignee of said Armstrong, a tract of land containing 250 acres in Davidson County on the south side of Cumberland about three miles below the mouth of Red River. Surveyed for Robert Nelson by himself Apr 20, 1786 in consequenceof a Warrant No. 850. Located Apr 14, 1785.

Page   204 - ROBERT NELSON - NC - No. 374 - Reg. Apr 24, 1788
By an Act for the relief of the Officers and Soldiers of the Continental Line, in consideration of the bravery and zeal of Josep Wilkins, a private in the said line, granted unto Robert Nelson, assignee of Josep Wilkins, a tract of land containing 640 acres in Davidson County on the north side of Cumberland River near two miles from Clarksville. Adjoining Robert Nelson, assignee of John Bell, Adam Boyd, Evan Shelby's line. Surveyed for Robert Nelson by himself July 20, 1786 in consequence of a Military Warrant No. 2701. Located __ day of __ 1786. Sept 15, 1787.

Page   204 - ROBERT NELSON - NC - No. 387 - Reg. Apr 25, 1788
By an Act for the relief of the Officers and Soldiers of the Continental Line, in consideration of the bravery and zeal of Dempsy Green, a private in the said line, granted unto Robert Nelson, assignee of Dempsy Green, a tract of land containing 640 acres in Davidson County on both sides of Red River about three miles from Clarksville. Adjoining Adam Boyd, James Summers, and Col. Martin Armstrong. Surveyed for Robert Nelson by himself Aug 15, 1788 in consequence of a Military Warrant No. 2488. Located May 12, 1786. Sept 15, 1787.

Page   205 - ROBERT NELSON - NC - No. 385 - Reg. Apr 25, 1788
By an Act for the relief of the Officers and Soldiers of the Continental Line, in consideration of the bravery and zeal of Patrick Mulford, a private in the said line, granted unto Robert Nelson, assignee of Patrick Mulford, a tract of land containing 640 acres in Davidson County on Grove Creek a south fork of Big harpeth. Adjoining Malone Mullins, L. Clark's line. Surveyed for Robert Nelson by himself Aug 20, 1786 in consequence of a Military Warrant No. 2491. Located Apr 1, 1786. Sept 15, 1787.

Page   205 - ROBERT NELSON - NC - No. 252 - Reg. Apr 25, 1788
By an Act for the relief of the Officers and Soldiers of the Continental Line, in consideration of the bravery and zeal of James McCleland, a sergeant in the said line, granted unto Robert Nelson, assignee of James McCleland, a tract of land containing 429

acres in Davidson County on the east side of Big Harpeth River on the west boundary of Alex Nelson's claim. Adjoining John and Alex Nelson's survey. Surveyed for Robert Nelson by himself Apr 13, (blank) in consequence of a Military Warrant No. 258. Located Apr 6, 1784. Mar 7, 1786.

Page 205 - TIMOTHY DEMUMBRE - NC - No. 607 - Reg. Apr 25, 1788
By an Act for the relief of the Officers and Soldiers of the Continental Line, in consideration of the bravery and zeal of Timothy Demumbre, (blank) in the said line, granted unto said Demumbre a tract of land containing 1000 acres in Davidson County on the north side of Cumberland River on the head of the creek that empties into the river at McFarling's cabin. Adjoining Captain Vance's claim, Robert Nelson's line, and Joseph Fleming's line, also Weakley's line. Surveyed for Timothy Demumbre July 20, 1786 by Robert Nelson, D.S. in consequence of a Military Warrant No. 3278. Located April 6, 1786. Sept 15, 1787.

Page 206 - ROBERT HAYS - NC - No. 644 - Reg. Apr 25, 1788
By an Act for the relief of the Officers and Soldiers of the Continental Line, in consideration of the bravery and zeal of Edward Butler, a non-commissioned officer in the said line, granted unto Robert Hays, assignee of Edward Butler, a tract of land containing 1000 acres in Davidson County on Bizzells Salleen to join an entry of William Stuart on the upper side. Crossing Clarks Creek. Surveyed for Robert Hays by himself Apr 20, 1786 in consequence of a Military Warrant No. 1666. Located Dec 23, 1785. Nov 15, 1787.

Page 206 - ROBERT HAYS - NC - No. 645 - Reg. Apr 25, 1788
By an Act for the relief of the Officers and Soldiers of the Continental Line, in consideration of the bravery and zeal of William James, a private in the said line, granted unto Robert Hays, assignee of William James, a tract of land containing 640 acres in Davidson County on the north side of Cumberland River beginning at the mouth of Gibsons Creek, corner of Neelys Lick. Surveyed by Robert Hays for himself Oct 2, 1786 in consequence of a Military Warrant No. 876. Located Nov 12, 1784. Nov 15, 1787.

Page 207 - LEWIS BEARD - NC - No. 228 - Reg. Apr 26, 1788
By an Act for the relief of the Officers and Soldiers of the Continental Line, in consideration of the bravery and zeal of James Marr, a private in the said line, granted unto Lewis Beard, assignee of James Marr, a tract of land containing 640 acres in Davidson County on Harpeth River, south side of Cumberland River. Surveyed for Lewis Beard May 12, 1785 by David Hays, D.S in consequence of a Military Warrant No. 749. Located Apr 29, 1784. Mar 7, 1786.

Page 207 - LEWIS BEARD - NC - No. 227 - Reg. Apr 26, 1788
By an Act for the relief of the Officers and Soldiers of the Continental Line, in consideration of the bravery and zeal of Elijah Kidwell, a private in the said line, granted unto Lewis Beard, assignee of Elijah Kidwell, a tract of land containing 640 acres in Davidson County on Harpeth River south side of Cumberland and adjoining James Marr's south boundary. Surveyed for Lewis Beard May 12, 1785 by David Hays, D.S. in consequence of a Military Warrant No. 601. Located May 22, 1784. Mar 7, 1786.

Page   207 - STEPHEN CANTRILL - NC - No. 64 - Reg. Apr 26, 1788
By an Act for the relief of the Officers and Soldiers of tne Continental Line, in consideration of the services of Stephen Cantrill, one of the Commission Guards, was granted a tract of land containing 640 acres in Davidson County on Stewarts Creek a branch of Stones River. Which land was surveyed for Stephen Cantrilll Apr 12, 1785 by Robert Russell, D.S. in consequence of a Warrant No. 203. Located Jan 29, 1784. Oct 8, 1787.

Page   208 - STEPHEN CANTRILL - NC - No. 82 - Reg. Apr 26, 1788
By an Act for the relief of the Officers and Soldiers of the Continental Line, in consideration of the bravery and zeal of Briton George, a private in said line, granted unto Stephen Cantrill, assignee of Briton George, a tract of land containing 640 acres in Davidson County on Sulphur Fork of Red River. Adjoining lands of Morton Mauldon's Preemption. Surveyed for Stephen Cantrill Feb 17, 1786 by Henry Bradford, D.S. in consequence of a Military Warrant No. 358. Located Nov 9, 1785. Sept 15, 1787.

Page   208 - DANIEL HOGAN - NC - No. 86 - Reg. Apr 26, 1788
For 10 lbs per 100 acres paid by Daniel Hogan was granted a tract of land containing 640 acres in Davidson County on south side of Cumberland River on the west fork of Mill Creek. Adjoining Andrew Ewing, Thomas Hardiman, John Holiday, James Ray's Preemption, Hogans branch. Surveyed for Daniel Hogan Feb 9, 1785 by James Mulherin, D.S. in consequence of a Warrant No. 252. Located Feb 7, 1784. Apr 17, 1786.

Page   209 - WILLIAM BOWMAN - NC No. 220 - Reg. Apr 26, (1788)
By an Act for the relief of the Officers and Soldiers of the Continental Line, in consideration of the bravery and zeal of John Callihan, a private in the said line, granted unto William Bowan, assignee of John Callihan, a tract of land containing 640 acres in Davidson County on the waters of Stones River, between Stones and Tamers Creek. Adjoining Col. James Armstrong. Surveyed for William Bowman July 15, 1785 by Robert Hays, D.S. in consequence of a Military Warrant No. 877. Located Mar 9, 1785. Mar 7, 1786.

Page   209 - JACOB MATHEWS - NC - No. 132 - Reg. Apr 26, 1788
By an Act for the relief of the Officers and Soldiers of the Continental Line, in consideration of the bravery and zeal of Jacob Mathews, a private in the said line, was granted a tract of land containing 640 acres in Davidson County on Willis Creek. Surveyed for Jacob Mathews Feb 1, 1785 by William Murry, D.S. in consequence of a Military Warrant No. 300. Located Aug 9, 1784. Mar 14, 1786.

Page   209 - ISAAC MOORE, ESQ. - NC - No. 569 - Reg. Apr 26, 1788
By an Act for the relief of the Officers and Soldiers of the Continental line, in consideration of the bravery and zeal of Isaac Moore, a captain in said line, was granted a tract of land containing 3840 acres in Davidson County on the first creek above the Big Salt Lick on the north side known by the name of Taylors Creek. Surveyed for Isaac Moore Oct 27, 1785 by Ed Hickman, D.S. in consequence of a Military Warrant No. 1086. Located Apr 16, 1785. Sept 15, 1787.

Page   210 - ALEXANDER MARTIN - NC - No. 2 - Reg. Apr 26, 1788

By an Act for the relief of the Officers and Soldiers of the Continental Line, in consideration of the bravery and zeal of Alexander Martin, a colonel in said line, was granted a tract of land containing 2314 acres in Davidson County on Big Harpeth River above the mouth of the first creek above the Commissioners old line including a spring running into the river on the north side, at the mouth of the branch at a sappling marked RM. Surveyed for said Martin Apr 12, 1785 by Robert Nelson, D.S. in consequence of a Military Warrant No. 2. Located Oct 14, 1785. Mar 14, 1786.

Page   210 - ROBERT SPOTSWOOD RUSSELL - NC - No. 25 - Reg. Apr 28, 1788

For 10 lbs per 100 acres paid by Robert Spotswood Russell, granted unto said Russell a tract of land containing 640 acres in Davidson Countyon the west fork of Stewarts Creek. Surveyed for said Russell Apr 12, 1785 by said Russell, D.S. in consequence of a Warrant No. 400. Located and entered Apr 6, 1784. Apr 17, 1786.

Page   210 - SAMUEL HAYS - NC - No. 35 - Reg. Apr 28, 1788

For 10 lbs per 100 acres paid by Samuel Hays, was granted a tract of land containing 640 acres in Davidson County on the north side of Stones or Clores Creek a branch of Stones River, adjoining a corner to the land surveyed for Stones Lick, also to Col. John Donaldson. Surveyed for said Samuel Hays June 16, 1785 by Daniel Smith, D.S. in consequence of a Warrant No. 205. Located Jan 29, 1784. Apr 1786.

Page   211 - JOHN BLACKAMORE - NC - No. 61 - Reg. Apr 28, 1788

For 10 lbs per 100 acres paid by John Blackamore was granted a tract of land containing 640 acres in Davidson County on north side of Cumberland River above the mouth of Dry Creek. Surveyed for John Blackamore Sept 14, 1784 by James Sanders, D.S. in consequence of a Warrant No. 492. Located June 19, 1784. Apr 17, 1786.

Page   211 - JACOB CASTLEMAN - NC - No. 576 - Reg. Apr 28, 1788

By an Act for the relief of the Officers and Soldiers of the Continental Line, in consideration of the bravery and zeal of William Price, a private in the said line, granted unto Jacob Castleman, assignee of William Price, a tract of land containing 640 acres in Davidson County on the southside of Cumberland River on both sides of Stones Lick Creek adjoining Stewart's Preemption on the north. Surveyed for said Castleman Sept 18, 1786 by Moses Shelby, D.S. in consequence of a Military Warrant No. 951. Located July 19, 1784. Sept 15, 1787.

Page   211 - JESSEE ROBERTS - NC - No. 637 - Reg. Apr 28, 1788

By an Act for the relief of the Officers and Soldiers of the Continental Line, in consideration of the bravery and zeal of John Young, granted unto Jessee Roberts, an assignee of said John Young, a tract of land containing 640 acres in Davidson County on the north side of Cumberland at Barnes' southwest corner. Surveyed for Jesse Roberts __ day of __, 178_ by Robert Hays, D.S. in consequence of a Military Warrant No. (blank). Located (blank). Dated Nov 15, 1787.

Page   212 - ROBERT MONTGOMERY - NC - No. 170 - Reg. Apr 28, 1788

For 10 lbs per 100 acres paid by Robert Montgomery, was granted a tract of land containing 640 acres in Davidson County on the west fork of Bledsoes Creek, adjoining Horatio Rolls' line. Surveyed for Robert Montgomery June 14, 1785 by James Sanders, D.C. in consequence of a Warrant No. 93. Located Jan 14, 1784. Apr 17, 1786.

Page   212 - TIMOTHY ACUFF - NC - No. 179 - Reg. Apr 28, 1788
By an Act for the relief of the Officers and Soldiers of the Continental Line, in consideration of the bravery and zeal of Richard Evans, a private in the said line, granted unto Timothy Acuff, assignee of Richard Evans, a tract of land containing 640 acres in Davidson County between Stuarts and Fanning Creek on the waters of Stones River. Beginning at Col. James Armstrong's north east corner. Surveyed for Timothy Acuff by Robert Hays, D.S. in consequence of a Military Warrant No. 1223. Located Mar 8, 1785. Mar 7, 1786.

Page   212 - WILLIAM JENKINS - NC - No. 600 - Reg. Apr 28, 1788
By an Act for the relief of the Officers and Soldiers of the Continental Line, in consideration of the bravery and zeal of William Jenkins, a private in the said line, granted unto William Jenkins a tract of land containing 274 acres in Davidson County on the War Trace Creek of the Sulphur Fork of Red River. Surveyed for William Jenkins June 26, 1786 by Robert Nelson, D.S. in consequence of a Military Warrant No. 1943. Located Mar 25, 1786. Sept 15, 1787.

Page   213 - ROBERT NELSON - NC - No. 380 - Reg. May 1, 1788
By an Act for the relief of the Officers and Soldiers of the Continental Line, in consideration of the bravery and zeal of Jacob Mitchel, a private in the said line, granted unto Robert Nelson, assignee of Jacob Mitchel a tract of land containing 640 acres in Davidson County on Pasturs Creek, adjoining Samuel Cooling's line, Jones' Preemption, and Richard Thomas's line.   Surveyed for Robert Nelson by himself June 25, 1787 in consequence of a Military Warrant No. 25. Located March 21, 1786. Sept 15, 1787.

Page   213 - ROBERT NELSON - NC - No. 646 - Reg. May 1, 1788
By an Act for the relief for the Officers and Soldiers of the Continental Line, in consideration of the bravery and zeal of James Beard, a private in the said line, granted unto Robert Nelson, assignee of James Beard, a tract of land containing 640 acres in Davidson County on the east side of Big Harpeth on the north boundary of Nelson's claim. Adjoining Thomas Pastures' line and Alexander Nelson's line. Surveyed for Robert Nelson by himself June 19, 1787 in consequence of a Military Warrant No. 2975. Located Jan 20, 1787. Dec 8, 1787.

Page   213 - ROBERT NELSON - NC - No. 393 - Reg. May 1, 1788
By an Act for the relief of the Officers and Soldiers of the Continental Line, in consideration of the bravery and zeal of James Fletcher, a private in the said line, granted unto Robert Nelson, assignee of James Fletcher, a tract of land containing 640 acres in Davidson County on Goose Creek a south fork of Big Harpeth and adjoining Nelson's line and Melone Mullins. Surveyed for Robert Nelson Sept 25, 1786 in consequence of a Military Warrant No. 2121. Located May 12, 1786. Sept 15, 1787.

Page   214 - ROBERT NELSON - NC - No. 8 - Reg. May 1, 1788

By an Act for the relief of the Officers and Soldiers of the Continental Line, in consideration of the services of Col. Martin Armstrong, surveyor of lands, granted unto Robert Nelson, assignee of Col. Martin Armstrong, a tract of land containing 250 acres in Davidson County on the south side of Cumberland River about three miles below the mouth of Red River. Adjoining a corner made by James Sanders to Samuel Martin. Surveyed for Robert Nelson by himself Apr 29, 1786 in consequence of a Military Warrant No. 849. Located Apr 14, 1785. Oct 8, 1787.

Page   214 - ANDREW CROCKETT - NC - No. 173 - Reg. May 6, 1788

For 10 lbs per 100 acres paid by Andrew Crockett, was granted a tract of land containing 640 acres in Davidson County on Little Harper adjoining John Cockrill's north line. Surveyed for Andrew Crockett Oct 24, 1784 by John Bucchanan, D.S. in consequence of a Warrant No. 474. Located June 7, 1784. Apr 17, 1786.

Page   214 - JOHN CROCKETT - NC - No. 113 - Reg. May 6, 1788

For 10 lbs per 100 acres paid by John Crockett, was granted a tract of land containing 640 acres in Davidson County on the waters of Big and Little Harper. Adjoining William Collins and John Cockrill. Surveyed for John Crockett Oct 28, 1784 by John Bucchanan, D.S. in consequence of a Warrant No. 486. Located June 10, 1784. Apr 17, 1786.

Page   215 - JAMES CROCKETT - NC - No. 150 - Reg. May 6, 1788

For 10 lbs per 100 acres paid by James Crockett, was granted a tract of land containing 640 acres in Davidson County on the head waters of the middle fork of Station Camp Creek. Surveyed for James CrockettNov 27, 1784 by James Sanders, D.S. in consequence of a Warrant No. 471. Located June 7, 1784. Apr 17, 1786.

Page   215 - JAMES CROCKETT - NC - No. 108 - Reg. May 6, 1788

For 10 lbs per 100 acres paid by James Crockett, was granted a tract of land containing 640 acres in Davidson County on south fork of Little Harpeth. Adjoining John Cockrill's line. Surveyed for James Crockett Oct 29, 1784 by John Bucchanan, D.S. in consequence of a Warrant No. 472. Located June 7, 1784. Apr 17, 1786.

Page   215 - CHARLS GERRAD - NC - No. 32 - Reg. May 7, 1788

By an Act for the relief of the Officers and Soldiers of the Continental Line, in consideration of the bravery and zeal of Charles Gerrard, a lieutenant in the said line, granted unto Charles Gerrard a tract of land containing 2560 acres in Davidson County on the south side of Cumberland River including the mouth of Yellow Creek. Surveyed for Charles Gerrard Apr 8, 1784 by James Sanders in consequence of a Military Warrant No. 84. Located Oct 22, 1783. Mar 14, 1786.

Page   216 - ISAAC LINSEY - NC - No. 47 - Reg. May 14, 1788

By an Act for the relief of the Officers and Soldiers of the Continental Line, in consideration of the services of William Loggins, one of the Guards to the Commissioners, granted unto Isaac Linsey, assignee of William Loggins, a tract of land containing 320 acres in Davidson County on the mouth of Walls Creek on the north side of

Cumberland River. Surveyed for Isaac Linsey July 9, 1784 by James Sanders, D.S. in consequence of a Warrant No. 1. Located Oct 23, 1783. Oct 8, 1787.

Page 216 - WILLIAM TERREL LEWIS - NC - No. 618 - Reg. May 16, 1788

By an Act for the relief of the Officers and Soldiers of the Continental Line, in consideration of the bravery and zeal of Micajah Lewis, a captain in the said line, granted unto William Terrel Lewis, heir of Micajah Lewis, a tract of land containing 3840 acres in Davidson County on the south side of Cumberland River and on the third creek above Caney Fork on the south side of said river. Surveyed for William Terrel Lewis Oct 19, 1785 by Edwin Hickman, D.S. in consequence of a Military Warrant No. 54. Located July 16, 1785. Sept 15, 1787.

Page 216 - JOEL LEWIS - NC - No. 243 - Reg. May 16, 1788

By an Act for the relief of the Officers and Soldiers of the Continental Line, in consideration of the bravery and zeal of James Rainey, a private in the said line, granted unto Joel Lewis, assignee of Rainey, a tract of land containing 640 acres in Davidson County on both sides of east fork of Yellow Creek. Surveyed for Joel Lewis Apr 3, 1785 by Joseph Brock, D.S. in consequence of a Military Warrant No. 273. Located 11 Dec 1784. Mar 7, 1786.

Page 217 - MATHEW PAYNE - NC - No. 139 - Reg. May 19, 1788

For 10 lbs per 100 acres paid by Mathew Payne, was granted a tract of land containing 640 acres in Davidson County lying at the mouth of Kaspers Creek on the north side of Cumberland River. Adjoining George Maxell near Kaspers Creek, down Cumberland River to a bluff on said river, and John Blackamore's line. Surveyed for Mathew Payne June 25, 1785 by Daniel Smith, D.S. in consequence of a Warrant No. 526. Located June 15, 1784. Apr 17, 1786.

Page 217 - ADAM LYNN - NC - No. (blank) - Reg. June 2, 1788

By an Act for the relief of the Officers and Soldiers of the Continental Line, in consideration of the services of Col. Martin Armstrong, surveyor of lands, granted unto Adam Lynn, assignee of Col. Martin Armstrong, a tract of land containing 50 acres in Davidson County on Shanes Fork of Gaspers Creek. Surveyed for Adam Lynn Mar 17, 1787 by Robert Ewing, D.S. in consequence of an entry made in Armstrong's office May 3, 1785. Oct 8, 1787.

Page 217 - ADAM LYNN - NC - No. (blank) - Reg. June 2, 1788

By an Act for the relief of the Officers and Soldiers of the Continental Line, in consideration of the services of Col. Martin Armstrong, surveyor of lands, granted unto Adam Lynn, assignee of Col. Martin Armstrong, a tract of land containing 50 acres in Davidson County on Shanes Fork of Gaspers Creek. Surveyed for Adam Lynn by Robert Ewing, D.S. Mar 17, 1787 in consequence of an entry made Mar 16, 1786. Oct 8, 1787.

Page 218 - EUSEBIUS BUSHNELL - NC - No. 626 - Reg. July 18, 1788

By an Act for the relief of the Officers and Soldiers of the Continental Line, in consideration of the bravery and zeal of William Davis, a private in the said line, granted unto Eusebius Bushnell, assignee of William Davis, a tract of land containing 640 acres in

Page   218 - BUSHNELL & DOBBINS - NC - Reg. July 19, 1788

By an Act for the relief of the Officers and Soldiers of the Continental Line, in consideration of the bravery and zeal of Benjamin Lyles, a private in the said line, granted unto Eusebius Bushnell and William Dobbins, assignee of Benjamin Lyles, a tract of land containing 640 acres in Davidson County on the south side of Cumberland River to join an entry of Capt. Edwin Hickman No. 1646 of 640 acres. Surveyed for Bushnell and Dobbins Dec 12, 1785 by Robert Hays, D.S. in consequence of a Military Warrant No. 1672. Located Aug 13, 1785. Sept 15, 1787.

Page   218 - BUSHNELL & DOBBINS - NC - No. 623 - Reg. July 19, 1788

By an Act for the relief of the Officers and Soldiers of the Continental Line, in consideration of the bravery and zeal of Joseph Milliford, a private in the said line, granted unto Eusebius Bushnell and William Dobbins, assignees of Joseph Milliford, a tract of land containing 640 acres in Davidson County on the waters of Stones River on a small creek which is known by Bushnells Creek. Surveyed for Bushnell and Dobbins Sept 1, 1785 by Robert Hays, D.S. in consequence of a Military Warrant No. 1667. Located Sept 1, 1785. Sept 15, 1787.

Page   219 - BUSHNELL & DOBBINS - NC - No. 634 - Reg. July 19, 1788

By an Act for the relief of the Officers and Soldiers of the Continental Line, in consideration of the bravery and zeal of John Beaver, a sergeant in the said line, granted unto Eusebius Bushnell and William Dobbins, assignees of John Beavers, a tract of land containing 1000 acres in Davidson County on the waters of Stone River. Adjoining Isaac Shelby's corner. Surveyed for Bushnell and Dobbins by Ed. Hickman in consequence of a Military Warrant No. 1669. Located July 25, 1785. Sept 15, 1787.

Page   218 - BUSHNELL & DOBBINS - NC - No. 633 - July 19, 1788

By an Act for the relief of the Officers and Soldiers of the Continental Line, in consideration of the bravery and zeal of William Hayes, a sergeant in the said line, granted unto Eusebius Bushnell and William Dobbins, assignees of William Hayes, a tract of land containing 1000 acres in Davidson County on the south side of Cumberland River on Hickmans Creek joining Hickman's upper line of his survey No. 1646. Surveyed for Bushnell and Dobbins Dec 5, 1785 by Robert Hays, D.S. in consequence of a Military Warrant No. 1656. Located Sept 1, 1785. Sept 15, 1787.

Page   219 - BUSHNELL & DOBBINS - NC - No. 624 - Reg. July 19, 1788

By an Act for the relief of the Officers and Soldiers of the Continental Line, in consideration of the bravery and zeal of Daniel Jacobs, a sergeant in the said line, granted unto Eusebius Bushnell and William Dobbins, assignees of Daniel Jacobs, a tract of land containing 1000 acres in Davidson County on waters of Stones River. Beginning at Col. Shelby's corner. Surveyed for Bushnell and Dobbins Sept 2, 1785 by Robert Hays in consequence of Military Warrant No. 1674. Located July 24, 1785. Sept 15, 1787.

Page   220 - BUSHNELL & DOBBINS - NC - No. 632 - Reg. July 19, 1788

By an Act for the relief of the Officers and Soldiers of the Continental Line, in consideration of the bravery and zeal of Alanson Summons, a sergeant in the said line, granted unto Eusebius Bushnell and William Dobbins, assignees of Alanson Summers, a tract of land containing 1000 acres in Davidson County on the waters of Stones Creek. Beginning at Col. Shelby's line. Surveyed for Bushnell and Dobbins Sept 6, 1895 by Robert Hays, D.S. in consequence of a Military Warrant No. 1660. Located July 25, 1785. Sept 15, 1787.

Page   220 - BUSHNELL & DOBBINS - NC - No. 636 - Reg. July 19, 1788
By an Act for the relief of the Officers and Soldiers of the Continental Line, in consideration of the bravery and zeal of Jacob Dicky, a private in the said line, granted unto Eusebius Bushnell and William Dobbins, a tract of land containing 640 acres in Davidson Countyon the south side of Cumberland River. Beginning four hundred and eighty poles from where the Virginia line crosses Cumberland River. Surveyed for Bushnell and Dobbins Sept 14, 1785 by Robert Hays, D.S. in consequence of a Military Warrant No. 1683. Located Sept 1, 1785. Sept 13, 1787.

Page   220 - BUSHNELL & DOBBINS - NC - No. 629 - Reg. July 19, 1788
By an Act for the relief of the Officers and Soldiers of the Continental Line, in consideration of the bravery and zeal of Mathew Wood, a captain in the said line, granted unto Eusebius Bushnell and William Dobbins, assignees of Mathew Wood, a tract of land containing 1622 acres in Davidson County on the main East Fork of Stones River, adjoining Col. Isaac Shelby's corner. Surveyed for Bushnell and Dobbins Sept 7, 1785 by Edwin Hickman, in consequence of a Military Warrant No. 572. Located July 25, 1785. Sept 15, 1787.

Page   221 - BUSHNELL & DOBBINS - NC - No. 625 - Reg. July 19, 1788
By an Act for the relief of the Officers and Soldiers of the Continental Line, in consideration of the bravery and zeal of Jacob Givins, a private in the said line, granted unto Eusebius Bushnell and William Dobbins, assignees of Jacob Givins, a tract of land containing 640 acres in Davidson County on the waters of Stuarts Creek. Beginning at Capt. Moses Shelby's corner. Surveyed for Bushnell and Dobbins by Robert Hays, D.S. in consequence of a Military Warrant No. 686. Located July 25, 1785. Sept 15, 1787.

Page   221 - BUSHNELL & DOBBINS - NC - No. 627 - Reg. July 19, 1788
By an Act for the relief of the Officers and Soldiers of the Continental Line, in consideration of the bravery and zeal of John Ward, a fifer in the said line, granted unto Eusebius Bushnell and William Dobbins, a tract of land containing 1000 acres in Davidson County on both sides of the main West Fork of Stones River. Adjoining Col. Isaac Shelby's line. Surveyed for Bushnell and Dobbins by Edwin Hickman, D.S. in consequence of a Military Warrant No. 1677. Located Sept 1, 1785. Sept 15, 1787.

Page   221 - BUSHNELL & DOBBINS - NC - No. 630 - Reg. July 19, 1788
By an Act for the relief of the Officers and Soldiers of the Continental Line, in consideration of the bravery and zeal of Henry Cole, a drummer in the said line, granted unto Eusebius Bushnell and William Dobbins, assignees of Henry Cole, a tract of land containing 1000 acres in Davidson County on the waters of Stones River adjoining Col. Isaac Shelby's corner. Surveyed for Bushnell and Dobbins by Edwin Hickman, D.S. in consequence of a Military Warrant No. 1665. Located July 25, 1788. Sept 15, 1787.

Page   222 - BUSHNELL & DOBBINS - NC - No. 631 - Reg. July 19, 1788

By an Act for the relief of the Officers and Soldiers of the Continental Line, in consideration of the bravery and zeal of Isaac Hill, a private in the said line, granted unto Eusebius Bushnell and William Dobbins, assignees of Isaac Hill, a tract of land containing 228 acres in Davidson County on the waters of Stones River adjoining Major Blount's corner. Surveyed for Bushnell and Dobbins by Robert Hays, D.S. in consequence of a Military Warrant No. 1689. Located July 25, 1785. Sept 15, 1787.

Page   222 - BUSHNELL & DOBBINS - NC - No. 635 - Reg. July 19, 1788

By an Act for the relief of the Officers and Soldiers of the Continental Line, in consideration of the bravery and zeal of John Dykes, a private in the said line, granted unto Eusebius Bushnell and William Dobbins, assignees of John Dykes, a tract of land containing 640 acres in Davidson County on the south side of Cumberland River joining Captain Laton's south west corner of his survey No. 335. Surveyed for Bushnell and Dobbins by Robert Hays, D.S. in consequence of a Military Warrant No. 682. Located Aug 13, 1785. Sept 15, 1787.

Page   222 - THOMAS WOODWARD - NC - No. 561 - Reg. July 21, 1788

By an Act for the relief of the Officers and Soldiers of the Continental Line, in consideration of the bravery and zeal of John McDowell, a private in the said line, granted unto Thomas Woodward, assignee of John McDowell, a tract of land containing 640 acres in Davidson County on the north fork of Red River joining Noah Woodward's north west corner. Surveyed for Thomas Woodward Feb 18, 1786 by Sqr. Grant, D.S. in consequence of a Military Warrant No. 1231. Located Dec 29, 1784. Sept 15, 1787.

Page   223 - THOMAS MOLLOY - NC - No. 28 - Reg. July 21, 1788

By an Act for the relief of the Officers and Soldiers of the Continental Line, in consideration of the services of Thomas Kilgore, one of the Commission Guards, granted unto Thomas Molloy, assignee of Thomas Kilgore, a tract of land containing 320 acres in Davidson County joining said Molloy's Guard Right No. 696 and on Cumberland River. Surveyed for Thomas Molloy by himself Nov 4, 1785 in consequence of a Warrant No. 695. Located Mar 26, 1785. Oct 8, 1787.

Page   223 - THOMAS MOLLOY - NC - No. 8 - Reg. July 21, 1788

By an Act for the relief of the Officers and Soldiers of the Continental Line, in consideration of the service of William Daniel, one of the Commission Guards, granted unto Thomas Molloy, assignee of William Daniel, a tract of land containing 320 acres in Davidson County adjoining Abrm. Burgusse's west boundary. Surveyed for Thomas Molloy by himself Nov 4, 1785 in consequence of a Warrant No. 696. Located Mar 26, 1785. Oct 8, 1787.

Page   223 - JACOB MESSICK - NC - No. 515 - Reg. July 21, 1788

By an Act for the relief of the Officers and Soldiers of the Continental Line, in consideration of the bravery and zeal of Jacob Messick, a lieutenant in the said line, granted unto Jacob Messick a heir of said Messick, a tract of land containing 2560 acres in Davidson County on the south side of Cumberland River. Beginning on the bank of the river opposite John Rice's entry as assignee of Porter, joining Perry Gleaves' upper line.

Surveyed for said Messick Sept 5, 1785 by I. Roberts, D,S, in consequence of a Military Warrant No. 553. Located July 8, 1784. Sept 15, 1787.

Page   224 - JOHN VANCE - NC - No. 586 - Reg. July 21, 1788
          By an Act for the relief of the Officers and Soldiers of the Continental Line, in consideration of the bravery and zeal of John Vance, Esq., a captain in the said line, granted unto said John Vance a tract of land containing 3840 acres in Davidson County on the north side of Cumberland Riverat the mouth of Brushy Creek. Adjoining James McFarlin's corner, Robert Nelson's corner. Surveyed for John Vance Feb 13, 1786 by Robert Nelson in consequence of a Military Warrant No. 329. Located June 28, 1784. Sept 15, 1787.

Page   224 - PETER CATRON - NC - No. 111 - Reg. July 21, 1788
          For 10 lbs per 100 acres paid by Peter Catron, conveyed unto peter Catron a tract of land containing 640 acres in Davidson County on the west fork of Mill Creek, joining Jonathan Drakes boundary and John Foreman's Preemption on the bank of a spring branch, and William Simpson's east boundary line. Surveyed for Peter Catron Feb 10, 1785 in consequence of a Warrant No. 583. Located Aug 18, 1784. Apr 17, 1786.

Page   224 - NOAH WOODWARD - NC - No. 590 - Reg. July 21, 1788
          By an Act for the relief of the Officers and Soldiers of the Continental line, in consideration of the bravery and zeal of Samuel Simpson, a private in the said line, granted unto Noah Woodward, assignee of Samuel Simpson, a tract of land containing 640 acres in Davidson County in the north fork of Red River. Surveyed for Noah Woodward Feb 8, 1785 by Sqr. Grant, D.S. in consequence of a Military Warrant No. 901. Located Dec 21(9), 1784. Sept 15, 1787.

Page   225 - ROBERT MARLEY - NC - No. 325 - Reg. July 21, 1788
          By an Act for the relief of the officers and Soldiers of the Continental Line, in consideration of the bravery and zeal of James Murry, a private in the said line, granted unto Robert Marley, assignee of James Murry, a tract of land containing 640 acres in Davidson County on the east bank of Spring Creek on William Ross' south boundary line and Hodges Blount's line. Surveyed for Robert Marley May 1, 1786 by John Bucchanan, D.S. in consequence of a Military Warrant No. 1775. Located Jan 21, 1786. Aug 1, 1787.

Page   225 - ROBERT MARLEY - NC - No. 328 - Reg. July 21, 1788
          By an Act for the relief of the Officers and Soldiers of the Continental Line, in consideration of the bravery and zeal of George Barton, a private in the said line, granted unto Robert Marley, assignee of George Barton, a tract of land containing 640 acres in Davidson Countyon the waters of Spring Creek and joining William Ross' line. Surveyed for Robert Marley May 1, 1786 by Bucchanan, D.S. in consequence of a Military Warrant No. 2109. Located Jan 21, 1786. Aug 1, 1787.

Page   225 - ROBERT MARLEY - NC - No. 326 - Reg. July 21, 1788
          By an Act for the relief of the Officers and Soldiers of the Continental Line, in consideration of the bravery and zeal of Charles Anderson, a private in the said line, granted unto Robert Marley, assignee of Charles Anderson, a tract of land containing 640

acres in Davidson County. Beginning on Hodges Blount's south boundary line, being Marley's north west corner as assignee of James Murry. Surveyed for Robert Marley May 1, 1786 by John Bucchanan, D.S. in consequence of a Military Warrant No. 2106. Located Jan 21, 1786. Aug 1, 1787.

Page   226 - JAMES COLE MONTFLORENCE - July 22, 1788
            This indenture made 2 July 1788 between William Crutcher of Davidson County of one part and James Cole Montgomery of same place of other part.   William Crutcher sold unto James Cole Montflorence all the title, interest and property in the town of Nashville and known by No. 19 with one half of the title in interest and property in the said lot. The joint tenants of the said lot and William amd James may beat in erecting buildings on the said lot. Proven July 8, 1788.

Page   226 - LEVI HAND - July 22, 1788
            We, Samuel Barton, Thomas Molloy and James Shaw and Isaac Linsey, directors and trustees of the town of Nashville, conveyed unto Levi Hand the Lot No. 66 in Nashville and shall within three years erect, build and finish a well framed square log, brick or stone house with a brick or stone chimney. This July 26, 1784. July 8, 1788.

Page   226 - JOHN GIBSON - We, Samuel Barton, Thomas Molloy, James Shaw and Isaac Linsey, directors and trustees of the town of Nashville, conveyed unto John Gibson Lot No. 38 in Nashville and shall within three years to erect, build and finish a well framed square log, brick or stone house with a brick or stone chimney. This July 30, 1784. July 8, 1788.

Page   227 - WILLIAM PURNELL - July 22, 1788
            We, Samuel Barton, Thomas Molloy and James Shaw, directors and trustees of town of Nashville, conveyed unto William Purnell Lot No. 52 in Nashville and shall within three years erect, build and finish a well framed square log, brick or stone house with a brick of stone chimney. This 12 Apr 1784. July 8, 1788.

Page   227 - JAMES BIZWELL - July 22, 1788
            We, Samuel Barton, Thomas Molloy, James Shaw and Isaac Linsey, directors and trustees of the town of Nashville, conveyed unto James Bizwell Lot No. 28 in Nashville and shall within three years erect, build and finish a well framed square log, brick or stone house with a brick or stone chimney. This 26 July 1784. July 8, 1788.

Page   227 - WILLIAM MULHERIN - July 22, 1788
            We, Samuel Barton, Thomas Molloy, James Shaw and Isaac Linsey, directors and trustees of Nashville, conveyed unto William Mulherin Lot No. 6 in Nashville and within three years shall erect, build and finish a well framed square log house with a brick or stone chimney. This July 30, 1784. July 8, 1788.

Page   228 - JOHN TOPP - July 22, 1788
            This indenture made 17 May 1788, between Robert Nelson of Davidson County of one part and John Topp of same place of other part. Robert Nelson conveyed unto John Topp a tract of land containing 640 acres in Davidson County on Goose Creek a south fork of Big Harpeth that empties into said river at Governor Martin's upper line. Adjoining

Melone Mullins' corner, L. Clark's line and Allen's corner. Which land the said Nelson obtained by patent dated Sept 15, 1787 as assignee of Peter Mulford, a private in the Continental Line of North Carolina. This July 9, 1788.

Page   228 - JOHN TOPP - July 22, 1788
This indenture made 17 May 1788 between Robert Nelson of Davidson County of one part and John Topp of same place of other part. Robert Nelson conveyed unto John Topp a tract of land containing 160 acres in Davidson County on Grove Creek a south fork of Big Harpeth joining the south boundary of John Topp's other claim conveyed unto him by said Nelson. Which land being part of a tract of 640 acres of land granted to the said Nelson by patent dated Sept 15, 1787 as assignee of James Fletcher, a private in the Continental Line. This July 9, 1788.

Page   229 - WALKER & STUART - July 22, 1788
This indenture made 8 July 1788 between Isaac Linsey of Sumner County, North Carolina of one part and William Stuart and Samuel Walker of Davidson County of other part. Isaac Linsey conveyed unto William Stuart and Samuel Walker a tract of land containing 16 acres and 120 poles in Davidson County. It being a part of a patent of 320 acres of land granted to said Linsey by patent dated Oct 8, 1787, as assignee of William Loggins, a soldier in the Commission Guards &c. This July 8, 1788.

Page   229 - DANIEL HOGAN - July 22, 1788
This indenture made 8 July 1788 between Isaac Linsey of Sumner County, North Carolina of one part and Daniel Hogan of Davidson County of other part. Isaac Linsey conveyed unto Daniel Hogan a tract of land containing 8 acres and 60 poles in Davidson County on the north side of Cumberland River about one mile and a half from Nashville town. Beginning at the house and including the same to corner on the road, to John Kits' line, Stephen Ray's line, and Christian Crips' line, also Adam Hampton's line. Land being part of 320 acres granted to said Linsey by the State of North Carolina, grant dated 1 Oct 1787. Wit: William Stuart July 8, 1788.

Page   230 - JOHN HUNTER - July 23, 1788
This indenture made 7 June 1788 between Eusebius Bushnell and William Dobbins of one part and John Hunter of other part, both of Davidson County. Said Bushnell and Dobbins conveyed unto John Hunter a lot of one acre of ground in the town of Nashville and known as Lot No. 28, being the lot formerly granted unto James Biswell by the Commission of the town by deed dated July 26, 1784. This July 10, 1788.

Page   230 - RICE PORTER - July 23, 1788
This indenture made 8 July 1788 between Rice Porter of Davidson County of one part and John Forde of same place of other part. John Forde conveyed unto Rice Porter one tract of land lying on the head waters of Craighead Creek in Davidson County. Adjoining Harts' line and Swanson's line. This July 8, 1788.

Page   231 - JAMES DONNALLY - July 23, 1788
This indenture made 7 July 1788 between Isaac Linsey of Sumner County of one part and James Donnally of Davidson County of other part. Isaac Linsey conveyed unto

James Donnally a tract of land in Davidson County on Cumberland River and joining Col. Martin Armstrong. Proven by Daniel Hogan and Headon Wells July 8, 1788.

Page   231 - HEADON WELLS - July 23, 1788
             This indenture made 5 July 1788 between Isaac Linsey of Sumner County, NC , of one part and Headon Wells of Davidson County of other part. Isaac Linsey conveyed unto Headon Wells a tract of land in Davidson County on the north side of Cumberland River about one mile and a half from Nashville containing 16 acres and a half of land being on Thomas Creek. Land being part of 320 acres of land granted unto Isaac Linsey by State of North Carolina dated Oct 8, 1787. Proven by William Stuart and Daniel Hogan July 8, 1788.

Page   232 - DAVID EARHART - July 23, 1788
             This indenture made July 8, 1788 between Isaac Linsey of Sumner County, NC of one part and David Earhart of Davidson County of other part. Isaac Linsey conveyed unto David Earhart a tract of land in Davidson County on the north side of Cumberland River about one mile and a half from Nashville containing 8 acres and 115 poles. Adjoining Adam Hampton's line. Which contains 7 acres and 115 poles being part of a tract of 320 acres granted unto Isaac Linsey by patent dated Oct 8, 1787, No. 117. Registered in Book A, folio 216. Proven by William Stuart and Daniel Hogan July 8, 1788.

Page   232 - LARDNER CLARK - July 23, 1788
             We, Samuel Barton, Thomas Molloy, James Shaw and Isaac Linsey, directors and trustees of the town of Nashville, granted unto Lardner Clark Lot No. 46 in town of Nashville and shall within three years from date of conveyance build, erect and finish a well framed square log, brick or stone house with brick or stone chimney. This 26 July 1784. July 8, 1788.

Page   233 - EDWARD LUCAS - July 23, 1788
             This indenture made October 1787 between Thomas Molloy of Davidson County of one part and Edward Lucas of same place of other part. Thomas Molloy conveyed unto Edward Lucas a tract of land containing 384 acres in Davidson County on the north side of Cumberland River. Said land being part of a tract of 384 acres of land granted to Thomas Callendar by the State of North Carolina for his services as captain in the Continental Line and dated Mar 14, 1786, No. 49. This July 7, 1788.

Page   233 - EUSEBIUS BUSHNELL - July 23, 1788
             This indenture made Sept 1, 1787 between Anthony Crutcher of one part and Eusebius Bushnell of other part, both of Davidson County. Anthony Crutcher conveyed unto Eusebius Bushnell a certain half acre lot which lot the said Bushnell sold and deeded to James Lenear and A. Crutcher, the said lot in the town of Nashville and known as Lot No. 28. The said lot being formerly granted to James Biswell by the Commissioners of said town dated July 26, 1784. July 8, 1788

Page   234 - N. COONROD - July 24, 1788
             This indenture made July 9, 1788 between Isaac Linsey of Sumner County, North Carolina of one part and Nicholas Coonrod of Davidson County of other part. Isaac

Linsey conveyed unto Nicholas Coonrod a tract of land containing 68 acres. Another tract of land containing 108 poles which adjoins Christian Cripps corner. One other lot or parcel containing 127 poles and joining Christian Cripp's line. All lying and being in the place called Heatons Old Station and being part of a tract of 320 acres granted to said Linsey by patent dated Oct 8, 1787 as assignee of William Loggins, one of the Commission Guards &c. Proven by Headon Wells and Christopher Guise July 8, 1788.

Page   234 - FRANCIS PRINCE - July 24, 1788
(2nd page)   We, Samuel Barton, Thomas Molloy and James Shaw, directors and trustees for the town of Nashville, NC, conveyed unto Francis Prince the Lot No. 75 in Nashville and shall within three years of date of conveyance make the requisite buildings on the said lot. This August 16, 1784. July 10, 1788

Page   235 - ROBERT DENNING - July 24, 1788
This indenture made Sept 15, 1786 between William Polk, John Montgomery and Anthony Crutcher of the one part and Robert Denning of the other part. William Polk, John Montgomery and Anthony Crutcher conveyed unto Robert Denning a piece or lot of graound in the town of Clarksville and known as Lot No. 72 containing half an acre of land. July 8, 1788.

Page   235 - ROBERT DENNING - July 24, 1788
This indenture made Sept 15, 1786 between William Polk, John Montgomery and Anthony Crutcher of one part and Robert Denning of other part. William Polk, John Montgomery and Anthony Crutcher conveyed unto Robert Denning a piece or lot of land in the town of Clarksville and known as Lot No. (blank) and containing half an acre of land. July 8, 1788.

Page   235 - ROBERT DENNING - July 24, 1788
This indenture made Sept 15, 1786 between William Polk, John Montgomery and Anthony Crutcher of the one part and Robert Denning of the other part. William Polk, John Montgomery and Anthony Crutcher conveyed unto Robert Denning a piece or lot in the town of Clarksville, containing half an acre. The number of lot not inserted, but was entered on the back as Lot No. 68. July 8, 1788.

Page   236 - ROBERT DENNING
This indenture made Sept 15, 1786 between William Polk, John Montgomery and Anthony Crutcher of one part and Robert Denning of other part. William Polk, John Montgomery and Anthony Crutcher conveyed unto Robert Denning a piece or lot of land in the town of Clarksville and known as Lot. No. (blank), containing half an acre of land. Proven by Robert Nelson in Davidson County July 8, 1788. On the back was marked No. 66.

Page   236 - JACQUES CHESNIER - July 24, 1788
This indenture made June 18, 1788 between Timothy Demumbre of the town of Nashville, Davidson County, NC of one part and Jacques Chesnier of the town of Kaskias and County of Illinois of other part. Timothy Demumbre conveyed unto Jacques Chesnier all that plantation or tract of land in Davidson County, NC, on the north side of Cumberland River at the head of the creek that empties into the said river at McFarlin's

line. Adjoining Robert Nelson's line, Joseph Fleming's line, and Weakley's line. Containing 1000 acres, which land was granted unto Timothy Demumbre by the State of North Carolina by patent No. 607 and dated Sept 15, 1787. Recorded in Davidson County in Book A, folio 205 April 25, 1788. Proven by James Cole Montflorence July 7, 1788.

Page   237 - THOMAS MOLLOY - July 25, 1788
            This indenture made July 8, 1788 between Robert Nelson of Davidson County of one part and Thomas Molloy of same place of other part. Robert Nelson conveyed unto Thomas Molloy a tract of land containing 200 acres in Davidson County on the north side of Cumberland River about half mile above Whites Creek. The said tract being granted to said Nelson by the State of North Carolina by patent dated Oct 8, 1787, No. 12. July 8, 1788.

Page   237 - BUSHNELL & DOBBINS - July 24, 1788
            This indenture made Oct 20, 1787 between James Lenier of one part and Eusebius Bushnell and William Dobbins of other part. James Lenier conveyed unto said Bushnell & Dobbins a certain lot of a half acre of land in the town of Nashville and known as Lot No. 28, being the half of the lot formerly granted to James Biswell by the Commissioners for said town by deed dated July 26, 1784. July 7, 1788.

Page   238 - LEWIS ROBERTS - July 24, 1788
            This indenture made July 7, 1788 between William Mabane of Orange County, North Carolina of one part and Lewis Roberts of Kentucky in the State of Virginia of the other part. William Mabane conveyed unto Lewis Roberts a certain tract of land in Green County, North Carolina on the west fork of Big Harpeth River. Containing 1028 acres, Which deed of conveyance was executed to Lewis Roberts by Anthony Bledsoe held for the County of Davidson July 7, 1788 in consequence of a Power of Attorney from said Mabane to said Nelson. Proven by James Robertson Apr 8, 1788.

Page   238 - JOHN MARNEY - July 24, 1788
(2nd page)   This indenture made Nov 8, 1787 between Joshua Howard of Davidson County of one part and John Marney of same place of other part. Joshua Howard conveyed unto John Marney a tract of land containing 274 acres in Davidson County on both sides of Whites and Heatons Creeks. Adjoining Drakes' land. A tract of land granted unto Caleb Marchant for his services as a private in the Continental Line and No. 115, dated March 7, 1786. Proven by Molloy and Robert Heaton July 7, 1788.

Page   239 - LARDNER CLARK - July 28, 1788
            This indenture made Sept 4, 1784 between Levi Hand of Davidson County of one part and Lardner Clark of same place of other part. Levi Hand conveyed unto Lardner Clark all the lot or parcel of land known in the town of Nashville as Lot No. 66. Said lot deeded July 26, 1784 granted by the directors and trustees of town of Nashville. Proven by Daniel James in Davidson County July 10, 1788.

Page   239 - LARDNER CLARK - July 28, 1788
            This indenture made May 4, 1786 between William Purnell of Lincoln County, Virginia, gentleman, of the one part and William Wicoff and Lardner Clark of Davidson County of other part. William Purnell conveyed unto Wicoff and Clark a tract of land in

in the town of Nashville known as Lot No. 64, dated 13 July 1784 . Proven by Anthony Foster July 10, 1788.

Page   240 - ANTHONY HART - July 28, 1788
          This indenture made Jan 10, 1788 between Anthony Hart of Davidson County of one part and John Forde of same place of other part. John Forde conveyed unto Anthony Hart one tract of land on the head waters of Thomas Creek in Davidson County. July 8, 1788.

Page   240 - ADAM HAMPTON - July 28, 1788
          This indenture made July 8, 1788 between Isaac Linsey of Sumner County, North Carolina of one part and Adam Hampton of Davidson County of other part. Isaac Linsey conveyed unto Adam Hampton two lots or parcels of land, including the house wherein said Hampton now lives. Beginning at N. Coonrod's corner. Adjoining Christian Cripp's corner, David Earhart's corner, all being in in the place called Heatons Old Station and being part of a tract of 320 acres granted unto said Linsey by patent dated Oct 8, 1787, as assignee of William Loggins, a soldier in the Commissioners Guard &c. Proven by Chrisopher Guise and Headon Wells July 8, 1788.

Page   241 - JOHN RICE - July 28, 1788
          This indenture made July 5, 1788 between Isaac Linsey of Sumner County, NC of one part and John Rice of Davidson County, NC of other part. Isaac Linsey conveyed unto John Rice the several lots or parcels of land. One lot containing half acre. Beginning at Adam Hampton's line. One tract of land containing 608 poles. Adjoining N. Coonrod's line. Also one other lot containing 612 poles joining Christopher Guise's corner. All lands being in the place called Heaton's Old Station in Davidson County, being part of a tract of 320 acres granted to said Linsey by patent dated Oct 8, 1787 as assignee of William Loggins, one of the Commission Guards &c. Proven by Christopher Guise and Headon Wells July 8, 1788.

Page   241 - ISHAM LENIER - July 29, 1788
(2nd page)   This indenture made July 5, 1788 between Henry Lenier of Davidson County, NC of one part and Isham Lenier of same place of other part. Henry Lenier conveyed unto Isham Lenier333 acres, one third of land lying in the State of Georgia. All that part of Lot No. 25 lying joining the half lot sold by Julius Sanders to William Taitt with all the houses, battery and other improvements belonging which is now on the Lot No. 25, also one Lot No. 72 lying and being in the town of Nashville. Which said lots conveyed dated July 13, 1784 granted and conveyed by the directors and trustees of the town of Nashville to Julius Sanders. July 7, 1788.

Page   242 - JOHN SHANNON - July 29, 1788
          This indenture made July 8, 1788 between Morris Shean and Phebe Shean his wife of Davidson County of one part and John Shannon of same place of other part. Morris Shean and Phebe Shean conveyed unto John Shannon a tract of land containing 478 acres in Davidson County on the forks of Gaspers Creek. Said land being part of a tract of 640 acres granted unto said Shean dated Apr 17, 1786. July 8, 1788.

Page   242 - CHRISTOPHER GUISE - July 29, 1788
This indenture made July 9, 1788 between Isaac Linsey of Sumner County, North Carolina of one part and Christopher Guise of the other part. Isaac Linsey conveyed unto Christopher Guise a tract of land in Davidson County on the north side of Cumberland River about one mile and a half below Nashville containing 8 acres and 100 square poles. Adjoining John Ray's line, Christian Cripp's line. Which land containing 40 poles of land being part of a tract of 320 acres granted to said Linsey by patent dated 1787. Proven by N. Coonrod and Daniel Hogan July 9, 1788.

Page   243 - RICE PORTER - July 29, 1788
This indenture made July 9, 1788 between Rice Porter of Davidson County of one part and Robert Nelson of same place of other part. Robert Nelson conveyed unto Rice Porter a tract of land lying on the east boundary of said Nelson's other land which he got of Capt. Forde in Davidson County. Adjoining Forde's corner. July 9, 1788.

Page 243 - JOHN BLACKAMORE - July 29, 1788
This indenture made May 16, 1788 between Eusebius Bushnell and William Dobbins of Davidson County of one part and John Blackamore of same place of other part. Bushnell and Dobbins conveyed unto John Blackamore a tract of land in Sumner County, North Carolina and on the east fork of Stones River containing 1000 acres. Adjoining Isaac Shelby's corner. July 7, 1788.

Page   244 - ADAM HAMPTON - July 29, 1788
This indenture made July 9, 1788 between Barkley William Polk of Davidson County of one part and Adam Hampton of same place of other part. Barkley William Polk conveyed unto Adam Hampton all that lot or parcel of land known in the town of Nashville by Lot No. 4. Which said lot was by deed dated July 1784 granted by the directors and trustees of the town of Nashville. Proven by Samuel Barton and Thomas Crutcher July 9, 1788.

Page   244 - ABSOLOM HOOPER - July 30, 1788
This indenture made July 8, 1788 between Samuel Vernor of Davidson County of one part and Absolom Hooper of same place of other part. Samuel Vernor conveyed unto Absolom Hooper a tract of land containing 340 in Davidson County on the north side of Cumberland River about two miles and a half from Heatons Old Station and joins James Hollis' corner. Said land being granted unto Samuel Vernor by the State of North Carolina dated 8 Oct 1787, No. 31. Acknowledged by Elizabeth Vernor and James Cooper, administrators of the said Samuel Vernor, deceased, July 8, 1788 in consequence of a sale of the said lands made and obligation for a conveyance thereof given by the said Vernor in his lifetime, proven and recorded.

Page   245 - HUGH BRADSHAW - July 30, 1788
This indenture made July 8, 1788 between Samuel Vernor of Davidson County of one part and Hugh Bradshaw of same place of other part. Samuel Vernor conveyed unto Hugh Bradshaw a tract of land containing 300 acres in Davidson County on the north side of Cumberland River about two miles and a half from Heatons Old Station. Adjoining James Hollis' Preemption. Said tract being granted to said Vernor by State of North Carolina Oct

8 1787. Which deed of conveyance to said Bradshaw was executed asknowledged to him by Elizabeth Vernor and James Cooper administrators of the said Vernor, deceased, in Court July 8, 1788. In consequence as appears of the sale of the said lands made an obligation for a conveyance thereof given by the said Vernor in his lifetime and was proven by John Thomas.

Page   245 - OLIVE SHAW - July 30, 1788
        We, Samuel Barton, Thomas Molloy, James Shaw and Isaac Linsey, directors and trustees of the town of Nashville, conveyed unto Lot No. 10 in Nashville and shall within three years of date of conveyance, one well framed square log, brick or stone house with a brick or stone chimney. This 26 July 1788.   Acknowledged   by   Thomas   Mollow (Molloy) and James Shaw. July 9, 1788.

Page   246 - WILLIAM PURNELL - July 30, 1788
        We, Samuel Barton, Thomas Molloy, James Shaw and Isaac Linsey, directors and trustees of town of Nashville, conveyed unto William Purnell Lot No. 64 in Nashville and within three years of date of conveyance erect, build finish a well framed square log, brick and stone house with brick or stone chimney. This 30 July 1784. July 30, 1788.

Page   246 - JOHN NELSON - NC - No. 258 - Reg. Aug 13, 1788
        By an Act for the relief of the Officers and Soldiers of the Continental Line, in consideration of the bravery and zeal of John Nelson, a major in the said line, conveyed unto John Nelson a tract of land containing 4800 acres in Davidson County on Nelsons Creek a branch of Big Harpeth that empties in on the east side above the Commissioners Old Line. Adjoining Governor Martin's line. Surveyed for said John Nelson April 10, 1785 by Robert Nelson, D.S. in consequence of a Military Warrant No. 37. Located Mar 9, 1784. Mar 14, 1786.

Page   246 - JOHN NELSON - NC - No. 123 - Reg. Apr 13, 1788
        By an Act for the relief of the Officers and Soldiers of the Continental Line, in consideration for the bravery and zeal of Thomas May, a private in the said line, conveyed unto John Nelson, assignee of Thomas May, a tract of land containing 274 acres in Davidson County on the north side of Cumberland River and east boundary of William Lomax. Surveyed for John Nelson July 12, 1785 by Robert Nelson, D.S. in consequence of a Military Warrant No. 759. Located Apr 30, 1784. Mar 14, 1786.

Page   247 - EDWIN HICKMAN - NC - No. 550 - Reg. Aug 18, 1788
        By an Act for the relief of the Officers and Soldiers in the Continental Line, in consideration of the bravery and zeal of Hugh Tucker, a non-commissioned officer in the said line, conveyed unto Edwin Hickman, assignee of the heirs of Hugh Tuckers, a tract of land containing 1000 acres in Davidson County on the south side of Cumberland River about a mile and a half above the mouth of Roaring River. Adjoining Lieut. William Waters. Surveyed for Edwin Hickman for himself Jan 16, 1786 in consequence of a Military Warrant No. 2603. Located Jan 13, 1786. Sept 15, 1787.

Page   247 - EDWIN HICKMAN - NC - No. 568 - Reg. Aug 13, 1788
        By an Act for the relief of the Officers and Soldiers of the Continental Line,

in consideration of the bravery and zeal of John Trainer, a private in the said line, a tract of land containing 640 acres in Davidson County on the south side of Cumberland River below Drys Camp. Surveyed for said Hickman Dec 16, 1785 by Robert Hays, D.S. in consequence of a Military Warrant No. 1646. Located Aug 13, 1785. Sept 15, 1787.

Page   248 - THOMAS EVANS - NC - No. 469 - Reg. Aug 13, 1788

By an Act for the relief of the Officers and Soldiers of the Continental Line, in consideration of the bravery and zeal of Thomas Evans, a private in the said line, granted unto Thomas Evans a tract of land containing 640 acres in Davidson County on the south side of Cumberland River, about half a mile below the mouth of Bledsoes Creek. Surveyed for Thomas Evans Oct 6, 1785 by David Shelby, D.S. in consequence of a Military Warrant No. 1061. Located July 8, 1784. Sept 15, 1787.

Page   248 - WILLIAM HARGROVE - NC - No. 10 - Reg. Aug 13, 1788

By an Act for the relief of the Officers and Soldiers of the Continental Line, in consideration of the bravery and zeal of William Hargrove, a lieutenant in the said line, granted unto William Hargrove a tract of land containing 2560 acres in Davidson County on the north side of Cumberland River opposite the mouth of Wells Creek. Surveyed for said William Hargrove Feb 8, 1785 by Thomas Molloy, D.S. in consequence of a Military Warrant No. 314. Located Dec 23, 1784. Sept 18, 1786.

Page   248 - SAMUEL BUDD - NC - No. 11 - Reg. Aug 13, 1788

By an Act for the relief of the Officers and Soldiers of the Continental Line, in consideration of the bravery and zeal of Samuel Budd, a captain in the said line, granted unto said Budd a tract of land containing 3840 acres in Davidson County on both sides of Lick or Budds Creek on the side of Cumberland. Surveyed for said Budd Mar 10, 1785 by Joseph Brock, D.S. in consequence of a Military Warrant No. 729. Located Nov 30, 1784. Feb 14, 1786.

Page   249 - JOSEPH McDOWEL - NC - No. 33 - Reg. Sept 3, 1788

By an Act for the relief of the Officers and Soldiers of the Continental Line, in consideration of the bravery and zeal of John Brown, a captain in the said line, granted unto Joseph McDowel, assignee of said John Brown a tract of land containing 1737 acres in Davidson County on PLeasant Creek emptying into Cumberland River on the north side. Surveyed for said Joseph McDowel July 12, 1785 by William Murry, D.S. in consequence of a Military Warrant No. 800. Located Apr 11, 1783. Mar 14, 1786.

Page   249 - JAMES FOSTER - NC - No. 117 - Reg. Sept 5, 1788

For 10 lbs per 100 acres paid by James Foster, a tract of land containing 640 acres in Davidson County. Adjoining John Tuckers Preemption being about 600 yards north east of Foster's Spring, Cockrill's boundary, crossing a branch of the east fork of Mill Creek. Surveyed for said James Foster Aug 25, 1784 by John Bruce, D.S. in consequence of a Warrant No. 389. Located and entered April 5, 1784. Apr 17, 1786.

Page   249 - THOMAS CALLENDER - NC - No. 49 - Reg. Sept 27, 1788

By an Act for the relief of the Officers and Soldiers of the Continental Line, in consideration of the bravery and zeal of Thomas Callender, a captain in the said line, granted unto Thomas Callender a tract of land containing 3840 acres in Davidson County on the north side of Cumberland River and on a creek that falls into said river about three miles below Wells Creek. Beginning at the mouth of the first said creek. Surveyed for Thomas Callender Dec 6, 1784 by Thomas Molloy, D.S. in consequence of a Military Warrant No. 871. Located Aug 2, 1784. Mar 14, 1786.

Page   250 - JOHN SITGREAVES - NC - No. 792 - Reg. Oct 6, 1788

By an Act for the relief of the Officers and Soldiers of the Continental Line, in consideration of the bravery and zeal of Samuel Williams, a private in the said line, granted unto John Sitgreaves, assignee of Samuel Williams, a tract of land containing 640 acres in Davidson County on the east fork of Buffalo Creek running into the Tennessee River on the north side of said river. Surveyed for John Sitgreaves the __ day of __, __ by William Murry, D.S. in consequence of a Military Warrant No. 1456. Located May 9, 1785. 1788.

Page   250 - HARDY HOLMS - NC - No. 232 - Reg. Oct 6, 1788

By an Act for the relief of the Officers and Soldiers of the Continental Line, in consideration of the bravery and zeal of Hardy Holms a tract of land containing 2560 acres in Davidson County on the waters of Stones River on Thomas Creek joining the upper line of the preemption and joining Col. Martin Armstrong's corner. Surveyed for Hardy Holms Mar 12, 1785 by Robert Hays, D.S. in consequence of a Military Warrant No. 212. Located Feb 7, 1784. Mar 14, 1786.

Page   250 - ALEXANDER EWING - NC - No. 659 - Reg. Oct 23, 1788

By an Act for the relief of the Officers and Soldiers of the Continental Line, in consideration of the bravery and zeal of Leonard Davis, a private in the said line, granted unto Alexander Ewing, assignee of Leonard Davis, a tract of land containing 640 acres in Davidson County on both sides of Big Harpeth River. Beginning at William Gallaspy's corner, to Sharp's line, and to McGavock's line. Surveyed for Alexander Ewing by John Donaldson in consequence of a Military Warrant No. 1005. Located Dec 6, 1784. Dec 8, 1787.

Page   251 - ARCHIBALD BUTTS - NC - No. 267 - Reg. Oct 23, 1788

By an Act for the relief of the Officers and Soldiers of the Continental Line, in consideration of the bravery and zeal of Archibald Butts, a drummer in the said line, granted unto said Butts a tract of land containing 1000 acres in Davidson on the north side of Cumberland River and Red River. Beginning at a sulphur lick at a sweet gum marked E.C. Surveyed for said Butts Mar 26, 1785 by Joseph Brock, D.S. in consequence of a Military Warrant No. 401. Located July 24, 1784. Mar 7, 1786.

Page   251 - NATHANIEL LAURENCE - NC - No. 85 - Reg. Oct 23, 1788

By an Act for the relief of the Officers and Soldiers of the Continental Line, in consideration of the bravery and zeal of Nathaniel Laurence, a lieutenant in the said line, granted unto said Laurence a tract of land containing 2560 acres in Davidson County on the south side of Cumberland River and upon Spring Creek. Adjoining Walter Allen's survey. Surveyed for said Laurence Sept 28, 1784 by James Mulherin, D.S. in consequence of a Military Warrant No. 352. Located July 9, 1784. Mar 14, 1786.

Page   251 - RICHARD FENNER - NC - No. 274 - Reg. Oct 23, 1788
        By an Act for the relief of the Officers and Soldiers of the Continental Line, in consideration of the bravery and zeal of Richard Fenner, a lieutenant in the said line, was granted a tract of land containing 2560 acres in Davidson County on the waters of Station Camp on the north side of Cumberland River. Beginning at a corner of the heirs of Benjamin Porter, to Elmore Douglass' corner. Surveyed for said Richard Fenner Sept 19, 1786 by A. Foster, D.S. in consequence of a Military Warrant No. 399. Located Oct 17, 1784. Mar 22, 1787.

Page   252 - RICHARD FENNER - No. 21 - Reg. Oct 23, 1788
        By an Act for the relief of the Officers and Soldiers of the Continental Line, in consideration of the bravery and zeal of William Fenner in the said line, granted unto Richard Fenner heir of William Fenner a tract of land containing 2057 acres in Davidson County on both sides of Sulphur Fork of Red River. Beginning at Charles Thompson's boundary where Drake's Preemption intersects the same, and to William Rentfro's line. Surveyed for Richard Fenner June 8, 1785 by Robert Nelson, D.S. in consequence of a Military Warrant No. 332. Located Aug 2, 1784. Mar 14, 1786.

Page   252 - ROBERT FENNER - NC - No. 83 - Reg. Oct 23, 1788
        By an Act for the relief of the Officers and Soldiers of the Continental Line, in consideration of the bravery and zeal of Robert Fenner, a captain in the said line, granted unto Robert Fenner a tract of land containing 3840 acres in Davidson Countyon Blue Creek empting into Duck River on the north side, including the mouth of said creek and an island. Beginning at a lake and on the bank of the river. Surveyed for Robert Fenner Aug 7, 1785 by William Murry, D.S. in consequence of a Military Warrant No. 333. Located May 7, 1785. Mar 14, 1786.

Page   252 - WICUFF & CLARK - NC - No. 789 - Reg. Oct 23, 1788
        By an Act for the relief of the Officers and Soldiers of the Continental Line, in consideration of the bravery and zeal of Daniel Howell, a private in the said line, granted unto William Wicuff and Lardner Clark, assignees of the heirs of Daniel Howell, a tract of land containing 640 acres in Davidson County on the north side of Cumberland River about two miles above the mouth of Harpeth River. Surveyed for said Wicuff and Clark Mar 4, 1786 by Thomas Molloy, D.S. in consequence of a Military Warrant No. 1980. Located Dec 9, 1785. July 11, 1788.

Page   253 - WICUFF & CLARK - NC - No. 747 - Reg. Oct 24, 1788
        By an Act for the relief of the Officers and Soldiers of the Continental Line, in consideration for the bravery and zeal of William Hooper, a private in the said line, granted unto William Wicuff and lardner Clark, assignees of William Hooper, a tract of land containing 228 acres of land in Davidson County on Guise Creek adjoining a tract of 640 acres belonging to Jonathan Guise. Surveyed for said Wicuff and Clark Mar 30, 1786 by Thomas Molloy, D.S. in consequence of a Military Warrant No. 1688. Located Dec 2, 1785. July 10, 1788.

Page   253 - WIKOFF & CLARK - NC - No. 789 - Reg. Oct 24, 1788
        By an Act for the relief of the Officers and Soldiers of the Continental Line,

in consideration of the bravery and zeal of John Thompson, a private in the said line, granted unto William Wikoff and Lardner Clark, assignees of the heirs of John Thompson, a tract of land containing 640 acres in Davidson County on the south side of Cumberland River on the west boundary line of Captain John Davis' survey. Surveyed for Wikoff and Clark June 26, 1786 by Robert Nelson, D.S. in consequence of a Military Warrant No. 2161. Located Mar 24, 1786. July 10, 1788.

Page   253 - WILLIAM McGAVIOCK (McGAVOCK) - NC - No. 118 - Reg. OCT 24, 1788
        For 10 lbs per 100 acres paid by William McGaviock and was granted a tract of land containing 640 acres in Davidson County on both sides of Arringtons Creek an east branch of Big Harpeth River. Surveyed for William McGaviock Feb 2, 1785 by Samuel Moore, D.S. agreeable to a warrant issued from the Preemption Office, No. 191. Entered Jan 26, 1784. Signed Apr 16, 1700.

Page   254 - DAVID McGAVOCK - NC - No. 40 - Oct 24, 1788
        For 10 lbs per 100 acres paid by David McGavock was granted a tract of land containing640 acres in Davidson County beginning at a small branch at the outside of the river. Surveyed for David McGavock by himself in consequence of a Warrant No. 373, issued from the Preemption Office and located Mar 29, 1784. Apr 17, 1786.

Page   254 - ADAM HAMPTON - NC - Reg. Oct 24, 1788
        This indenture made 21 July 1788 between Isaac Linsey of Sumner County, NC of one part and Adam Hampton of Davidson County of other part. Isaac Hampton conveyed unto Adam Hampton a lot or parcel of land in Davidson County on mthe north side of Cumberland River adjoining Heatons Old Station. Containing 7 acres and 56 poles. This 9 April 1788.

Page   254 - THOMAS GREEN - NC - Oct 24, 1788
        This indenture made 4 Aug 1788 between Isham Lenear and Thomas Green, both of Davidson County. Isham Lenear conveyed unto Thomas Green a house and lot formerly Julius Sanders. This Oct 7, 1788.

Page   255 - LARDNER CLARK - NC - Oct 24, 1788
        This indenture made 14 Aug 1788 between Ebenezer Titus and his wife Rachel Titus of Davidson County of one part and Lardner Clark of same place of other part. Said Ebenezer Titus and his wife Rachel Titus conveyed unto Lardner Clark a tract of land containing 320 acres in Davidson County on the north waters of Little Harpeth. Adjoining William Collinsworth. Which land was granted to said Titus by patent dated Oct 8, 1787 in consideration of the services as one of the Commissioners Guard. This Oct 7, 1788. Proven by Robert Cartwright.

Page   255 - THOMAS GREEN - NC - Oct 24, 1788
        This indenture made 8 Oct 1788 between Thomas Hickman, Sheriff of Davidson County, NC of one part and Thomas Green of same place of other part.
Witnessed that Anthony H(illegible) in court on 3 day of Jan 1787 did then and there a suit which he prosecuted against Julius Sanders obtain judgement against him for 65 dollars 1S 2d, as did Eusebius Bushnell the same day against said Julius Sanders as the bail of a

93

certain William Hamilton for sum of L41.19S.4d. Said Thomas Green purchased one hald of Lot No. 25 containing about half an acre of land in the town of Nashville, late the property of the said Sanders granted to him by the Commissioners for said town by deed dated July 30, 1784 adjoining the half lot sold to William Taitt which half lot or half acre of land so sold. This Oct 8, 1788.

Page   256 - JOHN BROWN - NC - Oct 25, 1788
This indenture made 8 July 1788 between Francis Armstrong and Mary Armstrong his wife of Davidson County of one part and John Brown of same place of other part. Francis Armstrong and his wife Mary Armstrong conveyed unto John Brown a tract of land containing 100 acres in Davidson County. Beginning at Samuel Barton's corner on the road that leads from Armstrongs to Nowlands. Said land being part of a tract of 640 acres granted to said Armstrong by patent dated Apr 17, 1786. This Oct 7, 1788. Proven by Samuel Barton.

Page   256 - NICHOLAS LONG - NC - Oct 25, 1788
This indenture made 26 Sept 1786 between Jacob Mathews of the County of Northampton, North Carolina of one part and Nicholas Long of the County of Halifax, North Carolina of other part. Jacob Mathews conveyed unto Nicholas Long a tract of land containing 640 acres in Davidson County, NC on Wells Creek. Which land was granted by the State of North Carolina to said Jacob Mathews by deed dated Mar 14, 1786 in consideration of the bravery and zeal of said Mathews, a private in the Continental Line. Proven by Lewis Ford Long.

Page   257 - ROBERT THOMPSON - NC - Oct 27, 1788
This indenture made 8 Aug 1788 between James Thompson and Elizabeth Thompson his wife of one part and Robert Thompson of other part. James Thompson and Elizabeth Thompson his wife conveyed unto Robert Thompson a tract of land containing 200 acres in Davidson County. Beginning at James Thompson's survey of 640 acres. This Oct 7, 1788.

Page   257 - WILLIAM BLACKAMORE - NC - Oct 27, 1788
This indenture made 7 Oct 1788 between Eusebius Bushnell and William Dobbins of Davidson County of one part and William Blackamore of same place of other part. Said Bushnell and Dobbins conveyed unto William Blackamore a tract of land containing 640 acres in Davidson County lying on Moses Shelby's west boundary line. Which land was granted to Eusebius Bushnell and William Dobbins by patent dated 15 Dec 1787. Oct 7, 1788.

Page   258 - EZEKIEL SMITH - NC - Oct 27, 1788
This indenture made 15 Sept 1788 between Mark Nobles of Davidson County of one part and Ezekiel Smith of same place of other part. Mark Nobles conveyed unto Ezekiel Smith a tract of land containing 200 acres in Davidson County on the north side of Sycamore Creek on the first branch above Ramseys Fork. Which land was granted to said Nobles by patent dated Sept 4, 2787 as assignee of Col. Martin Armstrong. This Oct 7, 1788.

Page   258 - JOHN RICE - NC - Oct 27, 1788
        This indenture made 13 Aug 1788 between Eusebius Bushnell and William
Dobbins, both of Davidson County of one part and John Rice of same place of other part.
Said Bushnell and Dobbins conveyed unto John Rice a tract of land containing 640 acres in
Davidson Countyon the waters of Stones River on a small creek known by the name of
Bushnells Creek and on Major Blount's east boundary line and Bushnell's south west corner
of a 1000 acre survey No. 1660. This 10 Oct 1788.

Page   259 - WITHEREL LATIMORE - NC - Oct 27, 1788
        This indenture made this 3 Sept 1788 between Eusebius Bushnell and William
Dobbins of Davidson County of one part and Witherel Latimore of other part.   Said
Bushnell and Dobbins conveyed unto Witherel Latimore a tract of land containing 228 acres
in Davidson County on the waters of Stones River. Adjoining Major Blount's corner.   Oct
7, 1788.

Page   259 - BENJAMIN JOSLIN - NC - Oct 29, 1788
        This indenture made 7 Oct 1788 between Eusebius Bushnell and William
Dobbins of Davidson County of one part and Benjamin Joslin of the other part.   Said
Bushnell and Dobbins conveyed unto Benjamin Joslin a tract of land containing 1000 acres
in Davidson County on both sides of Stones River.   Adjoining Col. Isaac Shelby's corner.
Which land was granted to Bushnell and Dobbins by a patent dated Sept 15, 1787.   11 Oct
1788.

Page   260 - JAMES COLE MONTFLORENCE - Nov 6, 1788
        This indenture made 6 Oct 1788 between Anthony Crutcher of Davidson
County of one part and James Cole Montflorence of same place of other part.   Said
Crutcher conveyed unto James Cole Montflorence a tract of land containing 320 acres in
Davidson County on the north fork of Red River in the county of Sumner County including
a spring and improvement being one half of that tract of 640 acres of land granted unto
said Anthony Crutcher by State of North Carolina for the services of Thomas Smith, a
private in the Continental Line. 6 Nov 1788.

Page   260 - Charles Homer - NC - Nov 6, 1788
        This indenture made 3 Nov 1788 between Isadore Skerrett of Davidson
County of one part and Charles Homer of the town of Windson, County of Bertie, North
Carolina, merchant, of the other part. Said Isadore Skerrett conveyed unto Charles Homer
a tract of land containing 640 acres in Davidson Countyon the east fork of Stones River
above the first line run by the Commissioners in 1783 joining Capt. Welch's surveyon the
east.   Said land being granted to Isadore Skerrett for the services of Timothy Zealott, a
private in the Continental Line, also that the other tract of land in Davidson County on
the east fork of Stones River.

Page   261 - MARTIN ARMSTRONG & ANTHONY CRUTCHER - NC - No. 421(?) - Nov
        13, 1788
        By an Act for the relief of the Officers and Soldiers of the Continental Line,
in consideration of the bravery and zeal of John Ford, a lieutenant in the said line, granted
unto Martin Armstrong and Anthony Crutcher, assignees of John Ford, a tract of land

containing 2560 acres in Davidson County on Thompsons Creek on the south side of Cumberland River. Surveyed for Martin Armstrong and Anthony Crutcher Oct 1, 1784 by James Mulherin, D.S. in consequence of a Military Warrant No. 298. Located July 5, 1784. Sept 15, 1787.

Page   261 - WILLIAM McGUAIOH (McGAVOCK) - NC - No. 77 - Reg. Nov 13, 1788

By an Act for the relief of the Officers and Soldiers of the Continental Line, in consideration of the services of William McGuaioh, one of the Commissioners Guard, granted unto said McGuaioh a tract of land containing 320 acres in Davidson County on both sides of Arringtons Creek about three miles and a half above the mouth. Surveyed for William McGuaioh Feb 2, 1785 by Samuel Moore, D.S. agreeable to a Warrant No. 189. Located Jan 26, 1784. Oct 8, 1787.

Page   261 - NATHANIEL McCANN - NC - No. 527 - Nov 13, 1788

By an Act for the relief of the Officers and Soldiers of the Continental Line, in consideration of the bravery and zeal of Nathaniel McCann, a lieutenant in the said line, granted unto him a tract of land containing 2560 acres in Davidson County on the south side of Cumberland River on both sides of the first creek above the mouth of the Caney Fork on the south side of the river. Surveyed for Nathaniel McCann Oct 7, 1785 by Edwin Hickman, D.S. in consequence of a Military Warrant No. 191. Located July 16, 1785. Sept 15, 1787.

Page   262 - WILLIAM BUSH - NC - No. 28 - Reg. Nov 13, 1788

By an Act for the relief of the Officers and Soldiers of the Continental Line, in consideration of the bravery and zeal of William Bush, a lieutenant in the said line, granted unto him a tract of land containing 2560 acres in Davidson County on both sides of the East Fork of Thompsons Creek on the south side of Cumberland River and adjoining Capt. Ashe's south boundary. Surveyed for said William Bush Jan 16, 1785 by Joseph Brock, D.S. in consequence of a Military Warrant No. 175. Located Oct 8, 1784. Mar 14, 1786.

Page   262 - JOHN BUSH - NC - No. 546 - Reg. Nov 13, 1788

By an Act for the relief of the Officers and Soldiers of the Continental Line, in consideration of the bravery and zeal of John Bush, a lieutenant in the said line, granted unto him a tract of land containing 914 acres in Davidson County on the waters of Stuarts Creek. Beginning on the Commissioners Old Line. Surveyed for John Bush Mar 14, 1785 by B. William Pollock, D.S. in consequence of a Military Warrant No. 216. Located Feb 17, 1784. Sept 15, 1787.

Page   262 - FEDERICK HARGET - NC - No. 42 - Reg. Nov 13, 1788

By an Act for the relief of the Officers and Soldiers of the Continental Line, in consideration of the bravery and zeal of Federick Harget, a captain in the said line, granted unto Federick Harget a tract of land containing 1580 acres in Davidson County on Willow Creek and its waters. Surveyed for said Harget Feb 15, 1785 by William Murry, D.S. in consequence of a Military Warrant No. 226. Located Mar 9, 1784. Mar 14, 1786.

Page   263 - JOSEPH LOVE - NC - Nov 18, 1788

This indenture made between Robert Nelson of Davidson County of one part and Joseph Love of same place of other part. Robert Nelson conveyed unto Joseph Love a tract called and known by the name of the Spice Bottom containing 640 acres in Davidson County. This 16 Nov 1788.

Page   263 - JAMES COLE MONTFLORENCE - NC - Nov 18, 1788

This made 18 Nov 1788 between Lardner Clark of Nashville, Davidson County, NC, merchant, of one part and James Cole Montflorence of same place of other part. Lardner Clark conveyed unto James Cole Montflorence a tract of land in Davidson County and aforesaid land granted by State of North Carolina for the services of John Ford as a lieutenant in the Continental Line and deeded to said Clerk by Anthony Crutcher, Esq., of Nashville and indenture dated 7 Nov 1788. Deed signed and sealed and delivered in the presence of George Augustus Suggs and William Crutcher and John Thompson. Land containing 2560 acres on Thompsons Creek. 18 Nov 1788.

Page   264 - WILLIAM WICUFF

This indenture made 17 Nov 1788 between Robert Nelson of Davidson County of one part and William Wicuff, Jr. of Monmouth County, State of New Jersey of other part. Robert Nelson conveyed unto William Wicuff, Jr. all that tract of land in Davidson County on the north boundary of William Top's claim on Red River about three or four miles below Clarksville. Adjoining Topp's line. Containing 540 acres. Said land being part of tract of 1050 acres granted by State of North Carolina unto Robert Nelson for the services of Christopher Tenor, a private in the Continental Line, dated 15 Sept 1787. This 18 Nov 1788.

Page   264 - JAMES COLE MONTFLORENCE - NC - Nov 19, 1788

This indenture made Nov 18, 1788 between Jesse Reed and Elizabeth his wife of Davidson County of one part and James Cole Montflorence of same place of other part. Jessee Reed and Elizabeth his wife conveyed unto James Cole Montflorence a tract of land ccontaining 640 acres in Davidson County on south side of Big Barren River on a creek known by the name of Long Creek of Barren. Which land was granted to the said Jesse Reed by patent dated Sept 15, 1787. This 19 Nov 1788.

Page   265 - JAMES COLE MONTFLORENCE - NC - Nov 19, 1788

This indenture made Nov 18, 1788 between Jessee Reed and Elizabeth his wife of Davidson County of one part and James Cole Montflorence of same place of other part. Jessee Reed and Elizabeth his wife conveyed unto James Cole Montflorence a tract of land containing 640 acres in Davidson County on the south side of Big Barren River on one of the main fork of Big Barren. By patent dated Sept 15, 1787. This 19 Nov 1788.

Page   266 - LARDNER CLARK - NC - Nov 19, 1788

This indenture made Nov 7, 1788 between Anthony Crutcher of Davidson County of one part and Lardner Clark of same place of other part. Anthony Crutcher conveyed unto Lardner Clark a tract of land containing 2560 acres in Davidson County on the south side of Cumberland River on Thompsons Creek. This 19 Nov 1788.

Page   266 - JOSEPH CARTWRIGHT - NC - No. 525 - Reg. Nov 25, 1788
          By an Act for the relief of the Officers and Soldiers of the Continental Line,
in consideration of the bravery and zeal of Joseph Cartwright, a private in the said line,
granted unto Joseph Cartwright a tract of land containing 640 acres in Davidson County on
the north side of Cumberland River on a creek called Halfpone at the mouth of the south
fork of said creek. Which land was surveyed for said Cartwright by Sampson Williams, D.S.
in consequence of a Military Warrant No. 831. Located July 24, 1784. Sept 15, 1787. On
the back of which grant was an assignment to Federick Davis made thus, viz, We, Mary
Sawyers, Thomas Britt, Keziah Cartwright and Sarah Cartwright of State of North Carolina
and County of Pasquotank do for ourselves as heirs &c assigns of the State and County
aforesaid for the consideration of the full and just sum of six pounds currency of said
State. Witness and signed this 6 June 1788. Jan 6, 1789.

Page   267 - MARMADUKE SCOTT - NC No. 562 - Reg. Nov 25, 1788
          By an Act for the relief of the Officers and Soldiers of the Continental Line,
in consideration of the bravery and zeal of Marmaduke Scott, a private in the said line,
was granted a tract of land containing 640 acres in Davidson County on the north side of
Cumberland River and on the day fork of Bledsoe Creek. Adjoining James Mauldin's corner
and John Grant's corner.   Surveyed for said Scott Mar 6, 1787 by Sqr. Grant in
consequence of a Military Warrant No. 912. Located Mar 20, 1785. Sept 15, 1787. On
back of which grant was an assignment to Federick Davis made thus, viz, I, Marmaduke
Scott of Pasquotank County, North Carolina do for myself my heirs &c assign over all my
right estate title interest claim and demand to the with in granted to Federick Davis for
the sum of twenty pounds cash. Jan 6, 1789.

Page   267 - JOHN KOEN - NC - No. 421 - Reg. Nov 25, 1788.
          By an Act for the relief of the Officers and Soldiers of the Continental Line,
in consideration of the bravery and zeal of John Koen, a private in the said line, was
granted a tract of land containing 571 acres in Davidson County on the south side of
Cumberland River and on Spencers Creek. Adjoining Thomas Spencer's boundary. Surveyed
for said John Koen July 30, 1785 by James Mulherin, D.S. in consequence of a Military
Warrant No. 839. Located July 24, 1784. Sept 15, 1787. On the back of grant was an
assignment to Federick Davis made thus, viz, I, John Koen of Pasquotank County, North
Carolina do for myself my heirs &c assign over all my right estate title interest &c for the
sum of ten pounds currency. This 24 May 1788. Jan 6, 1789.

Page   268 - JESSEE HARRISON - NC - No. 473 - Nov 25, 1788
          By an Act for the relief of the Officers and Soldiers of the Continental Line,
in consideration of the bravery and zeal of Jesse Harrison, a private in the said line, was
granted a tract of land containing 274 acres in Davidson County on the south side of
Cumberland River about two miles above the mouth of Harpeth River adjoining Joseph
Ca(illegible)'s boundary. Surveyed for Jessee Harrison March 3, 1786 by Thomas Molloy,
D.S. in consequence of a Military Warrant No. 841. Located Nov 30, 1785. Sept 15, 1787.

Page   268 - JOHN BUCCHANAN - NC - No. 41 - Reg. Dec 1, 1788
          By an Act for the relief of the Officers and Soldiers of the Continental Line,
in consideration of the services of Col. M. Armstrong, surveyor of lands, granted unto John

Bucchanan. assignee of Col. M. Armstrong, a tract of land containing 200 acres in Davidson County on the west side of Stones River about four miles above the Old Station. Surveyed for John Bucchanan by himself Mar 2, 1786 in consequence of a service right of said Armstrong, entered Dec 6, 1785. Oct 8, 1787.

Page   269 - JOHN MULHERIN - NC - No. 37 - Reg. Dec 1, 1788
By an Act for the relief of the Officers and Soldiers of the Continental Line, in consideration of the services of Col. Martin Armstrong, surveyor of lands, granted unto John Mulherin, assignee of said Armstrong, a tract of land containing 396 acres in Davidson County on both sides of Mill Creek. Adjoining James Bosley's Preemption and James Bryant's boundary. Surveyed for John Mulherin by John Bucchanan, D.S. in consequence of the services of said Armstrong, No. 1064. Located June 27, 2785. Oct 8, 1787.

Page   269 - WILLIAM TURNBULL - NC - No. 649 - Dec 1, 1788
By an Act for the relief of the Officers and Soldiers of the Continental Line, in consideration of the bravery and zeal of Josiah Jackson, a private in the said line, granted unto William Turnbull, assignee of said Josiah Jackson, a tract of land containing 640 acres in Davidson County on the head waters of Spring Creek and joining Samuel Buchanan. Surveyed for William Turnbull Aug 3, 1786 by John Bucchanan, D.S. in consequence of a Military Warrant No. 1810. Located Mar 3, 1786. Dec 8, 1788.

Page   269 - WILLIAM TURNBULL - NC - No. 663 - Reg. Dec 1, 1788
By an Act for the relief of the Officers and Soldiers of the Continental Line, in consideration of the bravery and zeal of Thomas Warren, a private in the said line, granted unto William Turnbull, assignee of the heirs of Thomas Warren, a tract of land containing 640 acres in Davidson County on the head waters of Spring Creek and joining Samuel Buchanan. Surveyed for William Turnbull Aug 3, 1786 by John Buchanan, D.S. in consequence of a Military Warrant No. 2061. Located Mar 3, 1786. Dec 8, 1787.

Page   270 - JAMES MULHERIN - NC - No. 153 - Reg. Dec 1, 1788
For 10 lbs per 100 acres paid by James Mulherin and granted unto James Mulherin a tract of land containing 640 acres in Davidson County on the bank of Cumberland River. Adjoining Samuel McMurry's corner and James Todd's corner. Surveyed for James Mulherin Mar 24, 1785 by John Bucchanan, D.S. agreeable to a Warrant No. 87. Entered Jan 14, 1784. Apr 17, 1786.

Page   270 - ABRM. RISTON, JOHN & ELISHA RICE - NC - No. 307 - Reg. Dec 8, 1788
By an Act for the relief of the Officers and Soldiers of the Continental Line, in cnsideration of the bravery and zeal of John Vintress, a private in the said line, granted unto Abraham Riston, John Rice and Elisha Rice, assignees of John Vintress, a tract of land containing 640 acres in Davidson County on a small creek that comes into the main Tennessee River on the north side. Beginning at the south east corner of an Entry No. 1767. Surveyed for said Riston and Rice May 8, 1786 by Isaac Roberts, D.S. in consequence of a Military Warrant No. 2160. Located Feb 6, 1786. June 13, 1787.

Page   270 - ABM. RISTON, JNO. & ELISHA RICE - NC - No. 306 - Reg. Dec 8, 1788
By an Act for the relief of the Officers and Soldiers of the Continental Line,

in consideration of the bravery and zeal of Moses Simpson, a private in the said line, granted unto John Rice, Abraham Riston and Elisha Rice, assignees of said Simpson, a tract of land containing 640 acres in Davidson County. Beginning on the west bank of Stones River on John Buchanan's corner. Surveyed for said Rice and Riston Mar 10, 1786 by John Bucchanan, D.S. by virtue of a Military Warrant No. 2055. Located Dec 7, 1785. June 13, 1787.

Page   271 - ABRAHAM RISTON, JNO. & ELISHA RICE - NC - No. 295 - Reg. Dec 8, 1788

By an Act for the relief of the Officers and Soldiers of the Continental Line, in consideration of the bravery and zeal of Obediah Sowell, a private in the said line, granted unto said Riston and Rice, assignees of heirs of said Obediah Sowell, a tract of land containing 640 acres in Davidson County on a branch of Smith's Creek a fork of Caney Fork. Adjoining another survey as assignee of Nathan Stephens heirs of Henry Stevens. Surveyed for said Riston and Rice Feb 22, 1787 by James Sanders, D.S. in consequence of a Military Warrant No. 2584. Located Feb 10, 1787. June 13, 1787.

Page   271 - ABRAHAM RISTON, JNO. & ELISHA RICE - NC - No. 295 - Reg. Dec 8, 1788

By an Act for the relief of the Officers and Soldiers of the Continental Line, in consideration of the bravery and zeal of Nathaniel Nelson, a private in the said line, granted unto John Rice, Abraham Riston and Elisha Rice, assignees of the heirs of said Nelson, a tract of land containing 640 acres in Davidson County on the southside of Tennessee River. Beginning at the mouth of the third creek above the Virginia Line. Surveyed for said Riston and Rice May 9, 1786 by Isaac Roberts, D.S. in consequence of a Military Warrant No. 2038. Located Feb 6, 1786. June 13, 1787.

Page   271 - ABHM. RISTON, JNO. & ELISHA RICE - NC - No. 305 - Reg. Dec 8, 1788

By an Act for the relief of the Officers and Soldiers of the Continental Line, in consideration of the bravery and zeal of Jacob Ferrill, granted unto said Abraham Riston and John Rice and Elisha Rice, assignees of the heirs of Jacob Ferrill a tract of land containing 640 acres in Davidson County on the north side of Tennessee River. Beginning about half a mile above the first bluff that is on the river above the Virginia Line. Surveyed for said Riston and Rice. Warrant No. 1767. Feb 6, 1786.

Page   272 - ABRAHAM RISTON, JOHN & ELISHA RICE - NC - No. 301 - Reg. Dec 8, 1788

By an Act for the relief of the Officers and Soldiers of the Continental Line, in consideration of the bravery and zeal of John Martin, a private in the said line, granted unto said Riston and Rice, assignees of the heirs of John Martin, a tract of land containing 640 acres in Davidson County on the north side of Tennessee River. Beginning on the bank of said river opposite to the first island above the Virginia Line. Surveyed for said Rice and Riston May 7, 1786 by Isaac Roberts, D.S. in Consequence of a Military Warrant No. 2140. Located Feb 6, 1786. June 13, 1787.

Page   272 - JOHN RICE - NC - No. 293 - Reg. Dec 8, 1788

By an Act for the relief of the Officers and Soldiers of the Continental Line,

in consideration of the bravery and zeal of Levy Baker, a private in the said line, granted unto John Rice, assignee of Levy Baker, a tract of land containing 640 acres in Davidson County in the fork of Cumberland River joining his entry assignee of Porter, Neville's corner and Moore's line and corner and to Topps' line. Surveyed for John Rice June 26, 1786 by Robert Nelson in consequence of a Military Warrant No. 1088. Located July 8, 1784. Jan 13, 1787.

Page   272 - SOLOMON KITTS - NC - No. 300 - Reg. Dec 1788
By an Act for the relief of the Officers and Soldiers of the Continental Line, in consideration of the bravery and zeal of Asia Stokes, a private in the said line, granted unto Solomon Kitts, assignee of the heirs of Asia Stokes, a tract of land containing 640 acres in Davidson County on the south side of Cumberland River. Beginning at Captain James Taton's corner. Grant signed and dated June 13, 1787. Warrant No. 1687. Located Sept 1, 1785. Surveyed by Edwin Hickman.

Page   273 - ABRAHAM RISTON, JOHN & ELISHA RICE - NC - No. 299 - Reg. Dec 8, 1788
By an Act for the relief of the Officers and Soldiers of the Continental Line, in consideration of the bravery and zeal of Domina Dominas, a private in the said line, granted unto John Rice, Abraham Riston and Elisha Rice, assignees of the heirs of said Dominas, a tract of land containing 1000 acres in Davidson County on the middle fork of Drake Creek. Beginning at a corner of a 640 acre survey of Benjamin Sheppard. Surveyed for said Rice and Riston Mar 22, 1786 by Edwin Hickman, D.S. in consequence of a Military Warrant No. 2602. Located 1786. June 13, 1787.

Page   273 - ABRAHAM RISTON, JNO. & ELISHA RICE - NC - No. 309 - Reg. Dec 8, 1788
By an Act for the relief of the Officers and Soldiers of the Continental Line, in consideration of the bravery and zeal of Henry Stevens, a private in the said line, granted unto John Rice, Abraham Riston and Elisha Rice, assignees of the heirs of Henry Stevens, a tract of land containing 640 acres in Davidson County on Smiths Creek a fork of the Caney Fork. Adjoining William Sanders' line. Surveyed for said Rice and Riston Feb 22, 1787 by James Sanders, D.S. The grant dated June 13, 1787. Warrant No. 2582. Located Feb 10, 1787.

Page   273 - JOHN RICE - NC - No. 292 - Reg. Dec 8, 1788
By an Act for the relief of the Officers and Soldiers of the Continental Line, in consideration of the bravery and zeal of Jesse Lain, a private in the said line, granted unto John Rice, assignee of said Jessee Lain, a tract of land containing 640 acres in Davidson County on Millars Creek joining his other entry as assignee of William Ramsey. Surveyed for John Rice July 15, 1786 by Robert Nelson, D.S. The grant dated June 13, 1786. Warrant No. 865. Located June 20, 1785.

Page   274 - JOHN RICE, SAPPINGTON & CO. - NC - No. 302 - Reg. Dec 8, 1788
By an Act for the relief of the Officers and Soldiers of the Continental Line, in consideration of the bravery and zeal of Thomas Woolen, a private in the said line, granted unto John Rice Sappington & Co., assignees of Thomas Woolen, a tract of land

containing 640 acres in Davidson County on the west fork of Jones Creek joining Benjamin Thomas's survey. Surveyed for Rice Sappington & Co. March 20, 1787 in consequence of a Military Warrant No. 2254. Located Dec 7, 1785. June 13, 1787.

Page   274 - ABRAHAM RISTON, JNO. & ELISHA RICE - NC - 296 - Reg. Dec 8, 1788

By an Act for the relief of the Officers and Soldiers of the Continental Line, in consideration of the bravery and zeal of William Harris. a private in the said line, granted unto John Rice, Abraham Riston and Elisha Rice, assignees of the heirs of William Harris, a tract of land containing 640 acres in Davidson County on Stones River opposite to the Mill Dam Rock and Stones River. Surveyed for Rice and Riston Mar 10, 1786 by John Buchanan, D.S. in consequence of a Military Warrant No. 2129. Located Dec 7, 1785. June 13, 1787.

Page   274 - ABRAHAM RISTON, JNO. & ELISHA RICE - NC - No. 294 - Reg. Dec 8, 1788

By an Act for the relief of the Officers and Soldiers of the Continental Line, in consideration of the bravery and zeal of Dugald McConough, a private in the said line, granted unto John Rice, Abraham Riston and Elisha Rice, assignees of the heirs of Dugald McConough, a tract of land containing 640 acres in Davidson County on east bank of Stones River being corner to two surveys claimed by John Rice & Co. Surveyed for Rice and Riston Mar 10, 1786 by John Bucchanan, D.S. Dated June 13, 1787. Warrant No. 2142. Located Dec 7, 1785.

Page   275 - ABRAHAM RISTON, JNO. & ELISHA RICE - NC - No. 297 - Reg. Dec 9, 1788

By an Act for the relief of the Officers and Soldiers in the Continental Line, in consideration of the bravery and zeal of Samuel Griffin, a private in the said line, granted unto John Rice, Abraham Riston and Elisha Rice, assignees of the heirs of Samuel Griffin, a tract of land containing 640 acres in Davidson County on the east bank of Stones River opposite the Mill Dam Rock. Surveyed for Rice and Riston Mar 10, 1786 by John Buchanan, D.S. in consequence of a Military Warrant No. 3037. Located Dec 7, 1785. June 13, 1787.

Page   275 - RICE & SAPPINGTON - NC - No. 298 - Reg. Dec 9, 1788

By an Act for the relief of the Officers and Soldiers of the Continental Line, in consideration of the bravery and zeal of John Wright, a private in the said line, granted unto John Rice and John Sappington, assignees of the heirs of John Wright, a tract of land containing 640 acres in Davidson County on Kerrs Creek of Sulphur Fork of Red River adjoining Frayner's line, Christian Cripp's corner. Surveyed for said Rice and Sappington July 15, 1786 by Robert Nelson, D.S. in consequence of a Military Warrant No. 2060. Located July 22, 1785. June 13, 1787.

Page   275 - JOHN RICE - NC - No. 658 - Reg. Dec 9, 1788

By an Act for the relief of the Officers and Soldiers of the Continental Line, in consideration of the bravery and zeal of James Tracy, a private in the said line, granted unto John Rice, assignee of James Tracy, a tract of land containing 274 acres in Davidson County on the waters of East Fork of Mill Creek, being John Williamson's north west corner and Lewis Ruland's line. Surveyed for John Rice Apr 5, 1786 by John Bucchanan, D.S. in consequence of a Military Warrant No. 201. Located Nov 5, 1785. Dec 8, 1787.

Page   276 - ROBERT BURTON - NC - No. 308 - Reg. Dec 9, 1788
By an Act for the relief of the Officers and Soldiers of the Continental Line, in consideration of the bravery and zeal of Briton Johnston, a private in the said line, granted unto Robert Burton, assignee of the heirs of Briton Johnston, a tract of land containing 640 acres in Davidson County on a branch of Smiths Creek a fork of the Caney Fork adjoining John Rice's south boundary assignee of Ruben Sowell, heir of Obediah Sowell. Surveyed for Robert Burton Feb 22, 1787 by James Sanders, D.S. in consequence of a Military Warrant No. 1145. Located Feb 10, 1787. June 13, 1787.

Page   276 - HARDY JONES - NC - No. 233 - Reg. Dec 9, 1788
By an Act for the relief of the Officers and Soldiers of the Continental Line, in consideration of the bravery and zeal of Hardy Jones, a private in the said line, granted unto Hardy Jones a tract of land containing 360 acres in Davidson County on the south side of Cumberland River and on Spring Creek. Beginning at south east corner of Jessee Suter's survey. Surveyed for Hardy Jones Sept 25, 1784 by James Mulherin, D.S. in consequence of a Military Warrant No. 178. Located ___ __ 1784. Mar 7, 1786.

Page   276 - JOSEPH BROCK - NC - No. 24 - Reg. Dec 10, 1788
By an Act for the relief of the Officers and Soldiers of the Continental Line, in consideration of the services of Col. Martin Armstrong, surveyor of lands, granted unto Joseph Brock, assignee of said Armstrong, a tract of land containing 640 acres in Davidson County on the south side of Red River about five miles from the mouth. Beginning at Brock's other survey on Adam Boyd's line. Surveyed for Joseph Brock Sept 18, 1785 by Robert Nelson, D.S. in consequence of a service right of said Armstrong's Entry No. 1046. Located June 18, 1785. Oct 8, 1787.

Page   277 - JOSEPH BROCK - NC - No. 27 - Reg. Dec 10, 1788
By an Act for the relief of the Officers and Soldiers of the Continental Line, in consideration of the services of Col. Martin Armstrong, surveyor of lands, granted unto Joseph Brock, assignee of said Armstrong, a tract of land containing 640 acres in Davidson County on the south side of Red River about six miles from the mouth. Beginning at Martin Armstrong's corner on the bank of the river. Surveyed for Joseph Brock Apr 22, 1785 by Robert Nelson, D.S. in consequence of said Armstrong's Entry No. 562. Located Jan 10, 1785. Oct 8, 1787.

Page   277 - ELISHA DAVIS - Grant No. 196 - Reg. Jan 15, 1789
Registered to Silas Linton page 57 assigned to Elisha and was in the following words, viz, "Know all men by these presents that I, Silas Linton of the State of North Carolina and County of Camden for myself my heirs &c assign over all my right estate title and interest claim and demand to the within granted premises to Elisha Davis his heirs and assigns of the County and State aforesaid for the consideration of eight pounds currency of the State aforesaid. In witness whereof I have hereunto set my hand and seal this 2nd day of May 1788." Signed Silas Linton with seal affixed and attested Federick Coan and John Davis. Which assignment so made by said Linton to the said Elisha Davis was duly proven

by Federick Koan in Court for the County of Davidson Jan 6, 1789. Test Andrew Ewing, C.D.C. & D.R.

Page   277 - THOMAS McFARLIN - Jan 16, 1789

This indenture made 14 Oct 1788 between John Foreman of State of Virginia of one part and Thomas McFarlin of Davidson County, NC of other part. John Foreman conveyed to Thomas McFarlin one lot of an acre in the town of Nashville known as Lot No. 36, being the lot formerly granted to John Foreman by the Commissioners by deed dated July 30, 1784. Jan 7, 1789.

Page   278 - PETER TURNEY - Jan 16, 1789

This indenture made Mar 31, 1788 between Thomas Molloy of Davidson County of one part and Peter Turney of same place of other part. Thomas Molloy conveyed unto Peter Turney a tract of land containing 320 acres adjoining Absolom Burgess' west boundary and banks of Cumberland River. The said tract being granted to the said Thomas Molloy by the State of North Carolina dated Oct 8, 1787, No. 8. The said tract being likewise granted to said Thomas Molloy of Davidson County dated Oct 8, 1787, No. 28. July 7, 1789.

Page   278 - MICHAEL GLAVES - Jan 16, 1789

This indenture made Jan 9, 1789 between Zachariah Stull of one part and Michael Glaves of the other part, both of Davidson County. Zachariah Stull conveyed unto Michael Glaves a tract of land containing 100 acres in Davidson County and adjoining Stull's Old Field, McGavock's line, and Joseph Hannah's corner. It being part of 640 acres granted to said Stull by patent dated Apr 17, 1786 in right of Preemption. This Jan 9, 1789.

Page   279 - JOHN JOHNSTON - By assignment from John Hope - Jan 16, 1789

This indenture made July 8, 1788 between Lardner Clark of one part and John Hope of other part, both of Davidson County. Lardner Clark for the sum of 200 lbs current money of the said State to him the said Clark in hand paid by the said Hope and conveyed unto John Hope a tract of land containing 320 acres in Davidson County in the forks of Mill Creek being part of a tract of 640 acres granted to said Clark by patent dated Mar 7, 1786 assignee of Siskow (?). Joining John Tucker's corner. Said deed acknowledged by Said Clark to said Hope in Davidson County Jan 6, 1789. And on back of said deed was assignment made thus, viz, I do hereby acknowledge the sale of the within deed to John Johnston of Davidson County. This 25 Aug 1788 &c. Jan 6, 1789.

Page   279 - CURTICE WILLIAMS - NC - No. 44 - Reg. Jan 16, 1789

By an Act for the relief of the Officers and Soldiers of the Continental Line, in consideration of the services of Col. Martin Armstrong, surveyor of lands, granted unto Curtice Williams, assignee of said Armstrong, a tract of land containing 100 acres in Davidson County on the head of the first small creek above the Blooming Grove on the north side of Cumberland River. Surveyed for said Williams Feb 30, 1786 by Robert Nelson, D.S. in consideration of a service right. No. (blank). Located Dec 6, 1785. Oct 8, 1787.

Page   280 - HAMPTON & HAY - Jan 16, 1789

This indenture made June 20, 1788 between Eusebius Bushnell and William

Dobbins of Davidson County of one part and David Hay, Esq. and Adam Hampton, born of same place of other part. Eusebius Bushnell and William Dobbins conveyed unto Adam Hampton and David Hay the following tracts of land on the waters of Cumberland River, also a house and half lot in the town of Nashville on Cumberland River, to wit, All that tract of land being on the waters of Stones River being a Military claim of 1000 acres the Warrant No. 1669, located July 25, 1784, also one other tract of land on the waters of Stones River, being another Military claim of 1000 acres on Stones River, Warrant No. 1674, located July 17, 1784. Also another tract of land on the waters of Stones River, being another Military claim of 640 acres, Warrant No. 1686, located July 25, 1784, also another tract of land being on the east fork of Stones River, being another Military claim of 1622 acres, Warrant No. 572, located July 20, 1784. Also another tract of land on Hickman's Creek below Dyers' Camp being a Military claim, Warrant No. 1696, located Sept 1, 1784. Also one other tract of land in Sumner County on the south side of Cumberland River, joining Tatom's tract of 2560 acres, where the Virginia Line crosses said river, being a Military claim for 640 acres, Warrant No. 1682, located Aug 13, 1784. Also another tract of land on the waters of Stones River being a Military claim for 1000 acres, Warrant No. 1665, located July 25, 1784. Together with one half of a town lot in Nashville, it being the half of the lot known as Lot No. 9, granted unto Bushnell and Dobbins by James Lenier and Sarah Lenier his wife by indenture dated Oct 20, 1787 and released unto David Hay and Adam Hampton.   David Hay and Adam Hampton have become securities for the said Bushnell and Dobbins to the estate of Mark Robertson, deceased, for sum of L.598:16s current money is paid about the 25 Dec 1789. Witnesses: Thomas Crutcher and James Cole Montflorence. Dated Jan 10, 1789.

N.B. The interlining on the other side of 1000 acres lying Stones River Warrant No. 1674, located July 17, 1784, was occassioned by being omitted through over sight and the quantity, no. of the Warrant, time of location as it stands inter(illegible) was actually inserted in the original mortage. Test: Andrew Ewing, D.R.

Page   282 - JOHN KIRKPATRICK - Jan 19, 1789
            This indenture made Jan 7, 1789 between James Bosley and his wife Mary Bosley of one part and John Kirkpatrick of other part, all of Davidson County. James Bosley and his wife Mary Bosley conveyed unto John Kirkpatrick a tract of land containing 127 acres in Davidson County, joining John Cockrill's and Peter Turney's Preemptions and on the waters of the French Lick Branch. Beginning at a corner of said Bosley's Guard Right. Jan 7, 1789.

Page   282 - ELISHA DAVIS - Jan 19, 1789
            This indenture made May 5, 1787 between John Richardson of Pasquotank County, North Carolina of one part and Elisha Davis of Cambden (Camden), North Carolina of other part. John Richardson conveyed unto Elisha Davis a tract of land on the south side of Cumberland River and on the waters of Browns Creek adjoining Samuel Barton's and Francis Armstrong's Preemptions, also Hardiman's line, and Thomas Brown's line. Jan 6, 1789.

Page   283 - FEDERICK DAVIS - Jan 19, 1789
            This indenture made Aug 22, 1787 between John Jennings of Pasquotank County, North Carolina of one part and Federick Davis of same place of other part. John

Jenning conveyed unto Federick Davis a tract of land on south side of Cumberland River and on Spencers Creek in the County of Sumner. Beginning at John Koan's corner. Containing 365 acres. Proven by Federick Koan held for the County of Davidson Jan 6, 1789.

Page   283 - WILLIAM THOMPSON - NC - No. 423 - Reg. Jan 19, 1789

By an Act for the relief of the Officers and Soldiers of the Continental Line, in consideration of the bravery and zeal of William Thompson, a private in the said line, granted unto said Thompson a tract of land containing 428 acres in Davidson County on the North Cross Creek about five miles from Cumberland River adjoining the Preemption of Jesse Maxy. Surveyed for William Thompson Mar 15, 1786 by Thomas Molloy, D.S. in consequence of a Military Warrant No. 990. Located Nov 20, 1785. Sept 15, 1787.

Page   284 - ARGALIS GETER - Jan 19, 1789

This indenture made Jan 6, 1789 between Jonathan Drake of Davidson County of one part and Argalis Geter of same place of other part. Jonathan Drake conveyed unto Argalis Geter a tract of land containing 150 acres in Davidson County on both sides of Whites Creek adjoining Amos Heaton's corner on the bank of Heatons Creek and John Marney's line. This 6 Jan 1789.

Page   284 - ISAAC THOMAS - Jan 19, 1789

This indenture made Dec 9, 1788 between Thomas Molloy of Davidson County of one part and Isaac Thomas of same place of other part. Thomas Molloy conveyed unto Isaac Thomas a tract of land containing 228 acres in Davidson County on the south side of Cumberland River adjoining Mark Robertson's Preemption, James Bosley's corner on a high bluff of said river, James Robertson's line. Said land being granted by State of North Carolina to the said Thomas Molloy with Grant dated Feb 16, 1786 and No. 8. Jan 10, 1789.

Page   285 - ISAAC SHELBY - Jan 19, 1789

This indenture made Jan 9, 1789 between Laurence Thompson of Davidson County of one part and Isaac Shelby of Lincoln County, State of Virginia of other part. Laurence Thompson conveyed unto Isaac Shelby a tract of land containing 1000 acres in Davidson County on the waters of Stones River and adjoining Isaac Shelby's corner of a 5000 acre survey and Captain Montfort's line. Which said land was granted unto Eusebius Bushnell and William Dobbins, being the original grant dated Sept 15, 1787. Jan 9, 1789.

Page   285 - BUSHBELL & DOBBINS - Jan 19, 1789

This indenture made Oct 20, 1787 between James Lenier of Davidson County of one part and Eusebius Bushnell and William Dobbins of same place of other part. James Lenier conveyed unto said Bushnell and Dobbins one equal undivided half part of a certain lot of ground lying in the town of Nashville and known as Lot No. 9, it being that part of said lot which joins Lardner Clark. Proven by Thomas Smith Jan 10, 1789.

Page   286 - SAMUEL DEASON - Jan 19, 1789

This indenture made Jan 1, 1789 between James Bosley of Davidson County of one part and Samuel Deason of same place of other part. James Bosley conveyed unto

Samuel Deason a tract of land containing 100 acres in Davidson County on the south side of Cumberland River near the Stone Lick. Jan 6, 1789.

Page   286 - JOHN FORDE - Jan 19, 1789
This indenture made Jan 3, 1789 between James Bosley of Davidson County of one part and John Forde of same place of other part. James Bosley conveyed unto John Forde one half lot and house in the town of Nashville, known as Lot No. 8. This Jan 6, 1789.

Page   287 - LAURENCE THOMPSON - Jan 20, 1789
This indenture made Jan 9, 1789 between Eusebius Bushnell and William Dobbins of one part and Laurence Thompson of other part. Eusebius Bushnell and William Dobbins conveyed unto Laurence Thompson a tract of land containing 1000 acres in Davidson County on the waters of Stones River, adjoining Col. Isaac Shelby's corner, Capt. Montfort's corner. Which land was granted to said Bushnell and Dobbins dated Sept 15, 1787. This Jan 9, 1789.

Page   287 - WILLIAM MILLER - Jan 20, 1789
This indenture made Jan 8, 1789 between William Punell of Lincoln County, State of Virginia of one part and William Miller of same place of other part. William Purnell conveyed unto William Miller a tract of land in Davidson County and on the north side of Big Harpeth River. This Jan 9, 1789.

Page   288 - SAMUEL MARTIN - Jan 20, 1789
This indenture made Jan 8, 1789 between James Bosley and Mary Bosley his wife of Davidson County of one part and Samuel Martin of same place of other part. James Bosley and Mary Bosley his wife conveyed unto Samuel Martin a tract of land containing 50 acres in Davidson County. Which land was formerly occupied by Charles Baker, being part of a tract of 640 acres granted unto James Bosley by patent dated (blank). This Jan 9, 1789.

Page   288 - WM. & HUGH McCAMMENTS - Jan 20, 1789
This indenture made Nov 10, 1787 between Federick Stump of Davidson County of one part and William McCamments and Hugh McCamments, bpth of State of South Carolina, of other part. Federick Stump conveyed unto William and Hugh McCamments a tract of land containing 150 acres in Davidson County on the west of Jacob Stump's survey and on waters of Whites Creek, adjoining Federick Stump's line. Which land being granted by the State of North Carolina to the aforesaid Stump, grant dated Oct 8, 1787. No. 19. This Jan 8, 1789.

Page   289 - WILLIAM SHAW - Jan 20, 1789
This indenture made Oct 15, 1788 between Absolom Hooper and Elizabeth Hooper his wife of Davidson County of one part and William Shaw of same place of other part. Absolom Hooper and Elizabeth Hooper his wife conveyed unto William Shaw a tract of land containing 130 acres in Davidson County on the waters of Whites Creek, it being part of Samuel Vernor's Preemption. This Jan 5, 1789.

Page   289 - JOHN HUNTER - Jan 20, 1789

This indenture made Jan 5, 1789 between Jonathan Drake and his wife Lucy Drake of one part and John Hunter of other part, all of Davidson County. Jonathan Drake and his wife Lucy Drake conveyed unto John Hunter a tract of land containing 320 acres in Davidson County on the waters of Little Harpeth. Beginning on Benjamin Reed's boundary. Land being part of a tract of 640 acres granted unto said Drake by patent dated Oct 8, 1787, assignee of Mark Robertson, assignee of John Drake, a hunter in the Commissioners Guard &c. This Jan 5, 1789.

Page   290 - PATRICK O'NEAL - Jan 20, 1789

This indenture made Jan 5, 1789 between Jonathan Drake and his wife Lucy Drake of one part and Patrick O'Neal of other part, all of Davidson County. Jonathan Drake and his wife Lucy Drake conveyed unto Patrick O'Neal a tract of land containing 320 acres in Davidson County on waters of Little Harpeth. Said land being part of 640 acres granted unto said Drake by patent dated Oct 8, 1787 as assignee of Mark Robertson, assignee of John Drake, a hunter on the Commissioners Guard &c. This Jan 5, 1789.

Page   290 - FEDERICK STUMP - NC - No. 19 - Reg. Jan 21, 1789

By an Act for the relief of the Officers and Soldiers of the Continental Line, in consideration of the services of Col. Martin Armstrong, surveyor of lands, granted unto Federick Stump, assignee of Col. Martin Armstrong, a tract of land containing 150 acres in Davidson County on the west of Jacob Stump's survey and on the waters of Whites Creek. Surveyed for saud Federick Stump Feb 2, 1786 by Robert Nelson, D.S. in consequence of service right of said Armstrong No. 1876. Located Nov 21, 1785. Oct 8, 1787.

Page   291 - JOHN RICE - Jan 21, 1789 - State of Maryland

This indenture made June 21, 1788 between Abraham Riston of one part and John Rice of the other part, both of Davidson County. Abraham Riston conveyed unto John Rice one third of nineteen tracts of land in Davidson County, it being the lands which said Abraham Riston is entitled to of the land held by John Rice, Abraham Riston and Elisha Rice as tennents in common entered in Col. Martin Armstrong's office which is about 3860 acres. Seven of which tracts of land grants have been obtained for dated June 13, 1787. One tract containing 1000 acres, No. 299. Six other tracts of 640 acres each numbered as follows, 294, 295, 296, 297, 306, 309, which said lands as lying on the rivers of Cumberland and Tennessee and the waters emptying therein. Received of John Rice L.386 current money of Maryland, this 21 June 1788. Jan 5, 1789.

Page   291 - SOLOMON KITT - Jan 21, 1789

This indenture made Jan 15, 1788 between John Rice, Abraham Riston and Elisha Rice of Davidson County of one part and Solomon Kitt of town and County of Baltimore, State of Maryland of other part. Whereas the State of North Carolina, did by patent No. 301 dated June 13, 1787 granted unto John Rice, Abraham Riston and Elisha Rice, assignees of the heirs of John Martin, a certain tract of land containing 640 acres in Davidson County and on the north side of Tennessee River. Beginning on the bank of said river opposite the first island above the Virginia Line. Said Rice and Riston conveyed unto Solomon Kitt all the certain tract of land containing 640 acres in Davidson County. This Jan 5, 1789.

Page   292 - SOLOMON KITTS - Jan 21, 1789
          This indenture made Jan 15, 1788 between John Rice, Abraham Riston and
Elisha Rice of Davidson County of one part and Solomon Kitt of Baltimore town and county,
State of Maryland of other part. Whereas the State of North Carolina did by patent No.
305 dated June 13, 1787 granted unto said John Rice, Abraham Riston and Elisha Rice as
assignees of Jacob Ferrill, a certain tract of land containing 640 acres in Davidson County
on the north side of Tennessee River. Beginning about half a mile above the first bluff that
was on the river above the Virginia Line. Said land recited patent of State of North
Carolina by No. 305. This Jan 5, 1789.

Page   293 - SOLOMON KITT - Jan 21, 1789
          This indenture made Jan 15, 1788 between John Rice, Abraham Riston and
Elisha Rice of Davidson County of one part and Solomon Kitt of town and county of
Baltimore, State of Maryland, of other part. Whereas the State of North Carolina did by
patent No. 308, dated June 13, 1787 granted unto John Rice, Abraham Riston and Elisha
Rice, assignees to John Vintress, a tract of land containing 640 acres in Davidson County on
a small creek that comes into Tennessee River on the north side.Beginning at the southeast
corner of an Entry No. 1767. Said Rices and Riston conveyed unto Solomon Kitt the above
tract of land. This Jan 5, 1789.

Page   294 - SOLOMON KITT - Jan 21, 1789
          This indenture made Jan 15, 1788 between John Rice, Abraham Riston and
Elisha Rice of Davidson County of one part and Solomon Kitt of town and county of
Baltimore, State of Maryland. Whereas the State of North Carolina did by patent No. 304
dated June 13, 1787 granted unto John Rice, Abraham Riston and Elisha Rice, assignees of
the heirs of Nathaniel Nelson, a tract of land containing 640 acres in Davidson County on
the north side of Tennessee River. Said land was conveyed unto Solomon Kitt the said 640
acres. This 5 Jan 1789.

Page   295 - ALEXANDER COWAN, Esq. - Jan 22, 1789
          This indenture made July 14, 1788 between John Rice and Elisha Rice, late of
Davidson County of one part and Alexander Cowan of Hartford County, State of Maryland
of other part. John and Elisha Rice conveyed unto Alexander Cowan a tract of land
containing 1280 acres in Davidson County. Which said land was granted unto John Rice,
Abraham Riston and Elisha Rice as tenents in common by the State of North Carolina by
patent dated June 13, 1787 and No. 296 and 297. The first tract being on the east bank of
Stones River opposite to the Mill Dam Creek. Second numbered tract beginning on the east
side of Stones River opposite to the Mill Dam Rock. Said land conveyed unto Alexander
Cowan and was proven by Benjamin Howard and Solomon Hardwick and by Joel Reece,
attorney for John Rice. Jan 5, 1789.

Page   296 - THOMAS MOLLOY - NC - No. 28 - Reg. Jan 22, 1789
          By an Act for the relief of the Officers and Soldiers of the Continental Line,
in consideration of the services of Col. Martin Armstrong, surveyor of lands, granted unto
Thomas Molloy, assignee of said Armstrong, a tract of land containing 160 acres in Davidson
County joining the southern boundary of said Molloy's Guard Right No. 696. Surveyed for
Thomas Molloy by himself Nov 4, 1785 in consequence of a Service Right of said

Armstrong's No. 6, located Mar 26, 1785. Oct 8, 1787.

Page   297 - JAMES SHAW - NC - No. 240 - Reg. Feb 5, 1789
        For 10 lbs per 100 acres paid by James Shaw was granted a tract of land
containing 640 acres in Davidson County adjoining the river on the south and by Nelson on
the north. Beginning opposite to the mouth of the Lick Branch. Surveyed for James Shaw
May 10, 1784 by James Sanders agreeable to Warrant No. 146. Located Jan 16, 1784. July
10, 1788.

Page   297 - JAMES SHAW - NC - No. 87 - Reg. Feb 5, 1789
        By an Act for the relief of the Officers and Soldiers of the Continental Line,
in consideration for the bravery and zeal of Robert Bedwell, one of the Commissioners
Guards, granted unto James Shaw, assignee of Robert Bedwell, a tract of land containing
320 acres in Davidson County on the bank of the south Cross Creek, the south corner of
said Shaw's Guard Right No. 651. On Cumberland River. Surveyed for James Shaw Dec 7,
1785 by Thomas Molloy, D.S. in consequence of a Warrant No. 652. Located Jan 6, 1785.
July 10, 1789.

Page   297 - JAMES SHAW - NC - No. 83 - Reg. Feb 5, 1789
        By an Act for the relief of the Officers and Soldiers of the Continental Line,
in consideration of the bravery and zeal of William Purnell, granted unto James Shaw,
assignee of said Purnell, a tract of land containing 320 acres in Davidson County. Beginning
on the west side of the south Cross Creek. Surveyed for James Shaw Dec 7, 1785 by
Thomas Molloy, agreeable to a Warrant No. 651. Located Jan 6, 1785. July 10, 1788.

Page   298 - LARDNER CLARK & WM. WICUFF - NC - No. 232 - Reg. Feb 5, 1789
        For 10 lbs per 100 acres paid by Lardner Clark and William Wicuff was
granted a tract of land containing 640 acres in Davidson County adjoining Thomas
(illegible)'s line. Surveyed for said Clark and Wicuff Mar 18, 1786 by Thomas Molloy, D.S.
agreeable to Warrant No. 777. Located Dec 2, 1785. July 10, 1788.

Page   298 - THOMAS HARDIMAN - NC - No. 272 - Reg. Feb 5, 1789
        For 10 lbs per 100 acres paid by Thomas Hardiman was granted a tract of
land containing 640 acres in Davidson County on the upper south road on a small branch of
Browns Creek, it being Samuel Barton's beginning. Said land surveyed for said Hardiman
June 8, 1784 by Thomas Molloy, D.S. agreeable to a Warrant No. 163. Entered Jan 18,
1784. July 10, 1788.

Page   298 - JOHN DONALDSON - NC - No. 209 - Reg. Feb 5, 1789
        For 10 lbs per 100 acres paid by John Donaldson was granted a tract of land
containing 640 acres in Davidson County between Cumberland and Stones Rivers. Adjoining
Nathaniel Hay's line. Surveyed for John Donaldson by John Donaldson, D.S. agreeable to
Warrant No. 327. Entered Mar 3, 1784. July 10, 1788.

Page   299 - WILLIAM DONALDSON - NC - No. 204 - Reg. Feb 5, 1789
        For 10 lbs per 100 acres paid by William Donaldson was granted a tract of
land containing 640 acres in Davidson County in the forks between Cumberland and Stones

River, adjoining John Donaldson's line. Surveyed for William Donaldson Mar 22, 1786 by John Donaldson agreeable to a Warrant No. 620. Located Nov 13, 1784. July 10, 1788.

Page 299 - JOHN RICE - NC - No. 89 - Reg. Feb 9, 1789

By an Act for the relief of the Officers and Soldiers of the Continental Line, in consideration of the bravery and zeal of Francis Bullard, one of the Commissioners Guard, granted unto John Rice, assignee of Francis Bullard, a tract of land containing 320 acres in Davidson County on Smiths Creek a fork of Caney Fork adjoining Robert Burton. Surveyed for said John Rice Apr 22, 1787 by James Sanders, D.S. agreeable to a Warrant No. 793. Entered Mar 24, 1787. July 10, 1788.

Page 299 - JOHN TOPP - No. 461 - Reg. Feb 10, 1789

By an Act for the relief of the Officers and Soldiers of the Continental Line, in consideration of the services of Roger Topp, one of the Guards to the Commissioners, granted unto John Topp, heir of Roger Topp, a tract of land containing 960 acres in Davidson County on south side of Cumberland River on Browns Creek. Joining Thomas Hardiman's corner and Samuel Barton's corner thence with a conditional line between Barton and Mitchell's line. Surveyed for John Topp June 15, 1786 by James Mulherin, D.S. agreeable to a Warrant No. 329. Entry dated Mar 3, 1784. Nov 25, 1788.

Page 300 - JOHN TOPP - NC - No. 281 - Feb 10, 1789

For 10 lbs per 100 acres paid by Roger Topp, granted unto John Topp, heir of Roger Topp, a tract of land containing 640 acres in Davidson County on the waters of Bledsoes Creek. Joining Henry Loving's and Jacob Zigler's corners. Surveyed for said Topp May 9, 1785 agreeable to a Warrant No. 330. Entered Mar 3, 1784. Nov 25, 1788.

Page 300 - JONATHAN GUISE - NC - No. 529 - Reg. Mar 9, 1789

By an Act for the relief of the Officers and Soldiers of the Continental Line, in consideration of the bravery and zeal of William Collins, a private in the said line, granted unto Jonathan Guise, assignee of William Collins, a tract of land containing 640 acres in Davidson County on the south side of Cumberland River including the mouth of the first creek below Yellow Creek. Joining John Estes' boundary. Surveyed for Jonathan Guise Dec 19, 1784 by Thomas Molloy, D.S. in consequence of a Military Warrant No. 604. Located July 8, 1784. Sept 5, 1787.

Page 300 - FEDERICK STUMP - NC - No. 20 - Reg. Mar 10, 1789

By an Act for the relief of the Officers and Soldiers of the Continental Line, in consideration of the services of Martin Armstrong, surveyor of lands, granted unto Federick Stump, assignee of said Armstrong, a tract of land containing 100 acres in Davidson County on the west boundary of William Mitchel's Preemption on Whites Creek. Surveyed for Federick Stump Dec 4, 1785 by Robert Nelson, D.S. in consequence of a Service Right of said Armstrong No. 1109. Located July 9, 1785. Oct 8, 1787.

Page 301 - SAMUEL BARTON - NC - No. 244 - Reg. Feb 5, 1789

For 10 lbs per 100 acres paid by Samuel Barton, was granted a tract of land containing 640 acres in Davidson County on a creek called Knife Creek that empties into the Cumberland River on the north side about twelve miles below the mouth of Red River.

111

Surveyed for Samuel Barton Aug 1, 1785 by R. Nelson, D.S. agreeable to a Warrant No. 295. Located Feb 16, 1784. July 10, 1788.

Page   301 - SAMUEL BARTON - NC - No. 86 - Reg. Feb 5, 1789

By an Act for the relief of the Officers and Soldiers of the Continental Line, in consideration of the bravery and zeal of Jonas Manifee, one of the Commissioners Guard, granted unto Samuel Barton, assignee of said Manifee, a tract of land containing 320 acres in Davidson County on the waters of Big Harpeth. Joining Andrew Goff's corner and Thomas Spencer's corner. Surveyed for said Barton Nov 18, 1785 by John Bucchanan, D.S. in consequence of a Warrant No. 773. Located Nov 31, 1785. July 10, 1785.

Page   301 - SAMUEL BARTON - NC - No. 101 - Reg. Feb 5, 1789

For 10 lbs per 100 acres paid by Samuel Barton, was granted a tract of land containing 500 acres in Davidson County in Middle District on the north side of Duck River. Beginning on the west bank opposite to two small islands one hundred poles above a small spring which is about one mile above the mouth of Falling Creek and Lenears' corner. Surveyed for Samuel Barton July 16, 1785 by Henry Rutherford, D.S. in consequence of a Warrant No. 713. Signed July 10, 1788.

Page   302 - SAMUEL BARTON - NC - No. 244 - Reg. Feb 5, 1789

For 10 lbs per 100 acres paid by Samuel Barton was granted a tract of land containing 640 acres in Davidson County on a creek called Knife Creek that empties into the Cumberland River on the north side about twelve miles below the mouth of Red River. Surveyed for said Barton Aug 1, 1785 by R. Nelson, D.S. agreeable to a Warrant No. 295. Located Feb 16, 1784. July 10, 1788.

Page   301 - SAMUEL BARTON - NC - No. 86 - Reg. Feb 5, 1789

By an Act for the relief of the Officers and Soldiers of the Continental Line, in consideration of the bravery and zeal of Jonas Manifee, one of the Commissioners Guard, granted unto Samuel Barton, assignee of said Manifee, a tract of land containing 320 acres in Davidson County on the waters of Big Harpeth. Joining Andrew Goff's corner and Thomas Spencer's corner. Surveyed for said Barton Nov 18, 1785 by John Bucchanan, D.S. in consequence of a Warrant No. 773. Located Nov ?, 1785. July 10, 1788.

Page   301 - SAMUEL BARTON - NC - No. 101 - Reg. Feb 5, 1789

For 10 lbs per 100 acres paid by Samuel Barton was granted a tract of land containing 500 acres in Davidson County in Middle District on the north side of Duck River, on a small spring which is about one mile above the mouth of Falling Creek. Surveyed for said Barton July 16, 1785 by Henry Rutherford, D.S. in consequence of a Warrant No. 713. Signed July 10, 1788.

Page   302 - WILLIAM ROSS - NC - Mar 10, 1789

No. 2745. William Ross, assignee of John Lacky, 640 acres in Davidson County on the ridge between Red River and Station Camp Creek. Located June 23, 1787. July 28, 1787.

Page   302 - WILLIAM ROSS - NC - Mar 10, 1789
        No. 2663. William Ross assignee of Aaron Holloman, 640 acres in Davidson
County on the ridge between Red River and Station Camp Creek. Located 23 Jun 1787.
July 17, 1787.

Page   302 - WILLIAM ROSS - NC - Mar 10, 1789
        No. 2694. William Ross, assignee of John Lacky, 640 acres in Davidson
County. Located June 23, 1787. July 28, 1787.

Page   302 - PETER POITEVINT - NC - Mar 10, 1789
        No. 368.   Peter Poitevint, assignee of John Barnes, a soldier on the
Continental Line, 640 acres in Davidson County on the south side of Cumberland River
about one mile and half below Miller Sawyers' Entry of 1000 acres, on the bank of the
Cumberland River at the mouth of the third creek below the Cross Creek. Located 11 Sept
·1787.

Page   302 - WILLIAM BOWEN - NC - No. 84 - Mar 10, 1789
        By an Act for the relief of the Officers and Soldiers of the Continental Line,
in consideration of the bravery and zeal of Harris Shane, one of the Commissioners Guard,
granted unto William Bowen, assignee of Harris Shane, a tract of land containing 320 acres
in Davidson County on the north side of Cumberland River at the mouth of Kaspers Creek
adjoining Dixon's heirs. Surveyed for William Bowen by D. Smith Dec 19, 1785. Warrant
No. 196. Located Jan 8, 1784. July 10, 1788.

Page   303 - FELIX ROBERTSON & JOHN JACKSON - NC - No. 122 - Reg. Mar 10, 1789
        For 10 lbs per 100 acres paid by Felix Robertson and John Jackson, granted
unto them a tract of land containing 400 acres in Davidson County in Middle District on the
north side of Duck River including the mouth of North Fork. Joining Anthony Newman's
corner. Surveyed for said Robertson and Jackson July 25, 1785 by Ed Harris, D.S. in
consequence of a State Warrant No. 2159. Located May 15, 1784. July 10, 1788.

Page   303 - THOS. BARRELL, JUN. - NC - No. 477 - Reg. Mar 10, 1789
        By an Act for the relief of the Officers and Soldiers of the Continental line,
in consideration of the bravery and zeal of Thomas Barrell, a captain in the said line,
granted unto Thomas Barrell a tract of land containing 3840 acres in Davidson County on a
creek about six miles below the first timbered island below the Cross Creek, on the south
side of Cumberland River. Surveyed for Thomas Barrell Mar 10, 1785 by William Murry,
D.S. in consequence of a Military Warrant No. 578. Located Feb 17, 1785. Apr 15, 1787.

Page   303 - JONATHAN DRAKE - NC - No. 64 - Reg. Mar 10, 1789
        For 10 lbs per 100 acres paid by Jonathan Drake, granted unto Said Drake a
tract of land containing 1600 acres in Western District on both sides of the long fork above
the mouth of Spring Creek adjoining Benjamin Smith and John Frazier's on said fork.
Surveyed for said Drake Oct 5, 1785 by Ed Harris, D.S. Warrant No. 1816. Dated Apr 23,
1784. July 10, 1788.

Page   304 - DAVID WILSON - NC - No. 98 - Reg. Mar 10, 1789

For 10 lbs per 100 acres paid by David Wilson, was granted a tract of land containing 4096 acres in Davidson County in Middle District and on the north side of Duck River on Caney Spring Creek. Surveyed for David Wilson Mar 31, 1785 by Robert Weakley, D.S. in consequence of a Warrant No. 464. Entered Oct 25, 1783. July 10, 1788.

Page   304 - ALEXR. ROBERTSON - NC - No. 18 - Mar 10, 1789

For 10 lbs per 100 acres paid by Alexander Robertson, was granted a tract of land containing 1000 acres in Davidson County in Middle District on Duck River about five miles above the mouth of North Fork. Joining Anthony Numan's corner. Surveyed for Alexander Robertson July 25, 1785 by Henry Rutherford in consequence of a State Warrant No. 689. Dated Oct 28, 1783. July 10, 1788.

Page   304 - MARK ROBERTSON - NC - No. 70 - Reg. Mar 10, 1789

For 10 lbs per 100 acres paid by Mark Robertson, was given a tract of land containing 5000 acres in Middle District on the north side of Duck River on both sides of Bear Creek adjoining William Cocke on the west. Surveyed for said Robertson Feb 22, 1785 by Ed Harris, D.S. in consequence of a State Warrant No. 571. Oct 27, 1783. July 10, 1788.

Page   305 - JAMES ROBERTSON - NC - No. 44 - Reg. Mar 11, 1789

For 10 lbs per 100 acres paid by James Robertson, was granted a tract of land containing 3000 acres in Middle District on Weakleys Creek a west fork of Richland Creek of Elk River. Said creek marked at the mouth on a tree E.H. & R.W. Joining Robert Weakley's survey of 2000 acres. Surveyed for James Robertson Mar 26, 1786 by Ed Hickman, D.S. in consequence of a Warrant No. 8. Dated Jan 10, 1786. July 10, 1789.

Page   305 - JAMES ROBERTSON - NC - No. 71 - Reg. Mar 11, 1789

For 10 lbs per 100 acres paid by James Robertson, was granted a tract of land containing 2000 acres in the Western District on both sides of Loathatchee River a fork of Wolf River. Joining William Alston's of No. 561 and Thomas Talbot's No. 1440. Surveyed for James Robertson Apr 5, 1785 by Ed Harris, D.S. in consequence of a State Warrant No. 465. Oct 25, 1783. July 10, 1788.

Page   305 - JAMES ROBERTSON - NC - No. 76 - Reg. Mar 11, 1789

(2nd page)   For 10 lbs per 100 acres paid by James Robertson was granted a tract of land containing 1000 acres in the Western District on the Obion River adjoining John Dougan's No. 686 and James Dougan's No. 598(508) on said river. Surveyed for said Robertson Sept 18, 1785 by Ed Harris, D.S. in consequence of a State Warrant No. 1646. Apr 16, 1784. July 10, 1788.

Page   306 - JAMES ROBERTSON & HUGH LEEPER - NC - No. 81 - Reg. Mar 11, 1789

For 10 lbs per 100 acres paid by James Robertson and Hugh Leeper, was granted a tract of land containing 2034 acres in Middle District on the north side of Duck River, on both sides of Leepers Lick Creek and including Leepers Lick lying on the west side of the creek. Surveyed for James Robertson and Hugh Leeper Mar 21, 1785 by Robert Hays, D.S. in consequence of a State Warrant No. 730. Oct 21, 1783. July 10, 1788.

Page   306 - THOMAS SHARP SPENCER - NC - No. 94 - Reg. Mar 11, 1789

By an Act for the relief of the Officers and Soldiers of the Continental Line, in consideration of the bravery and zeal of Benjamin Fletcher, one of the Commissioners guard, granted unto Thomas Sharp Spencer, assignee of said Benjamin Fletcher, a tract of land containing 320 acres in Davidson County on the waters of Big Harpeth River on the little south road.   Surveyed for said Spencer Nov 17, 1785 by John Bucchanan, D.S. in consequence of a Warrant No. 273.   Feb 13, 1784.   July 10, 1788.

Page   306 - JOHN DONALDSON - NC - No. 203 - Reg. Mar 11, 1789

For 10 lbs per 100 acres paid by John Donaldson was granted a tract of land containing 640 acres in Davidson County on the south side of Cumberland River.   Which land was surveyed by the said Donaldson for himself Mar 6, 1786, Warrant No. 742, Jun 3, 1785. July 10, 1788.

Page   307 - ROBERT THOMPSON - NC - No. 175 - Reg. Mar 11, 1789

By an Act for the relief of the Officers and Soldiers of the Continental Line, in consideration of the bravery and zeal of Mathew Cates, a private in the said line, granted unto Robert Thompson, assignee of Mathew Cates, a tract of land containing 274 acres in Davidson County on the west side of Big Harpeth River joining Curtis Ivey's line. Surveyed for Robert Thompson Mar 20, 1785 by John Donaldson, D.S.   Warrant No. 1011. Located Dec 7, 1784.   Mar 7, 1786.

Page   307 - AMBROSE JONES - NC - No. 790 - Reg. Mar 12, 1789

By an Act for the relief of the Officers and Soldiers of the Continental Line, in consideration of the bravery and zeal of Corbin Hickman, a private in the said line, granted unto Ambrose Jones, assignee of said Hickman, a tract of land containing 640 acres in Sumner County on the north side of Cumberland River on the middle fork of Drakes Creek. Beginning one half mile below an improvement made by Morton Mauldin. Surveyed for Ambrose Jones Oct 13, 1784 by William Crutcher, D.S.   Warrant No. 3354.   Located Sept 12, 1787. July 10, 1788.

Page   307 - AMBROSE JONES - NC - No. 791 - Reg. Mar 12, 1789

By an Act for the relief of the Officers and Soldiers of the Continental Line, in consideration of the bravery and zeal of Daniel Ray, a private in the said line, granted unto Ambrose Jones, assignee of said Daniel Ray, a tract of land containing 640 acres in Davidson County on the east side of Stones River. Beginning above the mouth of second creek above the mouth of Stuarts Creek that falls into the said river on the east side. Surveyed for Ambrose Jones Jan 20, 1788 by William Nash, D.S.   Warrant No. 2741. Located Jan 8, 1788. July 10, 1788.

Page   308 - WILLIAM TAITT - NC - No. 759 - Reg. Mar 13, 1789

By an Act for the relief of the Officers and Soldiers of the Continental line, in consideration of the bravery and zeal of John Teller, a private in the said line, granted unto William Taitt, assignee of said John Teller, a tract of land containing 640 acres in Davidson County on the west side of Samuel Kessly's claim.   Beginning at Col. Martin Armstrong's corner, also Robert Nelson's corner, Reason's corner, and Stuart's line and to Armstrong's line. Surveyed for William Taitt Feb 29, 1787 by Robert Nelson, D.S.   Warrant

No. 3344. Located Feb 17, 1787. July 10, 1788.

Page   308 - WILLIAM TAITT - NC - No. 511 - Reg. Mar 13, 1789
            By an Act for the relief of the Officers and Soldiers of the Continental Line,
in consideration of the bravery and zeal of James Gifford, a private in the said line,
granted unto William Taitt, assignee of said James Gifford, a tract of land containing 428
acres in Davidson County on Red River. Joining the boundary of the heirs of Jacob Jones's
Preemption. Surveyed for William Taitt Jan 11, 1787 by B. William Pollock, D.S.   Warrant
No. 3081. Located Jan 10, 1787. Sept 15, 1787.

Page   308 - ROBERT HAYS - NC - No. 105 - Reg. Apr 16, 1789
            For 10 lbs per 100 acres paid by Robert Hays was granted a tract of land
containing 5000 acres in Middle District on Richland Creek of Elk River about nine or ten
miles north of southern boundary of the State. Joining on a small bluff on the west side of
said creek George Dougherty's corner. Surveyed for Robert Hays Mar 24, 1786 by Robert
Weakley, D.S. in consequence of a Warrant No. 2575, dated May 25, 1784. Signed July 10,
1788.

Page   309 - ROBERT HAYS - NC - No. 82 - Reg. Apr 16, 1789
            For 10 lbs per 100 acres paid by Robert Hays was granted a tract of land
containing 1000 acres in Middle District on the south side of Duck River on Caney Spring
Creek. Joining David Wilson's corner, Robert Weakley's line. Surveyed for Robert Hays by
Robert Weakley, D.S. in consequence of a Warrant No. 2640. Dated May 25, 1785. July 10,
1788.

Page   309 - BARTHOLOMEW & PETER TARDIVEAU - NC - Apr 17, 1789
            This indenture made 8 Apr 1789 between Lardner Clark of Davidson County
of one part and Bartholomew Tardiveau and Peter Tardiveau of other part. Lardner Clark
conveyed unto said Bartholomew and Peter Tardiveau a tract of land containing 511½ acres
in Davidson County in the fork between Cumberland River and Red River near where the
town of Clarksville is laid off and established.   Proven by Daniel Smith and John Hinds.
This April Term 1789.

Page   310 - SAMUEL HANDLEY - NC - No. 14 - Reg. Apr 18, 1789
            By an Act for the relief of the Officers and Soldiers of the Continental Line,
in consideration of the service of Col. Martin Armstrong, granted unto Samuel Handley,
assignee of said Armstrong, a tract of land containing 100 acres in Davidson County on
Cobbs Creek of Richland the waters of Red River adjoining Robert King's survey. Surveyed
for Samuel Handley June 25, 1785 by Robert Nelson, D.S. in consequence of a Service Right
of said Armstrong No. 740. Located Mar 26, 1785. Oct 8, 1787.

Page   310 - JOHN SCOTT - NC - Apr 17, 1789
            This indenture made 8 Apr 1789 between Daniel Roman, attorney for Marget
Allen, late of Davidson County and John of the County of Bedford, State of Pennsylvania
of the other part. Daniel Roman, attorney, conveyed unto John Scott a tract of land
on the north side of Sulphur Fork of Red River, the north boundary of Col. Ezekiel Polk's
survey of 640 acres. Attested by Federick Stump and Lewis Fordd. Apr Term 1789.

Page 311 - THOMAS CRAIGHEAD - NC - Apr 20, 1789
This indenture made between Lardner Clark and Thomas Craighead, both of Davidson County, NC. Lardner Clark conveyed unto Thomas Craighead a tract of land containing 200 acres in Davidson County on the south side of Cumberland River in the big bend below the mouth of Stones River. Joining Col. Armstrong's tract. This 10 Mar 1789. Witnessed by John Boyd and George Winters. Apr Term 1789.

Page 311 - JAMES BOSLEY - NC - Apr 20, 1789
This indenture made 5 Jan 1789 between Anthony Crutcher of Davidson County of one part and James Bosley of same place of other part. Anthony Crutcher conveyed unto James Bosley a certain lot of one half acre of land including the house that stands thereon in the town of Nashville known by its being next to the river, No. 8 being the lot formerly granted to Samuel Dunbad by the Commissioners for the said town by deed dated __ day of __ 178_. Apr Term 1789.

Page 312 - EDWARD CATHAM - NC - Apr 20, 1789
This indenture made 16 Nov 1788 between William Newell of the State of Virginia and County of Fayette of the one part and Edward Catham of same place of other part. William Newell conveyed unto Edward Catham one tract of land in Davidson County and on the head of Little Harpeth. Bounded by William Simpson, John Crockett's Preemption. Apr Term 1789.

Page 312 - ANDREW LUCUS - NC - Apr 20, 1789
This indenture made 26 (blank) 1789 between James Bosley of Davidson County of one part and Andrew Lucus of same place of other part. James Bosley conveyed unto Andrew Lucus one lot containing one acre of land in the town of Nashville and known as No. 82, being the lot formerly granted to George Neville by the Commissioners by deed dated July 6, 1785. Apr Term 1789.

Page 313 - JOEL RICE - NC - Apr 21, 1789
This indenture made 23 Mar 1789 between Thomas Hickman, Sheriff of Davidson County of one part and Joel Rice of same place of other part. Thomas Hickman conveyed unto Joel Rice two lots in the town of Nashville and known as Lot No. 61 and No. 80, late the property of John Armstrong and Jemima Chancey, granted to them by the Commissioners of the town. Apr Term 1789. Signed by John Pryor, D.S.

Page 313 - DAVID SHELBY - NC - Apr 21, 1789
This indenture made 3 Feb 1789 between Edwin Hickman of Davidson County of one part and David Shelby of Sumner County, NC of other part. Edwin Hickman conveyed unto David Shelby a tract of land in Davidson County on the south side side of Cumberland River on Hickmans Creek which runs into Cumberland below Dyers Camp. Land containing 640 acres. Apr Term 1789.

Page 314 - EDWIN HICKMAN - NC - Apr 21, 1789
This indenture made 5 Nov 1788 between Thomas Brasher of Davidson County of one part and Edwin Hickman of same place of other part. Thomas Brasher conveyed unto Edwin Hickman all that messuage (dwelling house) tenement and farm commonly called

117

and known by the name of Heaton Station in Davidson County formerly in the possession of Christian Cripps. 6 Nov 1788. Apr Term 1789.

Page   314 - THOMAS COMSTOCK - NC - No. 18 - Reg. Apr 21, 1789
By an Act for the relief of the Officers and Soldiers of the Continental Line, in consideration of the service of Col. Martin Armstrong, granted unto Thomas Comstock , assignee of Col. Martin Armstrong, a tract of land containing 100 acres in Davidson County on the north side of Cumberland River about two miles north of the mouth of Red River to include a cave spring. Surveyed for Thomas Comstock Aug 5, 1785 by R. Nelson, D.S. in consequence of a Service Right No. 818. Located 7 Apr 1785. Oct 8, 1787.

Page   315 - THOMAS JAMESON - NC - Apr 21, 1789
This indenture made 7 Apr 1789 between Anthony Crutcher of Davidson County of one part and Thomas Jameson of same place of other part. Anthony Crutcher conveyed unto Thomas Jameson one piece or lot in the town of Nashville known by Lot No. 45. Containing one acres of land. Apr Term 1789.

Page   315 - HUGH BELL - NC - Apr 21, 1789
This indenture made Apr 6, 1789 between James Bosley of Davidson County of one part and Hugh Bell of same place of other part. James Bosley conveyed unto Hugh Bell one tract of land in Davidson County on the south side of Cumberland River near the Stone Lick, containing 125 acres. Bounded by Cockrill's line and John Kirkpatrick's line. Apr Term 1789.

Page   316 - JOSEPH MARTIN - NC - Apr 21, 1789
This indenture made Apr 4, 1789 between Samuel Martin and Elizabeth Martin his wife of Davidson County of one part and Joseph Martin and Elizabeth Martin his wife of same place of other part. Samuel Martin and Elizabeth martin his wife conveyed unto Joseph Martin and Elizabeth Martin his wife a tract of land containing 357 acres in Tennessee County, North Carolina on the south side of Cumberland River at the mouth of a branch four or five miles below the mouth of Red River. The said tract of land be made to said Martin as assignee of Abraham Jenkins bearing date 15 of Sept 1787. Proven by George N(illegible) and James Frost April Term 1789.

Page   316 - MILCHER ISLER - NC - Apr 22, 1789
This indenture made Apr 7, 1789 between Adam Hampton of Davidson County of one part and Milcher Isler of the County of Tennessee, North Carolina. Adam Hampton conveyed unto Milcher Isler a tract of land containing 320 acres in the County of Tennessee on the Sulphur Fork of Red River. Beginning at William Graham's line. Which land was granted unto said Hampton by patent dated Oct 8, 1787. Apr Term 1789.

Page   317 - SAMUEL MARTIN - NC - Apr 22, 1789
This indenture made Apr 4, 1789 between Joseph Martin and his wife Elizabeth Martin of Davidson County of one part and Samuel Martin and Elizabeth Martin his wife of same place of other part. Joseph Martin and Elizabeth Martin his wife conveyed unto Samuel Martin a tract of land containing 320 acres in Davidson County on the east fork of Whites Creek. Beginning where David Rounseville's line crosses the east fork of

Page   317 - JAMES MENESS - NC - Apr 22, 1789
        This indenture made Apr 7, 1789 between James Scott of Davidson County of one part and James Meness of same place of other part. James Scott conveyed unto James Meness a tract of land containing 100 acres in Davidson County adjoining Scott's Preemption. Apr Term 1789.

Page   318 - BARTLETT SIMS - NC - Apr 22, 1789
        This indenture made Apr 8, 1789 between   Elijah   Robertson of one part and Bartlett Sims of other part.   Elijah   Robertson conveyed unto Bartlett Sims a tract of land containing 640 acres in Davidson County on the north side of Cumberland River and on Sycamore Creek adjoining Henry Rutherford's corner on Reading Blount's corner.   Elijah Robertson for himself his heirs executor and administrators do grant unto Bartlett Sims the land. Apr Term 1789.

Page   318 - MATHEW SIMS - NC - Apr 22, 1789
        This indenture made Apr 8, 1789 between Elijah Robertson of one part and Mathew Sims of other part.   Elijah Robertson conveyed unto Mathew Sims a tract of land containing 640 acres in Davidson County on the north side of the second small creek that runs into Cumberland River above McF(illegible) on the waters of said creek and joining Reading Blount's line. Apr Term 1789.

Page   319 - CHARLES ANINGTON - NC - Apr 22, 1789
        This indenture made Feb 4, 1789 between Philemon Thomas of Fayette County, State of Virginia of one part and Charles Annington of Sumner County, NC of other part.   Philemon Thomas conveyed unto Charles Annington a tract of land containing 300 acres in Davidson County on the Wartrace Creek a branch of the Sulphur Fork of Red River. Apr Term 1789.

Page   319 - JOHN EDMONDSON - NC - Apr 22, 1789
        This indenture made Mar 10, 1789 between Thomas Denton of Mercer County, Virginia of the one part and John Edmondson of Davidson County of other part.   Thomas Denton conveyed unto John Edmondson a tract of land containing 320 acres on the waters of Mill Creek in Donelson, State of North Carolina.   Proven by John Buchanan and John Edmondson. Apr Term 1789.

Page   320 - JOHN ERWINE - NC - Apr 23, 1789
        This indenture made Nov 11, 1788 between Thomas Hickman of Davidson County of one part and John Erwine of same place of other part.   By virtue of a suit instituted by John Erwine against James Lenear and James Martin Lewis defendant.   By virtue of a judgement an order of sale issued for the County Court of Davidson County attested by Andrew Ewing, clerk of said court. Sale of a house and lot No. 28 in the town of Nashville the undivided right of James Lenear, one of the defendants and Anthony Crutcher, by public sale by Thomas Hickman, Sheriff, sale on 29 Nov 1788. Apr Term 1789.

Page   320 - JAMES HOGGATT - NC - Apr 23, 1789
        This indenture made Feb 18, 1789 between James Bosley of County and State of North Carolina of one part and James Hoggatt of same place of other part.   James

Bosley conveyed unto James Hoggatt one tract of land in Davidson County on the south side of Cumberland River and containing 700 acres adjoining Isaac Thomas's corner and Samuel Deason's corner and McGavock's and John Bell's corner. This Apr Term 1789.

Page   321 - JOSHUA HADLEY - NC - Apr 23, 1789
        This indenture made Feb 8, 1789 between David Hay, Sheriff of Davidson County of one part and Joshua Hadley of same place of other part. Whereas Joshua Hadley in a court held for said County Jan 9, 1787 did then and there in a suit which he prosecuted again James Lenear as the bail of a certain James Allen obtains judgement in said court against the said Lenear against the estate of the said Lenear by virtue of which execution David Hay after legal notice given have sold at public auction to the said Joshua Hadley for the sum of fifteen pounds a tract of land containing 640 acres surveyed by virtue of a Warrant No. 3387 and entered in Col. Armstrong's office June 15, 1786. Said land lying between Calebs and Millers Creek. Beginning at John Elliott's corner, William Cox's line, Coonrod's line, Robert Nelson, James Nelson, Caleb Winters, and Armstrong's corner, and also another tract of land containing 640 acres Feb 17, 1787. Beginning on Miller and Bush Creek of 640 acres, Fleming's line, William Fennor's line. Apr Term 1789.

Page   322 - EDGAR & TAITT - NC - Apr 23, 1789
        This indenture made the same day of April 1789 between Thomas Hickman, Sheriff of Davidson County of one part and Edgar and William Taitt of same place of other part. By virtue of a suit by Guilford Dudley against Eusebius Bushnell in the County Court of Cumberland, the said Guilford Dudley recovered a judgement against Eusebius Bushnell for £55.12.7 3/4 and costs. Eusebius Bushnell May have had, held or could hold in a half lot and house No. 9 in the town of Nashville. The undivided right of William Dobbins and Eusebius Bushnell the defendant was exposed to public sale by Thomas Hickman, Sheriff, did on the 6th day of Apr 1789 Edgar and Taitt became the purchasers. Apr Term 1789.

Page   322 - EDGAR & TAITT - NC - Apr 24, 1789
        This indenture made Jan 6, 1789 between Thomas Hickman, Sheriff of Davidson County, of one part and Edgar and Taitt of same place of other part. By virtue of a suit against William Dobbins, sold at auction a house and half Lot No. 9 in the town of Nashville to Edgar and Taitt on 11 Nov 1788. April Term 1789.

Page   323 - WILLIAM TERRELL LEWIS - NC - Apr 24, 1789
        This indenture made Sept 24, 1788 between James Robertson of one part and William Terrell Lewis of other part, both of Davidson County. James Robertson conveyed unto William Terrell Lewis a certain half lot of one half acre of ground in the town of Nashville and known by No. 24, it being one half of the lot formerly granted to James Robertson by the Commissioners for said town by deed dated 15 Aug 1784 and adjoining the half lot now the property of John Sappington and sold to said Sappington by James Robertson. Apr Term 1789.

Page   323 - ISAAC JOHNSTON - NC - Apr 24, 1789
        This indenture made Apr 8, 1789 between William Collinsworth of Davidson County of one part and Isaac Johnston of same place of other part. William Collinsworth conveyed unto Isaac Johnston all that tract of land in Davidson County on Little Harpeth

River, being part of a tract granted unto said Collinsworth. The Warrant No. 315. Crossing Cockralls spring branch. Containing 320 acres. Apr Term 1789.

Page   324 - BEAL BOSLEY - NC - Nov 24, 1789
            This indenture made Apr 8, 1789 between Samuel Martin and Elizabeth Martin his wife of Davidson County of one part and Beal Bosley of same place of other part. Samuel Martin and Elizabeth Martin his wife conveyed unto Beal Bosley a tract of land containing 50 acres in Davidson County. The said land included an improvement formerly occupied by Charles Baker, being part of a tract of 640 acres granted unto James Bosley by patent dated _____. Apr Term 1789.

Page   324 - ISAAC THOMAS - NC - Apr 24, 1789
            This indenture made Feb 19, 1789 between James Bosley of Davidson County of one part and Isaac Thomas of same place of other part. James Bosley conveyed unto Isaac Thomas one tract of land in Davidson County on the south side of Cumberland River containing 62 acres, crossing Stones Lick Branch. Apr Term 1789.

Page   325 - GEORGE DOUGHERTY - NC - No. 3 - Reg. Apr 28, 1789
            By an Act for the relief of the Officers and Soldiers of the Continental Line, in consideration of the bravery and zeal of George Dougherty, a major in the said line, granted unto George Dougherty a tract of land containing 4800 acres in Davidson County on both sides of Walnut Creek. Surveyed for said Dougherty Mar 26, 1785 by Robert Hays, D.S. by virtue of a Military Warrant No. 18. Located (blank). 14 Mar 1786.

Page   325 - THOMAS ARMSTRONG - NC - No. 164 - Reg. Apr 28, 1789
            By an Act for the relief of the Officers and Soldiers of the Continental Line, in consideration of the bravery and zeal of Absolom Fowler, a private in the said line, granted unto Thomas Armstrong, assignee of Absolom Fowler, a tract of land containing 640 acres in Davidson County joining Col. James Armstrong's Entry of 7200 acres on the waters of Stones River the south side. Beginning at Lieut. Hardy Holms' corner. Surveyed for Thomas Armstrong Mar 12, 1785 by Robert Hays, D.S. in consequence of a Military Warrant No. 86. Located Mar 9, 1784. Mar 7, 1786.

Page   325 - THOMAS ARMSTRONG - NC - No. 48 - Reg. Apr 28, 1789
            By an Act for the relief of the Officers and Soldiers of the Continental Line, in consideration of the bravery and zeal of Thomas Armstrong, a captain in the said line, granted unto Thomas Armstrong a tract of land containing 3840 acres in Davidson County on the main West Fork of Stones River on the west side about five miles from the line ran by the Commissioners in 1783 and about a mile from the river to include two springs. Surveyed for Thomas Armstrong Mar 9, 1785 by Robert Hays, D.S. Signed Mar 14, 1786.

Page   326 - JAMES ARMSTRONG - NC - No. 35 - Reg. Apr 28, 1789
            By an Act for the relief of the Officers and Soldiers of the Continental Line, in consideration of the bravery and zeal of James Armstrong, a colonel in the said line, granted unto James Armstrong a tract of land containing 7200 acres in Davidson County on the waters of Stones River. Surveyed for James Armstrong Mar 8, 1785 by Robert Hays, D.S. in consequence of a Military Warrant No. 84. Located Feb 14, 1784. Mar 14, 1786.

Page   326 - WICUFF & CLARK - NC - No. 39 - Apr 28, 1789
By an Act for the relief of the Officers and Soldiers of the Continental Line, in consideration of the service of Col. Martin Armstrong, surveyor, granted unto Lardner Clark and William Wicuff, assignees of said Armstrong, a tract of land containing 228 acres in Davidson County on the east fork of Blooming Grove joining the east boundary of John Allison's claim. Surveyed for said Wicuff & Clark Mar 30, 1786 by Robert Nelson, D.S. in consequence of a Service Right of said Armstrong, No. 1612. Located Nov 9, 1786. Oct 8, 1787.

Page   326 - ROBERT WEAKLEY - NC - No. 33 - Apr 28, 1789
For 10 lbs per 100 acres paid by Robert Weakley was granted a tract of land containing 2000 acres in Western District on the waters of the Obion River and the north sides of said river. Beginning on Ephraim McLean's line and Blount's. Surveyed for Robert Weakley Sept 14, 1785 in consequence of a State Warrant No. 1787. Dated Apr 23, 1784. July 10, 1788.

Page   327 - ROBERT WEAKLEY - NC - No. 108 - Reg. Apr 28, 1789
For 10 lbs per 100 acres paid by Robert Weakley was granted a tract of land containing 2000 acres in Middle District on the north side of Duck River on both sides of Caney Spring Creek. Surveyed for Robert Weakley Apr 1, 1785 in consequence of a Warrant No. 1788. Dated Apr 16, 1784. July 10, 1788.

Page   327 - ROBERT WEAKLEY - NC - No. 57 - Reg. Apr 28, 1789
For 10 lbs per 100 acres paid by Robert Weakley was granted a tract of land containing 2000 acres in the Middle District on Weakleys Creek a west fork of Richland Creek of Elk River marked at the mouth with E.H. & R.V. Surveyed for Robert Weakley by himself Mar 25, 1786 in consequence of a State Warrant No. 1799. Dated Apr 23, 1784. July 10, 1788.

Page   327 - JAMES HOGGATT - NC - No. 489 - Apr 28, 1789
By an Act for the relief of the Officers and Soldiers of the Continental Line, in consideration of the bravery and zeal of James Spence, a private in the said line, granted unto James Hoggatt, assignee of said Spence, a tract of land containing 228 acres in Davidson County on the north side of Cumberland River on the Sulphur Creek adjoining Samuel Lewis' corner. Surveyed for James Hoggatt Mar 26, 1786 by Robert Nelson, D.S. in consequence of a Military Warrant No. 1741. Located Nov 12, 1785. Sept 15, 1787.

Page   328 - JAMES HOGGATT - NC - No. 29 - Apr 28, 1789
By an Act for the relief of the Officers and Soldiers of the Continental Line, in consideration of the service of Col. Martin Armstrong, surveyor, granted unto James Hoggatt, assignee of the said Armstrong, a tract of land containing 160 acres in Davidson County on the north side of Cumberland River and joining his other survey of 228 acres. Surveyed for James Hoggatt Mar 29, 1786 by Robert Nelson, D.S. in consequence of a Service Right of said Armstrong No. 446. Located Dec 21, 1785. Oct 8, 1787.

Page   328 - JAMES HOGGATT - NC - No. 25 - Apr 28, 1789
By an Act for the relief of the Officers and Soldiers of the Continental Line,

in consideration for the services of Col. Martin Armstrong, surveyor, granted unto James Hoggatt, assignee of said Col. Martin Armstrong, a tract of land containing 60 acres in Davidson County on the north side of Cumberland River at the mouth of Sulphur Creek, joining said Hoggatt's survey of 160 acres. Surveyed for James Hoggatt by Robert Nelson, D.S. in consequence of a Service Right of said Armstrong's No. 440. Located Nov 12, 1787. Oct 8, 1787.

Page   328 - JOHN ELLIOTT - NC - No. 93 - Reg. Apr 29, 1789
        By an Act for the relief of the officers and Soldiers of the Continental Line, in consideration of the bravery and zeal of Samuel Barton, one of the Commissioners Guard, granted unto John Elliott, assignee of said Barton, a tract of land containing 640 acres in Davidson County on the south side of Cumberland River between Cedar Creek and Thompsons Creek. Joining Nathaniel Jones' lowest corner on said river. Surveyed for John Elliott Apr 19, 1786 by John Bucchanan, D.S. agreeable to a Warrant No. 750. Dated June 24, 1785. July 10, 1788.

Page   329 - THOMAS HICKMAN - NC - No. 739 - Reg. Apr 29, 1789
        By an Act for the relief of the officers and Soldiers of the Continental Line, in consideration for the bravery and zeal of Nathaniel Smith, a private in the said line, granted unto Thomas Hickman, assignee of Nathaniel Smith, a tract of land containing 640 acres in Davidson County on the waters of the first creek that runs into the East Fork of Stones River on the east side above the mouth of Bradleys Lick Creek. Surveyed for said Thomas Hickman by James Sanders, D.S. in consequence of a Military Warrant No. 2776. Located Aug 30, 1787. July 11, 1788.

Page   329 - THOMAS HICKMAN- NC - No. 744 - Reg. Apr 29, 1789
        By an Act for the relief of the Officers and Soldiers of the Continental Line, in consideration of the bravery and zeal of James Davis, a private in the said line, granted unto Thomas Hickman, assignee of James Davis, a tract of land containing 640 acres in Davidson County on the east side above the mouth of Bradleys Lick Creek, adjoining Joseph Hendrick's line. Surveyed for Thomas Hickman by James Sanders, D.S. in consequence of a Military Warrant No. 1791. Located Aug 30, 1787. July 11, 1788.

Page   329 - THOMAS HICKMAN - NC - No. 742 - Reg. Apr 29, 1789
        By an Act for the relief of the officers and Soldiers of the Continental Line, in consideration of the bravery and zeal of Federick Cross, a private in the said line, granted unto Thomas Hickman, assignee of Federick Cross, a tract of land containing 640 acres in Davidson County on the waters of the first creek that runs in on the east side of Stones River above Bradleys Lick Creek. Surveyed for Thomas Hickman by James Sanders, D.S. in consequence of a Military Warrant No. 2712. Located Aug 30, 1787. July 10, 1788.

Page   330 - THOMAS HICKMAN - NC - No. 764 - Reg. Apr 29, 1789
        By an Act for the relief of the Officers and Soldiers of the Continental Line, in consideration of the bravery and zeal of Henry Dickinson, a private in the said line, granted unto Thomas Hickman, assignee of Henry Dickinson, a tract of land containing 274 acres in Sumner County on the waters of Caney Fork and adjoining John Marshall and Stockly Donelson. Surveyed for Thomas Hickman by James Sanders, D.S. in consequence of

123

a Military Warrant No. 3456. Located Aug 30, 1784. July 11, 1788.

Page   330 - GEORGE NEVILLES - NC - No. 173 - Reg. APR 29, 1789
By an Act for the relief of the Officers and Soldiers of the Continental Line, in consideration of the bravery and zeal of James Gambling, a private in the said line, granted unto George Nevilles, assignee of said James Gambling, a tract of land containing 350 acres in Davidson County on Red River adjoining a Preemption of James Rentfro's at the upper end. Surveyed for George Nevilles Aug 28, 1785 by B. William Pollock, D.S. in consequence of a Military Warrant No. 832. Located May 30, 1785. Mar 7, 1786.

Page   330 - THOMAS CUMSTOCK - NC - No. 45 - Reg. Apr 30, 1789
By an Act for the relief of the Officers and Soldiers of the Continental Line, in consideration of the services of Col. Martin Armstrong, surveyor, granted unto Thomas Cumstock, assignee of said Armstrong, a tract of land containing 100 acres in Davidson County on the north side of Cumberland about two miles north of the mouth of Red River. Surveyed for Thomas Cumstock Aug 5, 1785 by Robert Nelson, D.S. in consequence of a Service Right of said Armstrong, No. 1207. Located Aug 8, 1785. Oct 8, 1787.

Page   331 - NICHOLAS COONROD - NC - No. 498 - Reg. Apr 30, 1789
By an Act for the relief of the Officers and Soldiers of the Continental Line, in consideration of the bravery and zeal of William Holland, a private in the said line, granted unto Nicholas Coonrod, assignee of William Holland, a tract of land containing 640 acres in Davidson County on the north side of Cumberland about four or five miles below the mouth of a spring branch, adjoining Col. Martin Armstrong's line. Surveyed for Nicholas Coonrod Nov 10, 1785 by Robert Nelson, D.S. in consequence of a Military Warrant No. 715. Located Aug 2, 1784. Sept 15, 1787.

Page   331 - WILLIAM MURRY - NC - No. 16 - Reg. Apr 30, 1789
By an Act for the relief of the Officers and Soldiers of the Continental Line, in consideration of the services of Col. Martin Armstrong, surveyor, granted unto William Murry, assignee of said Armstrong, a tract of land containing 100 acres in Davidson County on the waters of the Hurricane Creek running into Stones River on the lower side. Surveyed for William Murry Apr 8, 1786 in consequence of a Service Right for said Armstrong, No. (blank). Located July 4, 1785. Oct 8, 1787.

Page   331 - WILLIAM MURRY - NC - No. 35 - Reg. Apr 30, 1789
By an Act for the relief of the Officers and Soldiers of the Continental Line, in consideration of the services of Col. Martin Armstrong, surveyor, granted unto William Murry, assignee of said Armstrong, a tract of land containing 163 acres in Davidson County. Surveyed for William Murry Apr 8, 1786 in consequence of a Service Right of said Armstrong. Entered 4 July 1785. Signed Oct 8, 1787.

Page   332 - JOHN DREW - NC - May 28, 1789
This indenture made 1 May 1789 between James Bosley of one part and John Drew of other part. James Bosley conveyed unto John Drew one half lot in the town of Nashville, known by Lot No. 8.

Page   332 - THOMAS CLARK - Nc - No. 29 - Reg. May 28, 1789

By an Act for the relief of the Officers and Soldiers of the Continental Line, in consideration of the bravery and zeal of Thomas Clark, a lieutenant in the said line, granted unto Thomas Clark a tract of land containing 2560 acres in Davidson County on the south side of Cumberland River. Beginning on the river bank opposite the upper end of the first island above the mouth of Red River Letitia Archer's corner. Surveyed for Thomas Clark Nov 30, 1784 by Henry Rutherford, D.S. in consequence of a Military Warrant No. 77. Located July 13, 1784. Mar 14, 1786.

Page   333 - WILLIAM HUGHLETT - NC - No. 551 - Reg. May 4, 1789

By an Act for the relief of the officers and Soldiers of the Continental Line, in consequence of the bravery and zeal of Abraham Vaughan, a private in the said line, granted unto William Hughlett, assignee of Abraham Vaughan, a tract of land containing 640 acres in Davidson County on both sides of the second large creek above Caleb's Preemption on the south side of Richland Creek. Surveyed for said Hughlett by Robert Nelson, D.S. in consequence of a Military Warrant No. 930. Located Jan 16, 1785. Sept 15, 1787.

Page   333 - STEPHEN CANTRELL - NC - No. 269 - Reg. May 4, 1789

For 10 lbs per 100 acres paid by Stephen Cantrell granted unto said Cantrell a tract of land containing 640 acres in Davidson County. Surveyed for said Cantrell Aug 6, 1784 by James Sanders, D.S. in consequence of a Warrant No. 316. Located Feb 28, 1784. July 13, 1788.

Page   333 - GEE BRADLEY - NC - No. 577 - Reg. June 19, 1789

By an Act for the relief of the officers and Soldiers of the Continental Line, in consideration of the bravery and zeal of Gee Bradley, a captain in the said line, granted unto Gee Bradley a tract of land containing 3840 acres in Davidson County on the south side of Cumberland River on a large creek below Harpeth River. Surveyed for Gee Bradley Nov 20, 1785 by John Buchanan, D.S. in consequence of a Military Warrant No. 323. Located July 31, 1784. Sept 15, 1787.

Page   334 - THOMAS HICKMAN - No. 758 - Reg. Jun 19, 1789

By an Act for the relief of the officers and Soldiers of the Continental Line, in consideration of the bravery and zeal of James Cannon, a private in the said line, granted unto Thomas Hickman, assignee of said James Cannon, a tract of land containing 640 acres in Davidson County on the first creek that empties into the east fork of Stones River above the mouth of Bradleys Creek on the east side. Surveyed for Thomas Hickman Sept 3, 1787 by James Sanders, D.S. in consequence of a Military Warrant No. 2638. Located Aug 30, 1787. July 13, 1788.

Page   334 - THOMAS ISBELL - NC - No. 484 - Reg. June 19, 1789

By an Act for the relief of the officers and Soldiers of the Continental Line, in consideration of the bravery and zeal of Hardy Alway, a private of the said line, granted unto Thomas Isbell, assignee of Hardy Alway, a tract of land containing 640 acres in Davidson County on the south side of Big Barren on a creek (large) known by the name of Long Creek of Barren River. Surveyed for Thomas Isbell Dec 7, 1786 by Thomas Hickman, D.S. in consequence of a Military Warrant No. 2784. Located Nov 24, 1786. Sept 15, 1787.

Page   334 - BLOUNT WHITMELL - NC - No. 616 - Reg. June 19, 1789

By an Act for the relief of the Officers and Soldiers of the Continental Line, in consideration of the bravery and zeal of Blount Whitmell, a subalternate in the said line, granted unto Blount Whitmell a tract of land containing 824 acres in Davidson County at the mouth of Big Harpeth River on the west side. Surveyed for Blount Whitmell Oct 14, 1785 by Robert Weakley, D.S. in consequence of a Military Warrant No. 342. Located June 28, 1784. Sept 15, 1787.

Page   335 - NATHANIEL HAYS - NC - No. 24 - Reg. June 19, 1789

For 10 lbs per 100 acres paid by Nathaniel Hays was granted a tract of land containing 640 acres in Davidson County including a spring which lies in the intrance into Jones Bent on the south side of Cumberland River adjoining John Donelson's line and corner of Hugh Hays. Surveyed for Nathaniel Hays June 17, 1785 by Daniel Smith, agreeable to a Warrant No. 655. Entered Jan 6, 1786. Apr 17, 1786.

Page   335 - HUGH HAYS - NC - No. 87 - Reg. Jun 19, 1789

For 10 lbs per 100 acres paid by Hugh Hays was granted a tract of land containing 640 acres in Davidson County lying at the entrance into Jones bend on the south side of Cumberland River. Surveyed for Hugh Hays Jun 18, 1785 by Daniel Smith agreeable to a Warrant No. 654. Located Jan 8, 1785. Apr 17, 1786.

Page   335 - JOHN McMURRY - NC - No. 143 - Jun 20, 1789

For 10 lbs per 100 acres paid by John McMurry was granted a tract of land containing 640 acres in Davidson County on the waters of Big Harpeth adjoining William Marshal's corner. Surveyed for John McMurry Feb 21, 1785 by John Buchanan, D.S. agreeable to a Warrant No. 612. Entry dated Oct 30, 1784. Apr 17, 1786.

Page   336 - JAMES TATUM - NC - No. 87 - Reg. Jun 22, 1789

By an Act for the relief of the Officers and Soldiers of the Continental Line, in consideration of the bravery and zeal of James Tatum, a lieutenant in the said line, granted unto said James Tatum a tract of land containing 2560 acres in Davidson County. Beginning on the bank of the Cumberland River and on the Virginia Line. Surveyed for James Tatum by Edwin Hickman 12 Aug 1785 in consequence of a Military Warrant No. 335. Located July 31, 1784. Mar 14, 1786.

Page   336 - JOHN BAPTIST ASHE - NC - No. 257 - Jun 22, 1789

By an Act for the relief of the Officers and Soldiers of the Continental Line, in consideration of the bravery and zeal of John Baptist Ashe, a lieutenant in the said line, granted unto John Baptist Ashe a tract of land containing 4450 acres in Davidson County on the north side of Tennessee River on Ashes Creek adjoining Joseph Brevard's corner. Surveyed for John Baptist Ashe Aug 12, 1785 by Henry Rutherford, D.S. in consequence of a Military Warrant No. 496. Located 9 May 1785. Mar 14, 1786.

Page   336 - JAMES COLE MONTFLORENCE - NC - No. 878 - Reg. July 2, 1789

By an Act for the relief of the Officers and Soldiers of the Continental Line, in consideration of the bravery and zeal of Samuel Griffis, a sergeant, granted unto James Cole Montflorence, assignee of said Griffis, a tract of land containing 1000 acres in

Davidson County on Weakleys Creek a west fork of Barton Creek on the south side of Cumberland River below Harpeth River adjoining James Cole Montflorence's corner. Surveyed for said Montflorence Mar 10, 1786 by Robert Weakley, D.S. in consequence of a Military Warrant No. 2125. Located Nov 23, 1785. Jan 17, 1789.

Page   337 - JOHN RICE - NC - No. 55 - Reg. July 17, 1789

By an Act for the relief of the Officers and Soldiers of the Continental Line, in consideration of the services of William Ramsey, a chain carrier to the Commissioners, granted unto John Rice, assignee of William Ramsey, a tract of land containing 640 acres in Davidson County on the head of John Milners Creek on the waters of Richland Creek. Surveyed for John Rice Feb 19, 1789 by Robert Nelson, D.S. in consequence of a Warrant No. 180. Entered Jan 24, 1784. Apr 25, 1789.

Page   337 - JOHN RICE - NC - No. 884 - Reg. July 17, 1789

By an Act for the relief of the Officers and Soldiers of the Continental Line, in consideration of the bravery and zeal of Jasper Lane, a private in the said line, granted unto John Rice, assignee of Jasper Lane, a tract of land containing 640 acres in Davidson County adjoining said Rice's claim as assignee of William Ramsey. Surveyed for John Rice Feb 19, 1789 by Robert Nelson, D.S. in consequence of a Military Warrant No. 865. Located June 20, 1785. Apr 25, 1789.

Page   337 - JOHN RICE - NC - No. 885 - Reg. Jul 17, 1789

By an Act for the relief of the Officers and Soldiers of the Continental Line, in consideration of the bravery and zeal of Ezekiel Realy, a private in the said line, granted unto John Rice, assignee of said Realy, a tract of land containing 428 acres in Davidson County adjoining his entry as assignee of William Ramsey. Surveyed for John Rice Feb 19, 1789 by Robert Nelson, D.S. Warrant No. 676. Located Oct 7, 1785. Apr 25, 1789.

Page   338 - JOHN RICE - NC - No. 779 - Reg. July 17, 1789

By an Act for the relief of the Officers and Soldiers of the Continental Line, in consideration of the bravery and zeal of Federick Blansell, a private in the said line, granted unto John Rice, assignee of said Federick Blansell, a tract of land containing 228 acres in Sumner County on the waters of the Caney Fork. Surveyed for John Rice Oct 16, 1787 by James Sanders, D.S. in consequence of a Military Warrant No. 1930. Located Sep 21, 1787. July 11, 1788.

Page   338 - JOHN RICE - NC - No. 54 - Reg. July 17, 1789

By an Act for the relief of the Officers and Soldiers of the Continental line, inconsideration of the services of Col. Martin Armstrong, surveyor, granted unto John Rice, assignee of said Armstrong, a tract of land containing 168 acres in Davidson County. Beginning on the east side of Mill Creek on John Buchanan's line, on Joseph Martin's line, James Bryant's line, and John Mulherin's corner. Surveyed for John Rice by John Bucchanan by virtue of a Service Right of said Armstrong. Entered July 7, 1785. Apr 25, 1789.

Page   338 - SOLOMON KITTS - NC - July 17, 1789

This indenture made 20 May 1789 between John Rice of Davidson County of one part and Solomon Kitts, Esq., merchant late of Baltimore Town Baltimore County, State of Maryland, of other part. John Rice conveyed unto Solomon Kitts a tract of land containing 640 acres in Davidson County on the headwaters of John Milner's Creek a branch of Richland Creek. Beginning at the north east corner of another tract of land late the property of said John Rice as assignee of William Ramsey. This July Term 1789.

Page   339 - SOLOMON KITTS - NC - Jul 17, 1789
This indenture made 20 May 1789 between John Rice of Davidson County of one part and Solomon Kitts, Esq., merchant of Baltimore Town in Baltimore County, State of Maryland, of other part. John Rice conveyed unto Solomon Kitts 640 acres in Davidson County on the headwaters of John Milner's Creek a branch of Richland Creek. July Term 1789.

Page   340 - SOLOMON KITT - NC - Jul 17, 1789
This indenture made 20 May 1789 between John Rice of Davidson County of one part and Solomon Kitt of Baltimore Town, Baltimore County, State of Maryland, of other part. John Rice conveyed unto Solomon Kitt a tract of land containing 428 acres in Davidson County on the headwaters of John Milner's Creek a branch of Richland Creek, adjoining a tract late the property of said John Rice as assignee of William Ramsey. July Term 1789.

Page   340 - ROBERT WEAKLEY - NC - Jul 22, 1789
This indenture made 6 July 1789 between Absolom Hooper of Davidson County of one part and Robert Weakley of same place of other part. Absolom Hooper conveyed unto Robert Weakley a tract of land containing 230 acres in Davidson County on the north of Cumberland River and on both sides of Whites Creek adjoining Peter Sides corner which was said Sides now belonging to Eleazer Hamilton's. Said land granted unto said Absolom Hooper by State of North Carolina aforesaid Oct 8, 1787 for the services of Col. Martin Armstrong, surveyor for the Continental Line of the State of North Carolina which grant is No. 33, and recorded. July Term 1789.

Page   341 - MARK BROWN SAPPINGTON - July 21, 1789
This indenture made July 1, 1789 between Thomas Molloy of Davidson County of one part and Mark Brown Sappington of same place of other part. Thomas Molloy conveyed unto Mark Brown Sappington a tract of land containing 250 acres in Davidson County on the north side of Cumberland River about a quarter of a mile above Whites Creek adjoining James Brown's corner. Said land being part of the land granted to Robert Nelson by State of North Carolina dated Oct 8, 1787, No. 12. Conveyed by said Nelson to said Molloy and also part of a tract of 640 acres granted to said Molloy as assignee of William Spencer's heirs. July Term 1789.

Page   342 - ADAM HOPE - July 21, 1789
This indenture made 6 July 1789 between Jason Thompson of Davidson County of one part and Adam Hope of same place of other part. Jason Thompson conveyed unto Adam Hope a tract of land containing 320 acres in Davidson County on Mill Creek. Which land said Jason Thompson obtained by patent dated Mar 7, 1786 as assignee of Alexander Rammage, a private in the Continental Line. July Term 1789.

Page   342 - JOHN HOPE - Jul 21, 1789
This indenture made 6 July 1789 between John Johnston of Davidson County of one part and John Hope of same place of other part. John Johnston conveyed unto John Hope a tract of land containing 320 acres in Davidson County on the north side of Cumberland River and on the waters of Dry Creek adjoining Daniel Frazer's line, Joseph Shaw's boundary and John Walker's corner. Said land being part of a tract granted to said Johnston out of the Territory's office for the State of North Carolina bearing date April 7, 1786. This July 7, 1789.

Page   343 - MARK BROWN SAPPINGTON - Jul 21, 1789
This indenture made 7 July 1789 between John Sappington of Davidson County of one part and Mark Brown Sappington of same place of other part. John Sappington conveyed unto Mark Brown Sappington a tract of land containing 200 acres in Davidson County on the south side of Cumberland River adjoining John Boyd's corner. July Term 1789.

Page   344 - JAMES RUSSELL - July 21, 1789
This indenture made July 6, 1789 between Jonathan Drake of Davidson County of one part and James Russell of same place of other part. Jonathan Drake conveyed unto James Russell a tract of land containing 30 acres in Davidson County adjoining Argolus Getor's corner on John Marney's line. The land being part of a Preemption of 640 acres granted to Benjamin Drake by patent and dated Apr 17, 1786. No. 169 by Benjamin Drake conveyed to Jonathan Drake by deed dated Apr 7, 1788. July 6, 1789.

Page   344 - WILLIAM McEWEN - July 21, 1789
This indenture made 9 July 1789 between Samuel Barton of Davidson County of one part and William McEwen of Kentucky in the State of Virginia of other part. Samuel Barton conveyed unto William McEwen a tract of land containing 320 acres in Davidson County on the waters of Big Harpeth River adjoining Andrew Goff's corner and Thomas Spencer's line. Which land was granted to said Barton by patent dated July 10, 1788 and No. 86. July Term 1789.

Page   345 - JAMES COLE MONTFLORENCE - NC - Jul 27, 1789
This indenture made Feb 17, 1789 between Robert Norris of Halifax Town, State of North Carolina of one part and James Cole Montflorence of Sumner County, NC of other part. Robert Norris conveyed unto James Cole Montflorence a tract of land containing 213 acres, being part of that whole tract of 640 acres granted unto said Robert Norris by the State aforesaid for the services of Daniel Valentine, the grant of which is No. 836, lying in Davidson County on the waters of Caney Fork adjoining Elijah Robertson's corner. July Term 1789.

Page   345 - WILLIAM TAITT - NC - July 27, 1789
This indenture made 18 Nov 1788 between Robert Nelson of Davidson County of one part and William Taitt of same place of other part. Robert Nelson conveyed unto William Taitt a tract of land containing 640 acres in Davidson County on the north side of Cumberland River joining Joseph Flemming's survey on a small creek that empties into the river at McFarlin's cabin about three quarters of a mile from the river. Which land was

granted to said Nelson by patent dated 15 Sept 1787. July Term 1789.

Page   346 - DAVID SHELBY - NC - July 28, 1789
            This indenture made 6 July 1789 between David Hay of Davidson County of
one part and David Shelby of Sumner County, NC of other part. David Hay conveyed unto
David Shelby one half of Lot No. 37 in town of Nashville containing and including the
house and other improvements thereon. July Term 1789.

Page   346 - SAMUEL McCULLOCH - NC - July 28, 1789
            This indenture made Mar 5, 1789 between John Baptist Ashe of the County of
Halifax, North Carolina of one part and Samuel McCulloch, son of Benjamin McCulloch of
same place of other part. John Baptist Ashe conveyed unto Samuel McCulloch a tract of
land containing 4450 acres in Davidson County on the north side of Tennessee River on
Ashe's Creek adjoining Alexander Bound's upper corner, Joseph Brevard's corner. Proven by
Howel Tatum. July Term 1789.

Page   347 - JOHN TUCKER - NC - July 28, 1789
            This indenture made 10 July 1789 between Mosses Shelby of one part and
John Tucker of Davidson County of other part. Mosses Shelby conveyed unto John Tucker a
tract of land containing 300 acres and No. 67 in the patent. Adjoining Edwin Hickman's
survey, Stuarts Creek a fork of Stones River. July Term 1789.

Page   348 - MATHEW MOORE - NC - July 29m 1789
            This indenture made Mar 18, 1789 between Thomas Isbell and Phebe Isbell of
Surry County, North Carolina of one part and Mathew Moore of same place of other part.
Thomas Isbell and Phebe Isbell conveyed unto Mathew Moore a tract of land containing 640
acres in Davidson County on the south side of Big Barren on a large creek known by the
name of Long Creek of Big Barren River. The same being confirmed by State of North
Carolina unto said Thomas Isbell by grant dated Sept 15, 1787. Proven by Edwin Hickman.
July Term 1789.

Page   349 - EDWIN HICKMAN - NC - July 29, 1789
            This indenture made 11 July 1789 between Mosses Shelby of Tennessee County
of one part and Edwin Hickman of Davidson County of other part. Mosses Shelby conveyed
unto Edwin Hickman a tract of land containing 300 acres in Davidson County adjoining
Mulherin's line, bank of Stuarts Creek. The said land being part of said Mosses Shelby's
Guard Right, the Warrant No. 242. July Term 1789.

Page   349 - CHRISTOPHER GUISE - NC - No. 42 - Reg. Aug 17, 1789
            By an Act for the relief of the Officers and Soldiers of the Continental line,
in consideration of the services of Col. Martin Armstrong, surveyor, granted unto
Christopher Guise, assignee of said Armstrong, a tract of land containing 100 acres in
Davidson County on the waters of Guises Creek. Surveyed for said Christopher Guise Jan
18, 1786 by William Murry, D.S. by virtue of a Service Right entered 9 Apr 1785. Dated
Oct 8, 1787.

Page   350 - ABSOLOM HOOPER - NC - No. 33, Reg. Aug 18, 1789

By an Act for the relief of the Officers and Soldiers of the Continental Line, in consideration of the services of Col. Martin Armstrong, surveyor, granted unto Absolom Hooper, assignee of the said Armstrong, a tract of land containing 230 acres in Davidson County on the north side of Cumberland on both sides of Whites Creek adjoining Peter Sides corner. Surveyed for said Hooper Sept 9, 1785 by Edwin Hickman by virtue of a Service Right of said Armstrong. Located Nov 4, 1784. Oct 8, 1787.

Page   350 - JACOB MOYERS - NC - No. 38 - Reg. Aug 24, 1789

By an Act for the relief of the Officers and Soldiers of the Continental line, in consideration of the services of Col. Martin Armstrong, surveyor, granted unto Jacob Moyers a tract of land containing 400 acres in Davidson County on the east side of Stones River adjoining Cornelius Rudles' line, also at the mouth of Searcys Creek. Surveyed for Jacob Moyers Apr 1, 1786 by John Bucchanan, D.S. by virtue of a Service Right of said Armstrong, entered Nov 19, 1785. Oct 8, 1787.

Page   350 - ANTHONY CRUTCHER - NC - No. 579 - Reg. Aug 27, 1789

By an Act for the relief of the Officers and Soldiers of the Continental Line, in consideration of the bravery and zeal of John Hamilton, a private in the said line, granted unto Anthony Crutcher, assignee of said Hamilton, a tract of land containing 640 acres in Davidson County on the north side of Cumberland River and on the north side of Sycamore Creek adjoining Crutcher's corner. Surveyed for said Crutcher Sept 30, 1786 by Robert Weakley, D.S. Warrant No. 1845. Located June 29, 1786. Sept 15, 1786.

Page   351 - CAPT. JOHN INGLES - NC - No. 414 - Reg. Aug 27, 1789

By an Act for the relief of the Officers and Soldiers of the Continental line, in consideration of the bravery and zeal of John Ingles, Esq., a captain in the said line, granted unto John Ingles a tract of land containing 3840 acres in Davidson County on the waters of Bledsoes Creek adjoining Robert Deshies south west corner, to Oratio Rolls' corner to Robert Montgomery's line and to David Wilson's corner and to Roger Topps' heirs. Including a Preemption of 640 acres obtained by Richard Hogan so that the bounds now contain 4480 acres. Surveyed for John Ingles May 20, 1785 by James Sanders, D.S. by virtue of a Military Warrant No. 294. Located Apr 4, 1785. Sept 15, 1787.

Page   351 - GEORGE MAXELL - NC - No. 2 - Reg. Aug 27, 1789

By an Act for the relief of the Officers and Soldiers of the Continental Line, in consideration of the services of George Maxell, one of the Guards to the Commissioners, granted unto George Maxell a tract of land containing 320 acres in Davidson County on Kaspers Creek. Beginning in Kasper Mansker's line on Kennedys branch, to Mathew Payne's land. Surveyed for George Maxell Jan 22, 1785 by Daniel Smith, D.S. agreeable to a Warrant No. 194. Entered Jan 27, 1784. Oct 8, 1787.

Page   352 - ANTHONY HART - NC - No. 574 - Reg. Sept 14, 1789

By an Act for the relief of the Officers and Soldiers of the Continental Line, in consideration of the bravery and zeal of Isaac Reddick, a private in the said line, granted unto Anthony Hart, assignee of the heirs of Isaac Reddick, a tract of land containing 640 acres in Davidson County on the north side of Cumberland River on the west fork of Little

Brush Creek the waters of Red River adjoining John Nichols' corner. Surveyed for Anthony Hart Sept 29, 1786 by Robert Weakley, D.S. by virtue of a Military Warrant No. 2957. Located Apr 29, 1786. Sept 15, 1787.

Page   352 - ANTHONY HART - NC - No. 573 - Reg. Sept 1, 1789
By an Act for the relief of the Officers and Soldiers of the Continental Line, in consideration of the bravery and zeal of Abraham Burk, a private in the said line, granted unto Anthony Hart, assignee of the heirs of Abraham Burk, a tract of land containing 640 acres in Davidson County on the south side of Big Barren River on a creek known by the name of Long Creek of Barren. Surveyed for said Hart Dec 7, 1786 by Thomas Hickman, D.S. in consequence of a Military Warrant No. 2707. Located Nov 24, 1786. Sept 15, 1787.

Page   352 - ANTHONY HART - NC - No. 72 - Sept 1, 1789
By an Act for the relief of the Officers and Soldiers of the Continental Line, in consideration of the bravery and zeal of Obediah Calvin, a private in the said line, granted unto Anthony Hart, assignee of Obediah Calvin, a tract of land containing 640 acres in Davidson County on the north side of Cumberland River adjoining a survey of Robert Weakley on the north which includes Turnbulls horse sturnp. Surveyed for Anthony Hart Oct 14, 1786 by Robert Weakley, D.S.   Warrant No. 3423. Located Apr 28, 1786.   July 13, 1788.

Page   353 - ANTHONY HART - NC - No. 716 - Reg. Sept 1, 1789
By an Act for the relief of the Officers and Soldiers of the Continental Line, in consideration of the bravery and zeal of Mosses Madry, a private in the said line, granted unto Anthony Hart, assignee of the heirs of Mosses Madry, a tract of land containing 640 acres in Davidson County on the head waters of Kerrs and Nelson Creeks above Col. Armstrong's claim. Surveyed for Anthony Hart July 30, 1786 by Robert Nelson, D.S. in consequence of a Military Warrant No. 3084. Located Apr 29, 1786. July 13, 1788.

Page   353 - ANTHONY HART - NC - No. 572 - Reg. Sept 1, 1789
By an Act for the relief of the officers and Soldiers of the Continental Line, in consideration of the bravery and zeal of Samuel Lassiter Lewis, a private in the said line, granted unto Anthony Hart, assignee of the heirs of Samuel Lassiter Lewis, a tract of land containing 640 acres in Davidson County lying the trace near the head of Gilkisons Creek adjoining on the trace that leads from Thompsons settlement up the Sulphur Fork. Surveyed for Anthony Hart July 30, 1786 by Robert Nelson, D.S. in consequence of a Military Warrant No. 2671. Located Apr 29, 1786. Sept 15, 1787.

Page   353 - ANTHONY HART - NC - No. 675 - Reg. Sept 1, 1789
By an Act for the relief of the Officers and Soldiers of the Continental Line, in consideration of the bravery and zeal of William Ricoes, a private in the said line, granted unto Anthony Hart, assignee of the heirs of William Ricoes, a tract of land containing 640 acres in Davidson County on the west of Turnbulls clay lick on the head of Milners Creek adjoining Titus' and Stump's line. Surveyed for Anthony Hart Dec 15, 1786 by Robert Nelson, D.S. in consequence of a Military Warrant No. 2815. Located Apr 29, 1786. Dec 12, 1787.

Page   354 - ANTHONY HART - NC - No. 678 - Reg. Sept 1, 1789

By an Act for the relief of the Officers and Soldiers of the Continental Line, in consideration of the bravery and zeal of John Sellers, a private in the said line, granted unto Anthony Hart, assignee of John Sellers, a tract of land containing 640 acres in Davidson County on the south side of Cumberland River on the west boundary of Captain Fawn's survey. Surveyed for Anthony Hart Dec 16, 1786 by Robert Nelson, D.S. in consequence of a Military Warrant No. 2763. Located May 12, 1786. Dec 8, 1787.

Page   354 - OBED ROBERTS - NC - No. 5 - Reg. Sept 1, 1789

By an Act for the relief of the Officers and Soldiers of the Continental Line, in consideration of the services of Col. Martin Armstrong, surveyor, granted unto Obed Roberts, assignee of said Armstrong, a tract of land containing 640 acres in Davidson County on Camp Creek, the north waters of Duck River. Surveyed for Obed Roberts May 4, 1785 by William Murry, D.S. by virtue of a Service Right of said Armstrong, No. (blank). Entry date ___ --, 1785.

Page   354 - JAMES WEST GREEN - NC - No. 532 - Reg. Sept 16, 1789

By an Act for the relief of the Officers and Soldiers of the Continental Line, in consideration of the bravery and zeal of James West Green, a surgeon in the said line, was granted a tract of land containing 4800 acres in Davidson County on the first big creek below Harpeth on the south side of Cumberland adjoining General Nash's south boundary. Surveyed for said James West Green June 25, 1785 by Joseph Brock, D.S. Warrant No. 430. Located Mar 18, 1785. Sept 15, 178_.

Page   355 - JESSEE REED to JAMES COLE MONTFLORENCE - Oct 8, 1789

This indenture made 19 Sept 1789 between Jesse Reed, Esq. of Davidson County of one part and James Cole Montflorence of same place of other part. Jessee Reed conveyed unto James Cole Montflorence a tract of land containing 640 acres in Davidson County all of which were granted by the State for the Officers and Soldiers of the Continental Line. The numbers of the warrants are: 2003, 3429, 2741, 3506, 3427, 2633, 3421, 3715, 3507, 2652, 3457, 3509, 3501 and 1877. All fourteen tracts of land of 640 acres each. Witnesses: George Nugg, Daniel James and Thomas Crutcher. Oct 5, 1789.

Page 1 - JOSEPH BROCK - NC - No. 841 - Reg. Oct 8, 1789
By an Act for the relief of the Officers and Soldiers of the Continental Line, in consideration of the bravery and zeal of James Harrington, a private in the said line, granted unto Joseph Brock, assignee of the heirs of James Harrington, a tract of land containing 640 acres in Davidson County on the north side of Cumberland River on the waters of the Sulphur Forks of Red River. Beginning at the trace that leads from Holley's to Red River Old Station. Surveyed for Joseph Brock July 14, 1788 by Anthony Foster, D.S. in consequence of Military Warrant No. 3351. Located June 21, 1788. Jan 17, 1789.

PAGE 1 - JOSEPH BROCK - NC - No. 832 - Reg. Oct 8, 1789
By an Act for the relief of the Officers and Soldiers of the Continental Line, in consideration of the bravery and zeal of Chas. Holland, a private in the said line, granted unto Joseph Brock, assignee of the heirs of said Holland, a tract of land containing 640 acres in Davidson County on the north side of Cumberland River. Surveyed for Joseph Brock Dec 11, 1787 by A. Foster, D.S. in consequence of a Military Warrant No. 3467. Located Nov 24, 1787. Jan 17, 1789.

Page 1 - JOSEPH BROCK - NC - No. 826 - Reg. Oct 8, 1789
By an Act for the relief of the Officers and Soldiers of the Continental Line, in consideration of the bravery and zeal of Dred Simpson, a private in the said line, granted unto Joseph Brock,assignee of the heirs of said Dred Simpson, a tract of land containing 640 acres in Davidson County on the north side of Cumberland River about one or two miles of the Buffalo Pasture. Surveyed for Joseph Brock Dec 20, 1787 by A. Foster, D.S. in consequence of a Military Warrant No. 3482. Located Nov 24, 1787. Jan 17, 1789.

Page 2 - JOSEPH BROCK - NC - No. 846 - Oct 8, 1789
By an Act for the relief of the Officers and Soldiers of the Continental Line, in consideration of the bravery and zeal of Robert Beach, a private of the said line, granted unto Joseph Brock, assignee of the heirs of said Brock, a tract of land containing 640 acres in Davidson County on the north side of Cumberland River on Bear Creek about four miles south of Buffalo Pasture. Surveyed for Joseph Brock Dec 21, 1787 by A. Foster, D.S. in consequence of a Military Warrant No. 3443. Located Nov 21, 1787. Jan 17, 1789.

Page 2 - PHILLIP BUCKNER - Oct 8, 1789
This indenture made 2 May 1789 between Joseph Brock of Spotsylvania County of one part and Phillip Buckner of the County of Caroline of the other part. Joseph Brock conveyed unto Phillip Buckner a tract of land containing 3200 acres on the north side of Cumberland River in Davidson County, NC, being the contents of five patents dated Jan 17, 1789 granted to Joseph Brock as assignee of sundry persons for Military Services, one of which lies about two miles from the Buffalo Pasture. One which lies on Boar Creek about four miles south of said Buffalo Pasture. One other lying on the Sulphur Forks of Red River near the trace that leads from Holly to Red River Old Station. The other lying near the Buffalo Pasture. 2 May 1789.

Page 4 - CHARLES GOWARD - NC - Oct 22, 1789

This indenture made 8 Aug 1789 between Lardner Clark of Davidson County of one part and Charles Gower of same place of other part. Lardner Clark conveyed unto Charles Goward all that entire half of town lot of one acre in Nashville, Davidson County and known by Lot No. 7. Oct 9, 1789.

Page 4 - ROBERT WEAKLEY - NC - Oct 22, 1789

This indenture made 9 Oct 1789 between Evan Shelby of Tennessee County, NC of one part and Robert Weakley of Davidson County of other part. Evan Shelby conveyed unto Robert Weakley a tract of land containing 320 acres in Tennessee County north of the Cumberland River about eighty poles below the first island in said river, above the mouth of Red River. It being half of a Preemption obtained by Ephraim Pratt. Oct 9, 1789.

Page 5 - GEORGE WALKER - NC - Oct 27, 1789

This indenture made 9 Oct 1789 between Lardner Clark of Davidson County of one part and George Walker of other part. Lardner Clark conveyed unto George Walker a certain parcel of ground in the town of Nashville and known as No. 57. Oct Term 1789.

Page 5 - ANTHONY FOSTER - NC - Oct 22, 1789

This indenture made 9 Oct 1789 between David Hay, Esq., High Sheriff of Davidson County, of one part and Anthony Foster of same place of other part. David Hay, High Sheriff, conveyed unto Anthony Foster a certain lot or parcel of ground No. 75 which lot was sold by virtue of an execution obtained by John Rains against Henry Lanier. Oct Term 1789.

Page 6 - LAWRENCE THOMPSON - NC - Oct 22, 1789

This indenture made 6 Oct 1789 between Eusebius Bushnell and William Dobbins of Davidson County of the one part and Lawrence Thompson of Sumner County of other part. Said Bushnell and Dobbins conveyed unto Lawrence Thompson a tract of land containing 640 acres in Davidson County on the south side of Cumberland River, adjoining an entry of Edwin Hickman No. 1646 of 640 acres and an entry and warrant No. 1672 assigned to Eusebius Bushnell and William Dobbins by Benjamin Lyles. Oct Term 1789.

Page 6 - SAMUEL EWING - NC - No. 226 - Reg. Oct 23, 1789

For 10 lbs per 100 acres paid by Samuel Ewing, was given a tract of land containing 640 acres in Davidson County on the north side of Red River on the west fork. Surveyed for Samuel Ewing Apr 28, 1786 by Robert Nelson, D.S. in consequence of a Warrant No. 610. Located Oct 21, 1784. July 10, 1788.

Page 7 - JOHN SAPPINGTON - NC - Oct 23, 1789

This indenture made 6 Aug 1789 between Thomas James of Davidson County of one part and John Sappington of same place of other part. Thomas James conveyed unto John Sappington all that entire town lot of one acre of land in town of Nashville and known as Lot No. 2. Oct 7, 1789.

Page 7 - JOHN MARNEY - NC - Oct 23, 1789
This indenture made Apr 7, 1789 between Thomas and George Blackamore of Davidson County of one part and John Marney of the other. Thomas and george Blackamore conveyed unto John Marney a tract of land containing 227 acres in Davidson County on both sides of Whites Creek, adjoining Heaton and Drake's Preemption on the bank of Heaton Creek. Proven by William Blackamore and Daniel Frazier. Oct Term 1789.

Page 8 - BENJAMIN JOSTLING - NC - Oct 23, 1789
This indenture made 1 Nov 1789 between Eusebius Bushnell and William Dobbins odf Davidson County of one part and Benjamin Jostling of same place of other part. Eusebius Bushnell and William Dobbins conveyed unto Benjamin Jostling a tract of land containing 640 acres on the waters of Stones River on a small creek which is known asBushnells Creek and on Major Blount's line and at Bushnell's corner of a 1000 acres No. 1660. Which grant was granted unto said Bushnell and Dobbins by patent dated Sept 15, 1787. Proven by William A. Pease and Louis Reily. Oct Term 1789.

Page 8 - WILLIAM SANDS - NC - Oct 23, 1789
This indenture made 6 Aug 1789 between John Sappington of Davidson County of one part and William Sands of same place of other part. John Sappington conveyed unto William Sands all that town lot in the town of Nashville and known as Lot No. 2 containing one acre of land. Proven by Josiah Love and James Cole Montflorence. Oct Term 1789.

Page 9 - ROBERT CRESWELL - NC - Oct 23, 1789
This indenture made 3 Oct 1789 between Eusebius Bushnell and William Dobbins of Davidson County of one part and Robert Creswell of Herford County, Maryland of other part. Eusebius Bushnell and William Dobbins conveyed unto Robert Creswell a tract of land containing 640 acres in Davidson County on the waters of Stuarts Creek the waters of Stones River a branch of Cumberland River, adjoining Moses Shelby's corner. Said land known by No. 265 granted to the said Bushnell and Dobbins, assignees of the heirs of Jacob Givin. Oct Term 1789.

Page 9 - WILLIAM ARMSTRONG - NC - Oct 27, 1789
This indenture made and signed between Hugh Thompson of one part and William Armstrong of other part, both of town of Nashville, NC. Hugh Thompson conveyed unto William Armstrong one lot of ground in the town of Nashville containing one acre of land and known as Lot No. 66. Proven by Isaac Woolard and John Parks. Oct Term 1789.

Page 10 - PHILEMON THOMAS - NC Oct 27, 1789
This indenture made Aug 1, 1789 between Eusebius Bushnell and William Dobbins of Davidson County of one part and Philemon Thomas of Woodford County, Kentucky of the other part. Said Bushnell and Dobbins conveyed unto Philemon Thomas a tract of land containing 1622 acres in Davidson County on the main east fork of Stones River, adjoining Isaac Shelby's 5000 acre survey, granted unto him for his services as Commissioner appointed to settle the claim of Preemption and lay off the boundary of land granted the Officers and Soldiers of the Continental Line of this State. Which land said Bushnell and Dobbins obtained by patents dated Sept 15, 1787, as assignees of Mathew Wood, a captain in the said line. Oct Term 1789.

Page   10 - PHILEMON THOMAS - NC - Oct 27, 1789

(2nd page)   This indenture made Aug 1, 1789 between Eusebius Bushnell and William Dobbins of Davidson County of one part and Philemon Thomas of Woodford County, Kentucky of other part. Said Bushnell and Dobbins conveyed unto Philemon Thomas a tract of land containing 1000 acres in Davidson County on the waters of the east fork of Stones River, adjoining Col. Isaac Shelby's corner. Which land said Bushnell and Dobbins obtained by patent dated Sept 15, 1787 as assignee of Henry Cole, a drummer in the Continental Line. Proven by Robert Weakley and Griswold Latimore. Oct Term 1789.

Page   11 - NATHANIEL OVERALL - NC - Oct 27, 1789

This indenture made 7 Oct 1789 between John Johnston of Davidson County of one part and Nathaniel Overall of same place of other part. John Johnston conveyed unto Nathaniel Overall a tract of land containing 320 acres in Davidson County on the north side of Cumberland River on the head waters of Dry Creek, adjoining Daniel Frazier's field. Said land granted unto said Johnston dated year of 1786. Oct Term 1789.

Page   12 - HUGH THOMPSON - NC - Oct 28, 1789

This indenture made Sept 17, 1789 between Lardner Clark of Davidson County of one part and Hugh Thompson of same place of other part. Lardner Clark conveyed unto Hugh Thompson all that town lot in Nashville and known as Lot No. 66 containing one acre of land, also that other town lot in Nashville and known as Lot No. 67 containing one acre of land. Proven by James Cole Montflorence. Oct Term 1789.

Page   12 - JAMES COLE MONTFLORENCE - NC - Oct 29, 1789

This indenture made 5 Aug 1789 between William Crutcher of Davidson County of one part and James Cole Montflorence of same place of other part. Said Crutcher conveyed unto James Cole Montflorence all his right and interest in that town lot of one acre in town of Nashville and known as Lot No. 19. Oct Term 1789.

Page   13 - THOMAS HICKMAN and JAMES COLE MONTFLORENCE - NC - Oct 29, 1789

This indenture made 1 Sept 1789 between Edwin Hickman of Davidson County of one part and Thomas Hickman and James Cole Montflorence of same place of other part. Edwin Hickman conveyed unto Thomas Hickman and James Cole Montflorence all that tract of land lying in Tennessee County, NC, on the north side of Cumberland River at the mouth of Brushy Creek, adjoining Headon Wells' corner, James McFarland's corner, and Robert Nelson's corner. Which tract was formerly granted by State of North Carolina to John Vance for his services. Proven by Joseph Brock and James White. Oct Term 1789.

Page   13 - EDWIN HICKMAN - NC - Oct 29, 1789

This indenture made 25 Apr 1789 between Thomas Hickman, as High Sheriff of Davidson County of one part and Edwin Hickman of same place of other part. Thomas Hickman conveyed unto Edwin Hickman a tract of land containing 640 acres in Davidson County at the mouth of Brushy Creek, adjoining James McFarland's corner, Robert Nelson's corner. Which tract of land was granted by State of North Carolina to John Vance for his services in the Continental line. Jan Term 1789 at the instance of David Shelby against James Lanier, John Vance and Joseph S(illegible).Oct Term 1789.

Page   14 -   JOSIAH LOVE, ESQ. - NC - Oct 29, 1789

This indenture made 2 Sept 1789 between John Forde of Davidson County of one part and Josiah Love, Esq. of same place of other part. John Forde conveyed unto Josiah Love all that half acre lot in town of Nashville and known as Lot No. 8. It being the half lot sold by Anthony Crutcher to James Bosley and by said Bosley to said John Forde being that half of said lot on the river of Cumberland containing one half acre of land. Oct Term 1789.

Page   14 -   JOSIAH LOVE, ESQ. - NC - Oct 29, 1789

This indenture made 20 May 1789 between John Forde of Davidson County of one part and Josiah Love of same place of other part. John Forde conveyed unto Josiah Love all that half town lot in town of Nashville and known as Lot No. 8 being the same half lot which John Forde purchased of James Bosley. Also all the lands the said John Forde holds and possesses and is entitled to in the District of Mero. Proven by Daniel James. Oct Term 1789.

Page   15 -   ANN STERN SINGLETARY & DAVID STERN SINGLETARY - Oct 29, 1789

I, John Stern Singletary of Davidson County, State of North Carolina, in consideration of the natural affection and love which I have and bear into my beloved children, Ann Stern Singletary and David Stern Singletary, have given and granted unto my daughter Ann Stern Singletary all and singular my household furniture of every kind together with one cow and calf, one heifer and one yearling heifer and to my son David Stern Singletary do give one cow and calf, one yearling and singular the goods and chattels unto said Ann Singletary and David Singletary. Test: John Thompson and James Thompson. Signed 22 Mar 1789. Signed John Stern Singletary. Acknowledged at Oct term 1789.

Page   15 -   DAVID HOOD - NC - Oct 31, 1789

This indenture made 5 Oct 1789 between Johnathan Drake of Davidson County of one part and David Hood of same place of other part. Johnathan Drake conveyed unto David Hood all that tract of land containing 41 acres in Davidson County on both sides of Whites Creek and joining Thomas James' boundary and Sarah Lucas' line and Ezekiel Smith's line. Oct Term 1789.

Page   16 -   JOHN NOWLAND - NC - Oct 31, 1789

This indenture made 10 Sept 1789 between Francis Armstrong of one part and John Nowland of other part, both of Davidson County. Francis Armstrong conveyed unto John Nowland tract of land on the south side of Cumberland River on the waters of Browns Creek adjoining Samuel Barton's Preemption on the south side it being the land occupied by John Nolen whereon he lives. Said land containing 137 acres. Proven by Benjamin Bonds and Samuel Barton. Oct Term 1789.

Page   16 -   JOHN KIRKPATRICK - NC - Oct 31, 1789

This indenture made Sept 3, 1789 between Ephraim McLane of Davidson County of one part and John Kirkpatrick of same place of other part. Ephraim McLane conveyed unto John Kirkpatrick a tract of land containing 113 acres in Davidson County on the north side of Cumberland River adjoining John Evans' line. Which land is part of two tracts the one granted to Ephraim McLane by patent dated Oct 8, 1787. The other granted to Green Hill dated Mar 7, 1786.   Proven by William Murry and Samuel Buchanan.   Oct Term 1789.

Page   17 - JOHN NEWEL - NC - Nov 2, 1789
              This indenture made 25 Apr 1789 between James Bosley of Davidson County of one part and John Newel of same place of other part.   James Bosley conveyed unto John Newel a tract of land containing 140 acres in Davidson County near the Stone Lick on south side of Cumberland River adjoining John Cockrill's corner and Peter Turney's line.   Proven by Bennett Searcy and Hugh Bell. Oct Term 1789.

Page   17 - JAMES ROBERTSON - NC - Nov 2, 1789
              This indenture made 22 Aug 1789 between Thomas Green of Davidson County of one part and James Robertson of same place of other part.   Thomas Green conveyed unto James Robertson the one half lot No. 25 containing one half acre of land in the town of Nashville. Which said half lot was conveyed to the said Green by Thomas Hickman, High Sheriff of Davidson County, by deed dated Oct 8, 1788 as property of Julius Sanders granted to him by the Commissioners by deed dated July 30, 1784 adjoining the half lot sold to William Taitt. Proven by Samuel Wilson and Justinian Cartwright. Oct Term 1789.

Page   18 - LARDNER CLARK - NC - Nov 2, 1789
              This indenture made 12 Dec 1787 between Joseph Brock of one part and Lardner Clark of other part. Joseph Brock conveyed unto Lardner Clark a tract of land of containing 475 acres in Davidson County on Red River adjoining Joseph Brock's line. Proven by John Curtis and Thomas Cunningham.Oct Term 1789.

Page   19 - JAMES CRABTREE - NC - Nov 2, 1789
              This indenture made 5 Oct 1789 between Johnathan Drake of Davidson County of one part and James Crabtree of same place of other part.   Jonathan Drake conveyed unto James Crabtree a tract of land containing 640 acres in Sumner County on the south of Cumberland River adjoining a preemption of 640 acres surveyed for said Crabtree on the lower side, and above Isaac Linsey's plantation he now lives on north east corner of preemption. Proven by Robert Weakley. Oct Term 1789.

Page   19 - SARAH LUCAS - NC - Nov 3, 1789   Examined
              This indenture made Sept 18, 1789 between Jonathan Drake of Davidson County of one part and Sarah Lucas of same place of other part. Jonathan Drake conveyed unto Sarah Lucas a tract of land containing 180 acres in Davidson County on east sides of Whites Creek adjoining Argoles Geters' line, and James Russell's corner. Proven by Robert Weakley. Oct Term 1789.

Page   20 - WILLIAM THOMAS - NC - Nov 3, 1789
              This indenture made Sept 19, 1789 between Isaac Thomas of Davidson County of one part and William Thomas of same place of other part. Isaac Thomas conveyed unto William Thomas a tract of land containing 228 acres in Davidson County on the south side of Cumberland River adjoining Mark Robertson's Preemption, James Bosley's corner, which land was granted by the State of North Carolina to Thomas Molloy by patent dated Feb 16, 1788. Oct Term 1789.

Page   20 -   WILLIAM THOMAS - NC - Nov 3, 1789

This indenture made Sept 19, 1789 between Isaac Thomas of Davidson County of one part and William Thomas of same place of other part. Isaac Thomas conveyed unto William Thomas a tract of land containing 72 acres in Davidson County on the south side of Cumberland River adjoining said river. Proven by Andrew Ewing and Andrew Cassellman. Oct Term 1789.

Page   21 -   ANDREW CUNNINGHAM - NC - Nov 4, 1789

This indenture made Aug 7, 1789 between David Shannon and Jane Shannon his wife of Davidson County of one part and Andrew Cunningham of the same place of other part. David Shannon and Jane Shannon his wife, conveyed unto Andrew Cunningham a tract of land in Davidson County on the north side of Cumberland River on the waters of Whites Creek and being part of said Shannon's Preemption. Land containing 100 acres being part of a tract of land granted to said David Shannon out of the secretary's office for the State of North Carolina dated Apr 7, 1786. Proven by James Ross, Samuel McCutchen and James McCutchen. Oct Term 1789.

Page   22 -   MARY HUNTER - NC - Nov 4, 1789

This indenture made Aug 25, 1786 between John Erwine of one part and Mary Hunter of the other part. John Erwine conveyed unto Mary Hunter a certain undivided right in a certain lot of one acre of land in the town of Nashville, known by the No. 28, being the lot formerly granted to James Biswell by the Commissioners of the said town by deed dated July 26, 1784. Proven by Samuel Martin. Oct Term 1789.

Page   22 - JAMES COLE MONTFLORENCE - NC - Nov 4, 1789

This indenture made Sept 19, 1789 between John Drew of Davidson County of one part and James Cole Montflorence of same place of other part. John Drew conveyed unto James Cole Montflorence all that half town lot in town of Nashville and known as Lot No. 8 being the said half lot conveyed unto John Drew by James Bosley by deed dated 1 May 1789 under the signature of James Bosley. Proven by George Walker and Anthony Foster. Oct Term 1789.

Page   23 -   ANDREW EWING - NC - Nov 5, 1789

This indenture made 7 July 1789 between Thomas Hickman, Esq. as High Sheriff of one part and Andrew Ewing of same place of other part. Thomas Hickman conveyed unto Andrew Ewing the goods and chattels &c of Adam Hampton, a certain town lot of one acre of ground in the town of Nashville known as Lot No. 4 which lot No. 4 was bid off by said Andrew Ewing for the sum of 20 pounds. Oct Term 1789.

Page   23 -   ROBERT MITCHEL - NC - Nov 5, 1789

This indenture made 27 Aug 1789 between Daniel James of Davidson County of one part and Robert Mitchel of same place of other part. Daniel James conveyed unto Robert Mitchel a certain lot of one acre the same being in town of Nashville and known as Lot No. 88, which said lot was conveyed to the said James by Samuel Barton, Thomas Molloy and James Shaw, directors and trustees of the town of Nashville by deed dated July 26, 1784. Oct Term 1789.

Page   24 - JOHN BLAIR - NC - No. 388 - Reg. Nov 7, 1789

By an Act for the relief of the Officers and Soldiers of the Continental Line, in consideration of the bravery and zeal of Hance Polligrew, non-commissioned officer in the said line, granted unto John Blair, assignee of Hance Polligrew (wounded), a tract of land containing 1000 acres in Davidson County on the waters of Spring Creek adjoining William Ross' boundary and Nathaniel Lawrence's corner. Surveyed for John Blair May 1, 1786 by John Buchanan, D.S. in consequence of a Military Warrant No. 2022. Located Jan 21, 1786. Sept 15, 1787.

Page   24 - JOHN BLAIR - NC - No. 382 - Reg. Nov 7, 1789

By an Act for the relief of the Officers and Soldiers of the Continental Line, in consideration of the bravery and zeal of William Bennett, a private in the said line, granted unto John Blair, assignee of the heirs of William Bennett, a tract of land containing 640 acres in Davidson County on the east fork of Spring Creek adjoining William Ross' corner. Surveyed for John Blair May 1, 1786 by John Buchanan, D.S. in consequence of a Military Warrant No. 2108. Located Feb 7, 1786. Sept 15, 1787.

Page   24 - THOMAS McCRORY - NC - No. 390 - Reg. Nov 7, 1789

By an Act for the relief of the Officers and Soldiers of the Continental Line, in consideration of the bravery and zeal of James Gardner, a private in the said line, granted unto Thomas McCrory, assignee of the heirs of James Gardner, a tract of land containing 640 acres in Davidson County on the first branch to the eastward from where the big south road leaves Big Harpeth waters. Surveyed for Thomas McCrory Apr 25, 1786 by John Buchanan, D.S. in consequence of a Military Warrant No. 1982. Located Sept 31, 1785. Sept 15, 1787.

Page   25 - JOHN LARKIN - NC - No. 539 - Reg. Dec 15, 1789

By an Act for the relief of the Officers and Soldiers of the Continental Line, in consideration of the bravery and zeal of Hugh Larkin, a sergeant in the said line, granted unto John Larkin, heir of Hugh Larkin, a tract of land containing 1000 acres in Davidson County on Jones Creek. Surveyed for John Larkin Nov 12, 1785 by John Buchanan, D.S. in consequence of a Military Warrant No. 168. Located July 8, 1784. Sept 15, 1787.

Page   25 - JAMES RUSSELL - NC - No. 32 - Reg. Dec 15, 1789

By an Act for the relief of the Officers and Soldiers of the Continental Line, in consideration of the services of Col. Martin Armstrong, surveyor, granted unto James Russell, assignee of said Armstrong, a tract of land containing 100 acres in Davidson County on the south side of Cumberland River adjoining Peter Poyner's line. Surveyed for James Russell Nov 28, 1785 by Thomas Molloy, D.S. agreeable to a location made July 2, 1785 and No. 1071. Oct 8, 1787.

Page   25 - AUTHUR TYNER - NC - No. 519 - Dec 30, 1789

By an Act for the relief of the Officers and Soldiers of the Continental Line, in consideration of the bravery and zeal of Authur Tyner, a private in the said line, granted unto him a tract of land containing 274 acres in Davidson County on second creek on the south side of Cumberland River below the Cross Creek adjoining Thomas Molloy's Guard Right. Surveyed for Authur Tyner Nov 13, 1786 by Thomas Molloy, D.S. in consequence of a Military Warrant No. 708. Located ___ __ 1786. Sept 15, 1787.

Page   26 - JAMES TATUM - NC - No. 650 - Reg. Dec 30, 1789
            By an Act for the relief of the Officers and Soldiers of the Continental Line,
in consideration of the bravery and zeal of Hezekieh Nations, a private in the said line,
granted unto John Nation an heir of Hezekiah Nations, a tract of land containing 640 acres
in Davidson County lying between the Clay Lick and and the Battleground on the head
drafts of Sycamore adjoining A. Hart's line. Surveyed for James Tatum Oct 16, 1786 by
Robert Nelson, D.S. in consequence of a Military Warrant No. 2535. Located June 15, 1786.
Dec 8, 1787.

Page   26 - JOHN DEADERICK - NC - Jan 13, 1790
            This indenture made 26 Dec 1790 between David Shelby of Sumner County of
one part and John Deaderick of Davidson County of other part. David Shelby conveyed unto
John Deaderick a half Lot No. 37 in the town of Nashville, the same being conveyed by
David Hay to the said David Shelby. Proven by David Hay and William A. Peas. Jan Term
1790.

Page   26 - WILLIAM JACKSON - NC - No. 653 - Reg. Jan 13, 1790
            By an Act for the relief of the officers and Soldiers of the Continental Line,
in consideration of the bravery and zeal of William Jackson, a private in the said line,
granted unto him a tract of land containing 274 acres in Davidson County on the east side
of Big Harpeth joining the north boundary of Alex. Nelson's claim.Surveyed for William
Jackson May 26, 1787 by Robert Nelson, D.S. Warrant No. 184. Located Feb 17, 1787.
Dec 8, 1787.

Page   27 - JAMES MULHERIN - NC - Jan 13, 1790
            This indenture made 5 Jan 1790 between John Blair of Davidson County of
one part and James Mulherin of same place of other part. John Blair conveyed unto James
Mulherin a tract of land containing 400 acres in Sumner County on the east waters of
Spring Creek adjoining Nathaniel Laurence. Said land being part of a grant issued to said
Blair containing 1000 acres originally, the warrant granted to Hance Pettigrew, No. 2022.
Proven by John Buchanan and Thomas McCrory. Jan Term 1790.

Page   27 - DANIEL ROWAN - NC - Jan 14, 1790
            I, James Bosley of Davidson County, NC, conveyed unto Daniel Rowan all
that tract of land in Davidson County. Beginning at Anthony Crutcher's line, two poles
from his spring to a stake in Dentons Lick, on Crutcher's field, and Sappington's line and
Bell's line. Containing 37½ acres. This 30 Apr 1787. Proven by James How and Levy
Hand. Jan Term 1790.

Page   28 - RALPH FLEMING - NC - Jan 14, 1790
            This indenture made Jan 6, 1790 between Robert Nelson of Tennessee County
of one part and Ralph Fleming of Davidson County of other part. Robert Nelson conveyed
unto Ralph Fleming a tract of land containing 640 acres on the north side of Nelsons
Creek, an east branch of Big Harpeth adjoining Thomas Pasture's and Alexander Nelson's
survey, to Robert Nelson's survey. Jan Term 1790.

Page   28 - WILLIAM MARRS - NC - Jan 14, 1790

This indenture made Jan 7, 1790 between Anthony Crutcher of Davidson County of one part and William Marrs of same place of other part. Anthony Crutcher conveyed unto William Marrs a tract of land containing 333 acres in Davidson County on Whites Creek and adjoining James Marrs' corner, and Marshall's line. Proven by Samuel Shannon, John Forde and Edwin Hickman. Jan Term 1790.

Page   29 - MARY & NANCY RUDDLE - NC - Jan 14, 1790

This indenture made Jan 5, 1790 between William Turnbull of Davidson County of one part and Mary and Nancy Ruddle, daughters of Col. Cornelius Ruddle, deceased, of Bourbon County, Kentucky of the other part. William Turnbull conveyed unto Mary and Nancy Ruddle a tract of land containing 354 acres in Sumner County, NC, on the head waters of Spring Creek. Said land being part of a grant issued the the said Turnbull containing 640 acres, originally the warrant granted to Josiah Jackson No. 1810. The grant dated Dec 8, 1787. Proven by Elijah Hamilton and James Williams. Jan Term 1790.

Page   29 - JAMES HALL - NC - Jan 15, 1790

This indenture made Jan 8, 1790 between Anthony Crutcher of Davidson County of one part and James Hall of same place of other part. Anthony Crutcher conveyed unto James Hall a tract of land containing 300 acres in Davidson County and on the north side of Cumberland River on Whites Creek and adjoining James Mayore's tract and Armstrong's line. Which said land was entered June 29, 1784, being part of a larger tract. Attested: John S. Singletary and Robert Taitt. Jan Term 1790.

Page   30 - JAMES DONNALDSON - NC - Jan 18, 1790

This indenture made Dec 1789 between James Maxel of Davidson County of one part and James Donnaldson of same place of other part. James Maxel conveyed unto James Donnaldson one lot of one acre of land in the town of Nashville and known as Lot No. 41, formerly granted to James Mulherin, Esq. by Samuel Barton, Thomas Molloy and James Shaw, directors and trustees of the town of Nashville by deed dated July 26, 1784 and afterwards by said Mulherin to James Maxel by deed dated Apr 4, 1785. Attest: John Forde. Jan Term 1790.

Page   30 - JAMES MAXEL - NC - Jan 18, 1790

This indenture made Mar 25, 1789 between John Stern Singletary of Davidson County of one part and James Maxel of same place of other part. John Stern Singletary conveyed unto James Maxel one lot of an acre of land in the town of Nashville and known as Lot No. 49, formerly granted to Thomas Fletcher by Samuel Barton, Thomas Molloy and James Shaw, directors and trustees of the town of Nashville, by deed dated July 26, 2784 and afterwards by said Fletcher to James Donnelly by deed dated Jan 4, 1785 and afterwards by said Donnelly to John Stern Singletary by deed dated Mar 15, 1787. Attested: David Hay and John Thompson. Jan Term 1790.

Page   31 - BENJAMIN BARNES - NC - Jan 18, 1790

This indenture made Dec 3, 1789 between Francis Armstrong of one part and Benjamin Barnes of other part, both of Davidson County. Francis Armstrong conveyed unto Benjamin Barnes a tract of land containing 100 acres in Davidson County on the south side of Cumberland River on the waters of Browns Creek and adjoining John Brown's line it being John Noleland's corner. Attested: Edwin Hickman and Samuel Barton. Jan Term 1790.

Page   31 - JAMES BOSLEY - NC - Jan 18, 1790
        This indenture made Nov 9, 1789 between Elijah Robertson and Sarah Robertson his wife of Davidson County of one part and James Bosley of same place of other part. Elijah Robertson and Sarah Robertson his wife conveyed unto James Bosley a tract of land containing 496 acres in Davidson County on the south side of Cumberland River on the waters of the French Lake branch and adjoining John Cockrill's boundary and McGavoc's corner. Attested: Robert Weakley, William Taitt, J. Cartwright, Mark Brown Sappington, Thomas Crutcher and William Nash. Jan Term 1790.

Page   32 - CHARLES LONGMIER - NC - Jan 18, 1790
        This indenture made Nov 23, 1789 between Robert Weakley of Davidson County of one part and Charles Longmier of Washington County, NC of other part. Robert Weakley conveyed unto Charles Longmier a tract of land containing 640 acres in Davidson County on the south side of Cumberland River on the waters of east fork of Stones River the waters of Cumberland River. Beginning at Longmier's corner of a 640 acre survey Warrant No. 3397 on Isadore Skerrett's line. Said 640 acres granted to Robert Weakley by the State of North Carolina by virtue of a Military Warrant No. 2252. Attested: Valentine Sevier, Ezekiel Smith and Samuel Weakley. Jan Term 1790.

Page   33 - CHARLES LONGMIER - NC - Jan 19, 1790
        This indenture made Nov 23, 1790 between Robert Weakley of Davidson County of one part and Charles longmier of Washington County, NC of other part. Robert Weakley conveyed unto Charles Longmier a tract of land containing 640 acres in Davidson County on the south side of Cumberland River on both sides of the east fork of Stones River the waters of Cumberland River and adjoining Isadore Skerrett's corner. Said land granted to Robert Weakley by the State of North Carolina by virtue of a Military Warrant No. 3397. Attested: Valentine Sevier, Ezekiel Smith and Samuel Weakley. Jan Term 1790.

Page   33 - THOMAS WILLIAMSON - NC - Jan 19, 1790
        This indenture made Nov 16, 1789 between Robert Weakley of Davidson County of one part and Thomas Williamson of same place of other part. Robert Weakley conveyed unto Thomas Williamson a tract of land containing 640 acres in Davidson County on the south side of Cumberland River on both sides of the east fork of Stones River the waters of Cumberland River and adjoining Griffith Rutherford's line on east fork of Stones River of a survey of 640 acres. Said land granted to Robert Weakley by the State of North Carolina by virtue of a Military Warrant No. 2487. Attested: Anthony Crutcher and Thomas Molloy. Jan Term 1790.

Page   34 - JAMES WILLIAMSON - NC - Jan 19, 1790
        This indenture made Jan 4, 1790 between Gasper Mansker of Sumner County, NC of one part and James Williamson of Davidson County of other part. Gasper Mansker conveyed unto James Williamson a parcel of land on the Wartrace Fork of Gaspers Creek in Davidson County and Sumner County, NC adjoining John Shannon's line, and Williamson and

Barnett's line. Conveyed by Gasper Mansker and Elizabeth to James Williamson said land. Jan Term 1790.

Page   34 - DAVID McGAVOCK - NC - Jan 20, 1790
This indenture made Aug 27, 1789 between John Mulherin, late Sheriff of Davidson County of one part and David McGavock of Montgomery County, State of Virginia of the other part. John Mulherin conveyed unto David McGavock a tract of land containing 640 acres by virtue of an execution from the Davidson County court, in behalf James McGavock against one Evan Baker and others, dated Jan Term 1785. Attested: James Mulherin and William Turnbull. Jan Term 1790.

Page   35 - JOSEPH SHAW - NC - Jan 21, 1790
This indenture made Jan 6, 1790 between Anthony Crutcher of Davidson County of one part and Joseph Shaw of same place of other part. Anthony Crutcher conveyed unto Joseph Shaw a tract of land containing 320 acres in Davidson County on the headwaters of Whites Creek and adjoining Joseph Kincaid's tract and Phillip Walker's tract, John Walker's tract and Ebenezer Titus' line. Attested: Robert Boyd and James Robertson. Jan Term 1790.

Page   35 - ROBERT BARNETT - NC - Jan 21, 1790
(2nd page)   This indenture made Jan 1, 1790 between Kasper Mansker of Sumner County, NC of one part and Robert Barnett of Davidson County of other part. Kasper Mansker conveyed unto Robert Barnett a tract of land containing 360 acres in Davidson County on the left hand fork of Kasper Creek and adjoining James Byrns' line. Kasper Mansker and Elizabeth conveyed unto Robert Barnett said land. Jan Term 1790.

Page   36 - WILLIAM OVERALL - NC - Jan 21, 1790
This indenture made __ day of the year 1790 between Turner Williams of Davidson County of one part and William Overall of same place of other part. Turner Williams conveyed unto William Overall a tract of land containing 320 acres in Davidson County on the north side of Cumberland River about three miles from Nashville town, it being a tract of land granted the said Turner dated 8 Oct 1787. Signed by Sampson Williams, attorney for Turner Williams. Jan Term 1790.

Page   37 - WIKOFF & CLARK - NC - No. 46 - Reg. Feb 3, 1790
For 10 lbs per 100 acres paid by Wikoff and Clark was granted a tract of land containing 250 acres in Middle District on Weakleys Creek a west fork of Richland Creek of Elk River and adjoining James Robertson's corner. Surveyed for Wikoff and Clark by Robert Weakley in consequence of a Warrant No. 41. Dated May 1, 1786. July 10, 1788.

Page   37 - WIKOFF & CLARK - NC - No. 57 - Reg. Feb 3, 1790
For 10 lbs per 100 acres paid by Wikoff and Clark was granted a tract of land containing 400 acres in the Western District on Reel Foot River on the south bank of river at the mouth of Pawpaw Creek. Frederick Miller's corner. Surveyed for Wikoff and Clark May 16, 1788 by Henry Rutherford in consequence of a Warrant No. 26. Dated Jan 12, 1786. July 10, 1788.

Page   37 - WIKOFF & CLARK - NC - No. 82 - Reg. Feb 3, 1790
            For 10 lbs per 100 acres paid by Wikoff and Clark was granted a tract of land
containing 390 acres in the Western District on Reelfoot River, adjoining Frederick Miller's
corner. Surveyed for Wikoff and Clark May 16, 1786 by Henry Rutherford in consequence
of a Warrant No. 24. Dated Jan 12, 1786. July 10, 1788.

Page   38 - WIKOFF & CLARK - NC - No. 54 - Feb 3, 1790
            For 10 lbs per 100 acres paid by Wikoff and Clark was granted a tract of land
containing 1000 acres being in the Western District on Reelfoot River and adjoining
Frederick Miller's corner. Surveyed for Wikoff and Clark May 16, 186 by Henry Rutherford,
D.S. in consequence of a Warrant No. 25. Dated Jan 12, 1786. July 10, 1788.

Page   38 - JOHN MACER - NC - No. 61 - Reg. Feb 3, 1790
            Filed with the deeds of jan 1790.
            An extract from the records in the Secretary's Office Dec 11, 1789. We have
granted unto John Macer, a captain, 1097 acres of land in Davidson County on the east fork
of Buffalo Creek on the north side of Tennessee River. Signed 14 Mar 1786. A copy.

Page   38 - ANDREW HAMPTON - NC - No. 740 - Reg. Feb 3, 1790
            By an Act for the relief of the Officers and Soldiers of the Continental Line,
in consideration of the bravery and zeal of John Marshal, a private in the said line, granted
unto Andrew Hampton, assignee of John Marshal, a tract of land containing 640 acres in
Davidson County on the west side of the Elk Fork of Red River. Surveyed for Andrew
Hampton Sept 25, 1787 by B. William Pollock, D.S. in consequence of a Military Warrant
No. 3474. Located Aug 17, 1787. July 11, 1788.

Page   39 - ROBERT WEAKLEY - NC - No. 1015 - Reg. Feb 3, 1790
            By an Act for the relief of the Officers and Soldiers of the Continental Line,
in consideration of the bravery and zeal of Benajah Yorkins, a private in the said line,
granted unto Robert Weakley, assignee of the heirs of Bebejah Yorkins, a tract of land
containing 640 acres in Davidson County on the east fork of Stones River about six or seven
miles above the first line run by the Commissioners in the year 1783 and adjoining Isadore
Skerrett's corner. Surveyed for Robert Weakley May 27, 1788 in consequence of a Military
Warrant No. 3397. Located Mar 22, 1788. May 18, 1789.

Page   39 - ROBERT WEAKLEY - NC - No. 1010 - Reg. Feb 3, 1790
            By an Act for the relief of the Officers and Soldiers of the Continental Line,
in consideration of the bravery and zeal of Jacob Deaderick, a private in the said line,
granted unto Robert Weakley, assignee of the heirs of said Jacob Deaderick a tract of land
containing 640 acres in Davidson County on the east fork of Stones River about one mile
above the first line run by the Commissioners in the year of 1783 and adjoining Martin
Armstrong's corner. Surveyed for Robert Weakley May 17, 1788 by said Weakley for
himself in consequence of a Military Warrant No. 2264. Located Mar 22, 1788. May 18,
1789.

Page   39 - ROBERT WEAKLEY - NC - No. 1012 - Reg. Feb 3, 1790
            By an Act for the relief of the Officers and Soldiers of the Continental Line,

in consideration of the bravery and zeal of Abraham Green, a private in the said line, granted unto Robert Weakley, assignee of the heirs of Abraham Green, a tract of land containing 640 acres in Davidson County on the east fork of Stones River and adjoining Griffith Rutherford's line of survey of 640 acres. Surveyed for Robert Weakley May 17, 1788 by Robert Weakley for himself in consequence of a Military Warrant No. 2487. Located Mar 22, 1788. May 18, 1789.

Page   40 - ROBERT WEAKLEY - NC - No. 1013 - Reg. Feb 3, 1790
By an Act for the relief of the Officers and Soldiers of the Continental Line, in consideration of the bravery and zeal of Nelson Zealots, a private in the said line, granted unto Robert Weakley, assignee of the heirs of said Nelson Zealots, a tract of land containing 640 acres in Davidson County on the waters of Half Pone Creek, between said creek and Sycamore Creek on the north side of Cumberland River and adjoining John Cummins' corner and Anthony Hart's corner. Surveyed for Robert Weakley Feb 5, 1788 by the said Weakley for himself in consequence of a Military Warrant No. 3396. Located June 3, 1786. May 18, 1789.

Page   40 - ABRAHAM KENNADY - NC - No. 963 - Reg. Mar 1, 1790
By an Act for the relief of the Officers and Soldiers of the Continental Line, in consideration of the bravery and zeal of Daniel Laurey, granted unto Abraham Kennady, assignee of said Daniel Laurey, a tract of land containing 640 acres in Davidson County between the hradwaters of Barton Creek and Cedar Creek and adjoining George Pirtle's corner and Philip Jones' corner. Surveyed for Abraham Kennady Nov 10, 1788 by John Buchanan, D.S. in consequence of a Military Warrant No. 2523. Located May 6, 1788. May 13, 1789.

Page   40 - CHRISTOPHER WILLIAM BROOKS - NC - No. 90 - Mar 1, 1790
By an Act for the relief of the Officers and Soldiers of the Continental Line, in consideration of the bravery and zeal of George Brooks, a sergeant in the said line, granted unto Christopher William Brooks, heir of G.J. Brooks, a tract of land containing 1000 acres in Davidson County on the south side of Cumberland River. Beginning at the bank of said river above the mouth of Yellow Creek and adjoining Captain William Armstrong's corner. Surveyed for Christopher William Brooks July 14, 1785 by Edward Harris, D.S. in consequence of a Military Warrant No. 312. Located Nov 30, 1784. Mar 14, 1786.

Page   41 - SAMPSON WILLIAMS - NC - No. 88 - Reg. Mar 1, 1790
By an Act for the relief of the Officers and Soldiers of the Continental Line, in consideration of the bravery and zeal of Thomas Fleming, a private in the said line, granted unto Sampson Williams, assignee of Thomas Fleming, a tract of land containing 640 acres in Sumner County on the little fork of Spencers Creek on the south side of Cumberland River and adjoining Samuel Motheral's survey. Surveyed for Sampson Williams Feb 15, 1788 by himself in consequence of a Military Warrant No. 1708. Located Mar 24, 1787. Jan 17, 1789.

Page   41 - WILLIAM SHAW - NC - No. 1027 - Reg. Mar 1, 1790
By an Act for the relief of the officers and Soldiers of the Continental Line,

147

in consideration of the bravery and zeal of John Best, a private in the said line, granted unto William Shaw, assignee of the heirs of John Best, a tract of land containing 640 acres in Davidson County on the north side of Cumberland River on the waters of Red River. Surveyed for William Shaw July 10, 1788 by Anthony Foster, D.S. in consequence of a Military Warrant No. 3442. May 17, 1788. May 13, 1789.

Page   41 - ROBERT NELSON - NC - No. 894 - Reg. Mar 1, 1790

By an Act for the relief of the Officers and Soldiers of the Continental Line, in consideration of the bravery and zeal of Samuel Pulley, a private in the said line, granted unto Robert Nelson, assignee of Samuel Pulley, a tract of land containing 640 acres in Davidson County on the north side of Cumberland River below the mouth of Blooming Grove and adjoining the lower boundary of John Shelby's survey. Surveyed by Robert Nelson for himself Apr 9, 1787. Dated Jan 13, 1789.

Page   42 - WILLIAM BOWMAN - NC - No. 734 - Reg. Mar 2, 1790

By an Act for the relief of the officers and Soldiers of the Continental Line, in consideration of the bravery and zeal of Samuel Morrow, a private in the said line, granted unto William Bowman, heir of James Bowman, assignee of Samuel Borrow, a tract of land containing 640 acres in Davidson County on the west and north side of the land William Harrison now lives on of the north fork of Red River and adjoining Framel's line. Surveyed for William Bowman by himself Mar 13, 1787 in consequence of a Military Warrant No. 2531. Located Jan 22, 1787. July 13, 1788.

Page   42 - DAVID HART - NC - No. 785 - Reg. Mar 2, 1790

By an Act for the relief of the Officers and Soldiers of the Continental Line, in consideration of the bravery and zeal of George Elmore, a private in the said line, granted unto David Hart, assignee of George Elmore, a tract of land containing 274 acres in Sumner County on the waters of Goose Creek and adjoining William Lander(?). Surveyed for David Hart Aept 29, 1787 by James Sanders, D.S. in consequence of a Military Warrant No. 776. Located Sept 21, 1787. July 11, 1788.

Page   42 - TURNER WILLIAMS - NC - No. 995 - Reg. Mar 2, 1790

By an Act for the relief of the Officers and Soldiers of the Continental Line, in consideraton of the bravery and zeal of William Elliott, granted unto Turner Williams, assignee of William Elliott, a tract of land containing 640 acres in Davidson County on Smiths Fork of Caney Fork and south side of Cumberland in Sumner County. Surveyed for Turner Williams Apr 19, 1788 by Sampson Williams, D.S. in consequence of a Military Warrant No. 2714. Located Apr 1, 1788. May 1, 1789.

Page   43 - ABRAHAM RISTON - NC - No. 1042 - Reg. Mar 2, 1790

By an Act for the relief of the Officers and Soldiers of the Continental Line, in consideration of the bravery and zeal of Larkin Staughn, a private in the said line, granted unto Abraham Riston, assignee of said Larkin Staughn, a tract of land containing 640 acres in Davidson County on Spencers Creek and adjoining George Pirtles and Charles Dungethn's corner. Surveyed for Abrahan Riston July 4, 1788 by John Buchanan, D.S. in consequence of a Military Warrant No. 944. Located Mar 28, 1788. May 13, 1789.

Page   43 - ROBERT THOMPSON - NC - No. 46 - Reg. Mar 2, 1790
By an Act for the relief of the Officers and Soldiers of the Continental Line, in consideration of the services of Col. Martin Armstrong, surveyor, granted unto Robert Thompson, assignee of said Armstrong, a tract of land containing 100 acres on the waters of Richland Creek adjoining James Thompson's corner. Which land was surveyed for the said Armstrong May 13, 1785 in consequence of a Service Right of said Armstrong, No. 676. Located Mar 5, 1785. Oct 5, 1787.

Page   43 - SAMUEL McGOWN - NC - No. 64 - Reg. Mar 2, 1790
By an Act for the relief of the Officers and Soldiers of the Continental Line, in consideration of the services of Col. Martin Armstrong, surveyor, granted unto Samuel McGown, assignee of said Armstrong, a tract of land containing 60 acres in Davidson County on Whites Creek, between Mitchel's and Glaves' Preemption. Surveyed for said McGown Apr 20, 1787 by Robert Nelson, D.S. in consequence of a Service Right of said Armstrong, No. 2867. Located July 24, 1786. May 18, 1789.

Page   44 - THOMAS MOLLOY - NC - No. 1043 - Reg. Mar 2, 1790
By an Act for the relief of the Officers and Soldiers of the Continental line, in consideration of the bravery and zeal of William Spencer, a private in the said line, granted unto Thomas Molloy, assignee of William Spencer, a tract of land containing 240 acres in Davidson County including the two hundred acres belonging to Robert Nelson on the north side of Cumberland River in cluding the mouth of Whites Creek and adjoining George Freeland's corner and William Stuarts' corner, and James Brown's corner and to Thomas James' south boundary and then to Peter Sides' east boundary. Surveyed for Thomas Molloy Jan 15, 1787 by said Molloy for himself in consequence of a Military Warrant No. 2587. Located Mar 8, 1786.

Page   44 - WILLIAM DOBBINS - NC - No. 149 - Reg. Mar 3, 1790
For 10 lbs per 100 acres paid by William Dobbins, assignee of Lardner Clark, was granted a tract of land containing 1000 acres in the Middle District on the south side of Duck River near the head of a small creek that empties in a small distance below the forks of Duck River. Surveyed for William Dobbins Mar 10, 1788 by Thomas Hickman, D.S. in consequence of a Warrant No. 49. Located Nov 6, 1787. Aug 11, 1789.

Page   44 - JAMES HOGGATT - NC - No. 62 - Reg. Mar 3, 1790
((2nd page)   By an Act for the relief of the Officers and Soldiers of the Continental Line, in consideration of the services of Col. Martin Armstrong, surveyor, granted unto James Hoggatt, assignee of said Armstrong, a tract of land containing 60 acres in Davidson County at the mouth of Sulphur Creek and adjoining James Hoggatt's other corner. Dated May 10, 1789. The above land was surveyed for said Hoggatt Mar 12, 1787 by Robert Nelson, D.S. in consequence of a Service Right of said Armstrong, No. 1752. Located Dec 1, 1786.

Page   45 - MARTIN ARMSTRONG & ANTHONY CRUTCHER - NC - No. 67 - Reg. Mar 3, 1790
By an Act for the relief of the Officers and Soldiers of the Continental Line, in consideration of the services of Col. Martin Armstrong, surveyor, granted unto Martin Armstrong and Anthony Crutcher a tract of land containing 500 acres in Davidson County

on the south side of Cumberland River adjoining Benjamin Pirtel's (Pirtle's) line and McMurry's line. Surveyed for said Armstrong and CrutcherAug 15, 1785 by James Mulherin, D.S. in consequence of a Service Right of said Armstrong, No. 738. Located Mar 25, 1785. May 18, 1789.

Page 45 - JOHN WINDSOR - NC - No. 279 - Reg. Mar 3, 1790

For 10 lbs per 100 acres paid by John Windsor was granted a tract of land containing 1000 acres in Western District on the waters of Big Hatchie River on the north side. Beginning on the northeast corner of William Barry Groves' survey No. 2144. Surveyed for John Windsor Nov 22, 1786 by Isaac Roberts, D.S. in consequence of a Warrant No. 1259. Dated June 24, 1785. Apr 25, 1789.

Page 45 - ELIAS FORT - NC - No. 957 - Mar 3, 1790

By an Act for the relief of the Officers and Soldiers of the Continental Line, in consideration of the bravery and zeal of Ephraim Grant, a private in the said line, granted unto Elias Fort, assignee of Grant's heirs, a tract of land containing 640 acres in Davidson County adjoining the corner of Suggs' 640 acres and John Herail's tract. Surveyed for said Fort June 12, 1788 by William Nash, D.S. in consequence of a Military Warrant No. 1491. May 15, 1788. May 18, 1789.

Page 46 - JAMES CAMPBELL - NC - No. 65 - Reg. Mar 13, 1790

By an Act for the relief of the Officers and Soldiers of the Continental Line, in consideration of the bravery and zeal of James Campbell, a captain in the said line, was granted a tract of land containing 2075 acres in Davidson County exclusive of a Guard Right of 320 acres included in the above survey in all 2375 acres, on the Barrens. Surveyed for James Campbell Oct 26, 1784 by Joseph Brock, D.S. in consequence of a Military Warrant No. 367. Located July 13, 1784. Mar 14, 1786.

Page 46 - SAMUEL SHANNON - NC - No. 63 - Reg. Mar 13, 1790

By an Act for the relief of the Officers and Soldiers of the Continental Line, in consideration of the services of Col. Martin Armstrong, surveyor, granted unto Samuel Shannon, assignee of said Armstrong, a tract of land containing82 acres in Davidson County on the waters of Whites Creek and joining John Crow Preemption. Surveyed for Samuel Shannon Mar 12, 1787 by Robert Ewing, D.S. in consequence of a Service Right of said Armstrong No. 3141. Located Jan 17, 1787. May 18, 1789.

Page 46 - MARTIN ARMSTRONG - NC - No. 426 - Reg. Mar 16, 1790

By an Act for the relief of the Officers and Soldiers of the Continental Line, in consideration of the bravery and zeal of Cornelius Rynn, a private in the said line, granted unto Martin Armstrong, assignee of Cornelius Rynn, a tract of land containing 640 acres in Davidson County on the south side of Richland Creek. Surveyed for Martin Armstrong June 10, 1785 by Robert Nelson, D.S. in consequence of a Military Warrant No. 389. Located Jan 16, 1785. Sept 15, 1787.

Page 47 - WILLIAM BECK - NC - No. 241 - Reg. Mar 16, 1790

By an Act for the relief of the Officers and Soldiers of the Continental line, in consideration of the bravery and zeal of George Row, a private in the said line, granted unto William Beck, assignee of George Row, a tract of land containing 640 acres in Davidson County on Bl(illegible) Creek running into Duck River on the north side. Surveyed for William Beck Aug 8, 1785 by William Murry, D.S. in consequence of a Military Warrant No. 514. Located May 7, 1785. Mar 17, 1786.

Page   47 - WILLIAM BECK - NC - No. 126 - Reg. Mar 16, 1790
By an Act for the relief of the officers and Soldiers of the Continental Line, in consideration of the bravery and zeal of Pierson, a private in the said line, granted unto William Beck, assignee of said Pierson, a tract of land containing 640 acres in Davidson County on the south side of Cumberland River adjoining the north boundary of Capt. Samuel Budds' survey on Lick Creek. Surveyed for William Beck Apr 4, 1785 by Joseph Brock, D.S. in consequence of a Military Warrant No. 513. Located Dec 11, 1784. Mar 14, 1786.

Page   47 - ROBERT GREER - NC - No. 1021 - Reg. Mar 17, 1790
By an Act for the relief of the Officers and Soldiers of the Continental line, in consideration of the bravery and zeal of Robert Greer, a lieutenant in the said line, granted unto said Greer a tract of land containing 1006 acres in Davidson County on the east branch of the Half Pone Creek adjoining Benjamin Bailey's corner and Jonathan Drake's corner and Cartwright's corner. Surveyed for Robert Greer by Robert Weakley in consequence of a Military Warrant No. 1214. Located Mar 16, 1786. May 18, 1789.

Page   48 - WILLIAM FAWN - NC - No. 67 - Reg. Mar 17, 1790
By an Act for the relief of the Officers and Soldiers of the Continental Line, in consideration of the bravery and zeal of William Fawn, a captain in the said line, granted unto him a tract of land containing 3840 acres in Davidson County on the fork of Elk Creek on the south side of Cumberland River. Surveyed for William Fawn Mar 4, 1785 by William Murry, D.S. in consequence of a Military Warrant No. 231. Located Mar 9, 1784. Mar 14, 1786.

Page   48 - SIMON WILLIAMS - NC - Mar 17, 1790
This indenture made 14 May 1787 between William Fawn of Warren County, North Carolina and Simon Williams of same place. William Fawn conveyed unto Simon Williams a tract of land containing 3840 acres in Davidson County on the fork of Elk Creek on the south side of Cumberland River. Said land was granted unto William Fawn by the State of North Carolina for his services as a Captain in the Continental Line, No. 67. Proven by Thomas Smith and William Williams.

Page   49 - ROBERT THOMPSON - NC - No. 1037 - Reg. Apr 10, 1790
By an Act for the relief of the Officers and Soldiers of the Continental Line, in consideration of the bravery and zeal of James Stephenson, granted unto Robert Thompson a tract of land containing 640 acres in Davidson County between Cedar Creek and Spencers Creek adjoining Philip Jones' corner and George Pirtle's corner. Surveyed for Robert Thompson July 4, 1788 by John Buchanan, D.S. in consequence of a Military Warrant No. 3477. Located Mar 28, 1788. May 18, 1789.

Page   49 -   JOHN LOPP - NC - Apr 12, 1790
        This indenture made 8 Feb 1788 between Lewis Beard of Rowan County, North Carolina of one part and Capt. John Lopp, Jur. of same place of other part. Lewis Beard conveyed unto Capt. John Lopp a tract of land containing 640 acres in Davidson County on Harpeth River south side of Cumberland River. Said land being surveyed in the name of Lewis Beard under a Military Warrant No. 749 in the name of John Moor and transferred to said Lewis Beard by No. 228 and signed Mar 7, 1786. Proven by Nat Beard, William Bodenhamer, John McNairy and Jacob Dufner(?). Apr Term 1790.

Page   50 -   ROBERT CARTWRIGHT - NC - No. 179 - Reg. Apr 29, 1790
        For 10 lbs per 100 acres paid by Robert Cartwright was granted a tract of land containing 640 acres in Davidson COunty on the south side of the public land of Gasper Lick. Surveyed for said Cartwright by Squire Grant, D.S. Apr 16, 1786 in consequence of a Warrant No. 279. Entry date Feb 13, 1784. July 10, 1788.

Page   50 -   THOMAS TALBOT - NC - No. 106 - Reg. Apr 29, 1790
        For 10 lbs per 100 acres paid by Thomas Talbot was granted a tract of land containing 1000 acres in Western District on both sides of Loosiehatchie River adjoining James Robertson's survey of No. 460 on said river on the south. Which said land was surveyed for said Talbot Sept 15, 1785 by Ed Harris, D.S. in consequence of a Warrant No. 1440. Dated Jan 27, 1784. July 10, 1788.

Page   50 -   THOMAS TALBOT - NC - No. 13 - Reg. Apr 30, 1790
        For 10 lbs per 100 acres paid by Thomas Talbot, was granted a tract of land containing 2000 acres in Middle District lying on Duck River adjoining Thomas and Alexander Greer's corner. Surveyed for said Talbot Mar 4, 1786 by William Madlin(?), D.S. in consequence of a Warrant No. 1434 from the State dated Jan 27, 1784. Grant signed July 10, 1788.

Page   51 -   JOHN BUCCHANAN - NC - No. 1024 - Reg. Apr 30, 1790
        By an Act for the relief of the Officers and Soldiers of the Continental Line, in consideration of the bravery and zeal of William Browneau,   granted unto John Bucchanan, assignee of said Browneau, a tract of land containing 640 acres in Davidson County on the waters of Bartons Creek adjoining General Pirtle's corner and Ruth's Preemption. Surveyed for John Bucchannan by himself Nov 15, 1788 in consequence of a Military Warrant No. 3241. Located Nov 15, 1788. May 18, 1789.

Page   51 -   JOHN BUCCHANAN - NC - No. 944 - Reg. Apr 30, 1790
        By an Act for the relief of the Officers and Soldiers of the Continental Line, in consideration of the bravery and zeal of Ephraim Wyatte, granted unto John Bucchanan, assignee of said Wyatte's heirs, a tract of land containing 640 acres in Davidson County on Cedar Lick Creek adjoining William Slades' corner. Surveyed for said Bucchanan by himself Dec 4, 1788 in consequence of a Military Warrant No. 2479. Located Nov 15, 1788. May 13, 1789.

Page   52 -   JOHN BUCCHANAN - NC - No. 1020 - Reg. Apr 30, 1790
        By an Act for the relief of the Officers and Soldiers of the Continental Line,

in consideration of the bravery and zeal of Henry Richards, granted unto John Buchanan, assignee of the heirs of Henry Richards, a tract of land containing 640 acres in Davidson County on Stones River adjoining the survey of John Rice. Surveyed for John Buchanan by himself May 2, 1786 in consequence of a Military Warrant No. 1981. Located Dec 31, 1785. May 18, 1789.

Page   52 - EPHRAIM McLANE - NC - No. 159 - Reg. Apr 30, 1790
        For 10 lbs per 100 acres paid by Ephraim McLane was granted a tract of land containing 2500 acres being in the Western District on the waters of Obion River and on the north side of said river adjoining Hougan's & Blount's corner. Surveyed for Ephraim McLane Sept 14, 1785 by Henry Rutherford, D.S. in consequence of a Warrant No. 2219. Dated May 21, 1784. July 10, 1788.

Page   52 - EPHRAIM McLANE - NC - No. 151 - Reg. Apr 30, 1790
        For 10 lbs per 100 acres paid by Ephraim McLane was granted a tract of land containing 5000 acres in the Middle District on the north side of Duck River and on Knob and Snow Creeks branches of said river. Surveyed by Ephraim McLane, D.S. Aug 23, 1788 in consequence of a Warrant No. 1567. Dated Apr 1, 1784. Nov 27, 1789.

Page   53 - ROBERT BRANK & WILLIAM McLANE - NC - No. 150 - Reg. May 1, 1790
        For 10 lbs per 100 acres paid by Robert Brank and William McLane was granted a tract of land containing 1000 acres in Middle District on the north side of Duck River. Surveyed for Robert Brank and William McLane Aug 25, 1788 by Ephraim McLane, D.S. in consequence of a Warrant No. 1939. Apr 29, 1784. Nov 14, 1789.

Page   53 - STEPHEN CANTRELL - NC - No. 958 - Reg. May 1, 1790
        By an Act for the relief of the Officers and Soldiers of the Continental Line, in consideration of the bravery and zeal of Patrick McClure, a non-commissioned officer, granted unto Stephen Cantrell, assignee of said Patrick McClure, a tract of land containing 1000 acres in Davidson County on the north side of Cumberland River. Beginning at the upper end of second bluff below the Virginia Line. Surveyed for Stephen CantrellMar 4, 1787 by Thomas Hickman, D.S. in consequence of a Military Warrant No. (not listed). Located Nov 1, 1785. May 18, 1789.

Page   53 - EPHRAIM McLANE - NC - No. 123 - Reg. May 1, 1790
        For 10 lbs per 100 acres paid by Ephraim McLane was granted a tract of land containing 1000 acres in the Western District on the south side of Duck River about two miles south of the mouth of Falling Creek. Surveyed for said McLane July 6, 1785 by H. Rutherford, D.S. in consequence of a Warrant No. 2213. Dated May 20, 1784. July 10, 1788.

Page   54 - WHEELER & UNDERWOOD - NC - No. 110 - Reg. May 3, 1790
        By an Act for the relief of the Officers and Soldiers of the Continental Line, in consideration of the bravery and zeal of Empory Wheeler, a private in the said line, granted unto Mourning Wheeler and Elizabeth Underwood as heirs of E. Wheeler, a tract of land containing 640 acres in Davidson County and on the south side of Cumberland River and waters of Mill Creek adjoining the corner of John Foreman's Preemption. Surveyed for

said Wheeler and Underwood Apr 22, 1785 by John Buchanan, D.S. in consequence of a Military Warrant No. 710. Located Aug 5, 1784. Mar 7, 1786.

Page   54 - LARDNER CLARK - NC - No. 64 - Reg. May 3, 1790
          By an Act for the relief of the Officers and Soldiers of the Continental line, in consideration of the services of Col. Martin Armstrong, surveyor, granted unto Lardner Clark, assignee of said Armstrong, a tract of land containing 150 acres in Davidson County. Beginning at the bank of Stones River being the beginning corner of Cornelius Russells line. Surveyed for Lardner Clark May 2, 1786 by John Buchanan, D.S in consequence of a Service Right of said Armstrong, No. 1595. Located Nov 26, 1785. May 18, 1789.

Page   54 - THOMAS MARTIN & SAMUEL MARTIN - NC - No. 274 - May 12, 1790
          For 10 lbs per 100 acres paid by Thomas Martin and Samuel Martin was granted a tract of land containing 640 acres in Davidson County. Surveyed for said Martins Nov 26, 1785 by Thomas Molloy, D.S. in consequence of a Warrant No. 374. Dated Mar 29, 1784. July 12, 1788.

Page   55 - WICUFF & CLARK - NC - No. 876 - Reg. May 12, 1790
          By an Act for the relief of the Officers and Soldiers of the Continental Line, in consideration of the bravery and zeal of Frederick Bagwell, a private in the said line, granted unto William Wicuff and Lardner Clark, assignees of said Frederick Bagwell, a tract of land containing 640 acres in Davidson County about two or three miles south of Cumberland River near Thomas Fains (?) claim between the south Cross Creek and the next creek below. Surveyed for said Wicuff and Clark Oct 4, 1786 by Thomas Molloy, D.S. in consequence of a Military Warrant No. 2110. Located Apr 25, 1786. Jan 17, 1789.

Page   55 - WICUFF & CLARK - NC - No. 625 - Reg. May 12, 1790
          By an Act for the relief of the Officers and Soldiers of the Continental Line, in consideration of the bravery and zeal of James Caps, a corporal in the said line, granted unto William Wicuff and Lardner Clark, assignees of said Capps' heirs, a tract of land containing 1000 acres in Davidson County on the south side of Cumberland River about three miles below the big timbered island below the Cross Creeks. Surveyed for said Wicuff and Clark Mar 10, 1786 by Thomas Molloy, D.S. in consequence of a Military Warrant No. 2117. Located Dec 1, 1785. Jan 17, 1789.

Page   55 - LARDNER CLARK - NC - No. 823 - May 12, 1790
          By an Act for the relief of the Officers and Soldiers of the Continental Line, in consideration of the bravery and zeal of Jessee Robinson, a corporal in the said line, granted unto Lardner Clark, assignee of Jessee Robinson, a tract of land containing 1000 acres in Davidson County on the waters of West Harpeth River adjoining Major Absolom Tatum's corner. Surveyed for Lardner Clark Nov 20, 1785 by B. William Pollock, D.S. in consequence of a Military Warrant No. 844. Located Jan 28, 1785. Jan 17, 1789.

Page   56 - ANTHONY HART - NC - No. 845 - Reg. May 12, 1790
          By an Act for the relief of the Officers and Soldiers of the Continental Line, in consideration of the bravery and zeal of John Mills, a private in the said line, granted unto Anthony Hart, assignee of the heirs of John Mills, a tract of land containing 640 acres

in Davidson County on the head of Browns Creek Sulphur Fork of Red River adjoining Col. Armstrong. Surveyed for Anthony Hart July 29, 1786 by Robert Nelson, D.S. in consequence of a Military Warrant No. 2812. Located Apr 12, 1786. Jan 17, 1789.

Page   56 - ANTHONY HART - NC - No. 848 - Reg. May 12, 1790
        By an Act for the relief of the Officers and Soldiers of the Continental Line, in consideration of the bravery and zeal of Laurence Colbert, a private in the said line, granted unto Anthony Hart, assignee of said Colbert, a tract of land containing 640 acres in Davidson County on the dividing ridge between the waters of Sycamore and Half Pone Creek adjoining John Cummins' corner. Surveyed for Anthony Hart Feb 1, 1787 by R. Weakley, D.S. in consequence of a Military Warrant No. 3422. Located Apr 8, 1786. Jan 17, 1789.

Page   56 - ANTHONY HART - NC - No. 877 - Reg. ,ay 12, 1790
        By an Act for the relief of the Officers and Soldiers of the Continental Line, in consideration of the bravery and zeal of Morris Bailey, a private in the said line, granted unto Anthony Hart, assignee of Morris Bailey, a tract of land containing 640 acres in Davidson County on the west fork of Spring Creek the waters of Sycamore Creek adjoining Samuel Morsone's corner and John Nichols' corner. Surveyed for Anthony Hart Feb 1, 1787 by R. Weakley, D.S. in conseqence of a Military Warrant No. 3420. Located Apr 28, 1786. Jan 17, 1789.

Page   57 - ISAAC NEALY - NC - No. 194 - Reg. May 12, 1790
        For 10 lbs per 100 acres paid by Isaac Nealy was granted a tract of land containing 640 acres in Davidson County on the north side of Cumberland River adjoining the corner of the heirs of William Neeley's Preemption and Jessee Maxwell's line. Surveyed for said Isaac Neely Apr 10, 1786 by James Sanders, D.S. in consequence of a Warrant No. 66. Located Jan 6, 1784. July 10, 1788.

Page   57 - WILLIAM & SAMUEL NEELY - NC - No. 213 - Reg. May 12, 1790
        For 10 lbs per 100 acres paid by William and Samuel Neely was granted a tract of land containing 640 acres in Davidson County on the north side of Cumberland River adjoining the public survey and John Walker's line. Surveyed for William and Samuel Neely Apr 10, 1786 by James Sanders, D.S. in consequence of a Warrant No. 65. Located Jan 6, 1784. July 10, 1788.

Page   57 - JOHN ESTIS - NC - No. 268 - Reg. May 12, 1790
        For 10 lbs per 100 acres paid by John Estis was granted a tract of land containing 640 acres in Davidson County on the bank of Cumberland River. Surveyed for John Estis Dec 3, 1784 by Thomas Molloy, D.S. in consequence of a Military Warrant No. 349. Located Mar 11, 1784. July 10, 1786.

Page   58 - SAMUEL McCUTCHEN - NC - No. 246 - Reg. May 12, 1790
        For 10 lbs per 100 acres paid by Samuel McCutchen was granted a tract of land containing 640 acres in Davidson County on Little Harpeth River. Surveyed for Samuel McCutchen Feb 6, 1786 in consequence of a Warrant No. 259. Located Feb 9, 1784. July 10, 1788.

Page   58 -   JOHN McCUTCHEN - NC - No. 960 - Reg. May 13, 1790

By an Act for the relief of the Officers and Soldiers of the Continental Line, in consideration of the bravery and zeal of Edmerit Haddock, a private in the said line, granted unto John McCutchen, assignee of said haddock, a tract of land containing 228 acres in Davidson County on the north side of the east fork of Stones River on a branch of the same adjoining Robert Weakley's corner on the east side of a ridge and Gen. Mathew Lock's line. Surveyed for John McCutchen June 13, 1788 by Robert Weakley, D.S. in consequence of a Military Warrant No. 1235. Located Mar 22, 1788. May 18, 1789.

Page   58 -   DAVID SHELTON - NC - No. 443 - Reg. May 13, 1790

By an Act for the relief of the Officers and Soldiers of the Continental line, in consideration of the bravery and zeal of Nathan Thompson, a private in the said line, granted unto David Shelton, assignee of said Nathan Thompson, a tract of land containing 640 acres in Davidson County on the south side of Cumberland River adjoining James Sanders' corner. Surveyed for David Shelton Sept 8, 1786 by James Sanders, D.S. in consequence of a Military Warrant No. 764. Located July 4, 1785. Sept 15, 1787.

Page   59 -   ISAAC DRAKE - NC - No. 218 - Reg. May 13, 1790

For 10 lbs per 100 acres paid by Isaac Drake was granted a tract of land containing 640 acres in Davidson County on the waters of Hays Creek a branch of Big Harpeth River, adjoining Drake's spring. Surveyed for Isaac Drake by John Buchanan, D.S. in consequwnce of a Warrant No. 128. Located Jan 15, 1784. July 10, 1788.

Page   59 -   ISAAC DRAKE - NC - No. 57 - Reg. May 13, 1790

By an Act for the relief of the officers and Soldiers of the Continental Line, in consideration of the services of Col. Martin Armstrong, surveyor, granted unto Isaac Drake, assignee of said Armstrong, a tract of land containing 50 acres in Davidson County on Heatons Lick branch about three quarters of a mile above Heatons Lick. Surveyed for Isaac Drake Nov 12, 1786 by Thomas Molloy, D.S. in consequence of a Service Right of said Armstrong, No. 2040. Located Jan 21, 1786. May 18, 1789.

Page   59 -   DANIEL DUNHAM - NC - No. 180 - Reg. May 13, 1790

For 10 lbs per 100 acres paid by Daniel Dunham was granted a tract of land containing 640 acres in Davidson County beginning on the north side of Little Harpeth Creek and adjoining Samuel Crockett's west boundary. Surveyed for Daniel Dunham Nov 9; 1785 by Thomas Molloy, D.S. in consequence of a Warrant No. 120. Located Jan 15, 1784. July 10, 1788.

Page   60 -   JOHN CUMMINS - NC - No. 1025 - Reg. May 13, 1790

By an Act for the relief of the Officers and Soldiers of the Continental Line, in consideration of the bravery and zeal of Howell Gillum, a sergeant in the said line, granted unto John Cummins, assignee of said Gillum, a tract of land containing 1000 acres in Davidson County on the north side of Cumberland River on the dry fork of Half Pone Creek adjoining Nehemiah Long's corner and Samuel Marsone's corner and John Drake's line. Surveyed for John Cummins May 10, 1788 by Robert Weakley, D.S. in consequence of a Military Warrant No. 420. Located Mar 9, 1786. May 13, 1789.

Page   60 - THOMAS THOMPSON - NC - No. 255 - Reg. May 13, 1790

For 10 lbs per 100 acres paid by Thomas Thompson was granted a tract of land containing 640 acres in Davidson County on the south side of Cumberland River and waters of Browns Creek adjoining Jonathan Drake's corner and William Simpson's line. Surveyed for Thomas Thompson July 15, 1785 by James Mulherin, D.S. in consequence of a Warrant No. 132. Located Jan 15, 1784. July 13, 1788.

Page   60 - SAMUEL SHANNON - NC - No. 881 - Reg. May 13, 1790

By an Act for the relief of the Officers and Soldiers of the Continental Line, in consideration of the bravery and zeal of Robert Acock, a private in the said line, granted unto Samuel Shannon, assignee of said Acock, a tract of land containing 228 acres in Davidson County on the waters of Whites Creek adjoining Joseph Kinkaid's corner and John Crow's boundary, and James Mears' south boundary line. Surveyed for Samuel Shannon Mar 12, 1787 by Robert Ewing, D.S. in consequence of a Military Warrant No. 1482. Located Dec 22, 1785. Jan 17, 1789.

Page   61 - STEPHEN CANTRILL - NC - No. 1020 - Reg. May 14, 1790

By an Act for the relief of the Officers and Soldiers of the Continental Line, in consideration of the bravery and zeal of Moses Weaver, a private in the said line, granted unto Stephen Cantrell, assignee of Moses Weaver, a tract of land containing 274 acres in Davidson County on the head branches of the second creek above Bradleys Lick on the east branches of the east fork of Stones River adjoining Stockley Donelson's corner. Surveyed for Stephen Cantrill Nov 1, 1787 by John Donelson, D.S. in consequence of a Military Warrant No. 1678. Located Sept 21, 1787. May 13, 1789.

Page   61 - BARNABAS BOILS - NC - No. 1032 - Reg. May 14, 1790

By an Act for the relief of the Officers and Soldiers of the Continental Line, in consideration of the bravery and zeal of John Pettie, a private in the said line, granted unto Barnabas Boils, assignee of said Pettie, a tract of land containing 228 acres in Davidson County on the east fork of Whites Creek adjoining James Brown's north boundary. Surveyed for Barnabas Boils Mar 1, 1787 by Thomas Molloy, D.S. in consequence of a Military Warrant No. 1821. Located Nov 1, 1785. May 13, 1789.

Page   61 - WILLIAM STUART - NC - No. 757 - Reg. May 17, 1790

(2nd page)   By an Act for the relief of the Officers and Soldiers of the Continental Line, in consideration of the bravery and zeal of William Stuart, a private in the said line, granted unto William Stuart a tract of land containing 640 acres in Davidson County on the north side of Cumberland River on the first big creek above the line about two and a half miles above the mouth of said creek. Surveyed for William Stuart Dec 28, 1785 by Robert Hays, D.S. in consequence of a Military Warrant No. 659. Located July 13, 1784. July 11, 1788.

Page   62 - JOSEPH BROCK - NC - No. 867 - Reg. May 14, 1790

By an Act for the relief of the Officers and Soldiers of the Continental Line, in consideration of the bravery and zeal of William Gifford, a private in the said line, granted unto Joseph Brock, assignee of the heirs of William Gifford, a tract of land containing 640 acres in Davidson County on the north side of Cumberland River on the west boundary of said Brock's survey of No. 3443. Surveyed for Joseph Brock Dec 21, 1787 by Anthony Foster, D.S. in consequence of a Military Warrant No. 3349. Located Nov 24, 1787. Jan 17, 1788.

Page 62 - CHARLES SNYDER - NC - May 14, 1790
This indenture made Mar 25, 1790 between Lardner Clark of Nashville of one part and Charles Snyder of same place of other part. Lardner Clark conveyed unto Charles Snyder all that part of a town lot in Nashville, which lot is known as Lot No. 11. Beginning on the Main Street at the corner of the land now opened from the Main Street to said Lardner Clark's present dwelling house at the right hand corner going to the said house from the said Main Street. Test: James Cole Montflorence. Apr Term 1790.

Page 63 - JOHN McGAIOCH - NC - May 14, 1790
This indenture made Jan 2, 1790 between Thomas Molloy of Davidson County of one part and John McGaioch of same place of other part. Thomas Molloy conveyed unto John McGaioch a tract of land containing 103 acres in Davidson County about half a mile east of Whites Creek adjoining Robert Weakley's corner and James Brown's west boundary, and Thomas James' boundary. Being part of a tract of 640 acres granted to said Molloy by the State of North Carolina as assignee of the heirs of William Spencer for his services as a soldier in the Continental line per Military Warrant No. 2587. Test: Mark Brown Sappington and James Hoggatt. Apr Term 1790.

Page 64 - FREDERICK STUMP - NC - May 15, 1790
This indenture made Mar 23, 1790 between David Rounsevall of Davidson County of one part and Frederick Stump of same place of other part. David Rounsevall conveyed unto Frederick Stump a tract of land containing 3 acres in Davidson County on Whites Creek, being part of the tract of land whereon the said David Rounsevall now lives and which said David Rounsevall obtained as his Preemption Right in the Cumberland Country on the north side of said Preemption and west of said creek. Test: David Hay and Charles Snyder. Apr Term 1790.

Page Page 64 - ISAAC ROUNSEVALL - NC - May 15, 1790
This indenture made Mar 23, 1790 between Frederick Stump of Davidson County of one part and Isaac Rounsevall of same place of other part. Frederick Stump conveyed unto Isaac Rounsevall a tract of land containing 6 acres in Davidson County on Whites Creek, being part of the tract of land whereon the said Frederick Stump now lives and which said Frederick Stump obtained as his Preemption Right in Cumberland Country on the south side of said Preemption and west side of said creek. Test: David Hay and Charles Snyder. Apr Term 1790.

Page 65 - MICHAEL GLAVES - NC - May 15, 1790
This indenture made Dec 21, 1789 between Sampson Williams, Sheriff of Davidson County of one part and Michael Glaves of same place of other part. The Sheriff was directed to sale the goods and chattels of Daniel Chambers which Dennis Condry recovered of said Chambers. Sheriff sold unto Michael Glaves a tract of land containing 640 acres on the south fork of Whites Creek adjoining William Loggin's Preemption, Joseph Love's west boundary, John Walker's boundary, and Stephen Ray's north boundary. Test:

Page   65 - JAMES MAXEL - NC - May 17, 1790
        This indenture made Apr 5, 1790 between Joel Rice of Davidson County of
one part and James Maxel of same place of other part.   Joel Rice conveyed unto James
Maxel all that town lot in the town of Nashville known as Lot No. 61 containing one acre.
Apr Term 1790.

Page   66 - ISAAC DRAKE - NC - May 17, 1790
        This indenture made Apr 12, 1790 between Benjamin Drake of Davidson
County of one part and Isaac Drake of same place of other part.   Benjamin Drake conveyed
unto Isaac Drake a tract of land in Davidson County containing 101 acres on a fork of
Whites Creek adjoining Sarah Lucas' corner and Amos Heaton's line.   In witness whereof the
said Benjamin Drake, Jun. signed sealed and delivered the day and date above mentioned.
Apr Term 1790.

Page   66 - JAMES COOPER - NC - May 17, 1790
        This indenture made Mar 30, 1790 between William Loggins of Davidson
County of one part and James Cooper of same place of other part.   William Loggins
conveyed unto James Cooper a tract of land containing 300 acres in Davidson County on the
east fork of Whites Creek adjoining David Rounsevall's line and Loggins' Preemption, being
part of a tract of 640 acres granted to said Loggins by patent dated Apr 17, 1786. Tested:
James Hollis and Thomas Molloy. Apr Term 1790.

Page   67 - BENJAMIN GARRIS - NC - May 17, 1790
        This indenture made June 23, 1787 between Jessee Underwood, Elizabeth and
Mourning Wheeler of North Hampton County of North Carolina of one part and Benjamin
Garris of same place of other part. Jessee Underwood, Elizabeth and Mourning Wheeler
conveyed unto Benjamin Garris a tract of land containing 640 acres in Davidson County on
the south side of Cumberland River and waters of Mill Creek adjoining John Foreman's
Preemption. Said land was granted to Mourning Wheeler and Elizabeth Underwood
co-heirsess Empyry Wheeler, deceased which they were entitled to agreeable to an Act of
Assembly for the said Empery Wheeler's service in the North Carolina Continental services.
The grant bearing date Mar 7, 1786 and Numbered 110. Signed: Jessee Underwood, L.S.,
Elizabeth Underwood, L.S., John Vaughn, L.S., Mourning Vaughn, L.S. Test: Gen. Sharp
Garris, Susannah Garris and John Wade. Apr Term 1790.

Page   68 - JOHN COONROD - NC - May 17, 1790
        This indenture made Feb 16, 1790 between Martin Armstrong and Mary his
wife of Surry County, North Carolina of one part and John Coonrod of same place of other
part. Martin Armstrong and Mary his wife conveyed unto John Coonrod one tract of land
containing 640 acres in Davidson County on the south side of Richland. Said land being a
tract formerly granted to said Martin Armstrong by patent dated Sept 15, 1787 and No. 476.
Signed by Martin Armstrong, L.S. and Mary Armstrong, L.S. Test: William Hughlett, John
Rice, Martin Armstrong, Jr., and John Dixon. Apr Term 1790.

Page   68 - JOHN RICE - NC - May 17, 1790
(2nd page)   This indenture made Apr 10, 1790 between Hugh Bradshaw of Davidson
County of one part and John Rice of same place of other part. Hugh Bradshaw conveyed

unto John Rice a tract of land containing 70 acres in Davidson County on the north side of Cumberland River and on the waters of Whites Creek adjoining a line that divided said Bradshaw and Anthony Hart's boundary. Test: John Dixon and Robert Ewing. Apr Term 1790.

Page 69 - WILLIAM, DAVID & JAMES SHAW - NC - May 18, 1790

This indenture made the __ day of April 1790 between William Shaw, Sr. of Davidson County of one part and William Shaw, James Shaw and David Shaw all sons of James and Anner Shaw of Dickson County of same place of other part. William Shaw, Sr. in consideration of the natural love and affection for the said William Shaw, David Shaw and James Shaw, the sons of James and Anner Shaw, all that right of ferry on the Cumberland River at the town of Nashville, Davidson County, granted by the Court of Pleas and Quarter Sessions of Davidson County to the said James Shaw the father of William, David and James Shaw, with the necessary land for a road or roads from the several ferrylandings to the main County Road also the ferryhouse now built on the river bank on the north side of the river and known by Numbers 31 and 14 containing each one acre of land. Test: Joseph Shaw. Apr Term 1790.

Page 70 - WILLIAM SHAW, Senior - NC - May 18, 1790

This indenture made __ day of April 1790 between James Shaw of one part and William Shaw, Senior, of other part, both of Davidson County. James Shaw conveyed unto William Shaw, Senior, all the right title, interest and property in the ferry granted to James Shaw by the County of Davidson, cross Cumberland River at the town of Nashville, together with such parcel or portion of my lands adjoining said river on the north side, also two lots in town of Nashville and known as Lot No. 31 and Lot No. 14. Apr Term 1790.

Page 70 - JAMES HOGGATT - NC - May 18, 1790

This indenture made Jan 13, 1790 between Thomas Jamison of Davidson County of one part and James Hoggatt of same place of other part. Thomas Jamison conveyed unto James Hoggatt one lot in the town of Nashville known as Lot No. 45 containing one acre of land. Test: Robert Weakley and William Gallaspie. Apr Term 1790.

Page 71 - BEAL BOSLEY - NC - May 18, 1790

This indenture made __ day of __ 1789 between James Bosley of Davidson County of one part and Beal Bosley of same place of other part. James Bosley conveyed unto Beal Bosley all that tract of land containing 224 acres in Davidson County on the south side of Cumberland River on the Clover Hollow Beach (Creek) adjoining Samuel Deason's corner and James Hoggatt's corner. Test: Richard Shaffer and Hardy Allard. Apr Term 1790.

Page 71 - JAMES RUSSELL - NC - May 18, 1790

This indenture made Apr 13, 1790 between Argolas Jetor of Davidson County of one part and James Russell of same place of other part. Argolas Jetor conveyed unto James Russell all that land on the north side of Cumberland River on the east side of Whites Creek, including the house where the said Russell now lives, containing 10 acres of land. Test: Eleazer Hamilton and Samuel Deason. Apr Term 1790.

Page   72 -   JOHN BROWN - NC - May 18, 1790

This indenture made Oct 1, 1789 between Joseph Brock of Davidson County of one part and John Brown of the District of Sentucket, State of Virginia of the other part. Joseph Brock conveyed unto John Brown a certain lot or parcel of land in Davidson County, NC, on the north side of Cumberland River on the west side of a survey of No. 3443 made for said Joseph Brock. Containing 640 acres granted unto said Brock by patent No. 867 and dated Jan 1789. Wit: Peter Catlett, Jun. by virtue of a Power of Attorney and executed Mar 29, 1789. The Probate - New York. 1st day of Oct 1789 before me, James M. Hughs, one of the Masters in Chancery for the State, approved Joseph Brock, grantor within named by Peter Catlett, his attorney who acknowledged that he executed said indenture. Signed: James Hughs, May Court.

Page   72 -   FEDERICK STUMP - NC - May 19, 1790

This indenture made Mar 11, 1790 between Samuel Martin of one part and Federick Stump of other part, both of Davidson County. Samuel Martin conveyed unto Federick Stump a tract of land containing 320 acres in Davidson County on the east fork of Whites Creek adjoining David Rounsevall's line, Mitchel's corner and William Loggins' corner. Land being part of a tract granted to William Loggins by patent dated Apr 17, 1786. Test: Thomas Martin, Francis Fordne and William Loggins. Apr Term 1790.

Page   73 -   LARDNER CLARK - NC - May 19, 1790

This indenture made Dec 7, 1789 between Martin Armstrong of Surrey County, North Carolina of one part and Lardner Clark of Davidson County, NC, of other part. Martin Armstrong conveyed unto Lardner Clark a tract of land containing 2500 acres of land granted by the State to said Martin Armstrong and Anthony Crutcher for the services of Lieut. John Forde, land on the south side of Cumberland River on Thompsons Creek. Test: James Cole Montflorence. Apr Term 1790.

Page   73 -   WILLIAM BLEAKAMORE - NC - May 19, 1790

This indenture made Apr 15, 1790 between Thomas Hickman of Davidson County of one part and William Blackamore of same place of other part. Thomas Hickman conveyed unto William Blackamore a tract of land containing 640 acres in Davidson County on the first creek that runs into the east fork of Stones, on the east side above the mouth of Bradleys Lick Creek adjoining Joseph Hendricks' line. Said land granted to Thomas Hickman by State on the 11 July 1788. Test: Ed Hickman and Robert Weakley. Apr Term 1790.

Page   74 -   JOHN HANNAH - NC - May 19, 1790

This indenture made Apr 12, 1790 between Samuel Moore of Lincoln County, State of Virginia of one part and John Hanna of Tennessee County, North Carolina of other part. Samuel Moore conveyed unto John Hannah a tract of land containing 320 acres in Davidson County on the south side of Cumberland River on the waters of Harpeth River. Being half a Preemption granted to Samuel Moore by virtue of a Warrant No. 361, adjoining James Robertson's tract. Apr Term 1890.

Page   74 - ROBERT EWING - NC - May 19, 1790

This indenture made Feb 26, 1790 between Ephraim McLane of Davidson

County of one part and Robert Ewing of same place of other part.   Ephraim McLane conveyed unto Robert Ewing a tract of land containing 65 acres in Davidson County on the north side of the Cumberland River adjoining John Evans' line and McLane's 320 acres granted by patent dated 8 Oct 1787.   Conveyed by said Ephraim McLane, Junr.   Test: William Corbett and Samuel Allen.   Apr Term 1790.

Page   75 - SAMUEL McMURRY - NC - No. 238 - Reg. May 20, 1790
                For 10 lbs per 100 acres paid by Samuel McMurry was granted a tract of land containing 640 acres in Davidson County adjoining James Todd's line.   Which land was surveyed for Samuel McMurry Dec 6, 1784 by John Buchanan, D.S. in consequence of a Warrant No. 613.   Located Oct 13, 1784.   July 13, 1788.

Page   75 - EBENEZER BROOKS - NC - No. 216 - Reg. May 20, 1790
                For 10 lbs per 100 acres paid by Ebenezer was granted a tract of land containing 640 acres in Davidson County on Hurricane Creek a branch of Stones River adjoining said creek below on Old Buffalo Road.   Which land was surveyed for Ebenezer Brooks Aug 17, 1785 by John Buchanan, D.S. in consequence of a Warrant No. 435.   Located May 12, 1784.   July 13, 1788.

Page   76 - CHRISTOPHER FUNKHOUSER - NC - No. 205 - Reg. May 20, 1790
                For 10 lbs per 100 acres paid by Christopher Funkhouser was granted a tract of land containing 640 acres in Davidson County on both sides of Little Harpeth River. Surveyed for Christopher Funkhouser Sept 26, 1786 by John Donelson, D.S. in consequence of a Warrant No. 437.   Located Mar 10, 1784.   July 13, 1788.

Page   76 - WILLIAM MONTGOMERY - NC - No. 242 - Reg. May 21, 1790
                For 10 lbs per 100 acres paid by William Montgomery was granted a tract of land containing 640 acres in Davidson County on the south side of Cumberland River on the west fork of Big Harpeth near the forks and adjoining William Stuart's line.   Surveyed for William Montgomery Mar 3, 1786 by James Mulherin, D.S. in consequence of a Warrant No. 483.   Located June 9, 1784.   July 13, 1788.

Page   76 - HENRY HILAND - NC - No. 182 - Reg. May 21, 1790
                For 10 lbs per 100 acres paid by Henry Hiland was granted a tract of land containing 640 acres in Davidson County on both sides of Harpeth River including the mouth of Jones Creek.   Surveyed for Henry Hiland Oct 21, 1785 by Henry Rutherford in consequence of a Warrant No. 555.   Located July 27, 1784.   July 13, 1788.

Page   77 - WILLIAM TERRELL - NC - No. 190 - Reg. May 20, 1790
                For 10 lbs per 100 acres paid by William Terrell was granted a tract of land containing 640 acres in Davidson County on Overalls Creek a branch of Stones River adjoining Col. James Armstrong's 7200 acre survey.   Surveyed for William Terrell Mar 9, 1785 by B. William Pollock, D.S. in consequence of a Warrant No. 199.   Located Jan 28, 1784.   July 13, 1788.

Page   77 - ELIJAH GOWER, ELISHA GOWER & WILLIAM GOWER - NC - No. 263 -
                Reg. May 20, 1790

For 10 lbs per 100 acres paid by Elijah Gower, Elisha Gower and William Gower was granted a tract of land containing 640 acres in Davidson County beginning on the bank of Cumberland River. Surveyed for said Gowers by Thomas Molloy, D.S. in consequence of a Warrant No. 614. Located Nov 2, 1784. July 13, 1788.

Page   77 - JAMES MOORE - NC - No. 223 - Reg. May 20, 1790
        For 10 lbs per 100 acres paid by James Moore was granted a tract of land containing 640 acres in Davidson County on the east side of Mill Creek. Beginning at a tree below the mouth of Whites branch on the bank of said creek and adjoining Samuel McMurry's west boundary line. Surveyed for said James Moore by John Buchanan, D.S. in consequence of a Warrant No. 553. Located July 19, 1784. July 13, 1788.

Page   78 - THOMAS KENNEDY - NC - No. 321 - Reg. May 21, 1790
        For 10 lbs per 100 acres paid by Thomas Kennedy was granted a tract of land containing 640 acres in Davidson County on the south side of Cumberland and west side of Stones River, also the junction of Over(all) Creek with Stones River. Surveyed for Thomas Kennedy Jan 15, 1784 by James Mulherin, D.S. in consequence of a Warrant No. 365. Located Mar 18, 1784. July 13, 1788.

Page   78 - JOEL LAIN - NC - No. 266 - Reg. May 21, 1790
        For 10 lbs per 100 acres paid by Joel Lain was granted a tract of land containing 640 acres in Davidson County on Harpeth River below the mouth of Jones Creek adjoining Henry Hiland's line. Surveyed for Joel Lane Oct 22, 1785 by Henry Rutherford, D.S. in consequence of a Warrant No. 48. Located Jan 1, 1784.

Page   78 - ANDREW CROCKETT - NC - No. 258 - Reg. May 22, 1790
        For 10 lbs per 100 acres paid by Andrew Crockett was granted a tract of land containing 640 acres in Davidson County on the south side of Cumberland River and on the waters of Browns Creek adjoining Jonas Maniffee's corner and John Pain's line. Surveyed for Andrew Crockett Nov 13, 1784 by James Mulherin, D.S. in consequence of a Warrant No. 475. Located June 7, 1784. July 13, 1788.

Page   79 - WILLIAM SMITH - NC - No. 201 - Reg. May 21, 1790
        For 10 lbs per 100 acres paid by William Smith was granted a tract of land containing 640 acres in Davidson County on the east fork of Mill Creek adjoining Jason Thompson and Lardner Clark's corner and Cockrill's corner. Surveyed for William Smith by John Bucchanan Oct 4, 1785 in consequence of a Warrant No. 599. Located Oct 9, 1784. July 13, 1788.

Page   79 - WILLIAM LUCAS - NC - No. 186 - Reg. May 21, 1790
        For 10 lbs per 100 acres paid by William Lucas was granted a tract of land containing 640 acres in Davidson County adjoining Thomas Brown's boundary and John Dunham's line and William Gubbins' boundary, and Francis Armstrong's line. Surveyed for William Lucas June 10, 1785 by Thomas Molloy, D.S. in consequence of a Warrant No. 491. Located June 18, 1784. July 13, 1788.

Page   80 - JOHN DRAKE - NC - No. 21 - Reg. May 21, 1790

By an Act for the relief of the Officers and Soldiers of the Continental Line, in consideration of the services of Col. Martin Armstrong, surveyor, granted unto John Drake, assignee of said Armstrong, a tract of land containing 26 acres in Davidson County on the west side of Millers Creek of the Sulphur Fork of Red River adjoining Charles Thompson's line and Ralph Fleming's corner. Surveyed for John Drake Jan 30, 1786 by Robert Nelson, D.S. in consequence of a Service Right of said Armstrong, No. 1380. Located Sept 16, 1785. Oct 8, 1787.

Page   80 - JAMES BOSLEY - NC - No. 193 - Reg. May 21, 1790
For 10 lbs per 100 acres paid by James Bosley was granted a tract of land containing 640 acres in Davidson County. Beginning at a small tree below the Pond Spring and running to the bank of Cumberland River, and to west line of Bosley's tract No. 7, and to Bosley's tract No. 14. Surveyed for said James Bosley Mar 31, 1785 by Thomas Molloy, D.S. in consequence of a Warrant No. 43. Located Dec 31, 1783. July 13, 1788.

Page   80 - PETER RENTFRO - NC - No. 237 - Reg. May 21, 1790
For 10 lbs per 100 acres paid by Peter Rentfro was granted a tract of land containing 640 acres in Davidson County adjoining William Hay's corner. Surveyed for Peter Rentfro Nov 26, 1785 by Thomas Molloy, D.S. in consequence of a Warrant No. 581. Located Aug 17, 1784. July 13, 1788.

Page   81 - JONAS MANIFFEE - NC - No. 188 - Reg. May 22, 1790
For 10 lbs per 100 acres paid by Jonas Maniffee was granted a tract of land containing 584 acres in Davidson County on the south side of Cumberland River and on Browns Creek adjoining James Bosley's line and on the east boundary of the Public Survey which included the French Lick. Surveyed for Jonas Maniffee Mar 6, 1785 by James Mulherin, D.S. in consequence of a Warrant No. 529. Located July 17, 1784. July 13, 1788.

Page   81 - ROBERT THOMPSON - NC - No. 264 - Reg. May 22, 1790
For 10 lbs per 100 acres paid by Robert Thompson was granted a tract of land containing 640 acres in Davidson County joining William Collinsworth's Preemption on the south. Surveyed for Robert Thompson June 20, 1785 by B. William Pollock, D.S. in consequence of a Warrant No. 103. Located Jan 15, 1784. July 13, 1788.

Page   81 - JAMES BOSLEY - NC - No. 178 - Reg. May 22, 1790
For 10 lbs per 100 acres paid by James Bosley was granted a tract of land containing 640 acres in Davidson County. Beginning on the line run by the Commissioners about Dentons Lick and on a conditional line with George Freeland. Surveyed for James Bosley Mar 30, 1785 by Thomas Molloy, D.S. in consequence of a Warrant No. 19. Located Dec 26, 1783. July 10, 1788.

Page   82 - ALEXANDER EWING - NC - No. 909 - Reg. June 4, 1790
By an Act for the relief of the Officers and Soldiers of the Continental Line, in consideration of the bravery and zeal of Benjamin Brewington, a private in the said line, granted unto Alexander Ewing, assignee of said Benjamin Brewington, a tract of land containing 640 acres in Davidson County on both sides of Smiths Fork a branch of Caney Fork adjoining Stockley Donelson's line. Surveyed for Alexander Ewing Dec 20, 1787 by

John Donelson, D.S. in consequence of a Military Warrant No. 1515. Located Sept 21, 1787. Jan 17, 1789.

Page   82 - ANDREW BOYD - NC - No. 214 - Reg. June 4, 1790
        For 10 lbs per 100 acres paid by Andrew Boyd was granted a tract of land containing 640 acres in Davidson County on the head of Browns Creek adjoining Francis Armstrong's corner, the heirs of Nicholas Gentry's line, and Samuel Barton's line. Surveyed for Andrew Boyd Feb 14, 1785 by John Buchanan, D.S. agreeable to a Warrant No. 236. Entry date Feb 5, 1784. July 13, 1788.

Page   82 - THOMAS GILLISPIE - NC - No. 241 - Reg. June 4, 1790
        For 10 lbs per 100 acres paid by Thomas Gillispie was granted a tract of land containing 640 acres in Davidson County on the waters of Stones River adjoining Samuel McMurry's line and William Moores' line. Surveyed for Thomas Gillispie Apr 11, 1785 by John Buchanan, D.S. agreeable to a Warrant No. 628. Entered Nov 20, 1784. July 10, 1788.

Page   83 - COL. JOSEPH MARTIN - NC - No. 260 - Reg. June 4, 1790
        For 10 lbs per 100 acres paid by Col. Joseph Martin was granted a tract of land containing 640 acres in Davidson County on the waters of Stones River near Overalls Creek adjoining Colonel Armstrong's east boundary. Surveyed for Col. Joseph Martin Mar 10, 1785 by B. William Pollock, D.S. agreeable to a Warrant No. 600. Entered Oct 9, 1784. July 10, 1788.

Page   83 - WILLIAM COLLINSWORTH - NC - No. 254 - June 4, 1790
        For 10 lbs per 100 acres paid by William Collinsworth was granted a tract of land containing640 acres in Davidson County on the main Harpeth joining a Preemption belonging to Robert Thompson on the north. Surveyed for William Collinsworth June 20, 1785 by B. William Pollock, D.S. agreeable to a Warrant No. 448. Entered May 12, 1784. July 10, 1788.

Page   83 - GEORGE GILLISPIE - NC - No. 208 - Reg. June 4, 1790
        For 10 lbs per 100 acres paid by George Gillispie was granted a tract of land containing 640 acres in Davidson County on the south side of Big Harpeth River adjoining John Donelson's corner. Surveyed for George Gillispie Sept 22, 1786 by John Donelson, D.S. agreeable to a Warrant No. 714. Entered Apr 23, 1785. July 10, 1788.

Page   84 - JOSEPH MARTIN - NC - No. 184 - Reg. June 5, 1790
        For 10 lbs per 100 acres paid by Joseph Martin was granted a tract of land containing 640 acres in Davidson County on the south side of Cumberland River on Browns Creek chiefly on the upper side adjoining Thomas Hardiman's and James Bosley's line and on the road side leading from Bucchanan's to Nashville. Surveyed for Joseph Martin June 20, 1785 by James Mulherin, D.S. agreeable to a Warrant No. 387. Entered Mar 31, 1784. July 10, 1788.

Page   84 - JAMES TODD - NC - No. 249 - Reg. June 5, 1790
        For 10 lbs per 100 acres paid by James Todd was granted a tract of land containing 640 acres in Davidson County on the south side of Cumberland River adjoining

Stones River. Surveyed for James Todd July 10, 1784 by James Mulherin, D.S. agreeable to a Warrant No. 72. Entered Jan 10, 1784. July 10, 1788.

Page   84 - JAMES TODD - NC - No. 917 - Reg. June 7, 1790

By an Act for the relief of the officers and Soldiers of the Continental Line, in consideration of the bravery and zeal of Thomas Wood, a private in the said line, granted unto James Todd, assignee of said Thomas Wood's heirs, a tract of land containing 640 acres in Davidson County on the waters of Caney Fork adjoining a tract of James Mulherin as assignee of Ethelred Bailey's heirs. Surveyed for James Todd Dec 21, 1788 by James Mulherin, D.S. in consequence of a Military Warrant No. 2480. Located Nov 15, 1788. May 18, 1789.

Page   85 - THOMAS SHARPE - NC - No. 245 - Reg. June 7, 1790

For 10 lbs per 100 acres paid by Thomas Sharpe was granted a tract of land containing 640 acres in Davidson County adjoining Jessee Maxey's corner and Thomas Callendar's boundary. Surveyed for Thomas Sharpe Oct 31, 1785 by Thomas Molloy, D.S. agreeable to a Warrant No. 660. Entered Jan 10, 1785. July 10, 1788.

Page   85 - JESSEE MAXELL - NC - No. 88 - Reg. June 7, 1790

By an Act for the relief of the Officers and Soldiers of the Continental Line, in consideration of the bravery and zeal of James Franklin, one of the Commissioners Guards, granted unto Jessee Maxell, assignee of James Franklin, a tract of land containing 320 acres in Davidson County on the north side of Cumberland River. Beginning at the line of the heirs of Will Nealy's Preemption and corner of the Public Survey. Surveyed for Jesse Maxell Apr 10, 1786 by James Sanders, D.S. in consequence of a Warrant No. 687. Entered Feb 19, 1785. July 10, 1788.

Page   85 - ANDREW CROCKETT - NC - No. 36 - Reg. June 7, 1790

By an Act for the relief of the Officers and Soldiers of the Continental Line, in consideration of the services of Col. Martin Armstrong, surveyor, granted unto Andrew Crockett, assignee of said Armstrong, a tract of land containing 106 acres in Davidson County adjoining William Collinsworth's Preemption and Andrew Crockett's Preemption and also John Crockett's Preemption. Surveyed for Andrew Crockett May 4, 1785 by John Buchanan, D.S. in consequence of a Service Right of said Armstrong, No. 377. Located Oct 4, 1784. Oct 8, 1787.

Page   86 - THOMAS SHARPE SPENCER - NC - No. 95 - Reg. June 7, 1790

By an Act for the relief of the Officers and Soldiers of the Continental Line, in consideration of the bravery and zeal of Thomas Sharpe Spencer, one of the Commissioners Guards, granted unto Thomas Sharpe Spencer a tract of land containing 320 acres in Davidson County on the waters of Big Harpeth River. Surveyed for Thomas Sharpe Spencer Nov 17, 1785 by John Bucchanan, D.S. agreeable to a Warrant No. 272. Entered Feb 13, 1784. July 10, 1788.

Page   86 - JOSEPH DOUGHERTY - NC - No. 243 - Reg. June 7, 1790

For 10 lbs per 100 acres paid by Joseph Dougherty was granted a tract of land containing 640 acres in Davidson County on the south side of Cumberland River and on the waters of Big Harpeth. Surveyed for Joseph Dougherty Mar 3, 1786 by James Mulherin, D.S. agreeable to a Warrant No. 405. Entered June 10, 1784. July 10, 1788.

Page   86 - GEORGE SCOTT - NC - No. 220 - Reg. June 7, 1790

For 10 lbs per 100 acres paid by George Scott was granted a tract of land containing 640 acres in Davidson County on the south side of Cumberland River and on the waters of Big Harpeth on the south side of the East Fork. Surveyed for George Scott Mar 6, 1786 by James Mulherin, D.S. agreeable to a Warrant No. 514. Entered July 7, 1784. June 10, 1788.

Page   87 - WILLIAM COLLINSWORTH - NC - No. 230 - Reg. June 7, 1790

For 10 lbs per 100 acres paid by William Collinsworth was granted a tract of land containing 640 acres in Davidson County on Browns Creek adjoining the spring which William Ellis settled at. Surveyed for William Collinsworth Sept 13, 1787 by John Buchanan, D.S. agreeable to a Warrant No. 124. Entry dated Jan 15, 1784. July 10, 1788.

Page   87 - CORNELIUS RUDDELL - NC - No. 228 - Reg. June 7, 1790

For 10 lbs per 100 acres paid by Cornelius Ruddell was granted a tract of land containing 640 acres in Davidson County lying on Stones River about half a mile above the mouth of Searcys Creek. Surveyed for Cornelius Ruddell Nov 30, 1785 by John Bucchanan, D.S. agreeable to a Warrant No. 738. Entered May 30, 1785. July 10, 1788.

Page   87 - THOMAS DENTON - NC - No. 270 - Reg. June 7, 1790

For 10 lbs per 100 acres paid by Thomas Denton was granted a tract of land containing 640 acres in Davidson County near the spring being the waters of the east fork of Mill Creek. Surveyed for Thomas Denton Aug __, 1784 by John Bucchanan, D.S. agreeable to a Warrant No. 308. Entered Feb 19, 1784. July 10, 1788.

Page   88 - THOMAS MOLLOY - NC - No. 176 - Reg. June 7, 1790

For 10 lbs per 100 acres paid by Thomas Molloy was granted a tract of land containing 2500 acres in Davidson County. Beginning at the mouth of the first creek below Little Harpeth on George Neville's south boundary. Surveyed for Thomas Molloy by himself Sept 12, 1785 agreeable to a Warrant No. 24. Entered dated Dec 29, 1783.

Page   88 - EBENEZER TITUS - NC - No. 198 - Reg. June 7, 1790

For 10 lbs per 100 acres paid by Ebenezer Titus was granted a tract of land containing 640 acres in Davidson County on the waters of Big and Little Harpeth adjoining John Crockett's east corner and William Nevels' corner. Surveyed for Ebenezer Titus Nov 17, 1785 by John Bucchanan, D.S. agreeable to a Warrant No. 725. Entered May 7, 1785. July 10, 1788.

Page   88 - LEWIS ROBBARDS - NC - No. 206 - Reg. June 8, 1790

For 10 lbs per 100 acres paid by Lewis Robbards was granted a tract of land containing 640 acres in Davidson County on the south side of Cumberland River and adjoining Hay's line. Surveyed for Lewis Robards Mar 13, 1786 by John Donelson, D.S. agreeable to a Warrant No. 399. Entered Apr 6, 1784. July 10, 1788.

Page   89 - WILLIAM MOORE - NC - No. 200 - Reg. June 8, 1790
For 10 lbs per 100 acres paid by William Moore was granted a tract of land containing 640 acres in Davidson County on the waters of Stones River adjoiningSamuel McMurry's line and Thomas Gillespie's corner. Surveyed for William Moore Dec 6, 1784 by John Buchanan, D.S. agreeable to a Warrant No. 45. Entered Jan 1, 1784. July 10, 1788.

Page   89 - N. COONROD - NC - No. 224 - June 8, 1790
For 10 lbs per 100 acres paid by Nicholas Coonrod was granted a tract of land containing 640 acres in Davidson County on the south side of Cumberland on the head of Spring Creek. Surveyed for Nicholas Coonrod Aug 9, 1786 by James Sanders, D.S. agreeable to a Warrant No. 577. Entered Aug 13, 1784. July 10, 1788.

Page   89 - N. COONROD - NC - No. 259 - Reg. June 8, 1790
For 10 lbs per 100 acres paid by Nicholas Coonrod was granted a tract of land containing 640 acres in Davidson COunty on the south side of Cumberland River near to Bartons Creek. Surveyed for Nicholas Coonrod Dec 14, 1785 by B. William Pollock, D.S. in consequence of a Warrant No. 576. Entered Aug 13, 1784. July 10, 1788.

Page   90 - JASON THOMPSON - NC - No. 831 - Reg. June 8, 1790
By an Act for the relief of the Officers and Soldiers of the Continental Line, in consideration of the bravery and zeal of John Cronester, a private in the said line, granted unto Jason Thompson, assignee of John Cronester, a tract of land containing 640 acres in Davidson County on the waters of Mill Creek and Little Harpeth adjoining Ebenezer Titus' corner and Joseph Ferebus' boundary line, and Green Hill's line, and also to Benjamin Crockett's corner to William Collinsworth's boundary. Surveyed for Jason Thompson Oct 3, 1788 by John Bucchanan, D.S. in consequence of a Military Warrant No. 1139. Located July 4, 1788. Jan 17, 1789.

Page   90 - JAMES BOSLEY - NC - No. 235 - Reg. June 14, 1790
For 10 lbs per 100 acres paid by James Bosley was granted a tract of land containing 640 acres in Davidson County adjoining George Freeland's south west corner and on a conditional line with Elijah Robertson. Surveyed for James Bosley Mar 30, 1785 by Thomas Molloy, D.S. agreeable to a Warrant No. 7. Entered Dec 26, 1785. July 10, 1788.

Page   90 - GEORGE DAVIDSON - NC - No. 31 - Reg. June 28, 1790
By an Act for the relief of the Officers and Soldiers of the Continental Line, in consideration of the bravery and zeal of William Davidson, deceased, a Lieut Col. in the said line, granted unto George Davidson, heir of William Davidson, a tract of land containing 5760 acres in Davidson County on the north side of Tennessee River at the mouth of the first big creek below Dyers Creek. Surveyed for George Davidson by William Murry, D.S. in consequence of a Military Warrant No. 254. Located June 28, 1785. Mar 14, 1786.

Page   91 - JAMES MONTFLORENCE - NC - June 30, 1790
This indenture made 16 June 1790 between William Nash of Davidson County of one part and James Montflorence of same place of other part. William Nash conveyed unto James Montflorence the three military tracts of land. To wit, all that tract of land in

Davidson County on the north side of Cumberland River joining on the lower side of Capt. Andrew Armstrong's survey of 1286 acres, containing 640 acres of land about sixteen miles below said town of Nashville, also that the other tract of land in Davidson County on the waters of the first creek above Stones Lick Creek and on the north side of Stones River adjoining George Sugg's corner, No. 2236. Containing 640 acres about sixteen miles nearly southeast of Nashville. Also, that other tract of land in Davidson County on the waters of the first creek above Stones Lick Creek on the east side of Stones River adjoining Aquilla Sugg's corner, Warrant No. 1503. Containing 640 acres of land about fourteen miles from the town of Nashville. Proven by B. Searcy, A. Foster and William Crutcher.

Page   92 - JAMES COLE MONTFLORENCE - NC - June 30, 1790
           This indenture made 8 June 1790 between Elijah Robertson of Davidson County of one part and James Cole Montflorence of same place of other part. Elijah Robertson conveyed unto James Cole Montflorence all the ten following tracts of land of 1000 each and amounting to 10,000 acres, each in State of North Carolina in the Western District and on the waters of Mississippi. To wit, That tract of 1000 acres the grant of which is No. 200 lying on the south side of Loose Hatchee River adjoining Blount's survey No. 2456, and Blount's corner No. 2463. Also that other tract of 1000 acres grant No. 182 lying on the head of the south fork of Indian Creek of Big Hatchee River adjoining Blount's survey No. 2485 and Blount's No. 2464. Also that other tract of 1000 acres the grant of which is No. 226 on the waters of Indian Creek of Reelfoot River adjoining George Doughertys corner and Blount's corner. Also that other tract of 1000 acres the grant No. 243 on the waters of Reelfoot River adjoining Blount's corner and George Dougherty's corner. Also that other tract of 1000 acres the grant No. 235 On the head of Graves Creek and Spring Creek adjoining Blount's corner of No. 2316 and No. 2399 and No. 2315. Also that other tract of 1000 acres the grant No. 184 on the waters of Reelfoot River adjoining Blount's corner and George Dougherty's line. Also that other tract of land of 1000 acres No. 214 on Goose Creek adjoining Blount's survey No. 2311, Edward Harris' survey No. 234 and Martin Armstrong's No. 694 on said creek. Also that other tract of 1000 acres the grant No. 258 on the Lick Fork of Obion River adjoining Blount's survey No. 2442 and 2377 on said fork. Also that other tract of 1000 the grant No. 264 on the waters of Obion River adjoining Blount's corner, Abner Nash's corner. Also that other tract of 1000 acres the grant No. 175 on the waters of Obion River adjoining Blount's corner and Abner Nash's corner. The said ten tracts containing 10,000 acres of land conveyed unto James Cole Montflorence. Proven by John McNairy and Josiah Love the 13 June 1790.

Page   94 - WILLIAM NASH - NC - No. 940 - Reg. July 1, 1790
           By an Act for the relief of the Officers and Soldiers of the Continental Line, in consideration of the bravery and zeal of Isam Whitton, granted unto William Nash, assignee of the said Whitton's heirs, a tract of land containing 640 acres in Davidson County on the north side of Cumberland River joining on the lower side of Capt. Andrew Armstrong's survey of 1286 acres. Surveyed for William Nash by himself June 13, 1788 in consequence of a Military Warrant No. 2733. Located Apr 12, 1788. May 18, 1789.

Page   94 - WILLIAM NASH - NC - No. 938 - Reg. July 1, 1790
           By an Act for the relief of the Officers and soldiers of the Continental Line, in consideration of the bravery and zeal of Isaack Simmons, granted unto William Nash,

169

assignee of the heirs of said Simmons, a tract of land containing 640 acres in Davidson County on the waters of the first creek above Stones Lick Creek on the east side of Stones River adjoining Aquilla Suggs' Warrant No. 1503. Surveyed for William Nash by himself Nov --, 1788 in consequence of a Military Warrant No. 2235. Located Oct 18, 1788. May 18, 1789.

Page   94 - WILLIAM NASH - NC - No. 936 - Reg. July 1, 1790

By an Act for the relief of the Officers and Soldiers of the Continental Line, in consideration of the bravery and zeal of Richard Colbert, granted unto William Nash, assignee of the heirs of Richard Colbert, a tract of land containing 640 acres in Davidson County on the waters of the first creek above Stones Lick Creek on the east side of Stones River adjoining George Sugg's corner, No. 2236. Surveyed for William Nash by himself May 11, 1788 in consequence of a Military Warrant No. 1499. Located Nov 12, 1788. May 18, 1789.

Page   95 - JAMES COLE MONTFLORENCE - NC - July 1, 1790

This indenture made 2 June 1790 between Anthony Hart of Davidson County of one part and James Cole Montflorence of the town of Nashville of other part. Anthony Hart conveyed unto James Cole Montflorence sixteen following Military tracts of land of 640 acres each amounting to 10,240 acres of land in the District of Mero, State of North Carolina. To wit, All that tract of land of 640 acres in Tennessee County, NC. Beginning on the first large creek on the south side of Cumberland River above the Virgonia Line including the fork of said creek. Granted by the State of NC to John Forde and by said Forde conveyed to said Anthony Hart by deed. Also all that other tract of 640 acres in Tennessee County, NC, on the trace near the head of Gibsons Creek adjoining on the trace that leads from Thompson's Settlement up the Sulphur Fork. All that other tract of 640 acres in Tennessee County, NC, on the west fork of Spring Creek the waters of Sycamore Creek adjoining Samuel Marsham's corner and John Nichols' line. All that other tract of 640 acres in Tennessee County, NC, on the west survey made by Federick Stump which last survey includes Turnbull's Clay Lick, and the Military Warrant No. 2815, granted for the services of William Reeves. Also all that other tract of 640 acres in Tennessee County on the southern boundary of the above mentioned survey of said Federick Stump adjoining the Military Warrant No. 2957, granted for the services of Isaac Reddick. Also that other tract of 640 acres in Tennessee County on the eastern boundary of the aforesaid survey of said Stump, the Military Warrant No. 2763 granted for the services of John Sellers. Also that other tract of 640 acres in Tennessee County on the north fork of McAdoes Creek joining of survey of John Drake's on the west the Military Warrant No. 3415, granted for the services of Charles Brooks. Also that other tract of 640 acres in Tennessee County on the west fork of Little Brush Creek waters of Red River joining a survey of John Nichols on the north, all which seven last mentioned tracts of land are within the present settlement of Mero District. Also that other tract of land of 640 acres in Tennessee County on the north side of Cumberland River joining a survey of Robert Weakley on the north. The Military Warrant No. 3423 granted for the services of Obid Calvin. Also that other tract of 640 acres in Sumner COunty on the south side of the Caney Fork River joining an entry of John Hayward of 100 acres on the west the Military Warrant No. 2485, granted for the services of Randall Cross. Also that other tract of 640 acres in Sumner County on the waters of Collins River one of the branches of Caney Fork joining an entry made by Thomas Hickman in 1788 on the west. The Military Warrant No. 2492, granted for the services of Lewis Morgan. Also that other tract of 640 acres in Sumner County on Collins River about seven miles above the mouth of said river. The Warrant No. 2809, grantedfor the services of Richard King. Also that other tract of land of 640 acres in Sumner County on the waters of Caney Fork between Mulherin and Hickmans Creeks joining an entry made by Thomas Hickman in 1788, the Military Warrant No. 2665. Granted for the services ofJames Hammon. Also that other tract of 640 acres in Sumner County on the waters of Caney Fork between Mulherin and Hickmans Creeks. The Warrant No. 2483, grantedfor the services of Abraham Applewhite. Also that other tract of 640 acres of land in Sumner County on the headwaters of Hickmans Creek of the Caney Fork joining an entry made by Thomas Hickman in 1788. And also that tract of 640 acres in Sumner County on the south sides of Big Barren River and on a fork of said river, joining an entry of Joshua Davis on the south. Entered 2 Dec 1786. The Military Warrant No. 2707, granted for the services of Abraham Buck and 2249, for the services of William Wright. Proven by George Walker, Elijah Robertson and William A. Peas.

Page 97 - JOHN GRAY BLOUNT & THOMAS BLOUNT - NC - No. 175 - Reg. July 2, 1790

For 10 lbs per 100 acres paid by John Gray Blount and Thomas Blount was granted a tract of land containing 1000 acres being in the Western District on the waters of Obion River adjoining Blount's corner and Abner Nash's corner. Surveyed for said Blounts Oct 3, 1785 by Henry Rutherford, D.S. in consequence of a Warrant from the State No. 2452. Dated May 25, 1784. July 10, 1788.

Page 97 - JOHN GRAY BLOUNT & THOMAS BLOUNT - NC - No. 182 - July 2, 1790

For 10 lbs per 100 acres paid by John Gray Blount and Thomas Blount was granted a tract of land containing 1000 acres in the Western District on the head of the south fork of Indian Creek of Big Hatchee River adjoining said Blount's No. 2485 and No. 2464 on said creek. Surveyed for said Blounts Sept 8, 1785 by Edward Harris, D.S. in consequence of a Warrant No. 2483. Dated May 25, 1784. July 10, 1788.

Page 97 - JOHN GRAY BLOUNT & THOMAS BLOUNT - NC - No. 184 - Reg. July 2, 1790

For 10 lbs per 100 acres paid by John Gray Blount and Thomas Blount was granted a tract of land containing 1000 acres in the Western District on the waters of Reelfoot River adjoining Blount's boundary. Surveyed for said Blounts Sept 17, 1785 by Henry Rutherford, D.S. in consequence of a Warrant No. 2318. Dated May 25, 1784. July 10, 1788.

Page 98 - JOHN GRAY BLOUNT & THOMAS BLOUNT - NC - No. 200 - Reg. July 2, 1790

For 10 lbs per 100 acres paid by John Gray Blount and Thomas Blount was granted a tract of land containing 1000 acres in the Western District on the south side of Loshatchee River adjoining said Blount's survey of No. 2456 and No. 2463 on said river adjoining Blount's corner of No. 2463. Surveyed for said Blounts Sept 6, 1785 by Edward Harris, D.S. in consequence of a Warrant No. 2457. Dated May 25, 1784. July 10, 1788.

Page   98 - JOHN GRAY BLOUNT & THOMAS BLOUNT - NC - No. 243 - Reg. July 2, 1790

For 10 lbs per 100 acres paid by John Gray Blount and Thomas Blount was granted a tract of land containing 1000 acres in the Western District on the waters of Reelfoot River adjoining Blount's corner and George Dougherty's line. Surveyed for said Blounts Sept 17, 1785 by Henry Rutherford, D.S. in consequence of a Warrant No. 2320. Dated May 25, 1784. July 10, 1788.

Page   98 - JOHN GRAY BLOUNT & THOMAS BLOUNT - NC - No. 264 - Reg. July 2, 1790

For 10 lbs per 100 acres paid by John Gray Blount and Thomas Blount was granted a tract of land containing 1000 acres in the Western District on the waters of Obion River adjoining Blount's corners and Abner Naphs' corner. Surveyed for said Blounts Oct 3, 1785 by Henry Rutherford, D.S. in consequence of a Warrant No. 2384. Dated May 25, 1784. July 10, 1788.

Page   99 - JOHN GRAY BLOUNT & THOMAS BLOUNT - NC - No. 235 - Reg. July 2, 1790

For 10 lbs per 100 acres paid by John Gray Blount and Thomas Blount was granted a tract of land containing 1000 acres in the Western District on the heads of Grove Creek and adjoining said Blounts of No. 2315 and No. 2399 on said creek and joining Blount's corner of No. 2316 and No. 2315. Surveyed for said Blounts Oct 5, 1785 by Edward Harris, D.S. in consequence of a Warrant No. 2316. Dated May 25, 1784. July 10, 1788.

Page   99 - JOHN GRAY BLOUNT & THOMAS BLOUNT - NC - No. 258 - Reg. July 2, 1790

For 10 lbs per 100 acres paid by John Gray Blount and thomas Blount was granted a tract of land containing 1000 acres in the Western District on the Lick Fork of Obion River adjoining said Blounts of No. 2442 and No. 2377 on said Fork. Surveyed for said Blounts Oct 1, 1785 by Edward Harris, D.S. in consequence of a Warrant No. 2323. Dated May 25, 1784. July 10, 1788.

Page   99 - JOHN GRAY BLOUNT & THOMAS BLOUNT - NC - No. 226 - Reg. July 2, 1790

For 10 lbs per 100 acres paid by John Gray Blount and Thomas Blount was granted a tract of land containing 1000 acres in the Western District on the waters of Indian Creek of Reelfoot River adjoining George Dougherty's corner. Surveyed for said Blounts Sept 17, 1785 by Henry Rutherford, D.S. in consequence of a Warrant No. 2319. Dated May 25, 1784. July 10, 1788.

Page   100 - JOHN GRAY BLOUNT & THOMAS BLOUNT - NC - No. 214 - Reg. July 2, 1790

For 10 lbs per 100 acres paid by John Gray Blount and Thomas Blount was granted a tract of land containing 1000 acres in the Western District on Grove Creek adjoining said Blount's No. 2311, Edward Harris' No. 234 and Martin Armstrong's No. 694 on said creek and joining Blount's corner. Surveyed for said Blounts Oct 4, 1785 by Edward Harris, D.S. in consequence of a Warrant No. 2310. Dated May 25, 1784. July 10, 1788.

Page   100 - WILLIAM OVERALL & MARTIN KING - NC - No. 212 - Reg. July 2, 1790

For 10 lbs per 100 acres paid by William Overall and Martin King was granted a tract of land containing 640 acres in Davidson County on the south side of Cumberland River and on Overall Lower Creek near the mouth. Surveyed for said Overall and King Jan 8, 1786 by James Mulherin, D.S. in consequence of a Warrant No. 301. Entered Feb 10, 1784. July 10, 1788.

Page   100 - JAMES FRAZOR - NC - No. 251 - Reg. July 3, 1790

For 10 lbs per 100 acres paid by James Frazor was granted a tract of land containing 640 acres in Davidson County on Drakes Creek. Surveyed for said Frazor Dec 28, 1785 by Henry Bradford, D.S. in consequence of a Warrant No. 394. Entered Apr 5, 1784. July 10, 1788.

Page   101 - JOHN GRAY BLOUNT & THOMAS BLOUNT - NC - No. 233 - Reg. July 10, 1790

For 10 lbs per 100 acres paid by John Gray Blount and Thomas Blount was granted a tract of land containing 1000 acres in the Western District on the south fork of Obion River adjoining Blount's of No. 2453 and No. 2323 on said river. Surveyed for said Blounts Oct 1, 1785 by Edward Harris, D.S. in consequence of a Warrant No. 2377. Dated May 25, 1784. July 10, 1788.

Page   101 - JOHN GRAY BLOUNT & THOMAS BLOUNT - NC - No. 224 - Reg. July 10, 1790

For 10 lbs per 100 acres paid by John Gray Blount and Thomas Blount was granted a tract of land containing 1000 acres in the Western District on the waters of Obion River adjoining James Martin's corner. Surveyed for said Blounts Oct 3, 1785 by Henry Rutherford, D.S. in consequence of a Warrant No. 2445. Dated May 25, 1784. July 10, 1788.

Page   101 - JOHN GRAY BLOUNT & THOMAS BLOUNT - NC - No. 242 - Reg. July 10, 1790

For 10 lbs per 100 acres paid by John Gray Blount and Thomas Blount was granted a tract of land containing 1000 acres in the Western District on the south side of Loos Hatcher River adjoining said Blounts of No. 2460 and No. 2464 and No. 2457 on said river. Surveyed for said Blounts Sept 26, 1785 by Edward Harris, D.S. in consequence of a Warrant No. 2463. Dated May 25, 1784. July 10, 1788.

Page   102 - JOHN GRAY BLOUNT & THOMAS BLOUNT - NC - No. 181 - Reg. July 10, 1790

For 10 lbs per 100 acres paid by John Gray Blount and Thomas Blount was granted a tract of land containing 1000 acres in the Western District on the south side of Looshatcher River adjoining said Blounts of No. 2463, No. 2467 and No. 2433. Surveyed for said Blounts Sept 7, 1785 by Edward Harris, D.S. in consequence of a Warrant No. 2464. Dated May 25, 1784. July 10, 1788.

Page   102 - JOHN GRAY BLOUNT & THOMAS BLOUNT - NC - No. 188 - Reg. July 10, 1790

For 10 lbs per 100 acres paid by John Gray Blount and Thomas Blount was granted a tract of land containing 1000 acres in the Western District on Glove Creek adjoining Blounts of No. 2310, No. 2315 and Martin Armstrong No. 694 on said creek also Blount's corner of No. 2315. Surveyed for said Blounts Oct 4, 1785 by Edward Harris, D.S. in consequence of a Warrant No. 2811. Dated May 25, 1785. July 10, 1788.

Page   102 - ELIJAH ROBERTSON - NC - No. 336 - Reg. July 10, 1790
For 50 shilling for 100 acres paid by Elijah Robertson was granted a tract of land containing 100 acres in the Western District on the north side of Woolf River above the mouth of Looshatcher adjoining William Alston and Thomas Talbot's corner. Surveyed for Elijah Robertson Sept 5, 1785 by Edward Harris, D.S. in consequence of a (incomplete). Dated May 18, 1789.

Page   103 - ELIJAH ROBERTSON - NC - No. 337 - Reg. July 10, 1790
For 50 shillings per 100 acres paid by Elijah Robertson was granted a tract of land containing 500 acres in the Western District on the east side of Harris Fork of Obion River adjoining Carter's corner. Surveyed for Elijah Robertson Oct 6, 1785 by Edward Harris, D.S. in consequence of a Warrant No. 1996. Dated May 18, 1789.

Page   103 - ELIJAH ROBERTSON - NC - No. 817 - Reg. July 10, 1790
By an Act for the relief of the Officers and Soldiers of the Continental Line, in consideration of the bravery and zeal of Peter Black, a private in the said line, granted unto Elijah Robertson, assignee of the heirs of Elijah Robertson, a tract of land containing 640 acres in Davidson County on the waters of Caney Fork. Surveyed for Elijah Robertson June 10, 1788 by James Mulherin, D.S. in consequence of a Military Warrant No. 3300. Located Mar 22, 1788. Oct 21, 1788.

Page   103 - ELIJAH ROBERTSON - NC - No. 807 - Reg. July 10, 1790
By an Act for the relief of the Officers and Soldiers of the Continental Line, in consideration of the bravery and zeal of Estridge Nelson, a private in the said line, granted unto Elijah Robertson, assignee of the heirs of Estridge Nelson, a tract of land containing 640 acres in Davidson County on the waters of Caney Fork adjoining Col. John Pointer's tract. Surveyed for Elijah Robertson Jule 11, 1788 by James Mulherin, D.S. in consequence of a Military Warrant No. 3317. Dated Mar 22, 1788. Oct 29, 1788.

Page   104 - ELIJAH ROBERTSON - NC - No. 809 - Reg. July 10, 1790
By an Act for the relief of the Officers and Soldiers of the Continental Line, in consideration of the bravery and zeal of Thomas Riley, a private in the said line, granted unto Elijah Robertson, assignee of Thomas Riley, a tract of land containing 640 acres in Davidson County on the waters of Caney Fork. Surveyed for Elijah Robertson June 10, 1788 by James Mulherin, D.S. in consideration of a Military Warrant No. 3322. Entry dated Mar 22, 1788. Oct 21, 1788.

Page   104 - DAVID ALLISON - NC - July 23, 1790
This indenture made 29 June 1790 between Elijah Robertson of Davidson County of one part and David Allison of same place of other part. Elijah Robertson conveyed unto David Allison a tract of land containing 5000 acres in the Middle District on

the south side of Duck River and on both sides of Fountain Creek adjoining William Gilbert's corner and Globe Creek. Proven by George Suggs and James Hoggatt. July Term 1790.

Page   105 - JOHN DAVES - NC - July 23, 1790
This indenture made 12 Dec 1789 between Martin Armstrong of Surry County, NC of one part and John Daves of Craven County, NC of other part. Martin Armstrong conveyed unto John Daves a tract of land on the north side of Cumberland River in Davidson County being part of said Armstrong's tract of 306 acres adjoining James Shaw's Preemption and Eatons Old Station. Proven by James Cole Montflorence. July Term 1790.

Page   105 - JAMES COLE MONTFLORENCE - NC - July 23, 1790
This indenture made 10 Apr 1790 between Sampson Williams, Esq., High Sheriff, of Davidson County of one part and District of Mero and James Cole Montflorence of same place of other part. Sampson Williams, in pursuance of an order of the Court of Pleas and Quarter Sessions, at the instance of John Sappington, Esq. to expose to sale the Lot No. 2 in the town of Nashville. Taken by attachment at the suit of John Sappington as the property of William Sands and the said James Cole Montflorence being the highest bidder became the purchaser. All that town lot containing 1 acre of land. Test: Jessee Reed. July Term 1790.

Page   106 - PHILIP PHILIPS & MICHAEL CAMPBELL - NC - July 26, 1790
This indenture made 17 July 1790 between Joseph Sitgresser of Davidson County of one part and Philip Philips and Michael Campbell of same place of other part. Joseph Sitgresser conveyed unto Philip Philips and Michael Campbell a tract of land containing 640 acres in Davidson County on the east side of Buffalo River running into the Tennessee River on the north side. July Term 1790.

Page   107 - MARY HUNTER - NC - July 27, 1790
This indenture made 11 Jan 1790 between David Hay, Esq. and Adam Hampton of Davidson County of one part and Mary Hunter of same place of other part. Where as Eusebius Bushnell, William Dobbins of Davidson County on the 23 day of June 1788 by their certain deed indented and inrolled, in consideration of 598£, 16 shillings money, to them in hand is paid. Did bargain and sell unto David Hay and Adam Hampton and their heirs and assignees forever. The nine following tracts of land on the waters of Cumberland River. Also a house and half acre lot in the town of Nashville and on Cumberland River. David Hay and Adam Hampton became security for the said Eusebius Bushnell and William Dobbins unto the estate of Mark Robertson, deceased, for the sum of 598£, 16 shillings of money, which sum is payable the 25 Dec 1789. Witnessed by Thomas C(illegible) and James Cole Montflorence. If any of the enumerated tracts of land were sold or conveyed before the acknowledging of the within mortgage, then they are considered as void and not part of the land &c. David Hay and Adam Hampton did convey unto Mary Hunter all and singular the said land &c. Proven by John Thompson and Nathaniel Johnston and Griswold Latimore. July Term 1790.

Page   109 - ROBERT WEAKLEY - NC - July 29, 1790
This indenture made 15 Feb 1790 between Ephraim McLane of Davidson

County of one part and Robert Weakley of same place of other part. Ephraim McLane conveyed unto Robert Weakley a tract of land containing 2000 acres in the Western District on the waters of Obion River on the north side of said river adjoining Dugan's and Blount's corner and the south end of a tract of 2500 acres, lovated by said Weakley and granted to the said Ephraim McLane by patent dated 10 July 1788. Proven by James Cole Montflorence.

Page 109 - JAMES COLE MONTFLORENCE - NC - July 29, 1790

This indenture made 28 July 1790 between Robert Weakley of Davidson County of one part and James Cole Montflorence of same place of other part. Robert Weakley conveyed unto James Cole Montflorence a tract of land containing 2000 acres in the Western District on the waters of the Obion River on the north side of said river adjoining Blount's corner. It being the south end of a tract of 2500 acres, located by Robert Weakley. Also that other tract in the Western District on the waters of Obion River on the north side of said river adjoining Ephraim's (line) and Blount's line. Proven by Anthony Foster and Howel Tatum.

Page 110 - ROBERT WEAKLEY - NC - July 29, 1790

This indenture made 29 July 1790 between James Cole Montflorence of Davidson County, District of Mero, of one part and Robert Weakley of same place of other part. James Cole Montflorence conveyed unto Robert Weakley a tract of land containing 2000 acres in the Western District on the waters of the Obion River on the north side of said river adjoining Dugan's and Blount's corners and Ephraim McLane's line. Also four sound and sensible negro or mulatto slaves in Davidson County, between the age of ten and twenty five years old. Proven by Anthony Foster and Howel Tatum.

Page 111 - WILLIAM NASH - NC - Aug 2, 1790

This indenture made 17 June 1790 between James Cole Montflorence of Davidson County of one part and William Nash of same place of other part. James Cole Montflorence conveyed unto William Nash the three following Military tracts of land. To wit, All that tract of land in Tennessee County, NC, on the north side of Cumberland River, joining the lower side of Captain Andrew Armstrong's survey of 1286 acres containing 640 acres about 16 miles below the town of Nashville, also that other tract of land in Davidson County on the first creek above Stones Lick Creek and on the east side of Stones River adjoining George Sugg's corner of No. 2236 and containing 640 acres about 16 miles nearly southeast of Nashville. Also that other tract of land in Davidson County on the waters of the first creek above Stones Lick Creek on the east side of Stones River and joining west corner of Aquilla Suggs' and on the west boundary of Suggs' Warrant No. 1503 and containing 640 acres about 14 miles from the town of Nashville. Delivered on or before 1 July 1791 two young and likely negro or mulatto slaves between the age of twelve and tewnty five, sound and healthy. Proven by Anthony Foster, Bennett Searcy and William Crutcher. July Term 1790.

Page 112 - ANTHONY HART - NC - Aug 2, 1790

This indenture made 23 June 1790 between James Cole Montflorence of Davidson County of one part and Anthony Hart of same place of other part. James Cole Montflorence conveyed unto Anthony Hart the sixteen following Military tracts of land in the District of Mero, NC. To wit, All that tract of land in Tennessee County, NC on the south side of Cumberland River above the Virginia Line, including the fork of the said creek. Containing 640 acers granted by the State of North Carolina to John Forde and by said Forde conveyed to said Anthony and by said Anthony Hart to James Cole Montflorence. Also all that other tract in Tennessee County on the trace near the head of Gibsons Creek adjoining the trace that leads from Thompsons Settlement up the Sulphur Fork. Containing 640 acres of land. Also that other tract of land in Tennessee County on the west fork of Spring Creek the waters of Sycamore Creek adjoining Samuel Morison's corner and John Nichols' corner. Containing 640 acres of land. Also that other tract of land in Tennessee County on the west Turnbulls Clay Lick joining a survey made by Federick Stump, No. of the Military Warrant No. 2815. Granted for the services of William Reves. Also that other tract of land in Tennessee County on the boundary of Stump's survey on Turnbulls Clay Lick. No. of Military Warrant No. 2957. Granted for the services of Isaac Reddick. Also that other tract of land of 640 acres in Tennessee County on the eastern boundary of said Stump, the Military Warrant No. 2763. Granted for the services of John Cellers. Also that other tract of 640 acres in Tennessee County on the north side of Cumberland River joining a survey of Robert Weakley on the north, the Military Warrant No. 3423. Granted for the services of Obid Calvin. Also that other tract of 640 acres in Tennessee County on the north of McAdoes Creek, joining a survey of John Drake's on the west. The Military Warrant No. 3415. Granted for the services of Charles Brooks. Also that other tract of 640 acres in Tennessee County on the west fork of Little Brush Creek the waters of Red River joining a survey of John Nichols No. 3516. Granted for the services of William Holland. Also that other tract of 640 acres in Sumner County, NC, on the south side of Caney Fork adjoining an entry of John Haywood of 1000 acres, on the west. The Military Warrant No. 2485 and granted for the services of Randall Cross. Also another tract of 640 acres in Sumner County on the waters of Collins River one of the branches of Caney Fork joining an entry made by Thomas Hickman in 1788, on the west. Warrant No. 2492. Granted for the services of Lewis Morgan. Also that other tract of 640 acres in Sumner County on the Collins River about seven miles above the mouth of said river, Warrant No. 2809. Granted for the services of Richard King. Also that other tract of 640 acres in Sumner County on the waters of Caney Fork, between Mulherin and Hickmans Creek joining an entry made by Thomas Hickman in 1788. Warrant No. 2665, granted for the services of James Hammon. Also that other tract of 640 acres in Sumner County on the waters of Caney (Fork) between Hickmans and Mulherins Creek. Warrant No. 2483, granted for the services of Abraham Applewhite. Also that other tract of 640 acres in Sumner County on the south side of Big Barren River on a fork of said river joining an entry of Joshua Davis on the south, entered Dec 2, 1786. And also that other tract of 640 acres in Sumner County on the headwaters of Hickmans Creek of the Caney Fork joining an entry made by Thomas Hickman in 1788 on the west. The Military Warrants for two last tracts are numbered 2707. Granted for the services of Abraham Duck and No. 2249. Granted for the services of William Wright. Proven by Elijah Robertson and Anthony Foster. 27 July 1790.

Page   114 - JOHN BLACKAMORE - NC - Aug 3, 1790
            This indenture made 8 May 1790 between Thomas Hickman of Davidson County of one part and John Blackamore of same place of other part. Thomas Hickman conveyed unto John Blackamore a tract of land containing 640 acres in Davidson County on

the east fork of the first creek that empties into the east fork of Stones River above the mouth of Bradleys Lick Creek on the east side and joining Joseph Hendrick's corner. Grant No. 758. Proven by Thomas Johnston and William Crutcher. July Term 1790.

Page   114 - ISAAC ROUNDSEVALL - NC - Aug 3, 1790
This indenture made 15 July 1790 between Isaac Rounsevall of Davidson County of one part and Federick Stump of same place of other part. Federick Stump conveyed unto Isaac Rounsevall a tract of land containing 3 acres in Davidson County on Whites Creek. Proven by Mitchel O'Neal and John Burrow. July Term 1790.

Page   115 - JOSHUA THOMAS - NC - Aug 3, 1790
This indenture made 29 June 1790 between Sampson Williams, Sheriff of Davidson County of one part and Joshua Thomas of Davidson County of other part. The Sheriff was directed by the Court of Pleas and Quarter Sessions held on first Monday in Oct 1789, to sell a certain tract of land whereon Nicholas Baker then lived, to levy on the goods and chattels &c of Evan Baker the sum of 57 £ and 3 shillings which David Wilson recovered against him, the said Evan Baker. Land in Davidson County containing 640 acres on the north side of Cumberland about two miles from the town of Nashville. Granted in the year 1786, Apr 17 and registered Oct 24, 1788 and sold the same to said Joshua, the highest bidder.July Term 1790.

Page   115 - ADAM LYNN - NC - Aug 3, 1790
This indenture made between John Shannon and Adam Lynn, both of Davidson County. John Shannon conveyed unto Adam Lynn all that tract of land in Davidson County on the Shanes Fork of Gaspers Creek, being part of Morris Shanes' Preemption the south west corner. Containing 40 acres. Proven by Francis Byrd and Edward Williams. July Term 1790.

Page   116 - WILLIAM GALLASPY - NC - Aug 4, 1790
This indenture made 17 July 1790 between John Sappington of Davidson County of one part and William Gallaspy of same place of other part. John Sappington conveyed unto William Gallaspy a tract of land containing 320 acres in Davidson County on the south side of Cumberland River and on Mill Creek adjoining on the east side of the creek about 100 yards above the Old Trace leading to Stones River, Ebenezer Titus' Preemption. Proven by James Cole Montflorence. July Term 1790.

Page   117 - FEDERICK STUMP - NC - Aug 4, 1790
This indenture made 15 July 1790 between Dederick Stump of Davidson County of one part and David Rounsevall of same place of other part. David Rounsevall coonveyed unto Federick Stump a tract of land containing 1½ acres in Davidson County on Whites Creek. Being part of that tract whereon David now lives. July Term 1790.

Page   117 - GEORGE CUMMINS - NC - Aug 4, 1790
This indenture made 14 July 1789 between John Blair of Davidson County of one part and George Cummins of same place of other part. John Blair conveyed unto George Cummins a tract of land containing 600 acres in Sumner County on both sides of Spring Creek adjoining James Mulherin's corner and Nathaniel Laurence's boundary. Being

178

part of a tract of 1000 acres as by a patent granted to said John Blair dated 5 Sept 1787 and No. 388. July Term 1790.

Page   118 - THOMAS BYRD - NC - Aug 4, 1790
            This indenture made between Adam Lynn and Thomas Byrd, both of Davidson County. Adan Lyn conveyed unto Thomas Byrd a tract of land containing 50 acres in Davidson County on Shanes Fork of Gaspers Creek, it being the land where on the said Byrd now lives. Test: Andrew Ewing. July Term 1790.

Page   118 - ELEAZER HAMILTON - NC - Aug 4, 1790
            This indenture made 16 July 1790 between Pleasant Lockart of Davidson County of one part and Eleazer Hamilton of same place of other part. Pleasant Lockart conveyed unto Eleazer Hamilton a tract of land containing 32 acres in Davidson County on Whites Creek the north side of Cumberland River and joining Robert Weakley's corner and John Marney's line, and Elijah Hamilton's corner and to Robert Weakley's corner. Proven by Daniel Rowan and Rice Porter. July Term 1790.

Page   119 - THEODORUS MALETT - NC - Aug 4, 1790
            This indenture made 19 Sept 1789 between Elijah Robertson and Sarah his wife of Davidson County of one part and Theodorus Malett of other part. Elijah Robertson conveyed unto Theodorus Malett a tract of land containing 640 acres. Granted to the said Elijah Robertson by virtue of a Military Warrant granted unto Isaac Dunbar, No. 3307, lying in the County of Sumner, NC. Beginning on the waters of the Caney Fork River to the corner to his tract as assignee of the heirs of Robert Nixon. Proven by Anthony Crutcher and Rice Curtis. July Term 1790.

Page   119 - LEANDER HUGHS - NC - Aug 6, 1790
            This indenture made 17 July 1790 between Federick Stump of Davidson County of one part and Leander Hughs of same place of other part. Federick Stump conveyed unto Leander Hughs a tract of land containing 100 acres in Davidson County on a branch of Whites Creek and bounded by lands of William Mitchel and Federick Stump. Proven by George Blackamore and William Black. July Term 1790.

Page   120 - DAVID SHELBY - NC - Aug 6, 1790
            This indenture made 23 Sept 1789 between James Shaw of one part and David Shelby of other part, both of Davidson County. James Shaw conveyed unto David Shelby a tract of land containing 640 acres in Davidson County on the north side of Cumberland River opposite to the town of Nashville. Said land was originally granted to said James Shaw by patent dated 10 July 1788. Proven by Thomas Masten and William Baldwin. July Term 1790.

Page   120 - WILLIAM BLACKAMORE - NC - Aug 6, 1790
            This indenture made 15 Apr 1790 between Moses Shelby of Tennessee County of one part and William Blackamore of Davidson County of other part. Moses Shelby conveyed unto William Blackamore a tract of land containing 600 acres in Davidson County on the Stuarts Creek the waters of Stones River, being part of a tract of land containing 1200 acres granted to the said Shelby. Adjoining Edwin Hickman and John Tucker's lands.

179

Wit: Edwin Hickman and Matthew Talbot. July Term 1790.

Page   121 - JOHN LANCASTER - NC - Aug 6, 1790
                    This indenture made 1 Oct 1789 between Isaac Linsey of Sumner County, NC
of one part and John Lancaster of Davidson County of other part. Isaac Linsey conveyed
unto John Lancaster a tract of land containing 7 acres and 60 poles in Davidson County on
the north side of Cumberland River about one mile and a half from Nashville adjoining
Stephen Ray's line and Martin Armstrong's line. Being part of a tract of 320 acres of land
granted unto Isaac Linsey by State of North Carolina dated __ of ___ 178_ and No. __.
Proven by Lewis Forde and Phoenix Cox. July Term 1790.

Page   121- TIMOTHY DEMUMBRE - NC - Aug 7, 1790
                    This indenture made 15 July 1790 between James Hoggatt of Davidson County
of one part and Timothy Demumbre of same place of other part. James Hoggatt conveyed
unto Timothy Demumbre one piece or lot in town of Nashville and known as Lot No. 45 and
containing one acre together with all and every part and parcel thereof. Wit: John Dickson
and Bennett Searcy. July Term 1790.

Page   122 - THOMAS HARDIMAN - NC - Aug 7, 1790
                    This indenture made 7 July 1790 between Sampson Williams, Sheriff of
Davidson County of one part and Thomas Hardiman of· same place of other part. Said
Sheriff was directed to levy of the goods and chattels, lands and tenements of James
Lanier, Henry Lanier and Anthony Crutcher the sum of 200£ which Thomas Hardiman
recovered against the said Laniers and Crutcher, and costs. Said Sheriff levied on a tract
of land one undivided moiety granted to Martin Armstrong and Anthony Crutcher by patent
dated May 18, 1789, No. 67. Containing 500 acres in Davidson County on the south side of
Cumberland River and joining Benjamin Pettit's line and Murry's line. The said patent
granted to Col. Martin Armstrong and the said Crutcher dated May 18, 1789, No. 67 the
said Thomas Hardiman being the highest bidder purchased the same. Wit: Bennett Searcy.
July Term 1790.

Page   123 - JOSEPH LOVE - NC - Aug 7, 1790
                    This indenture made 12 July 1790 between Daniel Frazer of Davidson County
of one part and Joseph Love of same place of other part. Daniel Frazer conveyed unto
Joseph Love a tract of land containing 284 acres in Davidson County on both sides of
Whites Creek adjoining a Preemption known by Hollis' Preemption. The same being the
west end of a tract of land granted Daniel Frazer by the State of North Carolina 17 Apr
1786, No. 104. July Term 1790.

Page   123 - JAMES ROSS - NC - Aug 7, 1790
                    This indenture made 5 July 1790 between Samuel Shannon of Davidson County
of one part and James Ross of same place of other part. Samuel Shannon conveyed unto
James Ross a tract of land containing 92 acres in Davidson County on the north side of
Cumberland River and waters of Whites Creek and joining David Shannon's line. Said land
being granted to Samuel Shannon by State of North Carolina dated 17 Jan 1789. July Term
1790.

Page   124 - LARDNER CLARK - NC - Aug 9, 1790
          This indenture made 25 Apr 1789 between Thomas Hickman, Esq., High
Sheriff of Davidson County of one part and Lardner Clark of same place of other part.
Thomas Hickman conveyed unto Lardner Clark all that tract of land containing 640 acres in
Davidson County on the south side of Sulphur Fork of Red River adjoining William
Gilkerson's line, Benjamin Hardin's corner. Which said tract was executed at the instance
of James Cole Montflorence by virtue of a writ of venditione exponias from the Court of
Pleas and Quarter Sessions of Davidson County, dated Jan 1789 and against the heirs of
William Gubbins, deceased, which said land being sold at public sale to the said Lardner
Clark, the highest bidder on the 4 April 1789. July Term 1790.

Page   125 - JOHN SMITH - NC - Aug 9, 1790
          This indenture made 29 June 1790 between Michael Glaves of Davidson
County of one part and John Smith of same place of other part. Michael Glaves conveyed
unto John Smith a tract of land containing 320 acres in Davidson County on the waters of
Whites Creek adjoining Stephen Wray's line and William Loggins' line and John Walker's line.
Wit: Sampson Williams and William Loggins. July Term 1790.

Page   125 - GEORGE, JOHN & JAMES MAYFIELD - NC - Aug 9, 1790
          This indenture made 26 May 1790 between Isaac Mayfield of Davidson County
of one part and George, John and James Mayfield of same place of other part. Isaac
Mayfield conveyed unto George, John and James Mayfield a tract of land containing 480
acres in Davidson County on the waters of Mill Creekand joining Thomas Denton's boundary
and William Overall's line and John Henderson's line. Wit: Samuel Barton and William
Matlock. July Term 1790.

Page   126 - LARDNER CLARK - NC - Aug 9, 1790
          This indenture made 15 Aug 1785 between Jessee Hughes of Davidson County
of one part and Lardner Clark of same place of other part. Jessee Hughes conveyed unto
Lardner Clark all that lot or parcel of land known by Lot No. 67 in the town of Nashville.
Which said lot was by deed dated 30 July 1784 granted and conveyed by the directors and
trustees of town of Nashville to said Jessee Hughes. Wit: S. Singletary and Thomas
McFarland. July Term 1790.

Page   127 - JOHN WILLIAMS - NC - Aug 9, 1790
          This indenture made 29 June 1790 between John Boyd of Davidson County of
one part and John Williams of same place of other part. John Boyd conveyed unto John
Williams one lot of an acre in town of Nashville and known as Lot No. 60, being the lot
granted by Samuel Barton, Thomas Molloy and James Shaw, directors and trustees of town
of Nashville to John Boyd by deed dated 26 Jyly 1784. Test: Adam Binkley, James Alcorn
and John Boyd, Jr. July Term 1790.

Page   127 - BARTHOLOMEW STOVALL - NC - Aug 10, 1790
          This indenture made 5 June 1790 between John Brown of Davidson County of
one part and Bartholomew Stovall of same place of other part. John Brown conveyed
unto Bartholomew Stovall a tract of land containing 100 acres in Davidson County on the
south side of Cumberland River and on the west fork of Mill Creek adjoining Walker's

north west corner. Being a part of said Brown's Preemption. July Term 1790.

Page   128 - THOMAS MOLLOY - NC - No. 176 - Reg. Aug 10, 1790
        For 10 lbs per 100 acres paid by Thomas Molloy was granted a tract of land
containing 2500 acres in Davidson County. Beginning at the mouth of the first creek below
Little Harpeth on George Neville's boundary. Surveyed for Thomas Molloy by himself Sept
12, 1785 agreeable to a Warrant No. 24. Entered Dec 29, 1783. July 10, 1788.

Page   128 - ELIJAH ROBERTSON - NC - No. 106 - Reg. Aug 10, 1790
        For 10 lbs per 100 acres paid by Elijah Robertson was granted a tract of land
containing 5000 acres in Middle District on the south side of Duck River on both sides of
Fountain Creek adjoining William Gilbert's corner. Surveyed for Elijah Robertson Feb 27,
1785 by Stockley Donelson in consequence of a Warrant No. 1043. Dated Oct 29, 1783.
July 10, 1788.

Page   128 - THOMAS BROWN - NC - No. 192 - Aug 10, 1790
        For 10 lbs per 100 acres paid by Thomas Brown was granted a tract of land
containing 640 acres in Davidson County adjoining Francis Hodges' boundary and Francis
Armstrong's corner. Surveyed for Thomas Brown Nov 6, 1785 by Thomas Molloy, D.S. in
consequence of a Warrant No. 401. Entered Nov 9, 1784. July 10, 1788.

Page   129 - WILLIAM NASH - NC - No. 937 - Reg. Aug 10, 1790
        By an Act for the relief of the Officers and Soldiers of the Continental Line,
in consideration of the bravery and zeal of Daniel Elmore, private, granted unto William
Nash, assignee of the heirs of William Nash, a tract of land containing 640 acres in
Davidson County on the east fork of the first creek above Stones Lick Creek on the east
side of Stones River adjoining John Logan's corner. Surveyed for William Nash by himself
May 12, 1788 in consequence of a Military Warrant No. 1512. Located Apr 3, 1788. May
18, 1789.

Page   129 - WILLIAM NASH - NC - No. 939 - Reg. Aug 10, 1790
        By an Act for the relief of the Officers and Soldiers of the Continental Line,
in consideration of the bravery and zeal of Foster Reaves, a private, granted unto William
Nash, assignee of the heirs of Foster Reaves, a tract of land containing 640 acres in
Davidson County on the waters of the west fork of the first creek above Stones Lick Creek
the east side of Stones River. Surveyed for William Nash May 14, 1788 by said Nash in
consequence of a Warrant No. 2762. Located April 1788. May 18, 1789.

Page   129 - WILLIAM NASH - NC - No. 732 - Reg. Aug 10, 1790
        By an Act for the relief of the Officers and Soldiers of the Continental Line
in consideration of the bravery and zeal of Ezekiel Rigley, a private, granted unto William
Nash, assignee of Ezekiel Rigley, a tract of land containing 640 acres in Davidson County
on the east side of Stones River. Surveyed for William Nash by himself Feb 10, 1787 in
consequence of a Military Warrant No. 2577. Located Jan 1, 1787. July 11, 1788.

Page   130 - JOHN DONELSON - NC - No. 983 - Reg. Aug 11, 1790
        By an Act for the relief of the Officers and Soldiers of the Continental Line,

in consideration of the bravery and zeal of John Fusmon, a private, granted unto John Donelson, assignee of said John Fusmon, a tract of land containing 640 acres in Davidson County on both sides of Harpeth river adjoining Curtis Ivy's line. Surveyed by John Donelson for himself Mar 10, 1787 in consequence of a Military Warrant No. 2604. Located Dec 18, 1786.

Page   130 - JOHN LOGUE - NC - No. __ - Reg. Aug 11, 1790
        By an Act for the relief of the Officers and Soldiers of the Continental Line, in consideration of the bravery and zeal of James Gurley, a corporal, granted unto John Logue, assignee of James Gurley, a tract of land containing 1000 acres in Davidson County on the south side of Cumberland River on the first creek above Stones Lick Creek the waters of Stones River. Surveyed for John Logue Mar 20, 1788 by William Nash, D.S. in consequence of a Military Warrant No. 1737. Located Jan 28, 1786. May 18, 1789.

Page   130 - LEWIS REELING - NC - No. 202 - Reg. Aug 11, 1790
        For 10 lbs per 100 acres paid by Lewis Reeling was granted a tract of land containing 640 acres in Davidson County on the waters of Mill Creek adjoining William Overall's corner and James Mayfield's corner. Surveyed for Lewis Reeling Aug 25, 1785 by John Bucchanan, D.S. in consequence of a Warrant No. 727. Entered May 13, 1785. July 13, 1788.

Page   131 - ANDREW GOFF - NC - No. 215 - Reg. Aug 11, 1790
        For 10 lbs per 100 acres paid by Andrew Goff was granted a tract of land containing 640 acres in Davidson County on the waters of Big Harpeth and joining William and John Donnalson's corner. Surveyed for Andrew Goff Nov 18, 1785 by JOhn Bucchanan, D.S. in consequence of a Warrant No. 657. Entered Jan 8, 1785. July 13, 1788.

Page   131 - JOHN WALKER - NC - No. 217 - Reg. Sept 6, 1790
        For 10 lbs per 100 acres paid by John Walker was granted a tract of land containing 640 acres in Davidson County on the north side of Cumberland River adjoining William and Samuel Neely's line, Isaac Neely's line and James Men(illegible)'s line. Surveyed for John Walker Apr 13, 1786 by James Sanders, D.S. in consequence of a Warrant No. 686. Entered Feb 19, 1785. July 10, 1788.

Page   131 - JOHN FORDE - NC - No. 874 - Oct 4, 1790
        By an Act for the relief of the Officers and Soldiers of the Continental Line, in consideration of the bravery and zeal of Jonathan Lewis, a private in the said line, granted unto John Forde, assignee of Jonathan Lewis, a tract of land containing 274 acres in Davidson County on the north side of Cumberland, joining John Rice's claim and west Benney Tatum. Surveyed for John Forde Aug 20, 1787 by Robert Nelson, D.S. in consewuence of a Military Warrant No. 1642. Located May 8, 1787. Jan 17, 1789.

Page   132 - SAMUEL FINLEY - NC - Oct 13, 1790
        This indenture made 11 Oct 1790 between Joseph Dougherty of the District of Kentucky in the State of Virginia of one part and Samuel Finley od same place of other part. Joseph Dougherty conveyed unto Samuel Finley a tract of land containing 640 acres in Davidson County on the south side of Cumberland River and on the waters of Big

Harpeth. Which land was granted to said Dougherty by the State of North Carolina in right of Preemption by patent dated July 10, 1788 and No. 243. Oct Term 1790.

Page   132 - JOHN FORDE - NC - No. 896 - Reg. Nov 3, 1790

By an Act for the relief of the Officers and Soldiers of the Continental Line, in consideration of the bravery and zeal of Peter Coward, a private in the said line, granted unto John Forde, assignee of said Peter Coward, a tract of land containing 640 acres in Davidson County on the north side of Cumberland River on the waters of Battle Ground Creek adjoining David McCries' corner of a survey of 1000 acres on the waters of said creek. Surveyed for John Forde July 6, 1786 by Thomas Hickman, D.S. in consequence of a Military Warrant No. 2447. Located June 15, 1786. Jan 17, 1789.

Page   133 - COL. HARDY MURFREE - NC - No. 39 - Reg. Oct 22, 1790

By an Act for the relief of the Officers and Soldiers of the Continental Line, in consideration of the bravery and zeal of Hardy Murfree. colonel in the said line, granted unto him a tract of land containing 5760 acres in Davidson County on Murfrees Fork a branch of the west fork of Big Harpeth. Surveyed for Hardy Murfree July 17, 1784 by James Mulherin, D.S. in consequence of a Military Warrant No. 107. Located Feb 7, 1780. Mar 17, 1786.

Page   133 - BENJAMIN LOGAN - NC - Oct 22, 1790

This indenture made 11 Oct 1790 between Isaac Drake of Davidson County of one part and Benjamin Logan of Lincoln County, State of Virginia of other part. Isaac Drake conveyed unto Benjamin Logan a tract of land containing 640 acres in Davidson County on the waters of Hays Creek a branch of Big Harpeth River. Which land was granted to said Drake by the State of North Carolina by patent dated July 13, 1788 and No. 218. Oct Term 1790.

Page   134 - JOSEPH ERWINE - NC - Nov 3, 1790

This indenture made 1 Oct 1790 between John Forde of Davidson County of one part and Joseph Irvin of Guilford County, North Carolina of other part. John Forde conveyed unto Joseph Irvin a tract of land containing 640 acres on the north side of Cumberland River on the waters of Battle Ground Creek. Wit: Sampson Williams and Anthony Hart. Oct Term 1790.

Page   134 - MARTIN GARDNER SHEPPARD - NC - No. 751 - Reg. Nov 8, 1790

By an Act for the relief of the Officers and Soldiers of the Continental Line, in consideration of the bravery and zeal of Jeremiah Jackson, a private in the said line, granted unto Martin Gardner Sheppard, assignee of said Jeremiah Jackson, a tract of land containing 640 acres in Davidson County on the waters of Sulphur Fork of Red River. Surveyed for said Sheppard July 20, 1787 by Justinian Cartwright, D.S. in consequence of a Military Warrant No. 1498. Located Sept 25, 1786. July 11, 1788.

Page   135 - COL. JAMES GLASGOW - NC - No. 560 - Reg. Nov 8, 1790

By an Act for the relief of the Officers and Soldiers of the Continental Line, in consideration of the bravery and zeal of Giles Webb, a private in the said line, granted unto James Glasgow, assignee of Giles Webb, a tract of land containing 640 acres in

Davidson County on the south side of Cumberland River adjoining another boundary of Jonathan Drake's Preemption at Drakes Lick. Surveyed for said Glasgow July 9, 1785 by Ed. Harris, D.S. in consequence of a Military Warrant No. 149. Located Jan 5, 1784. Sept 15, 1789.

Page   135 - JAMES GLASGOW - NC - No. 53 - Reg. Nov 8, 1790

By an Act for the relief of the Officers and Soldiers of the Continental Line, in consideration of the services of Col. Martin Armstrong, surveyor, granted unto James Glasgow, assignee of said Armstrong, a tract of land containing 1428 acres in Davidson County on Goose Creek on the north side of Cumberland River adjoining William Holdenesse's corner and Thomas Donaho's line. Surveyed for James Glasgow Mar 17, 1784 by James Sanders, D.S. in consequence of a Service Right of said Armstrong. Located Nov 5, 1784. Oct 8, 1787.

Page   135 - JAMES GLASGOW - NC - No. 922 - Nov 8, 1790

By an Act for the relief of the Officers and Soldiers of the Continental Line, in consideration of the bravery and zeal of William Ecols, a sergeant in the said line, granted unto James Glasgow, assignee of said William Echols, a tract of land containing 1000 acres in Davidson County on the north side of Cumberland River and on Sycamore Creek. Surveyed for James Glasgow by William Nash, D.S. in consequence of a Military Warrant No. 1110. Located Jan 30, 1785. May 18, 1789.

Page   136 -JAMES GLASGOW - NC - No. 923 - Reg. Nov 8, 1790

By an Act for the relief of the Officers and Soldiers of the Continental Line, in consideration of the bravery and zeal of William B(illegible), a private in the said line, granted unto James Glasgow a tract of land containing 640 acres in Davidson County on the waters of Cedar Lick Creek adjoining a corner of Col Martin Armstrong. Surveyed for James Glasgow July 4, 1788 by John Bucchanan, D.S. in consequence of a Military Warrant No. 1318. Located Mar 2_, 1788. May 18, 1789.

Page   136 - JOHN WHITSETT - NC - No. 966 - Reg. Nov 8, 1790

By an Act for the relief of the Officers and Soldiers of the Continental Line, in consideration of the bravery and zeal of William Cone (Cane), a private in the said line, granted unto John Whitsett, assignee of the heirs of William Cone, a tract of land containing 640 acres in Davidson County on both sides of Smiths Fork a branch of Caney Fork. Surveyed for John Whitsett Apr 24, 1787 by John Donelson, D.S. in consequence of a Warrant No. 2118. Located Feb 24, 1787. May 18, 1789.

Page   136 - JOHN McPHERSON - NC - No. 530 - Reg. Nov 9, 1790

By an Act for the relief of the Officers and Soldiers of the Continental Line, in consideration of the bravery and zeal of Duncan McPherson, a private in the said line, granted unto John McPherson, assignee of the heirs of Duncan McPherson, a tract of land containing 640 acres in Davidson County on the north side of Cumberland River and south of Red River, about a mile and half or two miles south of the mouth of Parsons Creek adjoining Jones' Preemption. Surveyed for John McPherson Mar 15, 1786 by Robert Nelson, D.S. in consequence of a Military Warrant No. 2612. Located Oct 11, 1785. Sept 15, 1787.

Page   137 - JOHN ELLIOTT - NC - No. 970 - Reg. Nov 9, 1790

By an Act for the relief of the Officers and Soldiers of the Continental Line, in consideration of the bravery and zeal of Cornelius Englin, a private in the said line, granted unto John Elliott, assignee of the heirs of Cornelius Englin, a tract of land containing 640 acres in Davidson County on the west fork of Cedar Lick Creek. Beginning at a tree 40 poles west of where the Buffalo path leads from the Cedar Lick crosses the fork. Surveyed for John Elliott Mar 20, 1783 by John Bucchanan, D.S. in consequence of a Military Warrant No. 440. Located Nov 14, 1785. May 18, 1789.

Page   137 - JOSEPH MITCHEL - NC - No. 197 - Reg. Nov 9, 1790

By an Act for the relief of the Officers and Soldiers of the Continental Line, in consideration of the bravery and zeal of Joseph Mitchel, a private in the said line, granted unto Joseph Mitchel a tract of land containing 274 acres in Davidson County on the waters of Stones River, joining Henry Winburn's 389 acre survey. Surveyed for Joseph Mitchel Mar 13, 1785 by Barclay William Pollock, D.S. in consequence of a Military Warrant No. 146. Located Feb 7, 1784. Mar 7, 1786.

Page   137 - PETER TURNEY - NC - No. 96 - Reg. Nov 9, 1790

By an Act for the relief of the Officers and Soldiers of the Continental Line, in consideration of the bravery and zeal of Peter Turney, a sergeant in the Commissioner's guard &c, granted unto Peter Turney a tract of land containing 640 acres in Davidson County adjoining the corner of Capt. James Bradley and a branch of Indian Camp Creek. Surveyed for Peter Turney May 20, 1785 by John Bucchanan, D.S. agreeable to a Warrant No. 723. Entered May 4, 1785. July 10, 1788.

Page   138 - JOHN KIRKPATRICK - NC - Nov 9, 1790

This indenture made 12 Oct 1790 between James Thompson of County of Davidson, District of Mero of one part and John Kirkpatrick of same place of other part. James Thompson conveyed unto John Kirkpatrick a tract of land containing 274 acres in Davidson County on the waters of Richland Creek adjoining Francis Hodges' corner and Thomas Finney's corner. Which land was granted to James Thompson by patent dated 7 Mar 1786. Wit: Russell Gower and John Thompson. Oct Term 1790.

Page   138 -JOHN KIRKPATRICK - NC - Nov 9, 1790

This indenture made 12 Oct 1790 between Robert Thompson of Davidson County, District of Mero, of one part and John Kirkpatrick of same place of other part. Robert Kirkpatrick conveyed unto John Kirkpatrick a tract of land containing 100 acres in Davidson County on the south side of Cumberland River on the waters of Richland Creek adjoining James Thompson's corner and Finney's line. Which land was granted unto Robert Thompson by patent dated 8 Oct 1787. Wit: Russell Gower and John Thompson. Oct Term 1790.

Page   139 -THOMAS HARDIMAN - NC - Nov 10, 1790

This indenture made 11 Oct 1790 between William Blackamore of Davidson County of one part and Thomas Hardiman of same place of other part. William Blackamore conveyed untoThomas Hardiman a tract of land containing 600 acres in Davidson County on Stuarts the waters of Stones River, being part of a tract of 1200 acres. Adjoining Edwin

Hickman's corner and John Tucker's line. Which land was granted to Moses Shelby by the State of North Carolina for his service on the Guard. Oct Term 1790.

Page   139 - THOMAS HARDIMAN - NC - Nov 10, 1790
            This indenture made 11 Oct 1790 between Edwin Hickman of Davidson County of one part and Thomas Hardiman of same place of other part. Edwin Hickman conveyed unto Thomas Hardiman a tract of land containing 300 acres in Davidson County on Stuarts Creek. The said land being part of Moses Shelby's Guard Right. Which land was granted to the said Shelby by the State of North Carolina by patent dated (blank) and No. (blank).Oct Term 1790.

Page   140 - JAMES CRABTREE - NC - Nov 10, 1790
            This indenture made 8 July 1788 between Morris Shean and Theba Shean his wife of Davidson County of one part and James Crabtree of same place of other part. Morris Shean and Theba Shean conveyed unto James Crabtree a tract of land containing 162 acres in Davidson County and Sumner County on the Wartrace Fork of Gaspers Creek adjoining Simeon Kuykendall's corner and Gasper Mansker's line. Said land being part of a tract of 640 acres granted to said Shean by patent dated Apr 17, 1786. Test: Robert Hays, Young Ewing and Daniel Rowan. Oct Term 1790.

Page   140 - JAMES CROCKETT - NC - Nov 10, 1790
            This indenture made 27 July 1790 between Christopher Funkhouser of Sumner County, NC of one part and James Crockett of Montgomery County, State of Virginia, of other part.   Christopher Funkhouser conveyed unto James Crockett a tract of land containing 640 acres in Davidson County on both sides of Little Harpeth River. Said land was granted unto said Funkhouser by the State of North Carolina by patent dated July 10, 1788 and No. 205. Test: Hopkins Lacy and James Hoggatt. Oct Term 1790.

Page   141 - EDWIN HICKMAN - NC - Nov 11, 1790
            This indenture made 11 Oct 1790 between Thomas Hardiman of Davidson County of one part and Edwin Hickman of same place of other part. Thomas Hardiman conveyed unto Edwin Hickman 640 acres in Davidson County on the waters of Browns Creek adjoining Samuel Barton's line. Which said land was granted to said Hardiman by State of North Carolina by patent dated July 10, 1788 and No. 272. Oct Term 1790.

Page   141 - JONATHAN F. ROBERTSON - NC - Nov 11, 1790
            This indenture made 11 Oct 1790 between James Robertson of Davidson County of one part and Jonathan F. Robertson of same place of other part.   James Robertson conveyed unto Jonathan F. Robertson a tract of land containing 640 acres in Davidson County. Beginning about half a mile below an improvement made by Russell Gower on the bank of Cumberland River. Which land was granted to said James Robertson by State of North carolina by patent dated Apr 17, 1786 and No. 73. Oct Term 1790.

Page   142 - JOHN BOSLEY - NC - Nov 11, 1790
            This indenture made 11 Oct 1790 between James Robertson of Davidson County of one part and John Bosley of same place of other part.   James Robertson conveyed unto John Bosley a tract of land containing 335 acres in Davidson County on the

south side of Cumberland River. Which said land was granted to said Robertson by the state in right of the Military Service of James Marr by patent dated Sept 15, 1787 and No. 580. Oct Term 1790.

Page   143 - ROBERT EDMONDSON - NC - Nov 12, 1790
         This indenture made 11 Oct 1790 between James Foster of Davidson County of one part and Robert Edmondson of same place of other part. James Foster conveyed unto Robert Edmondson a tract of land containing 200 acres, it being a part of said James Foster's Preemption, in Davidson County adjoining John Cockrill's boundary and John Tucker's Preemption. Which land was granted unto said Foster by the State by patent dated Apr 17, 1786 and No. 117. Oct Term 1790.

Page   143 - JOHN CHILDERS - NC - Nov 12, 1790
         This indenture made 23 Aug 1790 between John Newell of Davidson County of one part and John Childers of same place of other part. John Newell conveyed unto John Childers a tract of land containing 144 acres in Davidson County near the Stone Lick on the south side of Cumberland River adjoining John Cockrill's corner and Peter Turney'd line. Test: Andrew Ewing, Andrew Cassellman and Susannah Ewing. Oct Term 1790.

Page   144 - JOHN BOYD, JUNIOR - NC - Nov 12, 1790
         We, Samuel Barton, Thomas Molloy, James Shaw and Joel Rice and David Hays, directors and trustees of the town of Nashville, conveyed unto John Boyd, Junior, a lot No. 148 in the town of Nashville. Oct Term 1790.

Page   144 - JOHN BOYD, SENIOR - NC - Nov 12, 1790
         We, Samuel Barton, Thomas Molloy, James Shaw, Joel Rice and David Hay, directors and trustees of town of Nashville, conveyed unto John Boyd, Senior, a lot No. 150 in town of Nashville. Oct Term 1790.

Page   144 - DAVID MAXEL - NC - Nov 12, 1790
         We, Samuel Barton, Thomas Molloy, James Shaw, Joel Rice and David Hay, directors and trustees of town of Nashville, conveyed unto David Maxel a lot No. 97 in town of Nashville. Oct Term 1790.

Page   145 - GEORGE RIDLEY - NC - Nov 15, 1790
         This indenture made 11 Oct 1790 between John Caffrey of Davidson County of one part and George Ridley of same place of other part. John Caffrey conveyed unto George Ridley a tract of land containing 640 acres in Davidson County on both sides of Stones Creek a branch of Stones River and about three miles above Stones Lick. Which land was granted unto said Caffrey by the State by patent dated Apr 17, 1786 and No. 142. Oct Term 1790.

Page   145 - NANCY SHEPPARD - NC - No. 697 - Reg. Nov 15, 1790
         By an Act for the relief of the Officers and Soldiers of the Continental Line, in consideration of the bravery and zeal of Hardy Hynes, a private in the said line, granted unto Nancy Sheppard, assignee of the heirs of Hardy Hynes, a tract of land containing 640 acres in Davidson County on the waters of Sulphur Fork of Red River. Surveyed for said

188

Sheppard July 20, 1787 by Justinian Cartwright, D.S. in consequence of a Military Warrant No. 1760. Located Sept 25, 1786. July 11, 1788.

Page   145 - NANCY SHEPPARD - NC - No. 694 - Reg. Nov 15, 1790

By an Act for the relief of the Officers and Soldiers of the Continental Line in consideration of the bravery and zeal of James Pollard, a private in the said line, granted unto Nancy Sheppard, assignee of said Pollard, a tract of land containing 640 acres in Davidson County on the waters of Sycamore. Surveyed for said Nancy Sheppard July 19, 1787 by Justinian Cartwright, D.S. in consequence of a Military Warrant No. 1750. Located Sept 25, 1786. July 11, 1788.

Page   146 - NANCY SHEPPARD - NC - No. 667 - Reg. Nov 16, 1790

By an Act of the relief of the Officers and Soldiers of the Continental Line, in consideration of the bravery and zeal of William Parker, a private in the said line, granted unto Nancy Sheppard a tract of land containing 640 acres in Davidson County on Hayes Creek which empties into Tennessee River on the north side. Beginning about three miles from the mouth of said creek at the corner of Benjamin Sheppard's entry No. 2302. Surveyed for said Nancy Sheppard Apr 20, 1786 by Isaac Roberts, D.S. in consequence of a Military Warrant No. 2090. Located Dec 23, 1785. Dec 8, 1787.

Page   146 - NANCY SHEPPARD - NC - No. 675 - Reg. Nov 16, 1790

By an Act for the relief of the Officers and Soldiers of the Continental Line, in consideration of the bravery and zeal of William Mills, a private in the said line, granted unto Nancy Sheppard a tract of land containing 640 acres in Davidson County on the waters of the Sulphur Fork of Red River adjoining James Brun's corner. Surveyed for said Nancy Sheppard July 19, 1789 by J. Cartwright in consequence of a Military Warrant No. 2093. Located Sept 25, 1786. July 11, 1788.

Page   146 - NANCY SHEPPARD - NC - No. 696 - Reg. Nov 16, 1790

By an Act for the relief of the Officers and Soldiers of the Continental Line, in consequence of the bravery and zeal of Henry Lambert, a private in the said line, granted unto Nancy Sheppard, assignee of the said Lambert, a tract of land containing 640 acres in Davidson County on the waters of Kaspers Creek. Surveyed for Nancy Sheppard July 20, 1787 by Justinian Cartwright in consequence of a Military Warrant No. 2082. Located Sept 25, 1786. July 11, 1788.

Page   147 - NANCY SHEPPARD - NC - No. 666 - Reg. Nov 16, 1790

By an Act for the relief of the Officers and Soldiers of the Continental line, in consideration of the bravery and zeal of Nehemiah Bennett, a private in the said line, granted unto Nancy Sheppard, assignee of Nehemiah Bennett, a tract of land containing 640 acres in Davidson County on a small creek that empties into the north side of tennessee River and known by the name of Indian Creek adjoining the corner of Thomas Berry's entry No. 139. Surveyed for Nancy Sheppard Apr 20, 1786 by Isaac Roberts, D.S. in consequence of a Military Warrant No. 1796. Located Dec 23, 2785. Dec 8, 1787.

Page   147 - NANCY SHEPPARD - NC - No. 693 - Reg. Nov 16, 1790

By an Act for the relief of the Officers and Soldiers of the Continental Line,

in consideration of the bravery and zeal of Hardy Johnston, a private of the said line, granted unto Nancy Sheppard, assignee of said Johnston, a tract of land containing 640 acres in Davidson County on the waters of Sulphur Fork of Red River adjoining James Brun's corner. Surveyed for said nancy Sheppard July 20, 1787 by Justinian Cartwright in consequence of a Military Warrant No. 1769. Located Sept 25, 1786.

Page   145 - NANCY SHEPPARD - NC - No. 691 - Reg. Nov 16, 1790
By an Act for the relief of the Officers and Soldiers of the Continental Line, in consideration of the bravery and zeal of Halladay Hathcock, a private in the said line, granted unto Nancy Sheppard, assignee of said Hathcock, a tract of land containing 640 acres in Davidson County on the waters of Sycamore. Surveyed for said Nancy Sheppard July 19, 1797 by Justinian Cartwright, D.S. in consequence of a Military Warrant No. 1763. Located Sept 25, 1786. July 11, 1788.

Page   148 - NANCY SHEPPARD - NC - No. 668 - Reg. Nov 16, 1790
By an Act for the relief of the Officers and Soldiers of the Continental line, in consideration of the bravery and zeal of Nathaniel Cooper, a private in the said line, granted unto Nancy Sheppard, assignee of the heirs of Nathaniel Cooper, a tract of land containing 640 acres in Davidson County on the north side of Tennessee River. Beginning where the Virginia Line strikes said river. Surveyed for Nancy Sheppard Feb 20, 1786 by Isaac Roberts, D.S. in consequence of a Military Warrant No. 2086. Located Jan 12, 1786. Dec 8, 1787.

Page   148 - NANCY SHEPPARD - NC - No. 692 - Reg. Nov 16, 1790
By an Act for the relief of the Officers and Soldiers of the Continental Line, in consideration of the bravery and zeal of Thomas Callaway, a private in the said line, granted unto Nancy Sheppard, assignee of said Callaway, a tract of land containing 640 acres in Davidson County on the waters of Kaspers Creek. Surveyed for Nancy Sheppard July 20, 1787 by J. Cartwright, D.S. in consequence of a Military Warrant No. 1865. Located Sept 25, 1786. July 11, 1788.

Page   149 - GEORGE AUGUSTUS SUGG - NC - No. 902 - Reg. Nov 23, 1790
By an Act for the relief of the Officers and Soldiers of the Continental Line, in consideration of the bravery and zeal of Henry Humpries, a private in the said line, granted unto George Augustus Sugg, assignee of the said Henry Humpries, a tract of land containing 640 acres in Davidson County on the east side of the main east fork of Stones River adjoining Reed's (Read's) corner. Surveyed for George Augustus Sugg Mar 21, 1788 by William Nash in consequence of a Military Warrant No. 2457. Located Mar 1, 1786. Jan 17, 1789.

Page   149 - GEORGE AUGUSTUS SUGG - NC - No. 921 - Reg. Nov 23, 1790
By an Act for the relief of the Officers and Soldiers of the Continental Line, in consideration of the bravery and zeal of John Peters, a private in the said line, granted unto George Augustus Sugg, assignee of said John Peters, a tract of land containing 640 acres in Davidson County on the main east fork of Stones River adjoining John Read's corner. Surveyed for George A. Sugg May 11, 1788 by William Nash in consequence of a Military Warrant No. 2213. Located Apr 5, 1788. May 18, 1789.

Page   149 - DANIEL JAMES - NC - No. 908 - Reg. Dec 27, 1790
By an Act for the relief of the Officers and Soldiers of the Continental Line, in consideration of the bravery and zeal of William Cason, a private in the said line, granted unto Daniel James, assignee of William Cason, a tract of land containing 640 acres in Davidson County on the north side of Cumberland on the waters of Station Camp Creek adjoining Elmore Douglass and David Looney. Surveyed for said Daniel James by himself Nov 20, 1787 in consequence of a Military Warrant No. 522. Located Jan 3, 1786. Jan 17, 1789.

Page   150 - SAMUEL WILSON - Territory of the United States of America south of the
                Ohio - Jan 21, 1791
This indenture made 13 Oct 1789 between John Rice and Elisha Rice of Davidson County, NC of one part and Samuel Wilson of Hartford County, State of Maryland of other part. John and Elisha Rice conveyed unto Samuel Wilson a tract of land containing 640 acres in Davidson County on both sides of Stones River adjoining Major John Bucchanan's corner. Patent No. 306 dated June 13, 1787. Proven by Edward Pratt and P.H. Lee. Jan Term 1791.

Page   150 - PATRICK PEADEN - Territory of the U.S.A. south of the Ohio - Jan 21, 1791
I, William Ross of the County of Pitt and State of North Carolina sold unto Patrick Peaden a tract of land containing 640 acres in Davidson County on Red River, which said land was taken up by William Ross assignee of the heirs of Gray Tucker by virtue of a Military Warrant No. 2694. Grant dated July 28, 1787. Land adjoining the heirs of John Lackey. Proven by William Corbitt, John Corbitt and Roderick Williams. Jan Term 1791.

Page   151 - JOHN WILLIAMS - Territory of the United States &c - Jan 21, 1791
I, Ambrose Jones of Pitt County, North Carolina conveyed unto John Williams of same place, a tract of land containing 640 acres in Davidson County on the east side of Stones River. Which land was taken up by said Ambrose Jones assignee of Daniel Ray, a Military Warrant No. 2741. Grant dated July 10, 1788. Land beginning above the mouth of the second creek, above the mouth of Stuarts, that falls into said river. Proven by William Corbitt. Jan Term 1791.

Page   151 - JOHN THOMPSON - Territory of the United States - Jan 21, 1791
This indenture made 21 Oct 1790 between William Nash of one part and John Thompson of the other part. The said Nash of Davidson County and John Thompson of Russell County, State of Virginia. William Nash conveyed unto John Thompson a tract of land containing 640 acres in Davidson County on the east fork of the first creek above Stones Lick Creek, the east side of Stones River adjoining John Logue's corner. Proven by David Hay, Andrew Ewing and Andrew Casselman. Jan term 1791.

Page   152 - JOHN THOMPSON - Territory of the United States - Jan 21, 1791
This indenture made 21 Oct 1790 between William Nash of Davidson County of one part and John Thompson of Russell County, Virginia of other part. William Nash conveyed unto John Thompson a tract of land containing 640 acres in Davidson County on the waters of the West Fork of the first creek aboveStones Lick Creek on the east side of

Stones River. Proven by David Hay, Andrew Ewing and Andrew Cassellman. Jan Term 1791.

Page   153 ~ JAMES SHAW - Territory of the United States &c - Jan 22, 1791
                This indenture made 3 Nov 1790 between John Shelby of Sullivan County, North Carolina of one part and James Shaw of Davidson County of other part. John Shelby conveyed unto James Shaw a tract of land containing 350 acres in Davidson County on the Blooming Grove Creek. Land being part of a tract of 2500 acres granted to the said John Shelby by the State of North Carolina. Grant dated Oct 8, 1787 and No. (blank). Proven by John Caffrey, Jacob Cassellman and James Bucchanan. Jan Term 1791.

Page   153 - JOHN BROWN - Territory of the United States &c - Jan 22, 1791
                This indenture made the __ day of Jan 1791 between James Shaw and John Brown of the District of Kentucky. James Shaw of District of Mero. James Shaw conveyed unto John Brown a tract of land containing 350 acres in the County of (blank) in the District of Mero. The said being part of a tract granted to John Shelby, Junior for public service, lying on Cumberland River and known by the Blooming Grove. Test: Bennett Searcy. Jan term 1791.

Page   154 - WILLIAM GUN - Territory of the United States &c - Jan 22 1791
                This indenture made 24 Dec 1790 between James Bosley and Mary Bosley his wife of Davidson County of one part and William Gun of same place of other part. James and Mary Bosley conveyed unto William Gun all that plantation or tract of land south of the river Ohio and County of Davidson on the south side of Cumberland River and on the waters of the French Lick branch adjoining the Public survey and McGavock's line. Land containing 493 acres of land. Proven by J.C. Montflorence and George Walker. 24 Dec 1790.

Page   155 - ELIZABETH CHAPMAN - Territory of the United States &c - Jan 24, 1791
                Samuel Barton, Thomas Molloy, James Shaw, Joel Rice and David Hay directors and trustees of the town of Nashville conveyed unto Elizabeth Chapman a lot of land No. 131 in the town of Nashville. This 6 Aug 1790. Jan Term 1791.

Page   155 - ELIZABETH CHAPMAN - Territory of the United States &c - Jan 24, 1791
                Samuel Barton, Thomas Molloy, James Shaw, Jorl Rice and David Hay, directors and trustees of the town of Nashville, conveyed unto Elizabeth Chapman a lot of land No. 158 in town of Nashville. This 6 Aug 1790. Jan term 1791.

Page   155 - RICHARD McGUIRE - Territory of the United States &c - Jan 24, 1791
                Samuel Barton, Thomas Molloy, James Shaw, Joel Rice and David Hay, directors and trustees of town of Nashville, conveyed unto Richard McGuire a lot of land No. 165 in the town of Nashville. Jan term 1791.

Page   156 - RICHARD McGUIRE - Territory of the United States &c - Jan 21, 1791
                Samuel Barton, Thomas Molloy, James Shaw, Joel Rice and David Hay, directors and trustees of town of Nashville, conveyed unto Richard McGuire a lot of land No. 101 in town of Nashville. Jan Term 1791.

Page   156 - JAMES COLE MONTFLORENCE - Territory of the United States &c -
          Jan 24, 1791
          Samuel Barton, Thomas Molloy, James Shaw, Joel Rice and David Hay,
directors and trustees of town of Nashville, conveyed unto James Cole Montflorence a   lot
of land No. 118 in the town of Nashville. This 6 Aug 1790. Jan Term 1791.

Page   156 - JAMES COLE MONTFLORENCE - Territory of the United States &c -
          Jan 24, 1791
          Samuel Barton, Thomas Molloy, James Shaw, Joel Rice and David Hay,
directors and trustees of the town of Nashville, conveyed unto James Cole Montflorence the
lot No. 122 in the town of Nashville. This 6 Aug 1790. Jan Term 1791.

Page   157 - JAMES COLE MONTFLORENCE - Territory of the United States &c -
          Jan 25, 1791.
          Samuel Barton, Thomas Molloy, James Shaw, Joel Rice and David Hay,
directors and trustees of the town of Nashville, conveyed unto James Cole Montflorence Lot
No. 124 in town of Nashville. This 6 Aug 1790. Jan Term 1791.

Page   157 - HYDER ALLY DAVIE - Territory of the United States &c - Jan 25, 1791.
          Samuel Barton, Thomas Molloy, James Shaw, Joel Rice and David Hay,
directors and trustees of the town of Nashville, conveyed unto Hyder Ally Davie the Lot
No. 155 in town of Nashville. This 6 Aug 1790. Jan Term 1791.

Page   THOMAS HANNAH - Territory of the United States &c - Jan 25, 1791
          Samuel Barton, Thomas Molloy, James Shaw, Joel Rice and David Hay,
directors and trustees of town of Nashville, conveyed unto Thomas Hannah the Lot No. 127
in town of Nashville. This 6 Aug 1790. Jan Term 1791.

Page   158 - DANIEL YOUNG - Territory of the United States &c - Jan 25, 1791
          This indenture made 13 Jan 1791 between Federick Stump of one part and
Daniel Young of other part, Both of Davidson County.   Federick Stump conveyed unto
Daniel Young a tract of land containing 320 acres in Davidson County on the east fork of
Whites Creek adjoining said Stump's corner, Mitchel's corner and William Loggins' corner.
Said land being part of a tract granted to William Loggins by patent dated Apr 17, 1786.
Jan Term 1791.

Page   158 - SAMUEL CURRY - Territory of the United States &c - Jan 26, 1791
          This indenture made 10 Jan 1791 between William Turnbull of Davidson
County of one part and Samuel Curry of same place of other part.   William Turnbull
conveyed unto Samuel Curry a tract of land containing 286 acres in Sumner County on the
waters of Spring Creek.   Said land being part of a tract issued to said Turnbull for 640
acres, the warrant originally granted to Josiah Jackson, No. 1810. The Grant dated Dec 8,
1787. Jan Term 1791.

Page   159 - JOHN NORFLEET - Territory of the United States &c - Jan 31, 1791
          This indenture made 29 July 1790 between Lemuel Laurence of Northampton
County, North Carolina of one part and John Norfleet of same place of other part.   Lemuel

Laurence conveyed unto John Norfleet a tract of land containing 640 acres in Davidson County between the Clay Lick and the Battle Ground in the head drafts of Sycamore and adjoining A. Hart's line, Reese's corner. Said land being a grant of land to James Tatum dated 8 Dec 1787. Test: Randolph Maddry, Isaac Walton and Abraham Rogers. Jan Term 1791.

Page   159 - MATTHEW PAYNE - Territory of the United States &c - Feb 1, 1791
          This indenture made 10 Apr 1789 between Thomas Hickman, High Sheriff of Davidson County of one part and Matthew Payne of same place of other part. Thomas Hickman sold unto Matthew Payne a lein all that tract of land in Davidson County on the waters of the Blooming Grove and adjoining John Hambleton's corner on John Shelby's line. Containing 640 acres. Which said tract was executed at the instance of John Turnbull by virtue of a writ of venditione exponas from the Worship Court of Pleas and Quarter Sessions for the County of Davidson County, dated Jan term 1789 and against the heirs of William Gubbins, deceased. Matthew Payne the highest bidder on the 10 Apr 1789. Test: Justinian Cartwright and Lardner Clark. Jan Term 1791.

Page   160 - WILLIAM COOEN - Territory of the United States &c - Feb 1, 1791
          This indenture made 18 May 1790 between Argolis Jeter of Davidson County and William Coon of same place. Argolis Jeter conveyed unto William Coven a tract of land containing 100 acres in Davidson County on both sides of Whites Creek adjoining Amos Heaton's corner on the bank of Heatons Creek and James Russell's line. Proven by John Topp and Elijah Gower. Jan Term 1791.

Page   160 - WILLIAM GUN - Territory of the United States &c - Feb 1, 1791
          This indenture made 29 Nov 1790 between Theodore Mallett of Davidson County of one part and William Gun of other part. Theodore Mallett conveyed unto William Gun a tract of land containing 640 acres by deed of conveyance from Elijah Robertson granted unto said Robertson by virtue of a Military Warrant granted unto Isaac Dunbar No. 3307, land being in Sumner Countyon the waters of Caney Fork River adjoining his tract as assignee of the heirs of Robert Dixon. Test: James Meclin, John Grimes and William Black. Jan Term 1791.

Page   161 - MITCHEL to THOMAS SMITH - Territory of the United States &c -
          Feb 1, 1791
          This indenture made 12 Apr 1790 between William Mitchel of Davidson County of one part and Thomas Smith of same place of other part. William Mitchel conveyed unto Thomas Smith a piece of land containing 208 acres in Davidson County on a branch of Whites Creek and joining Joseph Love's line and Mitchel's line and William Loggin's line. Proven by Thomas Hardiman, William Nash and James Foster. Jan Term 1791.

Page   161 - WILLIAM TURNBULL - Territory of the United States &c - Feb 2, 1791
          This indenture made 11 Jan 1791 between James Mulherin of Davidson County of one part and William Turnbull of same place of other part. James Mulherin conveyed unto WilliamTurnbull a tract of land containing 22 acres in Davidson County on the waters of Mill Creek adjoining Mulherin's Preemption. Said land being part of James Mulherin's

Preemption No. 87 the grant dated Apr 17, 1786. Jan Term 1791.

Page   162 - THOMAS HICKMAN - Territory of the United States &c - Feb 2, 1791
        This indenture made 1 Dec 1790 between James Hoggatt of Mero District and
Davidson County of one part and Thomas Hickman of same place of other part.   James
Hoggatt conveyed unto Thomas Hickman a tract of land containing 160 acres in Davidson
County on the north side of Cumberland River on Sulphur Creek adjoining said Hoggatt's
survey of 228 acres.   The grant of which is No. 29.   Proven by Adam Hampton and John
Cockrill. Jan Term 1791.

Page   162 - THOMAS HICKMAN - Territory of the United States &c - Feb 2, 1791
        This indenture made 1 Dec 1790 between James Hoggatt of Davidson County
and Mero District of one part and Thomas Hickman of same place of other part.   James
Hoggatt conveyed unto Thomas Hickman a tract of land in Davidson County and District of
Mero on the north side of Cumberland River on the Sulphur Creek, containing 228 acres.
Proven by Adam Hampton and John Cockrill. Jan Term 1791.

Page   163 - JOHN LUCAS - Territory of the United States &c - Feb 3, 1791
        This indenture made 12 Jan 1791 between Argolis Geter of the territory of
the United States south of the Ohio and County of Davidson of the one part and John Lucas
of the same place of the other part.   Argolis Geter conveyed unto John Lucas a tract of
land containing 40 acres in Davidson County on the west side of Whites Creek adjoining the
Widow Lucas' line. Jan Term 1791.

Page   163 - JOHN HAY - Territory of the United States &c - Feb 3, 1791
        This indenture made 13 May 1790 between Thomas Hickman of Davidson
County of one part and John Hay, son of David Hay and Ann Hay of the other part.
Thomas Hickman conveyed unto John Hay a half town lot in the town of Nashville being one
half of that town which lies next to the public lot, which half town lot contains one hald
acre. Proven by John Edmiston and Daniel James. Jan Term 1791.

Page   164 - JAMES LEE - Territory of the United States &c - Feb 3, 1791
        This indenture made 4 Nov 1790 between John McFarlin of North Carolina of
one part and James Lea of same place of other part. John McFarlin conveyed unto James
Lea one Lot No. 78 in the town of Nashville. Lot being the lot formerly granted to the
said McFarlin by the Commissioners of said town by deed dated 16 Aug 1784. Proven by
Andrew Ewing and William Ewing. Jan Term 1791.

Page   164 - ANDREW LUCAS - Territory of the United States &c - Feb 5, 1791
        This indenture made 12 Jan 1791 between William Lucas of Berkley County,
Virginia of one part and Andrew Lucas of Davidson County of other part. William Lucas
conveyed unto Andrew Lucas a tract of land in Davidson County and joining Francis
Armstrong's line. Being the upper end of a tract of 640 acres granted to said William
Lucas by the State of North Carolina by patent dated July 10, 1788, No. 186. Jan Term
1791.

165 - BENJAMIN CASSELLMAN - Territory of the United States &c - Feb 3, 1791
    This indenture made 12 Jan 1791 between William Lucas of Berkley County,
Virginia of one part and Benjamin Cassellman of the territory of the United States south of
the Ohio, and County of Davidson County of other part. William Lucas conveyed unto
Benjamin Cassellman a tract of land containing 320 acres in Davidson County adjoining
Andrew Lucas' corner and Francis Armstrong's line and Thomas Brown and John Dunam's
line, William Gubbin's boundary. The land being the lower end of a patent dated July 10,
1788 and No. 186. Jan Term 1791.

Page   165 - DAVID SHELTON - Territory of the United States &c - Feb 4, 1791
    For 10 for 100 acres paid by David Shelton was granted a tract of land
containing 640 acres in Davidson County beginning on the bank of Cumberland at the mouth
of Caney Fork . Running down Cumberland. Which land was surveyed for said Shelton Oct
15, 1785 by Edwin Hickman, D.S. in consequence of a Warrant No. 536. Entered July 19,
1784. July 10, 1788.

Page   166 - DANIEL WILLIAMS, SENIOR - Territory of the United States &c -
        Feb 4, 1791
    This indenture made 13 Dec 1790 between Thomas Thompson of Davidson
County of one part and Daniel Williams, Senior, of same place of other part. Thomas
Thompson conveyed unto Daniel Williams a tract of land containing 278 acres in Davidson
County adjoining William Simpson's boundary and Thompson's Pond and Lewis' boundary.
The patent dated 10 July 1788, registered Folio 60, May 13, 1790. Proven by Sampson
Williams, Jason Thompson and William Rutherford. Jan term 1791.

Page   166 - JOHN CLEVER - Territory of the United States &c - Feb 4, 1791
    North Carolina No. 800. By an Act for the relief of the Officers and Soldiers
of the Continental Line, in consideration of the bravery and zeal of Jacob Clever, a private
in the said line, granted unto John Clever, son and heir of Jacob Clever, a tract of land
containing 320 acres in Davidson County on the north side of theTennessee River. Surveyed
for said Clever by Henry Rutherford, D.S. in consequence of a Warrant No. 1006. Located
May 26, 1784. Nov 28, 1788.

Page   167 - EVAN SHELBY - Territory of the United States &c - Feb 5, 1791
    North Carolina, No. 210. For 10 lbs per 100 acres paid by Evan Shelby was
granted a tract of land containing 640 acres in Davidson County on Ashers Creek adjoining
David Wilson's line, Federick Edwards' line, and Peter Looney's line, and also Henry
Loving's line. Surveyed for Evan Shelby Aug 26, 1786 by James Sanders, D.S. agreeable to
a Warrant No. 369. Entered Mar 23, 1784. July 13, 1788.

Page   167 - JOHN ANDERSON - Territory of the United States &c - Feb 5, 1791
    North Carolina, No. 961. By an Act for the relief of the Officers and
Soldiers of the Continental Line, in consideration of the bravery and zeal of Isham
Handcock, granted unto John Anderson, assignee of said Handcock, a tract of land
containing 1000 acres in Davidson County on the waters of the Caney Fork adjoining Elijah
Robertson's tract as assignee of Alexander Stockley's heirs, Thomas Hickman's line.
Surveyed for John Anderson Nov 18, 1788 by James Mulherin, D.S. in consequence of a

Military Warrant No. 540. Located Nov 5, 1788. May 18, 1789.

Page   167 - WILLIAM ROSS - Territory of the United States &c - Feb 5, 1791
        North Carolina No. 322. By an Act for the relief of the Officers and Soldiers
of the Continental line, in consideration of the bravery and zeal of Gray Tucker, a private
in the said line, granted unto William Ross, assignee of the heirs of said Tucker, a tract of
land containing 640 acres in Davidson County on the waters of Red River, adjoining the
heirs of John Tucker. Surveyed for William Ross by Sampson Williams, D.S. in consequence
of a Military Warrant No. 2694. Located June 23, 1787. July 26, 1787.

Page   168 - GEORGE PAYNE - Territory of the United States &c - Feb 5, 1791
        North Carolina, No. 280. For 10 lbs per 100 acres paid by George Payne was
granted a tract of land containing 640 acres in Davidson County on the west fork of Station
Camp Creek, adjoining David Looney's line and Hamilton's line. Surveyed for George Payne
Mar 8, 1786 by Henry Bradford, D.S. in consequence of a Warrant No. 744. Entered June
14, 1785. July 13, 1788.

Page   168 - ELIJAH ROBERTSON - Territory of the United States &c - Feb 5, 1791
        North Carolina No. 816. By an Act for the relief of the Officers and Soldiers
of the Continental Line, in consideration of the bravery and zeal of Isaac Dunbar, a private
in the said line, granted unto Elijah Robertson, assignee of the heirs of Isaac Dunbar, a
tract of land containing 640 acres in Davidson County on the waters of Caney Fork.
Surveyed for Elijah Robertson June 11, 1788 by James Mulherin, D.S. in consequence of a
Military Warrant No. 3307. Located Mar 22, 1788. Oct 13, 1788.

Page   168 - READING BLOUNTS - Territory of the United States &c - Feb 7, 1791
        North Carolina No. 680. By an Act for the relief of the Officers and Soldiers
of the Continental Line, in consideration of the bravery and zeal of Andrew Miller, a
private in the said line, granted unto Reading Blount a tract of land containing 640 acres in
Davidson County on the headwaters of the long fork of Sycamore Creek, adjoining Elisha
Hunt's corner. Surveyed for Reading Blount Jan 5, 1787 by Robert Weakley, D.S. in
consequence of a Military Warrant No. 2146. Located Mar 22, 1786. Dec 8, 1787.

Page   169 - READING BLOUNT - Territory of the United States &c - Feb 7, 1791
        North Carolina No. 408. By an Act for the relief of the Officers and Soldiers
of the Continental Line, in consideration of the bravery and zeal of James Tolafarrow, a
private in the said line, granted unto Reading Blount a tract of land containing 640 acres in
Davidson County on the ridge between Sycamore and Marron Bone to the road that leads to
Hollis'. Surveyed for Reading Blount Apr 18, 1786 by Robert Weakley, D.S. in consequence
of a Military Warrant No. 2549. Located Feb 23, 1786. Sept 15, 1787.

Page   169 - READING BLOUNT - Territory of the United States &c - Feb 7, 1791
        North Carolina No. 404. By an Act for the relief of the Officers and Soldiers
of the Continental Line, in consideration of the bravery and zeal of Timothy Oglesby, a
private in the said line, granted unto Reading Blount, assignee of Timothy Oglesby, a tract
of land containing 640 acres in Davidson County on the north side of Cumberland River on
the head of the first creek that runs into Cumberland River above McFarlin's cabin.

Surveyed for Reading Blount Sept 1, 1786 by Robert Weakley, D.S. in consequence of a Warrant No. 2148. Located Mar 22, 1786. Sept 15, 1787.

Page   169 - READING BLOUNT - Territory of the United States &c - Feb 7, 1791
North Carolina No. 406. By an Act for the relief of the Officers and Soldiers of the Continental Line, in consideration of the bravery and zeal of James Revell, a private in the said line, granted unto Reading Blount, assignee of said James Reverr, a tract of land containing 640 acres in Davidson County on the north branch of Morrow Bone Creek above the lower road that leads from Nashville to Red River. Surveyed for Reading Blount June 3, 1786 by R. Weakley, D.S. in consequence of a Warrant No. 2152. Located Mar 1786. Sept 15, 1787.

Page   170 - READING BLOUNT - Territory of the United States &c - Feb 7, 1791
North Carolina No. 916. By an Act for the relief of the Officers and Soldiers of the Continental Line, in consideration of the bravery and zeal of Abraham Woff, a private in the said line, granted unto Reading Blount, assignee of said Abraham Woff, a tract of land containing 640 acres in Davidson County on the head branches of the east fork of Stones River adjoining Major Reading Blount's south waters of a tract No. 2534 and Elijah Robertson's corner. Surveyed for Reading Blount May 26, 1788 by Robert Weakley, D.S. in consequence of a Military Warrant No. 2041. Located Mar 22, 1788. May 18, 1789.

Page   170 - READING BLOUNT - Territory of the United States &c - Feb 7, 1791
North Carolina No. 953. By an Act for the relief of the Officers and Soldiers of the Continental Line, in consideration of the bravery and zeal of Jessee Bagworth, a private in the said line, granted unto Major Reading Blount, assignee of said Jesse Bagworth, a tract of land containing 640 acres in Davidson County on the first creek, the first line run by the Commissioners in 1783 crosses running west from the east fork of Stones River. Surveyed for Reading Blount May 26, 1788 by Robert Weakley, D.S. in consequenceof a Military Warrant No. 2559. Located Mar 22, 1788. May 18, 1789.

Page   170 - READING BLOUNT - Territory of the United States &c - Feb 7, 1791
North Carolina No. 956. By an Act for the relief of the Officers and Soldiers of the Continental Line, in consideration of the bravery and zeal of Edward Thust, a private in the said line, granted unto Reading Blount, assignee of Edward Thust, a tract of land containing 640 acres in Davidson County on the east fork of Stones River near the head branches of the same, adjoining Elijah Robertson's north west corner of a tract No. 3202 and Blount and Robertson's corner. Surveyed for Reading Blount May 26, 1788 by Robert Weakley, D.S. in consequence of a Military Warrant No. 2552. Located Mar 22, 1788. May 18, 1789.

Page   171 - READING BLOUNT - Territory of the United States &c - Feb 8, 1791
North Carolina No. 955. By an Act for the relief of the Officers and Soldiers of the Continental Line, in consideration of the bravery and zeal of Nathan Willoughby, a private in the said line, granted unto Major Reading Blount, assignee of said Nathan Willoughby, a tract of land containing 640 acres in Davidson County on the east waters of Half Pone Creek adjoining Cartwright's line and Robert Greer's line. Surveyed for Reading Blount May 9, 1788 by Robert Weakley, D.S. in consequence of a Military Warrant No. 2039.

Located Mar 9, 1786. May 18, 1789.

Page   171 - READING BLOUNT - Territory of the United States &c - Feb 8, 1791
        North Carolina No. 411. By an Act for the relief of the Officers and Soldiers of the Continental Line, in consideration of the bravery and zeal of George Wood, a private in the said line, granted unto Reading Blount a tract of land containing 640 acres in Davidson County on the lower road that leads from Nashville to Red River on the first branch of Sycamore Creek that said road crosses, on the north side of said branch and out the south of a small Clay Lick on said road on said Blount's line. Surveyed for Reading Blount June 2, 1786 by Robert Weakley, D.S. in consequence of a Military Warrant No. 2040. Located Mar 1, 1786. Sept 15, 1787.

Page   171 - READING BLOUNT - Territory of the United States &c - Feb 8, 1791
        North Carolina No. 915. By an Act for the relief of the Officers and Soldiers of the Continental Line, in consideration of the bravery and zeal of George Thompson, a private in the said line, granted unto Reading Blount, assignee of said George Thompson, a tract of land containing 640 acres in Davidson County on the north side of Cumberland River on a west fork of Parsons Creek, the same being the waters of Red River, adjoining John Drake's Spring which runs into McAdoes Creek about two miles from the spring. Surveyed for Reading Blount June 23, 1786 by Robert Weakley, D.S. in consequence of a Military Warrant No. 2551. Located Mar 1, 1786. May 18, 1789.

Page   172 - ELIJAH ROBERTSON - Territory of the United States &c - Feb 8, 1791
        North Carolina No. 1093. By an Act for the relief of the Officers and Soldiers of the Continental Line, in consideration of the bravery and zeal of Charles Rains, a private in the said line, granted unto Elijah Robertson, assignee of said Charles Rains, a tract of land containing 640 acres in Davidson County on the north side of Cumberland River on the south side of the south fork of McAdoes Creek adjoining Robertson's line, Robert McCallough's corner. Surveyed for Elijah Robertson Apr 26, 1786 by Robert Weakley, D.S. in consequence of a Military Warrant No. 1839. Located Mar 16, 1786. Nov 14, 1789.

Page   172 - ELIJAH ROBERTSON - Territory of the United States &c - Feb 8, 1791
        North Carolina No. 90. By an Act for the relief of the Officers and Soldiers of the Continental Line, in consideration of the bravery and zeal of Nicholas Pea, one of the Commissioners Guard, granted unto Elijah Robertson, assignee of said Nicholas Pea, a tract of land containing 320 acres in Davidson County beginning at the north west corner of the Public Survey which includes the French Lick and joining George Freeland's Preemption and James Robertson and Elijah Robertson's Preemption. Surveyed for Elijah Robertson Nov 19, 1784 by Thomas Molloy, D.S. agreeable to a Warrant No. 18. Entered Dec 29, 1783. July 10, 1788.

Page   172 - RICHARD CROSS - Territory of the United States &c - Feb 9, 1791
        North Carolina No. 86. For 10 lbs per 100 acres paid by Richard Cross was granted a tract of land containing 5000 acres in the Western District on the north fork of Loos Hatchie River, adjoining Jno. McKnill Alexander No. 1010, and John Sitgreaves No. 2299 on said forl. Surveyed for Richard Cross by Ed. Harris, D.S. Sept 2, 1785 Warrant No.

1046. Located Oct 29, 1783. July 10, 1788.

Page   173 - ELIJAH ROBERTSON - Territory of the United States &c - Feb 9, 1791
            North Carolina No. 219. For 10 lbs per 100 acres paid by Elijah Robertson
was granted a tract of land containing 640 acres in Davidson County beginning on the line
of the Public Survey about the French Lick and joining John Cockrill's boundary. Surveyed
for Elijah Robertson Nov 19, 1784 by Thomas Molloy, D.S. in agreeable to a Warrant No. 19.
Entered Dec 29, 1783. July 10, 1788.

Page   173 - PATSEY ROBERTSON - Territory of the united States &c - Feb 9, 1791
            North Carolina No. 822. By an Act for the relief of the Officers and Soldiers
of the Continental Line, in consideration of the bravery and zeal of Abraham Steps, a
sergeant in the said line, granted unto Patsey Robertson, assignee of the heirs of said
Abraham Steps, a tract of land containing 1000 acres in Davidson County on the Caney Fork
adjoining James Mulherin's tract and Thomas Hickman's tract. Surveyed for Patsey
Robertson by James Mulherin, D.S. in consequence of a Military Warrant No. 3392. Located
June 14, 1788. Oct 21, 1788.

Page   173 - PATSEY ROBERTSON - Territory of the United States &c - Feb 9, 1791
            North Carolina No. 821. By an Act for the relief of the Officers and Soldiers
of the Continental Line, in consideration of the bravery and zeal of Stephen Roper, a
sergeant in the said line, granted unto Patsey Robertson, assignee of the heirs of Stephen
Roper, a tract of land containing 1000 acres in Davidson County on the waters of Caney
Fork adjoining a tract of Elijah Robertson, assignee of the heirs of Etridge Nelson, and Capt
John Painter's west boundary. Surveyed for Patsey Robertson by James Mulherin, D.S. in
consequence of a Military Warrant No. 3320. Located June 16, 1788. Oct 21, 1788.

Page   174 - READING BLOUNT - Territory of the United States &c - Feb 10, 1791
            North Carolina No. 410. By an Act for the relief of the officers and Soldiers
of the Continental Line, in consideration of the bravery and zeal of George Welch, a private
in the said line, granted unto Reading Blount, assignee of George Welch, a tract of land
containing 640 acres in Davidson County on the south branch of Sycamore Creek, above the
lower road that leads from Nashville to Red River. Surveyed for Reading Blount June 3,
1786 by Robert Weakley, D.S. in consequence of a Military Warrant No. 2555. Located Mar
1, 1786. Sept 15, 1787.
North Carolina] Examined
Beaufort County]
Elijah Robertson. Signed and Sealed this 25 Sept 1790. Wit: Cox C(i llegible) and John Gray
Blount.

Page   174 - READING BLOUNT - Territory of the United States &c - Feb 10, 1791
            North Carolina No. 403. By an Act for the relief of the Officers and Soldiers
of the Continental Line, in consideration of the bravery and zeal of Nathan Rymore, a
private in the said line, granted unto Reading Blount, assignee of Nathan Rymore, a tract of
land containing 640 acres in Davidson County on the south branches of Sycamore Creek
above the lower road that leads from Nashville to Red River. Surveyed for Reading Blount
June 2, 1786 by Robert Weakley, D.S. in consequence of a Military Warrant No. 2154.

Located Mar 1, 1786. Sept 15, 1787.

North Carolina]
Beaufort County] E. Robertson

Signed and Sealed 15 Sept 1790.

Page   175 - READING BLOUNT - Territory of the United States &c - Feb 10, 1791
            North Carolina No. 914. By an Act for the relief of the Officers and Soldiers
of the Continental Line, in consideration of the bravery and zeal of Nathan Murdock, a
private in the said line, granted unto Major Reading Blount, assignee of Nathan Murdock, a
tract of land containing 640 acres in Davidson County on the north branches of the east
fork of Stones River adjoining Elijah Robertson's corner of a tract No. 3262. Surveyed for
Reading Blount May 16, 1788 by Robert Weakley, D.S. in consequence of a Military Warrant
No. 2534. Located Mar 22, 1788. May 18, 1789.

North Carolina]
Beaufort County] Elijah Robertson.

Signed and Sealed 25 Sept 1791 by Cox Coart and John Gray Blount.

Page   175 - READING BLOUNT - Territory of the United States &c - Feb 10, 1791
            North Carolina No. 952. By an Act for the relief of the Officers and Soldiers
of the Continental Line, in consideration of the bravery and zeal of Clement Richards, a
private in the said line, granted unto Reading Blount, assignee of the heirs of Clement
Richards, a tract of land containing 640 acres in Davidson County on the waters of Caney
Fork. Beginning at a mountain at the head of the east fork of Stones River and about
thirty yards south of a tree marked with a number of different letters which was made by
the Guard in 1783 in a path crossing said mountain. Surveyed for Reading Blount Mar 18,
1788 by Robert Weakley, D.S. in consequence of a Military Warrant No. 2151. Located Feb
23, 1786. May 18, 1789.

North Carolina]
Beaufort County] Elijah Robertson

Signed and Sealed this 25 Sept 1790. Wit: Cox Coart and John Gray Blount.

Page   176 - READEN BLOUNT - Territory of the United States &c - Feb 11, 1791
            North Carolina No. 409. By an Act for the relief of the Officers and Soldiers
of the Continental line, in consideration of the bravery and zeal of George Shaffer, a
private in the said line, granted unto Readen Blount, assignee of the said George Shaffer, a
tract of land containing 640 acres in Davidson County on the north side of Cumberland
River, the north branch of Sycamore Creek on the lower road that leads from Nashville to
Red River, adjoining Henry Rutherford's corner. Surveyed for Readen Blount June 3, 1786
by Robert Weakley, D.S. in consideration of a Military Warrant No. 2547. Located Mar 16,
1786. Sept 15, 1787.

North Carolina]
Beaufort County] Elijah Robertson

Signed and Sealed this 25 Sept 1790. Wit: Cox Coart and John Gray Blount.

Page   176 - READING BLOUNT - Territory of the United States &c - Feb 11, 1791
            North Carolina No. 407. By an Act for the relief of the Officers and Soldiers
of the Continental Line, in consideration of the bravery and zeal of Absolom Smith, a

private in the said line, granted unto Reading Blount, assignee of said Absolom Smith, a tract of land containing 640 acres in Davidson County on the south branches of Sycamore Creek on the lower road that leads from Nashville to Red River. Surveyed for Reading Blount June 3, 1786 by Robert Weakley, D.S. in consequence of a Military Warrant No. 2545. Located Mar 1, 1786. Sept 15, 1787.

North Carolina   ]   Elijah Robertson
Beaufort County   ]

Signed and Sealed this 25 Sept 1790. Wit: Cox Coart and John Gray Blount.

Page   177 - READING BLOUNT - Territory of the United States &c - Feb 11, 1791

       North Carolina No. 405. By an Act for the relief of the Officers and Soldiers of the Continental Line, in consideration of the bravery and zeal of Daniel Harris, a private in the said line, granted unto Reading Blount, assignee of Daniel Harris, a tract of land containing 640 acres in Davidson County on the south branches of Sycamore Creek above the lower road that leads from Nashville to Red River. Surveyed for Reading Blount June 3, 1786 by Robert Weakley, D.S. in consequence of a Military Warrant No. 2656. Located Mar 1, 1786. Sept 15, 1787.

North Carolina   ]   Elijah Robertson
Beaufort County   ]

Signed and Sealed this 25 Sept 1790. Wit: Cox Coart and John Gray Blount.

Page   177 - READING BLOUNT - Territory of the United States &c - Feb 11, 1791

       North Carolina No. 681. By an Act for the relief of the Officers and Soldiers of the Continental Line, in consideration of the bravery and zeal of Lewis Strand, a private in the said line, granted unto Reading Blount, assignee fo said Lewis Strand, a tract of land containing 640 acres in Davidson County on Sycamore Creek above the upper road crossing said creek and adjoining a survey of Col. Hardy Murfree. Surveyed for Reading Blount Jan 4, 1787 by Robert Weakley, D.S. in consequence of a Military Warrant No. 2548. Located Mar 16, 1786. Dec 8, 1787.

North Carolina   ]   Elijah Robertson
Beaufort County   ]

Signed and Sealed this 25 Sept 1790. Wit: Cox Coart and John Gray Blount.

Page   178 - READING BLOUNT - Territory of the United States &c - Feb 11, 1791

       North Carolina No. 954. By an Act for the relief of the Officers and Soldiers of the Continental Line, in consideration of the bravery and zeal of Timothy Burden, a private in the said line, granted unto Reading Blount, assignee of said Timothy Burden, a tract of land containing 640 acres in Davidson County on the waters of Caney Fork. Beginning at said Blount's corner of a tract No. 2151 on the north east end of mountain at the head of the east fork of Stones River about thirty yards south of a beech tree marked with number of different letters which was made by the Guards in 1783 on a path crossing said mountain. Surveyed for Reading Blount Mar 18, 1788 by Robert Weakley, D.S. in consequence of a Military Warrant No. 2560. Located Feb 23, 1786. Mar 18, 1789.

North Carolina   ]   Elijah Robertson
Beaufort County   ]

Signed and Sealed this 25 Sept 1790. Wit: Cox Coart and John Gray Blount.

Page   178 - JOHN BUCCHANAN - Territory of the United States &c - Feb 14, 1791
North Carolina No. 89. By an Act for the relief of the Officers and Soldiers of the Continental Line, in consideration of the services of Martin Armstrong, surveyor, granted unto John Bucchanan, assignee of said Armstrong, a tract of land containing 138 acres in Davidson County on the waters of Mill Creek adjoining John Foreman's corner and James Menesses' line. Surveyed for John Bucchanan by himself Dec 24, 1788 in consequence of an entry dated Nov 15, 1788. Nov 26, 1789.

Page   179 - ROBERT THOMPSON - Territory of the United States &c - Feb 14, 1791
North Carolina No. 1088. By an Act for the relief of the Officers and Soldiers of the Continental Line, in consideration of the bravery and zeal of Stephen Joiners, a private in the said line, granted unto Robert Thompson, assignee of said Joiners' heirs, a tract of land containing 640 acres in Davidson County on the waters of Hurricane Creek adjoining Minos Cannon's corner. Surveyed for Robert Thompson Mar 14, 1789 by John Bucchanan, D.S. in consequence of a Military Warrant No. 1917. Located Dec 27, 1788. Nov 14, 1789.

Page   179 - NICHOLAS COONROD - Territory of the United States &c - Feb 14, 1791
North Carolina No. 282. For 10 lbs per 100 acres paid by Nicholas Coonrod was granted a tract of land containing 640 acres in Davidson County on the south side of Cumberland River. Beginning at bank of said river below a spring called Espey's Spring and a conditional line formerly made by Benjamin Logan. Surveyed for Nicholas Coonrod Apr 10, 1788 agreeable to a Warrant No. 26. Entered Dec 29, 1783. Nov 26, 1789.

Page   179 - JOHN CARTER - Territory of the United States &c - Feb 14, 1791
North Carolina No. 112. For 10 lbs per 100 acres paid by John Carter was granted a tract of land containing 1000 acres in the Western District in the fork of the Forked Deer River adjoining William Hawkins' corner and Martin Armstrong's line. Surveyed for John Carter Sept 5, 1785 by James Robertson, D.S. by virtue of a Warrant No. 596. Entered Oct 27, 1785. July 10, 1788.

Page   180 - BENJAMIN LUCAS - Territory of the United States &c - Feb 14, 1791
North Carolina No. 288. For 10 lbs per 100 acres paid by Benjamin Lucas was granted a tract of land containing 640 acres in Davidson County on Big Harpeth River adjoining William Collinsworth's Preemption. Surveyed for Benjamin Lucas June 21, 1785 by B. William Pollock, D.S. agreeable to a Warrant No. 490. Entered June 18, 1784. Nov 26, 1789.

Page   180 - LARDNER CLARK - Territory of the United States &c - Feb 15, 1791
North Carolina No. 88. By an Act for the relief of the Officers and Soldiers of the Continental Line, in consideration of the services of Martin Armstrong, surveyor, granted unto Lardner Clark, assignee of said Armstrong, a tract of land containing 228 acres in Davidson County on the waters of Mill Creek adjoining Thomas Fletcher's corner. Surveyed for Lardner Clark Mar 10, 1786 by John Bucchanan, D.S. in consequence of a Service Right of said Armstrong's No. 1572. Located Dec 19, 1785. Nov 17, 1789.

Page   180 - WICUFF & CLARK - Territory of the United States &c - Feb 15, 1791
North Carolina No. 186. By an Act for the relief of the Officers and Soldiers of the Continental Line, in consideration of the services of Martin Armstrong, surveyor, granted unto William Wicuff and Lardner Clark, assignees of said Armstrong, a tract of land containing 228 acres of land in Davidson County on the waters of Puzzle Creek about half a mile north of Cumberland River adjoining Absolom Sheperd's corner. Surveyed for said Wicuff and Clark Mar 11, 1786 by Thomas Molloy, D.S. No. 1702. Located Dec 9, 1788. Nov 14, 1789.

Page   181 - ARCHIBALD MARLIN - Territory of the United States &c - Feb 16, 1791
North Carolina No. 462. By an Act for the relief of the Officers and Soldiers of the Continental Line, in consideration of the bravery and zeal of Archibald Marlin, a private in the said line, granted unto said Marlin a tract of land containing 297 acres in Davidson County on both sides of Stones Creek a branch of Stones River adjoining JOhn Caffrey's corner. Surveyed for said Marlin April 26, 1786 by John Donelson, D.S. by virtue of a Military Warrant No. 848. Located Apr 18, 1785. Sept 15, 1787.

Page   181 - CHRISTOPHER GRICE - Territory of the United States &c - Feb 16, 1791
North Carolina No. 81. By an Act for the relief of the Officers and Soldiers of the Continental Line, in consideration of the services of Martin Armstrong, surveyor, granted unto Christopher Grice, assignee of said Armstrong, a tract of land containing 100 acres in Davidson County on Heatons Lick Branch adjoining Isaac Drake's boundary. Surveyed for Christopher Grice Feb 6, 1787 by Thomas Molloy, D.S. agreeable to a located dated Aug 18, 1786 and No. 2919. Nov 14, 1789.

Page   181 - JAMES THOMPSON - Territory of the United States &c - Mar 3, 1791
North Carolina No. 224. By an Act for the relief of the Officers and Soldiers of the Continental Line, in consideration of the bravery and zeal of John Stewart, a private in the said line, granted unto James Thompson, assignee of said John Stuart, a tract of land containing 274 acres in Davidson County on the waters of Richland Creek adjoining Thompson's corner, Francis Hodge's corner and Finney's corner. Surveyed for James Thompson May 12, 1785 by Robert Weakley, D.S. in consequence of a Warrant No. 454. Located June 9, 1784. Mar 17, 1786.

Page   182 - THOMAS HAMILTON - Territory of the United States &c - Mar 25, 1791
North Carolina No. 509. By an Act for the relief of the Officers and Soldiers of the Continental Line, in consideration of the bravery and zeal of James Cunningham, a private in the said line, granted unto Thomas Hamilton, assignee of James Cunningham, a tract of land containing 640 acres in Davidson County on the west side of Caney Fork adjoining John Nichols' tract of a 1000 acres at the mouth of third large creek above the mouth of said river. Surveyed for Thomas Hamilton Aug 5, 1786 by Edwin Hickman, D.S. in consequence of a Military Warrant No. 1938. Located July 29, 1786. Sept 15, 1787.

Page   182 - THOMAS HAMILTON - Territory of the United States &c - Mar 25, 1791
North Carolina No. 500. By an Act for the relief of the Officers and Soldiers of the Continental Line, in consideration of the bravery and zeal of Jeremiah McLain, a private in the said line, granted unto Thomas Hamilton, assignee of Jeremiah McLain, a

Page   182 - JAMES SCURLOCK - Territory of the United States &c - Mar 25, 1791
North Carolina No. 912. By an Act for the relief of the Officers and Soldiers of the Continental line, in consideration of the bravery and zeal of James Scurlock, a lieutenant, granted unto James Scurlock a tract of land containing 560 acres in Davidson County on both sides of Harpeth River adjoining Manifee's corner and John Nichols' corner. Surveyed for James Scurlock Feb 10, 1786 by John Donelson, D.S. in consequence of a Military Warrant No. 153. Located Dec 7, 1784. May 18, 1789.

Page   183 - WILLIAM JAMMERSON - Territory of the United States &c - Apr 6, 1791
North Carolina No. 594. By an Act for the relief of the officers and Soldiers of the Continental Line, in consideration of the bravery and zeal of William Montgomery, a private in the said line, granted unto William Jammerson, assignee of William Montgomery, a tract of land containing 640 acres in Davidson County on the south side of Cumberland River adjoining Dennis Reardon's line and in a small island in Bartons Creek. Surveyed for William Jammerson Sept 1, 1787 by Anthony Bledsoe, D.S. in consequence of a Military Warrant No. 1168. Located Aug 2, 1784. Sept 12, 1787.

Page   183 - GEORGE McLANE - Territory of the United States &c - Apr 9, 1791
North Carolina No. 40. For 10 lbs per 100 acres paid by George McLane was granted a tract of land containing 1000 acres in the Western District on Flat Creek and the waters thereof adjoining Thomas Gillaspie's corner. Surveyed for George McLane by Henry Rutherford, D.S. in consequence of a Warrant No. 2214. Located May 20, 1784. July 10, 1788.

Page   183 - JOSEPH KERE - Territory of the United States &c - Apr 22, 1791
North Carolina No. 967. By an Act for the relief of the Officers and Soldiers of the Continental line, in consideraton of the bravery and zeal of Daniel Heston, a private in the said line, granted unto Joseph Kere, assignee of said Daniel Hester, a tract of land containing 640 acres in Davidson County on the head of Gibsons Creek and Bucchanan's Spring Branch and on the north side of Cumberland River adjoining John Bucchanan's cornerand James Scott's line. Surveyed for Joseph Kere Mar 8, 1787 by John Donelson, D.S. in consequence of a Military Warrant No. 255. Located Dec 30, 1784. May 18, 1789.

Page   184 - JOHN JONES - Territory of the United States &c - Apr 26, 1791
North Carolina No. 854. By an Act for the relief of the Officers and Soldiers of the Continental Line, in consideration of the bravery and zeal of Samuel Thompson, a private in the said line, granted unto John Jones, assignee of said Samuel Thompson, a tract of land containing 640 acres in Davidson County being on the waters of Caney Fork adjoining James Walker's assignee of Thomas Wood. Surveyed for John Jones Nov 11, 1788 by James Mulherin, D.S. in consequence of a Military Warrant No. 2021. Located Nov 5, 1788. Jan 17, 1789.

Page   184 - STOCKLEY DONELSON - Territory of the United States &c - Apr 26, 1791
North Carolina No. 978. By an Act for the relief of the officers and Soldiers of the Continental Line, in consideration of the bravery and zeal of William Crawley, a private in the said line, granted unto Stockley Donelson, assignee of the heirs of William Crawley, a tract of land containing 640 acres in Davidson County on the south side of

Cumberland River, Jones Bluff adjoining James Robertson's corner. Surveyed for Stockley Donelson Mar 20, 1787 by John Donelson, D.S. in consequence of a Military Warrant No. 1831. Located Jan 26, 1786. May 18, 1789.

Page   184 - PETER CLOUD - Territory of the United States &c - Apr 26, 1791
North Carolina No. 158. By an Act for the relief of the Officers and Soldiers of the Continental Line, in consideration of the bravery and zeal of Daniel Johnston, a private in the said line, granted unto Peter Cloud, assignee of said Daniel Johnston, a tract of land containing 274 acres in Davidson County on Kaspers Creek on the north side of Cumberland River adjoining Kasper Mansker's corner and to a tree in the line of the Public Survey. Surveyed for Peter Cloud Sept 30, 1784 by James Sanders, D.S. in consequence of a Military Warrant No. 735. Located July 27, 1784. Mar 17, 1786.

Page   185 - MANN PHILIPS - Territory of the United States &c - Apr 26, 1791
North Carolina No. 609. By an Act for the relief of the Officers and Soldiers of the Continental Line, in consideration of the bravery and zeal of Thomas Andrews, a private in the said line, granted unto Mann Philips, assignee of said Thomas Andrews, a tract of land containing 640 acres in Davidson County on the south side of Big Barren River on the fifth creek that the Virginia Line crossestothe east of Red River adjoining Edwin Hickman's corner. Surveyed for Mann Philips Nov 17, 1786 by Thomas Hickman, D.S. in consequence of a Military Warrant No. 2258. Located Jan 7, 1786. Sept 15, 1787.

Page   185 - MANN PHILIPS - Territory of the United States &c - Apr 26, 1791
North Carolina No. 683. By an Act for the relief of the Officers and Soldiers of the Continental Line, in consideration of the bravery and zeal of Jordan Wilkins, a private in the said line, granted unto Mann Philips, assignee of the heirs of Jordan Wilkins, a tract of land containing 640 acres in Davidson County on the waters of Salleir to join entry of Lardner Clark No. 2605, on the north. Surveyed for said Mann Philips Mar 23, 1786 by Robert Hays, D.S. in consequence of a Military Warrant No. 2256. Located Dec 23, 1785. Dec 12, 1787.

Page   185 - MANN PHILIPS - Territory of the United States &c - Apr 26, 1791
North Carolina No. 684. By an Act for the relief of the Officers and Soldiers of the Continental Line, in consideration of the bravery and zeal of John Wilson, a private in the said line, granted unto Mann Philips, assignee of the heirs of John Wilson, a tract of land containing 640 acres in Davidson County to join an entry of 1000 acres No. 2347 on the upper line adjoining said line crossing the Sallein. Surveyed for Mann Philips Mar 29, 1786 by Robert Hay, D.S. in consequence of a Military Warrant No. 2075. Located Dec 23, 1785. Dec 12, 1787.

Page   186 - DR. JAMES WHITE - Territory of the United States &c - Apr 27, 1791
North Carolina No. 1011. By an Act for the relief of the Officers and Soldiers of the Continental Line, in consideration of the bravery and zeal of Thomas White, a captain in the said line, granted unto James White, heir of said Thomas White, a tract of land containing 3840 acres in Davidson County on a large bent of Cumberland River on the north west side of the first timbered island in said river below Heatons Station. Surveyed for James White Dec 21, 1787 by Robert Weakley, D.S. in consequence of a Military

Warrant No. 102. Located July 13, 1784. May 18, 1789.

Page 186 - WILLIAM McWHIRTER - Territory of the United States &c - Apr 27, 1791

This indenture made 12 Apr 1791 between Peter Cloud of Davidson COunty of one part and William McWhirter of same place of other part. Peter Cloud conveyed unto William McWhirter a tract of land containing 274 acres in Davidson County on Kaspers Creek adjoining Kasper Mansker's corner and on the line of the Public Survey. Apr Term 1791.

Page 187 - JOHN SHEHEN - Territory of the United States &c - Apr 27, 1791

This indenture made 29 Mar 1791 between Lardner Clark of Davidson County of one part and John Shehen, planter, of same place of other part. Lardner Clark conveyed unto John Shehen a tract of land containing 40 acres in Davidson County on the south side of Cumberland River at the forks of Mill Creek adjoining Lardner Clark's boundary of his Preemption as assignee of James Wilson's intersects the said fork. Apr Term 1791.

Page 187 - DANIEL COWAN - Territory of the united States &c - Apr 27, 1791

This indenture made 8 Feb 1791 between George Nevilles of Tennessee County and District of Mero of one part and Daniel Cowan of Davidson County of other part. George Nevilles conveyed unto Daniel Cowan a tract of land containing 640 acres in Davidson County on Big Harpeth. Beginning at the mouth of the first creek below Little Harpeth. Which land was granted unto said Nevilles by patent dated 10 July 1788. Test: Benjamin Koen and Elisha Rice. Apr Term 1791.

Page 188 - JOHN THOMPSON - Territory of the United States &c - Apr 27, 1791

This indenture made 14 Apr 1791 between James Thompson of Davidson County of one part and John Thompson of same place of other part. James Thompson conveyed unto John Thompson a lot of one acre of land in the town of Nashville and No. 48. It being the lot granted by Samuel Barton, Thomas Molloy and James Shaw, directors and trustees of the town of Nashville, granted unto said James Thompson, the deed dated 30 July 1784. Apr Term 1791.

Page 188 - TIMOTHY ANDERSON - Territory of the United States &c - Apr 28, 1791

This indenture made 13 Apr 1791 between Authur McAdoe of Lancaster County, State of South Carolina of one part and Timothy Anderson of same place of other part. Authur McAdoe conveyed unto Timothy Anderson one tract of land containing 640 acres in Tennessee County on the north side of Cumberland River adjoining Headon Wells' line. Apr Term 1791.

Page 188 - ELIZABETH McCUTCHEN, GRIZZEL McCUTCHEN & JANE McCUTCHEN - April 28, 1791

This indenture made 13 Apr 1791 between Lewis Reeling of Davidson County of one part and Elizabeth McCutchen, Grizzel McCutchen and Jane McCutchen of the other part. Lewis Reeling conveyed unto Elizabeth McCutchen, Grizzel McCutchen and Jane McCutchen the said Elizabeth McCutchen, relict of William McCutchen, a tract of land in Davidson County on the waters of Mill Creek and containing 200 acres and joining William Overall's corner and the corner of the heirs of James Mayfield, and Thomas Denton's boundary. The said land being part of said Lewis Reeling's 640 acres. The said Elizabeth McCutchen and her assigns during the whole term of the natural life of the said Elizabeth McCutchen only, and the said bargained after the decease of the said Elizabeth McCutchen remain in fee simple unto the aforesaid Grizzel McCutchen and Jane McCutchen her daughters of the said William McCutchen. The Grizzel and Jane and joint tenements their heirs and assigns forever. Apr Term 1791.

Page 189 - MARY & MARGET LEFEVER - Territory of the United States &c - Apr 21, (2nd page) 1791

North Carolina No. 284. For 10 lbs per 100 acres paid by Mary and Marget Lefever was granted a tract of land containing 640 acres in Davidson County on the south side of Cumberland River on both sides of James Hay's Spring Creek adjoining Joseph Hendrick's on the south bank of Cumberland River and James Hay's land and also Daniel Smith's corner. Surveyed for Mary and Marget Lefever June 7, 1788 by Daniel Smith, surveyor, agreeable to a Warrant No. 453. Entry dated May 18, 1784. Nov 26, 1789.

Page 190 - EDGAR & TAITT - Territory of the United States &c - Apr 28, 1791

This indenture made 27 Aug 1790 between John Forde of Davidson County of one part and Edgar & Taitt of same place of other part. John Forde conveyed unto said Edgar and Taitt a tract of land containing 640 acres in Davidson County, namely one tract of 640 acres and grant No. 904, dated Jan 17, 1879. Test: Joseph Sitgreaves and David Hay. Apr Term 1791.

Page 190 - THOMAS OVERTON - Territory of the United States &c - Apr 29, 1791

This indenture made and entered 21 Feb 1791 between Stockley Donelson of one part and Thomas Overton of other part. Stockley Donelson conveyed unto Thomas Overton a tract of land containing 640 acres in Davidson County on the south side of Cumberland River, Jones Bluff adjoining James Robertson's corner. Test: Andrew Jackson. Apr Term 1791.

Page 191 - ISAAC ROUNSEVALL - Territory of the United States &c - Apr 29, 1791

This indenture made 10 Mar 1791 between (blank) Rounsevall of Davidson County of the one part and Isaac Rounsevall of of same place of other part. (blank) Rounsevall conveyed unto Isaac Rounsevall a tract of land being part of David Rounsevall's Preemption, containing 160 acres in Davidson County on the west side of Whites Creek adjoining John Drake's line. Which land was granted unto David Rounsevall by patent dated 1786 and No. 11. Apr Term 1791.

Page 191 - COURSES OF THE FRENCH LICK SURVEY - April 29, 1791

Court of Davidson County, Jan Term 1791 directing the surveyors of said county to resurvey the Public tract including the French Lick agreeable to an original survey by the Commissioners in the year 1783 or 1784. Anthony Foster, surveyor, made return at April Term 1791 the survey including the French Lick agreeable to a former survey of the Commissioners made by Thomas Molloy, Esq., to wit, Beginning at a hickory eighteen poles below the mouth of the Lick Branch, running south sixty seven degrees west two hundred and twenty six poles to a hackberry, thence south thirty three degrees east four hundred and sixty two poles to an elm, thence north sixty seven east two hundred and twenty six poles to an ash, thence north thirty three degrees west one hundred and thirty five poles to the river, thence down the river with its meanders to the beginning. Which causes contains 640 acres of land. North sixty seven degrees east seventy five poles to the river, thence down the river with its meanders to intersect the black line, running north thirty three degrees west makes 21 acres. Whether the last mentioned courses belong to the survey or not is unknown as I have not got the return made by the Commissioners to the Assembly of North Carolina. James Moreland and Andrew Ewing, sworn chain carriers. Surveyed Feb 3rd 1791. Signed Anthony Foster, examinor." April Term 1791.

Page   192 - WILLIAM GUBBINS - Territory of the United States &c - Apr 27, 1791
North Carolina No. 100. By an Act for the relief of the Officers and Soldiers of the Continental Line, in consideration of the services of William Gubbins, an ensign in the Guard allowed the Commissioners for laying off the land, granted unto William Gubbins a tract of land containing 720 acres in Davidson County adjoining Thomas Finney's line and William Lucas' boundary. Surveyed for William Gubbins Dec 10, 1785 by Thomas Molloy, D.S. in consequence of a Warrant No. 762. Entry date Aug 22, 1785. Nov 14, 1789.

Page   192 - FEDERICK STUMP - NC - May 5, 1791
No. 76. We have granted unto Federick Stump 640 acres in Davidson County on the waters of Whites Creek adjoining David Rounsevall's line. This 17 April 1786.

Page   193 - JOHN FORDE - Territory of the United States &c - May 23, 1791
North Carolina No. 897. By an Act for the relief of the Officers and Soldiers of the Continental Line, in consideration of the bravery and zeal of Solomon Middleton, a private in the said line, granted unto John Forde, assignee of said Solomon Middleton, a tract of land containing 640 acres in Davidson County on the north side of Cumberland River on the waters of Persons Creek. Surveyed for John Forde July 5, 1786 by Robert Nelson, D.S. in consequence of a Military Warrant No. 921. Located May 12, 1786. Jan 17, 1789.

Page   193 - JOHN FORDE - Territory of the United States &c - May 23, 1791
North Carolina No. 898. By an Act for the relief of the Officers and Soldiers of the Continental Line, in consideration of the bravery and zeal of Joel Ballard, a private in the said line, granted unto John Forde, assignee of said Joel Ballard, a tract of land containing 640 acres in Davidson County on the north side of Cumberland River on Persons Creek. Surveyed for John Forde July 5, 1786 by Robert Nelson, D.S. in consequence of a Military Warrant No. 2445. Located May 12, 1786. Jan 17, 1789.

Page   193 - JOHN FORDE - Territory of the United States &c - May 23, 1791
North Carolina No. 899. By an Act for the relief of the Officers and Soldiers of the Continental Line, in consideration of the bravery and zeal of James Bond, a private in the said line, granted unto John Forde, assignee of James Bond, a tract of land containing 640 acres in Davidson County on the north side of Cumberland River on Persons Creek. Surveyed for John Forde July 5, 1786 by John Lockart, D.S. in consequence of a Military Warrant No. 727. Located May 12, 1786. Jan 17, 1789.

Page   194 - ISAAC RIGHT - Territory of the United States &c - May 24, 1791
North Carolina No. 1009. By an Act for the relief of the Officers and Soldiers of the Continental Line, in consideration of the bravery and zeal of David Pasmore, a private in the said line, granted unto Isaac Right, assignee of said David Pasmore, a tract of land containing 365 acres in Davidson County on the waters of Stones River adjoining Benjamin Floods beginning corner. Surveyed for Isaac Right Mar 2, 1786 by John Bucchanan, D.S. in consequence of a Military Warrant No. 417. Located Jan 18, 1786. May 18, 1789.

Page   194 - ROBERT WEAKLEY - Territory of the United States &c - May 24, 1791
North Carolina No. 1182. By an Act for the relief of the Officers and Soldiers of the Continental Line, in consideration of the bravery and zeal of Thomas Winstill, a private in the said line, granted unto Robert Weakley, assignee of the heirs of said Thomas Winstill, a tract of land containing 640 acres in Davidson County on the south side of Cumberland River on the waters of the east fork of Stones River adjoining a survey of said Weakley on the north. Warrant No. 3397. Joining Isadore Skerrett's line. Surveyed for said Weakley by himself July 28, 2790 in consequence of a Military Warrant No. 2252. Located Oct 1, 1789. Nov 30, 1790.

Page   194 - ROBERT NELSON - Territory of the United States &c - May 24, 1791
North Carolina No. 1184. By an Act for the relief of the Officers and Soldiers of the Continental Line, in consideration of the bravery and zeal of Taylor Jones, a private in the said line, granted unto Robert Nelson, assignee of Taylor Jones, a tract of land containing 640 acres in Davidson County on the east side of Big Harpeth River adjoining John Nelson's corner. Surveyed for Robert Weakley by himself Nov 12, 1786 in consequence of a Military Warrant No. 2195. Located July 22, 1785. Nov 30, 1790.

Page   195 - JASON THOMPSON - Territory of the United States &c - May 24, 1791
North Carolina No. 97. By an Act for the relief of the Officers and Soldiers of the Continental Line, in consideration of the services of Col. Martin Armstrong, surveyor, granted unto Jason Thompson, assignee of said Armstrong, a tract of land containing 104 acres in Davidson County on Mill Creek adjoining Joseph McDowel's corner. Surveyed for Jason Thompson Feb 24, 1789 by John Bucchanan, D.S. in consequence of the Service Right of said Armstrong. Located Jan 24, 1789. Nov 20, 1790.

Page   195 - JASON THOMPSON - Territory of the United States &c - May 24, 1791
North Carolina No. 1069. By an Act for the relief of the Officers and Soldiers of the Continental Line, in consideration of the bravery and zeal of Jonathan Davice, a private in the said line, granted unto Jason Thompson, assignee of said Jonathan Davice, a tract of land containing 640 acres in Davidson County on Mill Creek adjoining Joseph McDowel's corner. Surveyed for Jason Thompson Feb 22, 1789 by John Bucchanan, D.S. in consequence of a Military Warrant No. 3458. Located Dec 27, 1788. Nov 14, 1789.

Page   195 - JASON THOMPSON - Territory of the United States &c - May 24, 1791
North Carolina No. 1201. By an Act for the relief of the Officers and Soldiers of the Continental Line, in consideration of the bravery and zeal of Isaac Brown, a private in the said line, granted unto Jason Thompson, assignee of said Isaac Brown, a tract

of land containing 640 acres in Davidson County on the waters of Mill Creek adjoining Minos Cannon, Robert Thompson and Jason Thompson's corner. Surveyed for Jason Thompson Jan 28, 1791 by John Bucchanan, D.S. in consequence of a Military Warrant No. 3678. Located Jan 11, 1791. Mar 15, 1791.

Page   196 - JASON THOMPSON - Territory of the United States &c - May 24, 1791
        North Carolina No. 1085. By an Act for the relief of the Officers and Soldiers of the Continental Line, in consideration of the bravery and zeal of Joseph Alexander, a private in the said line, granted unto Jason Thompson, assignee of Joseph Alexander, a tract of land containing 640 acres in Davidson County on the east waters of Spring Creek adjoining William Ross' corner and John Blair's corner. Surveyed for Jason Thompson Mar 2, 1789 by John Bucchanan, D.S. in consequence of a Military Warrant No. 3441. Located Jan 24, 1789. Nov 14, 1789.

·Page   196 - JASON THOMPSON - Territory of the United States &c - May 24, 1791
        North Carolina No. 1097. By an Act for the relief of the Officers and Soldiers of the Continental Line, in consideration of the bravery and zeal of Peter Cotench, a private in the said line, granted unto Jason Thompson, assignee of Peter Cotench's assignees, a tract of land containing 640 acres in Davidson County on the east waters of Mill Creek adjoining Minos Cannon's corner. Surveyed for Jason Thompson Jan 20, 1789 by John Bucchanan, D.S. in consequence of a Military Warrant No. 3454. Located Jan 8, 1789. Nov 14, 1789.

Page   196 - MINOS CANNON - May 25, 1791
        North Carolina No. 1087. By an Act for the relief of the Officers and Soldiers of the Continental Line, in consideration of the bravery and zeal of Vinson Allhead, a private in the said line, granted unto Minos Cannon, assignee of the said Vinson Allhead, a tract of land containing 640 acres in Davidson County on the waters of Mill Creek the ridge between said creek and Stones River waters of the north edge of the Big Hurricane. Surveyed for Minos Cannon Dec 4, 1788 by John Bucchanan, D.S. in consequence of a Military Warrant No. 2105. Located Jan 2, 1787. Nov 14, 1789.

Page   197 - JOHN BOYD - Territory of the United States &c - May 25, 1791
        North Carolina No. 347. By an Act for the relief of the Officers and Soldiers of the Continental Line, in consideration of the bravery and zeal of Geffry Gains, a private in the said line, granted unto John Boyd, assignee of Anthony Gains, heir of Geffry Gains, a tract of land containing 640 acres in Davidson County on a branch of Spring Creek joining a survey of Col. Murphry's on the west. Surveyed for John Boyd Mar 20, 1785 by Joseph Brook, D.S. in consequence of a Military Warrant No. 737. Located Dec 16, 1784. Sept 15, 1787.

Page   197 - SAMPSON WILLIAMS - Territory of the United States &c - May 25, 1791
        North Carolina No. 1061. By an Act for the relief of the Officers and Soldiers of the Continental Line, in consideration of the bravery and zeal of Philip Coldin, a private in the said line, granted unto Sampson Williams, assignee of said Philip Coldin, a tract of land containing 428 acres in Davidson County on the north side of Cumberland River about five miles above Nashville town adjoining Ephraim McLean's boundary and the

Rev. Thomas Craighead's Preemption and on Swanson's line. Surveyed for Sampson Williams July 20, 1789 by said Williams himself in consequence of a Military Warrant No. 3424. Located July 18, 1789. Nov 14, 1789.

Page   197 - SAMPSON WILLIAMS - Territory of the United States &c - May 25, 1791
        North Carolina No. 1078. By an Act for the relief of the Officers and Soldiers of the Continental Line, in consideration of the bravery and zeal of James Henderson, a private in the said line, granted unto Sampson Williams, assignee of James Henderson, a tract of land containing 640 acres in Davidson County on the north side of Cumberland River on the dividing ridge between Goose Creek and Big Barren waters. Surveyed for Sampson Williams Oct 1, 1789 by Sampson Williams by himself in consequence of a Military Warrant No. 3667. Located Sept 5, 1789. Nov 14, 1789.

Page   198 - JOHN BUCCHANAN - Territory of the United States &c - May 25, 1791
        North Carolina No. 95. By an Act for the relief of the Officers and Soldiers of the Continental Line, in consideration of the services of Martin Armstrong, surveyor, granted unto John Bucchanan, assignee of said Armstrong, a tract of land containing 200 acres in Davidson County on the west side of Mill Creek on the first branch below the Big Hurricane and adjoining John Rice's line. Surveyed for John Bucchanan Aug 12, 1790 by the said Bucchanan for himself in consequence of a Service Right. Located July 29, 1789. Nov 30, 1790.

Page   198 - JOHN BUCCHANAN - Territory of the United States &c - May 26, 1791
        North Carolina No. 1199. By an Act for the relief of the Officers and Soldiers of the Continental Line, in consideration of the bravery and zeal of Aron Garner, a private in the said line, granted unto John Bucchanan, assignee of Aron Garner, a tract of land containing 640 acres in Davidson County on the waters of Stones River adjoining John Foreman's and John Forde's corner and Thomas Cotton's south boundary. Surveyed for John Bucchanan Dec 4, 1788 by said Bucchanan for himself in consequence of a Military Warrant No. 2722. Located Dec 3, 1787. Nov 30, 1790.

Page   198 - JOHN BUCCHANAN - Territory of the United States &c - May 26, 1791
        North Carolina No. 1185. By an Act for the relief of the Officers and Soldiers of the Continental Line, in consideration of the bravery and zeal of James Hutchens, a private in the said line, granted unto John Bucchanan, assignee of James Hutchens, a tract of land containing 640 acres in Davidson County on the waters of Mill Creek adjoining Thomas Denton's corner and John Rice's line. Surveyed for John Bucchanan July 28, 1789 by the said Bucchanan for himself in consequence of a Military Warrant No. 1095. Located Aug 25, 1787. Nov 30, 1790.

Page   199 - JOHN BUCCHANAN - Territory of the United States &c - May 26, 1791
        North Carolina No. 92. By an Act for the relief of the Officers and Soldiers of the Continental Line, in consideration of the services of Martin Armstrong, surveyor, granted unto John Bucchanan, assignee of said Armstrong, a tract of land containing 28 acres in Davidson County on the waters of Little Harpeth adjoining John Henderson's Preemption and the Guard Right line and Christopher Funkhouser's line and James Leeper's line. Surveyed for John Bucchanan July 27, 1790 by said Bucchanan for himself in

212

in consequence of the Service Right. Located Nov 7, 1789. Nov 30, 1790.

Page   199 - JOHN BUCCHANAN - Territory of the United States &c - May 26, 1791
        North Carolina No. 1183. By an Act for the relief of the Officers and
Soldiers of the Continental Line, in consideration of the bravery and zeal of John Harris, a
private in the said line, granted unto John Bucchanan, assignee of John Harris, a tract of
land containing 640 acres in Davidson County on the headwaters of Mill Creek   adjoining
the John Forde's and John Bucchanan's corners. Surveyed for John Bucchanan Dec 4, 1788
by said Bucchanan for himself in consequence of a Military Warrant No. 2730. Located Dec
3, 1787. Nov 30, 1790.

Page   199 - BENJAMIN DRAKE - Territory of the United States &c - May 28, 1791
        North Carolina No. 1072. By an Act for the relief of the Officers and
Soldiers of the Continental Line, in consideration of the bravery and zeal of Shadrack Cobb,
a private in the said line, granted unto Benjamin Drake, assignee of Shadrack Cobb, a tract
of land containing 640 acres in Davidson County on the north side of Cumberland River on
the head of the North Fork of McAdoes Creek. Surveyed for Benjamin Drake Apr 25, 1786
by Robert Weakley, D.S. in consequence of a Military Warrant No. 1922. Located Aug 17,
1785. Nov 14, 1789.

Page   200 - JOHN THOMPSON - Territory of the United States &c - June 1, 1791
        North Carolina No. 1079. By an Act for the relief of the Officers and
Soldiers of the Continental Line, in consideration of the bravery and zeal of William
Bunington, a private in the said line, granted unto John Thompson, assignee of William
Bunington, a tract of land containing 640 acres in Davidson County on the east waters of
Mill Creek adjoining Joseph McDowel's corner and Jason Thompson's corner. Surveyed for
John Thompson Mar 2, 1789 by John Bucchanan, D.S. in consequence of a Military Warrant
No. 2407. Located Jan 7, 1789. Nov 14, 1789.

Page   200 - BENJAMIN SHEPPARD - June 6, 1791
        North Carolina No. 370. By an Act for the relief of the Officers and Soldiers
of the Continental Line, in consideration of the bravery and zeal of Jacob Basdel, a private
in the said line, granted unto Benjamin Sheppard, assignee of Jacob Basdel, a tract of land
containing 640 acres in Davidson County on the north side of Cumberland River adjoining
Lieut. Nathaniel Williams' line and Capt. John Creddock's corner. Surveyed for Benjamin
Sheppard Mar 8, 1789 by Edwin Hickman, D.S. in consequence of a Military Warrant No.
2334. Located Feb 28, 1787.

Page   200 - GEORGE HOUSER - Territory of the United States &c - June 6, 1791
        North Carolina No. 50. For 10 lbs per 100 acres paid by George Houser was
granted a tract of land containing 5000 acres in the Western District on Housers Creek
about one mile above the mouth of said creek adjoining John Rights of No. 694 on said
creek on the south. Surveyed for George Houser Oct 3, 1785 by Edward Harris, D.S. in
consequence of a Warrant No. 691. Dated Oct 28, 1783. July 10, 1788.

Page   201 - THOMAS FINNEY - Territory of the United States &c - June 11, 1791
        North Carolina No. 37. By an Act for the relief of the Officers and Soldiers

213

of the Continental Line, in consideration of the bravery and zeal of Thomas Finney, a lieutenant in the said line, granted unto Thomas Finney a tract of land containing 2560 acres in Davidson County on Richland Creek on the south side of Cumberland River adjoining John Donelson's line and John Dunam's line also Isaac Johnston's corner and Daniel Dunam's corner also Francis Hodges' corner. Surveyed for Thomas Finney Feb 10, 1785 by Thomas Molloy, D.S. in consequence of a Military Warrant No. 108. Located Feb 7, 1784. Mar 10, 1786.

Page   201 - GEORGE LEEPER - Territory of the United States &c = June 21, 1791
            North Carolina No. 207. For 10 lbs per 100 acres paid by George Leeper was granted a tract of land containing 640 acres in Davidson County on the north side of Cumberland River adjoining James Clendening's line and a north branch of Station Camp also Peter Looney's line. Surveyed for George Leeper Sept 7, 1786 by James Sanders, D.S. in consequence of a Warrant No. 143. Entered Jan 16, 1784. July 10, 1788.

Page   201 - FEDERICK STUMP - Territory of the United States &c - June 25, 1791
            North Carolina No. 1. Granted unto Federick Stump one of the Guard to the Commissioners for laying off of the lands allotted to the Officers and Soldiers of the Continental Line of this state, a tract of land containing 320 acres in Davidson County on the north side of Cumberland River adjoining the mouth of Bull Run about four miles below Hestons Station. July 20, 1787.

Page   202 - STEPHEN BROOKS - Territory of the United States &c - June 25, 1791
            North Carolina No. 905. By an Act for the relief of the Officers and Soldiers of the Continental Line, in consideration of the bravery and zeal of John Mosland, a private in the said line, granted unto Stephen Brooks, assignee of John Mosland, a tract of land containing 640 acres in Davidson County on the waters of Stones River on the first creek above Stuarts Creek on the east side of said river. Surveyed for Stephen Brooks Oct 10, 1786 by William Nash, D.S. in consequence of a Military Warrant No. 3515. Located Oct 10, 1786. Jan 17, 1789.

Page   202 - STEPHEN BROOKS - Territory of the United States &c - June 25, 1791
            North Carolina No. 910. By an Act for the relief of the Officers and Soldiers of the Continental Line, in consideration of the bravery and zeal of William Glaughn, a private in the said line, granted unto Stephen Brooks, assignee of said William Glaughn, a tract of land containing 640 acres in Davidson County on the east side of Stones River on the first creek above Stones Lick Creek adjoining Thomas Thompson's corner. Surveyed for Stephen Brooks Oct 14, 1786 by William Nash, D.S. in consequence of a Military Warrant No. 2917. Located Oct 10, 1786. Jan 17, 1789.

Page   202 - STEPHEN BROOKS - Territory of the United States &c - June 25, 1791
            North Carolina No. 911. By an Act for the relief of the Officers and Soldiers of the Continental Line, in consideration of the bravery and zeal of William Goodman, a private in the said line, granted unto Stephen Brooks, assignee of William Goodman, a tract of land containing 640 acres in Davidson County on the first creek above Stones Lick Creek on the east side of Stones River . Surveyed for Stephen Brooks Oct 10, 1786 by William Nash, D.S. in consequence of a Military Warrant No. 2720. Located Oct 10, 1786. Jan 17,

Page   203 - JAMES BROWN - Territory of the United States &c - June 25, 1791
        North Carolina No. 1. For 10 lbs per 100 acres paid by James Brown was granted a tract of land containing 3980 acres in Middle District on Lytles Creek on the south side of Duck River adjoining Nicholas Long's corner. Surveyed for James Brown by Robert Weakley in consequence of a Warrant No. 417. Dated Oct 25, 1783. Apr 15, 1788.

Page   203 - JOSEPH BROCK - Territory of the United States &c - June 29, 1791
        North Carolina No. 847. By an Act for the relief of the Officers and Soldiers of the Continental Line, in consideration of the bravery and zeal of George Carter, a private in the said line, granted unto Joseph Brock, assignee of the heirs of George Carter, a tract of land containing 640 acres in Davidson County on the north side of Cumberland River near the Buffaloe Pasture on the south boundary of a survey of said Brooks of No. 3467. Surveyed for Joseph Brock by Anthony Foster in consequence of a Military Warrant No. 3339. Located Nov 24, 1787. Jan 17, 1789.

Page   203 - ABSOLOM TATUM - Territory of the United States &c - June 29, 1791
        North Carolina No. 11. By an Act for the relief of the Officers and Soldiers of the Continental Line, in consideration of the services of Major Absolom Tatum, one of the Commissioners Guard, granted unto said Tatum a tract of land containing 5000 acres in Davidson County on both sides of the west fork of Big Harpeth River near the county line. Surveyed for said Absolom Tatum by James Sanders, D.S. agreeable to a Warrant No. (blank). Entry dated July 21, 1784. Feb 16, 1786.

Page   204 - ROBERT NELSON - Territory of the United States &c - June 29, 1791
        North Carolina No. 247. By an Act for the relief of the Officers and Soldiers of the Continental Line, in consideration of the bravery and zeal of Robert Nelson, a sergeant in the said line, granted unto Robert Nelson a tract of land containing 357 acres in Davidson County adjoining James Shaw's Preemption on the south and Baker on the north and the end of the Conditional Line. Surveyed for Robert Nelson May 10, 1784 by James Sanders, D.S. in consequence of a Military Warrant No. 261. Located Mar 13, 1784. Mar 7, 1786.

Page   204 - JOHN NICHOLS - Territory of the United States &c - June 29, 1791
        North Carolina No. 93. By an Act for the relief of the Officers and Soldiers of the Continental Line, in consideration of the bravery and zeal of Andrew Haddock, a sergeant in the said line, granted unto John Nichols, assignee of Andrew Haddock, a tract of land containing 1000 acres in Davidson County on both sides of Big Harpeth River and joining James McGavock's Preemptionon the east and west sides also Manifee's line. Surveyed for John Nichols by John Donelson, D.S. in consequence of a Military Warrant No. 1076. Located Nov 13, 1784. Mar 14, 1786.

Page   204 - JOHN NICHOLS - Territory of the United States &c - June 29, 1791
        North Carolina No. 1039. By an Act for the relief of the officers and Soldiers of the Continental Line, in consideration of the bravery and zeal of William Venters, granted unto John Nichols, assignee of the heirs of William Venters, a tract of land

containing 640 acres in Davidson County on the first creek of Duck River which the line of Davidson County crosses going westward from Harpeth on the south side of said line. Surveyed for John Nichols Jan 14, 1787 by Thomas Molloy, D.S. in consequence of a Military Warrant No. 2587?. Located May 1, 1786. May 18, 1789.

Page   205 - MARTIN ARMSTRONG - Territory of the united States &c - July 1, 1791
          North Carolina No. 439. By an Act for the relief of the Officers and Soldiers of the Continental Line, in consideration of the bravery and zeal of Peter Harris, a non-commissioned officer in the said line, granted unto Martin Armstrong, assignee of Peter Harris, a tract of land containing 1000 acres in Davidson County on the south side of Cumberland River about three or four miles above Roaring River adjoining Edwin Hickman's corner. Surveyed for Martin Armstrong Mar 12, 1786 by Edwin Hickman, D.S. in consequence of a Military Warrant No. 1657. Located Jan 23, 1786. Sept 15, 1787.

Page   205 - MARTIN ARMSTRONG - Territory of the United States &c - July 1, 1791
          North Carolina No. 79. By an Act for the relief of the Officers and Soldiers of the Continental Line, in consideration of the services of Martin Armstrong, surveyor, granted unto Martin Armstrong a tract of land containing 400 acres in Davidson County on the north side of Cumberland River adjoining Mauldin's Military Right of 640 acres on the east and John Foreman's corner. Surveyed for Martin Armstrong Oct 10, 1786 by Anthony Foster, D.S. in consequence of the Service Right. Nov 27, 1789.

Page   205 - ALEXANDER REED - Territory of the United States &c - July 2, 1791
          North Carolina No. 83. By an Act for the relief of the officers and Soldiers of the Continental Line, in consideration of the services of Martin Armstrong, surveyor, granted unto Alexander Reed, assignee of the said Armstrong, a tract of land containing 15 acres in Davidson County on a branch of Whites Creek, north side of Cumberland River adjoining Ralston's boundary. Surveyed for Alexander Reed July 24, 1788 by Daniel James, D.S. in consequence of a Service Right of said Armstrong. Located (blank). Nov 14, 1789.

Page   206 - ALEXANDER REED - Territory of the United States &c - July 2, 1791
          North Carolina No. 85. By an Act for the relief of the Officers and Soldiers of the Continental Line, in consideration of the services of Martin Armstrong, surveyor, granted unto Alexander Reed, assignee of said Armstrong, a tract of land containing 228 acres in Davidson County on the north side of Cumberland River on a branch of Whites. Creek. Surveyed for Alexander Reed July 24, 1788 by Daniel James, D.S. in consequence of a Service Right. Located Mar 13, 1786. Nov 14, 1789.

Page   206 - ALEXANDER REED - Territory of the United States &c - July 2, 1791
          North Carolina No. 91. By an Act for the relief of the Officers and Soldiers of the Continental Line, in consideration of the services of Martin Armstrong, surveyor, granted unto Alexander Reed, assignee of said Armstrong, a tract of 200 acres in Davidson County on the ridge between Whites Creek and Manskers Creek on the north side of Cumberland River. Surveyed for Alexander Reed July 25, 1788 by Daniel James, D.S. in consequence of the Service Right of said Armstrong. Located Nov 25, 1785. Nov 14, 1789.

Page   206 - ALEXANDER REED - Territory of the United States &c - July 2, 1791
North Carolina No. 84. By an Act for the relief of the Officers and Soldiers of the Continental Line, in consideration of the service of Martin Armstrong, surveyor, granted unto Alexander Reed, assignee of said Eusebius Bushnell, assignee of said Armstrong, a tract of land containing 50 acres in Davidson County on the north side of Cumberland River on a branch of Whites Creek joining said Reed's No. 228 acre Service Right. Surveyed for Alexander Reed July 25, 2788 by Daniel James, D.S. in consequence of said Service Right. Located Mar 31, 1788. Nov 14, 1789.

Page   207 - ALEXANDER REED - Territory of the United States &c - July 2, 1791
North Carolina No. 82. By an Act for the relief of the Officers and Soldiers of the Continental Line, in consideration of the services of Martin Armstrong, surveyor, granted unto Alexander Reed, assignee of said Armstrong, a tract of land containing 100 acres in Davidson County on the waters of Manskers Creek called Linseys Fork adjoining Peter Cloud on the upper side. Surveyed for Alexander Reed July 26, 1788 by Daniel James, D.S. in consequence of a Service Right. Located Nov 24, 1785. Nov 14, 1789.

Page   207 - MATTHEW JONES - Territory of the United States &c - July 28, 1791
This indenture made 17 March 1791 between William Mabane of Orange County, North Carolina of one part and Matthew Jones of Chatham County, North Carolina of the other part. William Mabane conveyed unto Matthew Jones a tract of land containing 1028 acres in Davidson County adjoining Hugh's line and Grimes' line No. 2 Being one seventh part of a tract of land of 7200 acres granted to the heirs of Col. Robert Mabane, deceased, and surveyed by John Donelson, D.S. and laid of in lots by a scale of two hundred poles to the inch. Nov 28, 1784. As will more appear by the plot now in the possession of the said Mabane. July Term 1791.

Page   208 - JAMES MABANE - Territory of the United States &c - July 1791
This indenture made 24 Jan 1791 between William Mabane of Orange County, North Carolina of one part and James Mabane of same place of other part. William Mabane conveyed unto said brother James Mabane a tract of land containing 1028 acres in Davidson County on the west fork of Big Harpeth River, it being part of 7200 acre tract granted to the said William Mabane being heir of Col. Robert Mabane, deceased. Wit: Thomas Mulhollan and John Nichols. July Term 1791.

Page   208 - JOHN BOYD - Territory of the United States &c - July 28, 1791
We, Samuel Barton, Thomas Molloy, James Shaw, Joel Rice and David Hay, directors and trustees of the town of Nashville, conveyed unto John Boyd the lot of land No. 89 in the town of Nashville. This 17 May 1791. July Term 1791.

Page   209 - EZEKIEL NORRIS - Territory of the United States &c - July 28, 1791
This indenture made 3 Nov 1790 between John Shelby of Sullivan County, North Carolina of one part and Ezekiel Norris of Sumner County, NC of the other part. John Shelby conveyed unto Ezekiel Norris a tract of land containing 150 acres in Tennessee County on the waters of the Cumberland River on the north side of Cumberland River being part of a 2500 acre survey granted to the said Shelby by the State of North Carolina. Test: Anthony Foster and George A. Sugg. July Term 1791.

Page   209 - NATHANIEL ALEXANDER - Territory of the United States &c - July 28, 1791

North Carolina No. 72. By an Act for the relief of the officers and Soldiers of the Continental Line, in consideration of the bravery and zeal of Nathaniel Alexander, a sergeant in the said line, granted unto Nathaniel Alexander a tract of land containing 1000 acres in (blank) County on the north side of Tennessee River. Beginning on the bank of the river below the mouth of a large creek opposite to the middle of a large island. Surveyed for Nathaniel Alexander Aug 12, 1785 by William Murry, D.S. in consequence of a Military Warrant No. 781. Located May 7, 1785. Mar 14, 1786.

Page   210 - ROBERT BROWNFIELD - Territory of the United States &c - July 28, 1791

By an Act for the relief of the Officers and Soldiers of the Continental Line, in consideration of the bravery and zeal of Robert Brownfield, a sergeant in the said line, granted unto Robert Brownfield a tract of land containing 1000 acres Davidson County on the east fork of Buffalo Creek on the north side of Tennessee River. Surveyed for Robert Brownfield Aug 8, 1785 by William Murry, D.S. in consequence of a Military Warrant No. 780. Located May 7, 1785. Mar 14, 1786.

Page 210 - THOMAS TALBOT - Territory of the United States &c - July 28, 1791

This indenture made 15 Mar 1791 between Thomas Molloy of Davidson County of one part and Thomas Talbot of same place of other part. Thomas Molloy conveyed unto Thomas Talbot a tract of land containing 1250 acres in Davidson County beginning on the east bank of Big Harpeth at the mouth of the first creek below Little Harpeth on George Neville's south boundary, being the moiety of a tract of land of 2500 acres granted to said Thomas Molloy by the State of North Carolina for his services as surveyor in laying off the lands granted the Continental line as per entry No. 24. Test: Robert Childers, Andrew Greer, William Smith and Francis Clark. July Term 1791.

Page   211 - ABSALOM HOOPER - Territory of the United States &c - July 29, 1791

This indenture made 11 July 1791 between Benjamin Drake of Davidson County of one part and Absalom Hooper of same place of the other part. Benjamin Drake conveyed unto Absalom Hooper a tract of land containing 640 acres in Davidson County on the east waters of Whites Creek adjoining Dennis Cond(illegible)'s line, and Samuel Verner's line. The said land being a Preemption granted by the State of North Carolina to said Benjamin Drake, Sen., assignee of Charles Robertson Nov 26, 1789 and No. 286. July Term 1791.

Page   211 - ROBERT WEAKLEY - Territory of the United States &c - July 29, 1791

This indenture made 11 Mar 1791 between Thomas Molloy of Davidson County of one part and Robert Weakley of same place of the other part. Thomas Molloy conveyed unto Robert Weakley a tract of land containing 20 acres in Davidson County on Whites Creekadjoining John McGaugh's corner and the west bank of Whites Creek. Said land being part of a tract of 640 acres granted by the State of North Carolina to the said Thomas Molloy, assignee of the heirs of Authur Spence Aug 11, 1789, No. 1043. July Term 1791.

Page   212 - JOHN McNAIRY & MARY McNAIRY - July 29, 1791

This indenture made 3 Feb 1791 between William Dobbins of Sumner County, NC, in his own name ans in the name of Eusebius Bushnell of the one part and the Honorable John McNairy and Mary McNairy of Davidson County of the other part. By deed of conveyance dated June 23, 1788 Eusebius Bushnell in his own name and in the name of William Dobbins his co-partner, did mortgage to David Hay and Adam Hampton the nine tracts of land together with one half lot in town of Nashville for 598 pounds, sixteen shillings due the said Mary McNairy, then Mary Robertson, which sum was to be paid by 25 Dec 1789, else the equity of redemption of the aforesaid to be foreclosed. David Hay and Adam Hamptonassigned over to Mary Hunter now Mary McNairy on the 11th Jan 1790 the aforesaid mortgage. Test: John Overton. July Term 1791.

Page   211 - BENJAMIN DRAKE - Territory of the United States &c - July 29, 1791

North Carolina No. 286. For 10 lbs per 100 acres paid by Benjamin Drake was granted a tract of land containing 640 acres in Davidson County on the east waters of Whites Creek adjoining Dennis Condry's line and Samuel Vernor's line. Surveyed for Benjamin Drake Mar 29, 1785 by B. William Pollock, D.S. agreeable to a Warrant No. 228. Entered Jan 31, 1784. Nov 26, 1789.

Page   213 - JAMES MEARS - Territory of the United States &c - July 30, 1791

This indenture made 9 July 1791 between Samuel Shannonand his wife Jean Shannon of Davidson County of one part and James Mears of same place of the other part. Samuel Shannon and his wife Jean Shannon conveyed unto James Mears a tract of land containing 82 acres in Davidson County on the waters of Whites Creek adjoining John Crow's boundary. It being a tract of land granted to Samuel Shannon, assignee of Martin Armstrong May 18, 1789. Samuel Shannon and Jane Shannon, his wife, conveyed   unto James Mears said land 9 July 1791. Samuel Shannon L.S. Jane(Jean) Shannon L.S.   July Term 1791.

Page   213 - JAMES MEARS - Territory of the United States &c - July 30, 1791

This indenture made 9 July 1791 between Samuel Shannon and his wife Jane (Jean) Shannon of Davidson County of the one part and James Mears of same place of other part. Samuel Shannon and Jane Shannon conveyed unto James Mears a tract of land containing 136 acres in Davidson County on the waters of Whites Creek adjoining John Crow's boundary and James Ross' corner. Being part of a tract of 228 acres granted to the said Samuel Shannon, assignee of Robert Acock Jan 13, 1789. July Term 1791.

Page   214 - WILLIAM, JOSEPH, DANIEL & GEORGE BROWN - July 30, 1791

This indenture made 6 May 1791 between Federick Stump of Davidson County of one part and William Brown, Joseph Brown, Daniel Brown and George Brown, male heirs of James Brown, deceased, of the other part. Witnesseth that the said Federick Stump for the consideration of 200£ of lawful money paid by the aforesaid James Brown, deceased, before the sealing and signing of these present. The said Federick Stump conveyed unto William Brown, Joseph Brown, Daniel Brown and George Brown a tract of land containing 320 acres in Davidson County on the north side of Cumberland River about four miles below Heatons Old Station adjoining the mouth of Bull Run. Test: Samuel Barton, John Dixon nd Edmond Gamble. July Term 1791.

Page   214 - DAVID ALLISON - Territory of the United States &c - July 30, 1791
This indenture made 15 May 1790 between Thomas Martin of the one part and David Allison of other part. Thomas Martin conveyed unto David Allison a tract of land containing 640 acres in Tennessee County. Test: Daniel James. July Term 1791.

Page   215 - RICHARD JOHNIS - Territory of the United States &c - July 30, 1791
This indenture made 2 Nov 1790 between Lardner Clark of Davidson County of one part and Richard Johnis of same place of other part. Lardner Clark conveyed unto Richard Johnis a tract of land containing 320 acres in Davidson County on the east fork of Mill Creek. Granted by the State of North Carolina in a tract of 320 acres by patent dated 8 Mar 1787. Signed by Lardner Clark. Test: Sampson Williams, William Wicuff and John Boyd, Jr. July Term 1791.

Page   215 - MATTHEW PAYNE - Territory of the United States &c - Aug 1, 1791
This indenture made 3 July 1791 between Matthew Payne of Davidson County of one part and William Dobbins of Sumner County of other part. William Dobbins conveyed unto Matthew Payne a tract of land on the waters of Duck River. Test: Hopkins Lacy and John Omrie. July Term 1791.

Page   216 - BRADLEY GAMBREL - Territory of the United States &c - Aug 1, 1791
This indenture made 14 July 1791 between Thomas Hardiman of one part and Bradley Gambell of the other part, both of Davidson County on a branch of Mill Creek adjoining James Meness' line. Containing 30 acres. Test: Samuel Wilson and John Campbell. July Term 1791.

Page   216 - HUGH ROBISON - Territory of the United States &c - Aug 1, 1791
This indenture made 1 Feb 1791 between Thomas Thompson, Samuel Thompson and John Coots of Guilford County, North Carolina of one part and Hugh Robison of Rowan County, North Carolina of the other part. Thomas and Samuel Thompson and John Coots conveyed unto Hugh Robison a tract of land containing 460 acres on the waters of main river called Duck River in the Middle District adjoining Thomas Thompson's corner on Duck and John Coots' corner and also Samuel Thompson's corner. Test: James Boyd, John Boyd and Thomas Dick. July Term 1791.

Page   217 - JAMES HAMILTON - Territory of the United States &c - Aug 1, 1791
This indenture made 28 Dec 1790 between Thomas Molloy of Davidson County of one part and James Hamilton of same place of the other part. Thomas Molloy conveyed unto James Hamilton a tract of land containing 118 acres in Davidson County on the north side of Cumberland River and on the west sides of Whites Creek adjoining William Stuart's corner and Robert Weakley's corner. Said land being part of 640 acres granted to the said Molloy by the State of North Carolina as assignee of the heirs of William Spence for his services as a soldier in the Continental Line per Warrant No. 2587. Test: James Cotton. July Term 1791.

Page   217 - JAMES HOGGATT - Territory of the United States &c - Aug 1, 1791
(2nd page)   This indenture made 24 Jan 1791 between James Bosley of Davidson County of one part and James Hoggatt of same place of other part. James Bosley conveyed unto

James Hoggatt a tract of land containing 200 acres in Davidson County on the south side of Cumberland River adjoining John Boyd's corner. Test: Bennett Searcy, Elisha Rice, James Cole Montflorence and John Overton. July Term 1791.

Page 218 - WILLIAM BUCCHANAN - Territory of the United States &c - Aug 1, 1791
          This indenture made ___ day of ___ 1791 between John Forde of Davidson County of one part and William Bucchanan of same place of other part. John Forde conveyed unto William Bucchanan a tract of land containing 640 acres on the waters of Mill Creek and Stones River in Davidson County and District of Mero. Land joins John Foreman's Preemption which includes Mill Creek lick. Ths said land was granted unto John Forde in consequence of a warrant originally granted to (blank) No. 1559 and located Dec 3, 1788 and dated (blank). Test: Elijah Robertson and Adam Hampton. July Term 1791.

Page 218 - SAMUEL BARTON - Territory of the United States &c - Aug 2, 1791
          This indenture made 14 July 1791 between John Brown of one part and Samuel Barton of the other part, both of Davidson County. John Brown conveyed unto Samuel Barton a tract of land containing 50 acres in Davidson County on the waters of Browns Creek adjoining Brown's corner. Test: Andrew Ewing and Bennett Searcy. July Term 1791.

Page 219 - WILLIAM HAGGARD - Territory of the United States &c - Aug 2, 1791
          This indenture made 11 July 1791 between John Brown of Davidson County of one part and William Haggard of (blank) County in the District of Kentucky of other part. John Brown conveyed unto William Haggard a tract of land containing 50 acres in Davidson County on the waters of Browns Creek. Test: Andrew Ewing and Bennett Searcy. July Term 1791.

Page 219 - THOMAS TALBOT - Territory of the United States &c - Aug 2, 1791
          This indenture made 15 Apr 1791 between Hayden Wells of one part and Thomas Talbot of the other part, both of Davidson County. Hayden Wells conveyed unto Thomas Talbot a tract of land containing 290½ acres in Davidson County on the north side of Cumberland River adjoining Heaton's Old Station. Test: William Hickman and Stephen Wray. July Term 1791.

Page 220 - WILLIAM DOUGLASS - Territory of the United States &c - Aug 2, 1791
          This indenture made 1 Dec 1790 between Thomas Smith of Davidson County of one part and William Douglass of same place of other part. Thomas Smith conveyed unto William Douglass a tract of land containing 28 acres in Davidson County on a branch of Whites Creek adjoining Michael Glaves' line and Love's line. Test: John Smith, John Lancaster and Reuben Smith. July Term 1791.

Page 220 - JAMES THOMPSON - Territory of the United States &c - Aug 2, 1791
(2nd page)   This indenture made 14 July 1791 between Robert Thompson of one part and James Thompson of the other part, both of Davidson County. Robert Thompson conveyed unto James Thompson a tract of land containing 640 acres in Davidson County on the waters of Hurricane Creek adjoining Minnos Cannon's corner. Said land was originally granted to said Robert Thompson by the State of North Carolina by patent dated Nov 14,

1789 and No. 1088. Test Andrew Ewing and John Boyd, Jun. July Term 1791.

Page   221 - ELIJAH ROBERTSON - Territory of the United States &c - Aug 3, 1791
This indenture made 28 June 1791 between James Cole Montflorence of Davidson County of one part and Elijah Robertson of same place of the other part. James Cole Montflorence conveyed unto Elijah Robertson all the following tracts of land containing 1000 acres each and amounting to 10,000 acres in aforesaid territory in the Western District and on the waters of the Mississippi to wit, that tract of 1000 acres, Grant No. 200 lying on the south side of Loose Hatchie River adjoining Blount's survey No. 2456 and No. 2463 on said river. Beginning at Blount's corner of No. 2456 and Blount's No 2463 corner. Also that other tract of 1000 acres No. 182, lying on the head of the south fork of Indian Creek of Big Hatchee River and joining Blount's survey No. 2485 and No. 2464 on said creek. Also that other tract of 1000 acres the Grant No. 226 lying on the waters of Indian Creek of Reelfoot River adjoining George Dougherty's corner and Blount's corner. Also that other tract of 1000 acres the Grant No. 243 on the waters of Reelfoot River adjoining Blount's corner and George Dougherty's corner. Also that other tract of 1000 acres the Grant No. 235 on the head of Grove Creek and Spring Creek adjoining Blount's survey No. 2315 and No. 2399 on said creek adjoining Blount's corner of No. 2316 and No. 2399 and No. 2315. Also that nother tract of 1000 acres Grant No. 184 lying on the waters of Reelfoot River adjoining Blount's corner and George Dougherty's line. Also that other tract of 1000 acres Grant No. 214 lying on Goose Creek adjoining Blount's survey No. 2311, Edward Harris survey No. 234 and Martin Armstrong's No. 694 on said creek. Also that other tract of 1000 acres Grant No. 258 on the Lick Fork of Obion River adjoining Blount's survey No. 2442 and No. 2377 on said creek and joining Blount's curvey No. 2377. Also that other tract of 1000 acres Grant No. 264 on the waters of Obion River adjoining Blount's corner and Abner Nash's corner. Also that other tract of 1000 acres Grant No. 175 on the waters of Obion River adjoining Blount's corner and Abner Nash's corner. Test: Andrew Ewing and Andrew Cassellman. July Term 1791.

Page   222 - ELEZEAR HAMILTON - Territory of the United States &c - Aug 3, 1791
This indenture made 21 May 1791 between Thomas Molloy of Davidson County of one part and Eleazer Hamilton of same place of the other part. Thomas Molloy conveyed unto Eleazer Hamilton a tract of land containing 32 acres in Davidson County on the waters of Whites Creek adjoining Robert Weakley's corner and Thomas James' corner. Said land being part of a tract of 640 acres granted by the State of North Carolina to said Thomas Molloy as assignee of the heirs of William Spence for his service as a soldier in the Continental Line. Grant dated Aug 11, 1789 and No. 1043. Test: David Hamilton and James Hamilton. July Term 1791.

Page   222 - JOSEPH HANNAH - Territory of the United States &c - Aug 4, 1791
(2nd page)   North Carolina No. 285. For 10 lbs per 100 acres paid by Joseph Hannah was granted a tract of land containing 640 acres in Davidson County on Big Harpeth Creek where Alstons trace crosses said creek. Surveyed for Joseph Hannah May 20, 1788 by S. Williams, D.S. agreeable to an entry dated Apr 10, 1784. Nov 26, 1789.

Page   223 - JOHN DRAKE - Territory of the United States &c - Aug 4, 1791
This indenture made 11 July 1791 between Isaac Drake of one part and John

Drake of the other part, both of Davidson County. Isaac Drake conveyed unto John Drake a tract of land containing 50 acres in Davidson County on Heatons Lick branch about three quarters of a mile above Heatons Lick. Which land was granted to said Isaac Drake by the State of North Carolina by patent dated May 18, 1789 as assignee of Martin Armstrong. July Term 1791.

Page   223 - JAMES ESPEY - Territory of the United States &c - Aug 4, 1791
            North Carolina No. 98. By an Act for the relief of the Officers and Soldiers of the Continental Line, in consideration of the services of James Espey, one of the Commissioners Guards, granted unto James Espey a tract of land containing 320 acres in Davidson County in a large bent of the river on the north side of Cumberland River known by the name of Hoggatt Bent. Surveyed for James Espey Feb 5, 1788 by S. Williams, D.S. agreeable to an entry dated Jan 15, 1784. Nov 26, 1789.

Page   223 - JAMES ESPEY - Territory of the United States &c
            For 10 lbs per 100 acres paid by James Espey, assignee of George Green, granted unto said Espey a tract of land containing 640 acres in Davidson County on the east fork of Bledsoe Lick Creek running into Cumberland River on the north side adjoining Isaac Bledsoe's line and a corner of public land. Surveyed for said Espey Feb 8, 1786 by William Murry, D.S. agreeable to an entry dated Jan 30, 1784. Nov 26, 1789.

Page   224 - JAMES BROWN - Territory of the United States &c - Aug 4, 1791
            North Carolina No. 124. By an Act for the relief of the Officers and Soldiers of the Continental Line, in consideration of the bravery and zeal of William Morris, a private in the said line, granted unto James Brown, assignee of William Morris, a tract of land containing 640 acres in Davidson County on a small creek on the south side of the Sulphur Fork of Red River about four or five miles above Caleb Creek adjoining about three quarters of a mile above Jonathan Guise's Preemption. Surveyed for James Brown Jan 15, 1785 by Robert Nelson, D.S. in consequence of a Military Warrant No. 1065. Located July 14, 1784. Mar 14, 1786.

Page   224 - WILLIAM TERREL LEWIS - Territory of the United States &c - Aug 4, 1791
            North Carolina No. 287. For 10 lbs per 100 acres paid by William Terrel Lewis was granted a tract of land containing 320 acres in Davidson County on the south side of Cumberland River adjoining James Mulherin's Preemption and James Todd's line and Charles Robertson's Preemption. Surveyed for said William Terrel Lewis June 15, 1786 by James Mulherin, D.S. agreeable to an entry dated May 10, 1785. Nov 26, 1789.

Page   224 - ARCHIBALD BUCCHANAN - Aug 4, 1791
            North Carolina No. 283. For 10 lbs per 100 acres paid by Archibald Bucchanan was granted a tract of land containing 640 acres in Davidson County on the waters of Stones River including the place called Clover Bottom adjoining a bluff on said river about twelve poles above the mouth of a small dry branch and James Todd's line. Surveyed for said Bucchanan June 6, 1788 by Daniel Smith agreeable to an entry dated Dec 11, 1784. Nov 26, 1789.

Page   225 - JOHN MARNEY - Territory of the United States &c - Aug 9, 1791

This indenture made 15 July 1791 between Isaac Johnston of Davidson County of one part and John Marney of the other part and same place. Isaac Johnston conveyed unto said John Marney a tract of land containing 200 acres in Davidson County on Richland Creek. Beginning at a corner of a Preemption of 640 acres granted to Isaac Johnston, Grant dated (blank), No. 37 Warrant No. 76, entry dated Jan 1784. Test: Daniel Rowan. July Term 1791.

Page   225 - ANTHONY HART - Territory of the United States &c - Aug 15, 1791

This indenture made 29 June 1791 between James Cole Montflorence of the one part and Anthony Hart of the other part, both of Davidson County. James Cole Montflorence conveyed unto Anthony Hart the following tracts of military tracts of land of 640 acres each amounting in the whole to 10, 240 acres in the District of Mero, to wit, all that tract of land containing 640 acres in the County of Tennessee on the first large creek on the south side of Cumberland above the Virginia Line including the fork of the said creek. Granted by the State of North Carolina to John Forde and by him conveyed to said Hart and by said Hart to said Montflorence by deed. Also that other tract of 640 acres in the Tennessee County on the trace near the head of Gibsons Creek on the trace that leads from Thompsons Settlement up the Sulphur Fork east three hundred and twenty poles to a stake. Also that tract of land containing 640 acres in Tennessee County on the west fork of Spring Creek the waters of Sycamore Creek adjoining Samuel Marsham's corner and John Nichols' line. Also that tract of 640 acres in the Tennessee County on the west of a survey made by Federick Stump which includes Turnbulls Clay Lick and joining the west and south of Military Warrant No. 2815. Granted for the services of William Reves. Also that other tract of land containing 640 acres in Tennessee County on the southern boundary of the aforesaid survey of said Federick Stump adjoining the Military Warrant No. 2957. Granted for the services of Isaac Reddick. Also that other tract of 640 acres in Tennessee County on the eastern boundary of the aforesaid survey of said Stump, the Military Warrant No. 2763. Granted for the services of John Sellers. Also that other tract of 640 acres in Tennessee County on the north fork of McAdoes Creek, adjoining a survey of John Drakes on the west, the Military Warrant No. 3415. Granted for the services of Charles Brooks. Also that other tract of 640 acres in Tennessee County on the waters of Little Brush Creek waters of Red River adjoining a survey of John Nichols on the north, the Military Warrant No. 3516, granted for the services of William Holland all which last seven mentioned tracts of land was within the present settlement of Mero District. Also that other tract of 640 acres in the Tennessee County on the north side of Cumberland and joining a survey Robert Weakley's on the north, the Military Warrant No. 3423, granted for the services of Obed. Calvin. Also that other tract of 640 acres in Sumner County on the south side of the Caney Fork River joining an entry of John Haywood's 1000 acres, on the west, the Military Warrant No. 585, granted for the services of Randall Cross. Also that other tract of 640 acres in Sumner County on the waters of Collins River one of the branches of the Caney Fork joining an entry made by Thomas Hickman in 1788 on the west, the Military Warrant No. 2492, granted for the services of Lewis Morgan. Also that other tract of 640 acres in Sumner County on Collins River about seven miles from the mouth of said river, the Warrant No. 809, granted for the services of Richard King. Also that other tract of 640 acres in Sumner County on the waters of Caney Fork, between Mulherin and Hickmans Creek joining an entry made by Thomas Hickman in 1788, the Military Warrant No. 2665, granted for the services of James Hammonds. Also that other tract of 640 acres in Sumner County on the waters of the Caney Fork between Mulherin and Hickmans Creek, Warrant No. 2483, granted for the services of Abraham Applewhite. Also that other tract of 640 acres in Sumner County on the headwaters of Hickmans Creek of the Caney Fork joining on the west of an entry made by Thomas Hickman in 1788. Also that other tract of 640 acres in Sumner County on the south side of Big Barren River and on a fork of said the Red River, joining an entry of Joshua Davis' on the south, entered 2 Dec 1786, the Military Warrants of which two last mentioned tract No. 2707 granted for the service of Abraham Buck and 2249 for the services of William Wright. This 29 July 1791. July Term 1791.

Page 227 - JAMES TATUM - Territory of the United States &c - I, Howel Tatum of Davidson County have constituted , appointed and ordained James Tatum my true and lawful attorney for me to sell any of my lands in the District of Mero for money or such number of negroes &c. This 30 Apr 1791. Test: William Donelson, John Donelson and Samuel Donelson. Aug 16, 1791.

Page 227 - JOHN DONELSON - Territory of the United States &c - Sept 1, 1791
North Carolina No. 1202. By an Act for the relief of the Officers and Soldiers of the Continental Line, in consideration of the bravery and zeal of William Bailey, a private in the said line, granted unto John Donelson, assignee of the heirs of William Bailey, a tract of land containing 640 acres in Davidson County on the south side of Cumberland River adjoining Daniel Chambers' corner. Surveyed for John Donelson Apr 5, 1791 by the said Donelson for himself in consequence of a Military Warrant No. 3246. Located Dec 31, 1785. Nov 20, 1790.

Page 227 - JOSEPH ERWINE - Territory of the United States &c - Sept 3, 1791
This indenture made 1 Oct 1790 between John Williams of Davidson County of the one part and Joseph Erwine of same place of the other part. John Williams conveyed unto Joseph Erwine a tract of land containing one acre in the town of Nashville and known by No. 60. Being the lot granted by Thomas Molloy, Samuel Barton and James Shaw, directors and trustees of the town of Nashville, to John Boyd of the said town by deed dated 26 July 1784. Test: David Hay, Oct 1790.

Page 228 - NATHANIEL JONES - Territory of the United States &c - Sept 6, 1791
North Carolina No. 58. By an Act for the relief of the Officers and Soldiers of the Continental Line, in consideration of the bravery and zeal of Nathaniel Jones, heir of the said Samuel Jones, a tract of land containing 2560 acres in Davidson County on the south side of Cumberland River. Surveyed for Nathaniel Jones June 19, 1785 by John Bucchanan, D.S. in consequence of a Military Warrant No. 160. Located July 8, 1784. Mar 14, 1786.

Page 228 - JOSEPH McDOWEL - Territory of the United States &c - Sept 6, 1791
North Carolina No. 1074. By an Act for the relief of the Officers and Soldiers of the Continental Line, in consideration of the bravery and zeal of John Bartie, a private in the said line, granted unto Joseph McDowel, assignee of John Bartie, a tract of land containing 640 acres in Davidson County on the east side of Mill Creek. Surveyed for Joseph McDowel Dec 4, 1788 by John Bucchanan, D.S. in consequence of a Military

Warrant No. 2045. Located Jan 2, 1787. Nov 26, 1789.

Page   228 - JOSEPH McDOWEL - Territory of the United States &c - Sept 6, 1791
        North Carolina No. 1086. By an Act for the relief of the Officers and
Soldiers of the Continental Line, in consideration of the bravery and zeal of George
Faigan, a private in the said line, granted unto Joseph McDowel, assignee of George
Faigan, a tract of land containing 640 acres in Davidson County on Mill Creek adjoining
John Forde's corner. Surveyed for Joseph McDowel Dec 28, 1788 by John Buchanan, D.S.
in consequence of a Military Warrant No. 2031. Located Dec 27, 1788. Nov 14, 1789.

Page   229 - JOHN WALKER - Territory of the United States &c - Sept 20, 1791
        North Carolina No. 259. BY an Act for the relief of the Officers and
Soldiers of the Continental Line, in consideration of the bravery and zeal of John Walker, a
major in the said line, granted unto John Walker a tract of land containing 1709 acres in
Davidson County on a creek of Duck River empting in on the north side. Surveyed for
John Walker Aug 10, 1785 by William Murry, D.S. in consequence of a Military Warrant No.
240. Located Nov 9, 1784.

Page   229 - THOMAS HAYNES - Territory of the United States &c - Oct 22, 1791
        This indenture made 16 Jan 1787 between Ephraim Griffin of Gates County,
North Carolina and Thomas Haynes of Perquimans County, North Carolina of the other
part. Ephraim Griffin conveyed unto Thomas Haynes a tract of land containing 640 acres
in Davidson County on a branch of Sycamore Creek that runs in on the north side near the
old Buffalo path. Said land being a tract of land granted to David Edwards, assignee of
Elizabeth Ray, heir of Stephen Ray a private in the Continental Line and Grant No. 189,
dated 7 Mar 1786. Test: John Gordon, William Burke and Joshua Fletcher. This 9 Nov
1787.

Page   230- EPHRAIM GRIFFIN - Territory of the United States &c - Oct 22, 1791
        I, David Edwards of Edenton in Chowan County, North Carolina, conveyed
unto Ephraim Griffin of Gates County, North Carolina, a tract of land containing 640 acres
in Davidson County on a branch of Sycamore Creek that runs in on the north side near the
Old Buffalo Path. This 1 Jan 1787. Test: Henry H(illegible) and Samuel Jucah. 9 Nov
1787.

Page   230 - BENJAMIN BAILEY - Territory of the United States &c - Oct 22, 1791
        North Carolina No. 38. By an Act for the relief of the Officers and Soldiers
of the Continental Line, in consideration of the bravery and zeal of Benjamin Bailey, a
captain in the said line, granted unto Benjamin Bailey a tract of land 3840 acres in
Davidson County including a Preemption of 640 acres of land in said survey in all 4480
acres on the north side of Cumberland River and joining Half Pone Creek. Surveyed for
said Bailey Aug 10, 1784 by James Mulherin, D.S. in consequence of a Military Warrant No.
552. Located July 24, 1784. Mar 14, 1786.

Page   231 - DAVID EDWARDS - Territory of the United States &c - Oct 22, 1791
        North Carolina No. 199. By an Act for the relief of the Officers and
Soldiers of the Continental Line, in consideration of the bravery and zeal of Stephen Ray,

a private in the said line, granted unto David Edwards, assignee of Elizabeth Ray, heiress of Stephen Ray, a tract of land containing 640 acres in Davidson County on a branch of Sycamore Creek that runs in on the north side of the Old Buffalo path. Surveyed for David Edwards Mar 20, 1785 by Henry Rutherford, D.S. in consequence of a Warrant No. 701. Located Dec 7, 1784. Mar 7, 1786.

Page   231 - JOHN COOTS - Territory of the United States &c - Oct 28, 1791
            This indenture made 21 Feb 1789 between Thomas Thompson and Samuel Thompson of Guilford County, North Carolina of one part and John Coots of same place of the other part. Thomas and Samuel Thompson conveyed unto John Coots a tract of land containing 1020 acres being a part of a certain tract containing 4260 acres on the waters or main river called Duck River in Middle District. Beginning at a bluff on Duck River at Joseph Kirkpatrick's corner, Samuel Thompson's corner and Hugh Roberts' corner. Test: James Boyd, John Boyd and James Coots. 26 Oct 1791.

Page   232 - NIMROD WILLIAMS - Territory of the United States &c - Nov 3, 1791
            This indenture made 3 Aug 1791 between William Collinsworth of Davidson County of one part and Nimrod Williams of same place of other part. William Collinsworth conveyed unto Nimrod Williams a tract of land in Davidson County on Browns Creek adjoining William Ellis' spring. Which land was granted unto William Collinsworth by the State of North Carolina by patent dated 10 July 1788. Test: Andrew Ewing and Moses Shelby. Oct Term 1791.

Page   232 - WILLOUGHBY WILLIAMS - Territory of the United States &c - Nov 4, 1791
            North Carolina No. 1102. Byan Act for the relief of the Officers and Soldiers of the Continental Line, in consideration of the bravery and zeal of John Pevill, a private in the said line, granted unto Willoughby Williams, assignee of said John Pevill, a tract of land containing 640 acres in Davidson County on the north side of Cumberland River and on the north fork of Sycamore. Surveyed for Willoughby Williams Sept 11, 1789 by Thomas Johnston, D.S. in consequence of a Military Warrant No. 3019. Located Sept 11, 1789. June 17, 1790. Willoughby Williams of Dobbs County was paid by Joel Bunn of Nash County, North Carolina, sold and transferred unto Joel Bunn the land in the within grant. This 24 June 1790.

Page   233 - JAMES GLASGOW - Territory of the United States &c - Nov 4, 1791
            North Carolina No. 687. By an Act for the relief of the Officers and Soldiers of the Continental Line, in consideration of the bravery and zeal of James Harrison, a private in the said line, granted unto James Glasgow, assignee of Francis Harrison, heir of said James Harrison, a tract of land containing 640 acres in Davidson County on Sinking Creek a branch of the west fork of Red River on the west side adjoining William Ross' survey of 3016 acres. Surveyed for James Glasgow June 21, 1785 by Robert Nelson, D.S. in consequence of a Military Warrant No. 1568. Located Feb 12, 1785. Nov 16, 1787. James Glasgow of Dobbs County was paid by Burrel Bunn of Nash County, North Carolina the land contained on the within grant. 24 May 1790.

Page   233 - JOSEPH ROSS - Territory of the United States &c - Nov 4, 1791
            North Carolina No. 1080. By an Act for the relief of the Officers and

Soldiers of the Continental Line, in consideration of the bravery and zeal of James Hawley, a private in the said line, granted unto Joseph Ross, assignee of said James Hawley, a tract of land containing 640 acres in Davidson County on the north side of Cumberland River on Sycamore Creek adjoining William Ramsey's line and near the line of a survey of Col. James Glasgow and about a mile from the Cumberland River. Surveyed for Joseph Ross Oct 10, 1789 by Robert Weakley, D.S. in consequence of a Military Warrant No. 2265. Located Jan 17, 1789. Nov 26, 1789.

Page   233 - AQUILLA SUGG - Territory of the United States &c - Nov 5, 1791
(2nd page)   North Carolina No. 926.   By an Act for the relief of the Officers and Soldiers of the Continental Line, in consideration of the bravery and zeal of Meradith Berks, a private in the said line, granted unto Aquilla Sugg, assignee of the heirs of said Meradith Berks, a tract of land containing 640 acres in Davidson County on the waters of the east fork of the first creek above Stones Lick River adjoining Thomas Thompson's survey. Surveyed for Aquilla Sugg May 11, 1788 in consequence of a Military Warrant No. 1514. May 18, 1789. Located Apr 13, 1788.

Page   234 - LEMUEL HOGAN - Territory of the United States &c - Nov 5, 1791
            North Carolina No. 55. By an Act for the relief of the officers and Soldiers of the Continental Line, in consideration of the bravery and zeal of James Hogan, deceased, Brigadier General in the said line, granted unto Lemuel Hogan an heir of said James Hogan, a tract of land containing 12,000 acres in Davidson County on the south side of Cumberland River at the mouth of the Caney Fork. Surveyed for Lemuel Hogan June 28, 1785 by Edwin Hickman, D.S. in consequence of a Military Warrant No. 324. Located June 22, 1784. Mar 14, 1786.

Page   234 - JOSEPH ROSS - Territory of the United States &c - Nov 5, 1791
            North Carolina No. 1067. By an Act for the relief of the officers and Soldiers of the Continental Line, in consideration of the bravery and zeal of James Zailett, a private in the said line, granted unto Joseph Ross, assignee of James Zailett, a tract of land containing 640 acres in Davidson County on the south side of the Cumberland River on the north waters of of the east fork of Stones River above the first line run by the Commissioners in 1783 adjoining Isadore Skerrett's north east corner of a survey Warrant No. 3398 and also Matthew Lock' corner in John Welch's line. Surveyed for Joseph Ross Oct 15, 1789 by Robert Weakley, D.S. in consequence of a Military Warrant No. 3400. Located June 4, 1789. Nov 14, 1789.

Page   234 - HUGH LEWIS - Territory of the United States &c - Nov 5, 1791
            North Carolina No. 87. By an Act for the relief of the Officers and Soldiers of the Continental Line, in consideration of the services of Col. Martin Armstrong, surveyor, granted unto Hugh Lewis, assignee of said Armstrong, a tract of land containing 100 acres in Davidson County on Brush Creek adjoining John Titswood's line. Surveyed for Hugh Lewis Mar 14, 1789 by Robert Nelson, D.S. Nov 14, 1789.

Page   235 - WILLIAM WALKER - Territory of the United States &c - Nov 5, 1791
            North Carolina No. 615. By an Act for the relief of the Officers and Soldiers of the Continental Line, in consideration of the bravery and zeal of William

Walker, a sergeant in the said line, granted unto William Walker a tract of land containing 1000 acres in Davidson County on the south side of Sulphur Fork of Red River adjoining Benjamin Hardin's cornerand William Gubbins' corner. Surveyed for William Walker June 22, 1786 by Robert Weakley, D.S. in consequence of a Military Warrant No. 1878. Located Mar 22, 1786. Sept 15, 1787.

Page   235 - JAMES HAYS - Territory of the United States &c - Nov 5, 1791
North Carolina No. 290. For 10 lbs per 100 acres paid by James Hays was granted a tract of land containing 640 acres in Davidson County on the head of the first small creek of Cumberland River which runs in on the south side above Drakes Creek adjoining Joseph Hendricks' line and Isaac Lefever's land. Surveyed for James Hays June 7, 1788 by Daniel Smith in consequence of a Warrant No. 204. Entered Jan 29, 1784. Nov 26, 1789.

Page   235 - JAMES ROBERTSON - Territory of the United States &c - Nov 7, 1791
North Carolina No. 1341. By an Act for the relief of the Officers and Soldiers of the Continental Line, in consideration of the bravery and zeal of John Robertson, a private in the said line, granted unto James Robertson, assignee of said John Robertson, a tract of land containing 620 acres in Davidson County on the south side of Cumberland River opposite Neeleys Lick adjoining on the bank of Cumberland against Neely's island. Surveyed for James Robertson Apr 14, 1790 by John Donelson, D.S. in consequence of a Military Warrant No. 682. Located May 16, 1786. Nov 16, 1790.

Page   236 - JOHN GORDON - Territory of the United States &c - Nov 5, 1791
This indenture made 7 Jan 1787 between Joseph Bailey of Perquimans County, North Carolina of one part and John Gordon of same place of the other part. Joseph Bailey conveyed unto John Gordon a tract of land containing 1024 acres in Davidson County on the north side of Cumberland River on the Half Pone Creek adjoining said Bailey's east line. Said land being part of a tract of land granted to Captain Benjamin Bailey of 3840 acres being the bounty land allowed him for his service in the Continental line and by him given to his brother the said Joseph Bailey the said Grant No. 38 and dated Mar 14, 1786. Test: Hardy Murphree, Thomas Haynes and William Clemens. Nov 6, 1791.

Page   236 - JAMES ROBERTSON - Territory of the United States &c - Nov 7, 1791
North Carolina No. 571. By an Act for the relief of the Officers and Soldiers of the Continental Line, in consideration of the bravery and zeal of John Pendergrass, a private in the said line, granted unto James Robertson, assignee of John Pendergrass, a tract of land containing 274 acres in Davidson County on the south side of Cumberland River adjoining Daniel Chambers' corner. Surveyed for James Robertson Mar 23, 1786 by John Donelson, D.S. in consequence of a Military Warrant No. 271. Located Feb 1, 1785. Sept 15, 1787.

Page   237 - JOHN FOWLER - Territory of the United States &c - Nov 7, 1791
North Carolina No. 281. For 10 lbs per 100 acres paid by John Fowler who is heir of James Fowler, deceased, a tract of land containing 640 acres in Davidson County on second creek an eastern branch of Stones River adjoining the corner of the heirs of Elijah Oliver's land. Surveyed for John Fowler Sept 1, 1786 by Daniel Smith by virtue

of a Warrant No. 786. May 1, 1786. Nov 26, 1789.

Page   237 - THOMAS TAYLOR - Territory of the United States &c - Nov 7, 1791
                North Carolina No. 682. By an Act for the relief of the Officers and
Soldiers of the Continental Line, in consideration of the bravery and zeal of Benjamin
Jones, a private in the said line, granted unto Thomas Taylor, assignee of said Benjamin
Jones, a tract of land containing 320 acres in Davidson County on the east waters of
Whites Creek joining the north boundary of Absolom Hooper's and John Nelson's corner.
Surveyed for Thomas Taylor (date not listed) by Robert Nelson, D.S. in consequence of a
Military Warrant No. 3386. Located Sept 29, 1786. Dec 8, 1787.

Page   237 - MORGAN BRYANT - Territory of the United States &c - Nov 7, 1791
(2nd page)   North Carolina No. 90. By an Act for the relief of the Officers and Soldiers
of the Continental Line, in consideration of the services of Col. Martin Armstrong,
surveyor, granted unto Morgan Bryant, assignee of the said Armstrong, a tract of land
containing 100 acres in Davidson County on Sulphur Fork of Red River two miles above
Jacob Pennington's claim. Surveyed for Morgan Bryant June 27, 1789 by Thomas Johnston,
D.S. in consequence of a Service Right of said Armstrong, entered June 9, 1785. Nov 26,
1787.

Page   237 - JOHN STEWART - Territory of the United States &c - Nov 7, 1791
                North Carolina No. 99. By an Act for the relief of the Officers and Soldiers
of the Continental Line, in consideration of the services of John Stewart, one of the
Commissioners Guard &c, granted unto John Stewart a tract of land containing 320 acres
in Davidson County on both sides of the Sulphur Fork of Richland Creek of Red River.
Surveyed for John Stewart June 30, 1786 by James Sanders, D.S. in consequence of a
Warrant No. 365. Entered Mar 22, 1784. Nov 26, 1789.

Page   238 - RICHARD HIGHTOWER - Territory of the United States &c - Nov 7, 1791
                This indenture made 13 Aug 1791 between William Collinsworth of one part
and Richard Hightower of the other part, both of Davidson County. William Collinsworth
conveyed unto Richard Hightower a tract of land containing 640 acres in Davidson County
on a north branch of Little Harpeth adjoining James Leeper, John Henderson's line and
James Mayfield's boundary and Thomas Denton's line. Said land was granted unto the said
Collinsworth by the State of North Carolina by patent dated Oct 8, 1787 and No. 72. Test:
Andrew Ewing. Oct Term 1791.

Page   238 - JOHN MARNEY - Territory of the United States &c - Nov 9, 1791
                This indenture made 23 May 1791 between Thomas Molloy of Davidson
County of one part and John Marney of same place of the other part. Thomas Molloy
conveyed unto John Marney a tract of land containing 60 acres and 3/4 in Davidson County
on the waters of Whites Creek adjoining said Marney's land. Said land being part of tract
of 640 acres granted by the State of North Carolina to Thomas Molloy, assignee of the
heirs of William Spence for his services as a soldier in the Continental Line and grant
dated Aug 11, 1789 and No. 1043. Test: James How and David Hord. Oct Term 1791.

Page 239 - BENJAMIN CASSELLMAN - Territory of the United States &c - Nov 8, 1791
This indenture made 30 July 1791 between Andrew Lucas of Davidson County of the one part and Benjamin Cassellman of same place of the other part. Andrew Lucas conveyed unto Benjamin Cassellman a tract of land containing 1 acre of ground being in the town of Nashville and known as No. 82, being the lot formerly granted to George Nevilles by the Commissioners of the town of Nashville by deed dated Aug 16, 1784 and by said Neville to James Bosley July 6, 1785 and by him to said Lucas Feb 26, 1789. Oct Term 1791.

Page 239 - JOHN WILSON - Territory of the United States &c - Nov 8, 1791
This indenture made 30 Oct 1791 between Daniel Frazer of Davidson County of one part and John Wilson of same place of the other part. Daniel Frazer conveyed unto John Wilson a tract of land containing 160 acres in Davidson County on the waters of Whites Creek it being the east end of Daniel Frazer's Preemption Right adjoining John Duffell. Which land was granted to the said Daniel Frazer by the State of North Carolina by a patent dated Apr 17, 1786, No. 104. Oct Term 1791.

Page 240 - JAMES STUART - Territory of the United States &c - Nov 8, 1791
This indenture made 7 Nov 1791 between Charles Longmier of Washington County of one part and James Stuart of same place of the other part. Charles Longmier conveyed unto James Stuart a tract of land containing 640 acres in Davidson County on the south side of Cumberland on both sides of the east fork of Stones River the waters of the said Cumberland River. Proven by Daniel James and William M(illegible). 8 Nov 1791.

Page 240 - JAMES STUART - Territory of the United States &c - Nov 8, 1791
(2nd page) This indenture made 7 Nov 1791 between Charles Longmire of Washington County and James Stuart of same place of the other part. Charles Longmier conveyed unto James Stuart a tract of land containing 640 acres in Davidson County on the south side of Cumberland River and on the east fork of Stones River the waters of the said Cumberland adjoining James Stuart's survey No. 3397 on Isadore Skerrett's line. Land granted to Robert Weakley by the State of North Carolina by virtue of a Military Warrant No. 2252 and sold unto Charles Longmier by deed dated Nov 23, 1789. 8 Nov 1791.

Page 241 - JOHN McNAIRY, ESQ. - TERRITORY OF THE UNITED STATES &C - Nov 9, 1791
This indenture made 19 Aug 1791 between Lardner Clark, Esq. of Davidson County of one part and John McNairy, Esq. of same place of the other part. Lardner Clark conveyed unto John McNairy a tract of land containing 640 acres in Davidson County on Hurricane Creek a branch of Stones River adjoining James Bradley's corner and Henry Harrow's boundary. Wit: Bennett Searcy. Oct Term 1791.

Page 241 - ALSEE THOMPSON & ELIZABETH THOMPSON - Territory of the United States &c - Nov 9, 1791
I, Robert Thompson of Davidson County, for the love and affection for my sisters Alsee Thompson and Elizabeth Thompson, I hereby grant and bestow a certain tract or parcel of land containing 640 acres to be equally divided between them. Land in Davidson County on the east waters of Mill Creek adjoining Joseph McDowel's corner and

Jason Thompson's corner. Which land was granted unto John Thompson by the State of North Carolina by patent dated Nov 14, 1789 and No. 1079. This 12 Oct 1791. Wit: Andrew Ewing. Oct Term 1791.

Page 242 - JOHN McFARLIN - Territory of the United States &c - Nov 10, 1791
This indenture made 13 Oct 1791 between Joseph Shaw of the one part and John McFarlin of the other part, both of Davidson County. Joseph Shaw conveyed unto John McFarlin a tract of land containing 113 acres in Davidson County adjoining John Walker's north boundary and Kincade's corner and Philip Walker's line. Oct Term 1791.

Page 242 - JOHN SINGLETARY - Territory of the United States &c - Nov 10, 1791
I, James Thompson of Davidson County for the love and affection and good will for my grandson John Singletary, son of John S. Singletary and Catherine Singletary his wife, conveyed unto said John Singletary a tract of land containing 50 acres in Davidson County adjoining said Thompson's Preemption. Said land being part of the said James Thompson's Preemption granted to him by the State of North Carolina patent dated Apr 17, 1786. Test: Jessee Evans and Benjamin Joslin. Oct Term 1791.

Page 243 - SOLOMON SISSUMS - Territory of the United States &c - Nov 10, 1791
This indenture made 24 May 1791 between Reuben Smith of Edgecomb County, North Carolina of one part and Solomon Sissums of same place of the other part. Reuben Smith conveyed unto Solomon Sissums a tract of land containing 640 acres in Davidson County on the east fork of Buffalo Creek empting into the Tennessee on the north side adjoining William Smith's corner. Test: Joseph Hart and Elias Fort. Oct Term 1791.

Page 243 - JOSHUA THOMAS - Territory of the United States &c - Nov 11, 1791
This indenture made 8 Oct 1791 between John Thomas of Davidson County of one part and Joshua Thomas of same place of the other part. John Thomas conveyed unto Joshua Thomas a tract of land containing 100 acres in Davidson County on the north side of Cumberland River. Which said land is part of 640 acres granted unto John Thomas by patent dated Apr 17, 1786. Test: John Kirkpatrick and Eli Hamons. Oct Term 1791.

Page 244 - GOWERS - Territory of the United States &c - Nov 11, 1791
The Justices of Davidson County at July Term 1791 appointed us the subscribers Commissioners to divide according to quantity and quality a tract of land containing 640 acres on the south side of Cumberland River between Elijah Gower, Elisha Gower and William Gower said land being the contents of a patent granted to said Gowers dated 10 July 1788. Land numbered the lower division thereof No. 1, the middle division No. 2, and the upper division No. 3. Division No. 1 to William Gower. Second division No. 2 to Elisha Gower. And Division No. 3 to Elijah Gower. Signed 17 Aug 1791 by John Dickson, Thomas Hickman, Thomas McCrory and Robert Heaton.

Page 244 - JOHN DUFFELL - Territory of the United States &c - Nov 12, 1791
(2nd page) This indenture made 13 Oct 1791 between Daniel Frazer of Davidson County of one part and John Duffell of same place of the other part. Daniel Frazer conveyed unto John Duffell a tract of land containing 124 acres in Davidson County on the waters of

Whites Creek, it being part of a tract was Daniel Frazer's Preemption adjoining John Wilson's. Which land was granted to Daniel Frazer by the State of North Carolina by patent dated Apr 17, 1786 and No. 104. Oct Term 1791.

Page   245 - JOSHUA HADLEY & PATRICK TRAVERS - Territory of the United States
            Nov 14, 1791
            This indenture made 2 Feb 1787 between Curtis Ivy of one part and Joshua Hadley and Patrick Travers of Cumberland County of the other part. Curtis Ivy conveyed unto said Hadley and Travers a tract of land containing 2560 acres on both sides of Big Harpeth in Davidson County adjoining James Robertson. Said land being part of a tract of land granted him for his services in the Continental Line. (It being one part of a Preemption Right of about 200 acres included in the said 2560 acres not meant or intended to be conveyed or granted to the said Hadley and Travers). Wit: J. Dosden and George Blocker. 24 June 1788.

Page   245 - LEVI HAND - Territory of the United States &c - Nov 14, 1791
            This indenture made 30 Aug 1791 between James Bosley of Davidson County of one part and Levi Hand of same place of the other part. James Bosley conveyed unto Levi Hand a tract of land containing 100 acres on the south side of Cumberland River and near the Stone Lick, adjoining John McNairy's corner and Isaac Mason's line. Which said land was granted unto James Bosley by the State of North Carolina by patent. Test: John Bell and Samuel Weakley. Oct Term 1791.

Page   246 - PHILIPS & CAMPBELL - Territory of the United States &c - Nov 14, 1791
            This indenture made 13 Oct 1791 between Elijah Robertson of Davidson County of one part and Philip Philips and Michael Campbell of the District of Kentucky of the other part. Elijah Robertson conveyed unto said Philips and Campbell a tract of land containing 1207 acres including the plantation that I now live on. The 1207 acres of land are various tracts which was obtained by Preemption Right and Military Warrants granted by the State of North Carolina and entered 7 Mar 1786 and No. 1837 (illegible) 204 which (illegible) Ephraim Scurlock also the others a Warrant No. 3155. Located 20 Mar 1786 which also joins William Meelin , Sen., Isaac Roberts, John Cockrill and William Gun which all amounts to 1207 acres. Wit: Andrew Ewing. Oct Term 1791.

Page   246 - JOHN OVERTON - Territory of the United States &c - Nov 16, 1791
(2nd page)   This indenture made and entered 11 Aug 1791 between George Walker of one part and John Overton of the other part. George Walker conveyed unto John Overton a tract of land in Nashville containing one acre of land and known as Lot No. 52. Oct Term 1791.

Page   247 - ELIZABETH BENNETT - Territory of the United States &c - Nov 16, 1791
            This indenture made 7 July 1791 between Timothy Demumbre of one part and Elizabeth Bennett commonly (illegible) of the town and county aforesaid. Timothy Demumbre conveyed unto Elizabeth Bennett all that town lot of one acre of ground in Nashville and known as Lot No. 45. Wit: J.O.M. & B. Searcy. Oct Term 1791.

Page   247 - HOWEL TATUM - Territory of the United States &c - Nov 16, 1791
            This indenture made 15 Oct 1791 between Samuel Felin of Lincoln County,
State of Kentucky of one part and Howel Tatum of Davidson County of the other part.
Samuel Felin conveyed unto Howel Tatum a certain lot of 1 acre in the town of Nashville,
and known as Lot No. 34. Wit: Andrew Jackson and John Overton. Oct Term 1791.

Page   247 - JOSEPH ROSS - Territory of the United States &c - Nov 16, 1791
            North Carolina No. 352. For 10 lbs per 100 acres paid by Joseph Ross was
granted a tract of land containing 1000 acres in the Western District in the fork of Obion
River adjoining James Glasgow's corner. Surveyed for Joseph Ross Oct 10, 1787 by Isaac
Roberts, D.S. by virtue of a Warrant No. 1712. Dated May 8, 1787. Dec 16, 1789.

Page   248 - THOMAS SMITH - Territory of the United States &c - Nov 16, 1791
            This indenture made 3 Mar 1790 between William Loggins of Davidson
County of one part and Thomas Smith of same place of the other part. William Loggins
conveyed unto Thomas Smith a tract of land containing 20 acres in Davidson County on a
branch of Whites Creek adjoining Federick Stump's line. Wit: Reuben Smith, William
Hughes and Jessee Smith. Oct Term 1791.

Page   248 - PHILIPS & CAMPBELL - Territory of the United States &c - Nov 17, 1791
            This indenture made 13 Oct 1791 between Elijah Robertson of Davidson
County of one part and Philip Philips and Michael Campbell of the District of Kentucky of
the other part. Elijah Robertson conveyed unto said Philips and Campbell a tract of land
containing 2560 acres in Davidson County on the waters of the Caney Fork River which
said land is entered in four different tracts of 640 acres in the Military Land Office kept
in Nashville which was entered on the 22 Mar 1788 and surveyed by James Mulherin,
number of warrant of the first entry is No. 3314. Elijah Robertson of Thomas Smith of the
heirs of Thomas Harold adjoining his tract assignee of the heirs of William Digg at the
north west corner. Also the number of the second tract and warrant No. 3310 and entered
on the same day as the above, and adjoining Elijah Robertson as assignee of the heirs of
Evan Watkins on the west. Which was granted to the said heirs of William Diggs and
assigned to the said Robertson by Thomas Smith. Also the third warrant No. 3300 and
entered the same day as the other two above described and adjoining the said Robertson
tract as assignee of the heirs of Thomas Harold on the west and also the heirs of Peter
Black. Also the fourth, number of warrant No. 3311 and was entered on the same day as
the above and adjoining as assignee of Robert Nixon's corner. Which land was granted to
Samuel Gold, heir of Stephen Gold and assigned to said Robertson by Thomas Smith. Test:
Anthony Foster. Oct Term 1791.

Page   249 - JASON THOMPSON - Territory of the United States &c - Nov 18, 1791
            This indenture made 7 May 1791 between Thomas Thompson of one part and
Jason Thompson of the other part, both of Davidson County. Thomas Thompson conveyed
unto Jason Thompson a tract of land containing 192 acres in Davidson County adjoining
Thompson Pond and Thomas Thompson's Preemption. Test: William Armstrong and T.
Creighton. Oct Term 1791.

Page   249 - WILLIAM LOGGINS - Territory of the United States &c - Nov 18, 1791
(2nd page)   This indenture made 29 July 1791 between James Cooper of Davidson County of one part and William Loggins of same place of the other part. James Cooper conveyed unto William Loggins a tract of land containing 300 acres in Davidson County on the east fork of Whites Creek adjoining Loggin's Preemption. Land being part of a tract of 640 acres granted to the said Loggins by patent dated Apr 17, 1786. Proven by Thomas Smith. Oct Term 1791.

Page   Page 250 - MICHAEL ROBERTSON - Territory of the United States &c - Nov 22, 1791
        North Carolina No. 37. For 10 lbs per 100 acres paid by Michael Robertson was granted a tract of land containing 1500 acres in the Western District on the north side of Duck River. Beginning at the bank of said river bank about three miles above the mouth of Falling Creek, Martin Fifer's corner. Surveyed for said Robertson July 26, 1785 by Henry Rutherford in consequence of a Warrant No. 640, dated Oct 28, 1783. July 10, 1788.

Page   250 - ROBERT NELSON - Territory of the United States &c - Nov 24, 1791
        This indenture made 6 Nov 1791 between Samuel McGown of Davidson County of one part and Robert Nelson of Tennessee County of the other part. Samuel McGowan conveyed unto Robert Nelson a tract of land containing 60 acres on the east side of Whites Creek between Mitchel's and Glaves' Preemptions. Wit: John McNairy. 23 Nov 1791.

Page   250 - ALEXANDER EWING - The territory of the United States &c - Dec 5, 1791
        This indenture made 7 Nov 1791 between Robert Nelson of Tennessee County of one part and Alexander Ewing of Davidson County of the other part. Robert Nelson conveyed unto Alexander Ewing a tract of land containing 480 acres in Davidson County on Grove Creek the south side of Big Harpeth and adjoining Mullins and Patten's corners and said Nelson's corner. Test: Daniel James and John Edmiston. 12 Nov 1791.

Page   250   Nashville, Tennessee
(2nd page)   State of Tennessee   Aug 15, 1887
              Davidson County
        We the undersigned transcribers do hereby certify that we have correctly transcribed the foregoing Book (B) from the original and that we have compared said transcript, and certify that this foregoing Book (B) is a correct copy.
Signed and Sealed   R.A. Lasseter
before me this Aug 15/87   F.P. Provost
Rbt. Smith   H.C. Caffey

PAGE 1 - DANN HILL - Territory of the United States &c - Jan 25, 1792

This indenture made 10 Jan 1792 between John Topp of Davidson County of one part and Dann Hill of same place of the other part. John Topp conveyed unto Dann Hill a tract of land containing 100 acres in Davidson County about three miles from Nashville and on the east boundary of Ewin Hickman's, deceased, claim where on his widow now lives. Said land being part of a tract of 960 acres granted by the State of North Carolina to John Topp, heir of Roger Topp. Test: Thomas Hickman and Robert Heaton. Jan Term 1792.

Page 1 - JOSEPH LANE - Territory of the United States &c - Jan 25, 1792

This indenture made 9 Jan 1792 between Jarret Maniffee of the District of Kentucky and County of Lincoln of one part and Joseph Lane of the territory of the United States of America south of the River Ohio of the other part. Jarrett Maniffee conveyed unto Joseph Lane a tract of land containing 640 acres in Davidson County on north side of Big Harpeth. Which land was granted to the said Maniffee by the State of North Carolina by patent dated Apr 17, 1786 and No. 120. Aug 29, 1791.

Page 2 - JONAS MANIFFEE - Territory of the United States &c - Jan Term 1792

I, Jarret Maniffee of Bourbon County, District of Kentucky, appointed Jonas Maniffee of Davidson County my true and lawful attorney in fact for me and in my name to execute a deed in fee simple with common warrantry to Joseph Love of Davidson County the right to 640 acres of land known by the name of Jarret Maniffee's Preemption and entered Jan 9, 1784 and No. 482, lying on the south side of Big Harpeth River granted to me by the State of North Carolina by patent dated Apr 17, 1786 and No. 120, hereby giving and granting to my said attorney all my power and authority to make such conveyance to the said Love as above specified in as full. This 29 Aug 1791. Signed Abraham Byrd and William Route. 6 Sept 1791. in the sixteenth year of the Commonwealth of Virginia. John Edwards.

Page 2 - JOHN PILLOW - Territory of the United States &c - Jan 28, 1792

This indenture made 10 Jan 1792 between Samuel Barton of Davidson County of one part and John Pillow of same place of the other part. Samuel Barton conveyed unto John Pillow a tract of land containing 50 acres in Davidson County on the waters of Browns Creek. Which land was conveyed to the said Barton by John Brown by deed dated July 14, 1791 and to the said Brown by Francis Armstrong by deed dated July 8, 1788. Being part of the said Armstrong's Preemption. Jan Term 1792.

Page 3 - JESSEE HUTSON - Territory of the United States &c - Jan 30, 1792

This indenture made 9 Jan 1792 between Barnabeth Harrod of Davidson County of the one part and Jesse Hutson of same place of the other part. Barnabeth Harrod conveyed unto Jesse Hutson a tract of land containing 200 acres in Davidson County on Dry Creek on the north side of Cumberland River, being the west end of Barned Harrod's Preemption. Test: Henry Bradford and Thomas Blackamore. Jan Term 1792.

Page   3 -   JESSEE HUTSON - Territory of the United States &c - Jan 30, 1792
This indenture made 3 Jan 1792 between John Blackamore of the one part and Jesse Hutson of the other part, both of Davidson County. John Blackamore conveyed unto Jesse Hutson a tract of land containing 100 acres in Davidson County on the north side of Cumberland River, being part of a tract of 640 acres formerly granted to the said John Blackamore. Said tract adjoining Daniel Frazier's line. Wit: Thomas Blackamore and Henry Bradford. Jan Term 1791.

Page   4 -   WILLIAM NASH - Territory of the United States &c - Jan 1792
This indenture made 9 June 1791 between James Cole Montflorence of one part and William Nash of the other part, both of Davidson County. James Cole Montflorence conveyed unto William Nash the following tracts of land in Davidson County on the north side of Cumberland River joining the lower side of Capt. Andrew Armstrong's survey of 1280 acres and containing 640 acres of land about sixteen miles below Nashville, also that other tract of land in Davidson County on the waters of the first creek above Stones Lick Creek and on the east side of Stones River adjoining George Sugg's corner No. 2236. Also that other tract of land in Davidson County on the first creek above Stones Lick Creek on the east side of Stones River adjoining said Sugg's Warrant No. 1503. Said land containing 640 acres about fourteen miles from the town of Nashville , being the same tracts surveyed by William Nash to the said James Cole Montflorence by deed dated 16 June 1790. Wit: Bennett Searcy. Jan Term 1792.

Page   4 -   WILLIAM COCKE - Territory of the United States &c - Feb 3, 1792
(2nd page)   North Carolina No. 267. For 10 lbs per 100 acres paid by William Cocke was granted a tract of land containing 640 acres in Davidson County on the north side of Cumberland River, beginning at the mouth of Stones Spring branch and joins John Bucchanan's corner. Surveyed for said William Cocke Sept 7, 1785 by John Buchanan, D.S. in consequence of a Warrant No. 198. Entered Jan 28, 1784. July 10, 1788.

Page   5 -   ROBERT HAYS - Territory of the United States &c - Feb 3, 1792
This indenture made 9 Sept 1791 between William Cocke of Hawkins County of the one part and Robert Hays of Davidson County of the other part. William Cocke conveyed unto Robert Hays a tract of land containing 640 acres in Davidson County on the north side of Cumberland River adjoining John Buchanan's corner and James Scott's line. Wit: Andrew JacksonMark Mitchell and Thomas Searsey. Jan Term 1792.

Page   5 -   WILLIAM TUTON - Territory of the United States &c - Feb 7, 1792
North Carolina No. 879. By an Act for the relief of the officers and Soldiers of the Continental Line, in consideration of the bravery and zeal of Thomas Boyer, a private in the said line, granted unto William Tuton, assignee of said Boyer, a tract of land containing 640 acres in Davidson County on the north side of Cumberland River below the mouth of Red River adjoining John Menees' east boundary. Surveyed for William Tuton July 11, 1788 by William Crutcher, D.S. in consequence of a Military Warrant No. 3491. Located June 30, 1788. Jan 17, 1789.

Page   6 -   WILLIAM TUTON - Territory of the United States &c - Feb 7, 1792
North Carolina No. 994. By an Act for the relief of the Officers and

Soldiers of the Continental Line, in consideration of the bravery and zeal of Elthred Exum, a private in the said line, granted unto William Tuton, assignee of saud Exum, a tract of land containing 640 acres in Davidson County on Caney Fork adjoining to his tract as assignee of Samuel Scutchen's tract. Surveyed for William Tuton by James Mulherin, D.S. Nov 11, 1788 in consequence of a Military Warrant No. 1897. Located Nov 5, 1788. May 13, 1789.

Page   6 -   WILLIAM TUTON - Territory of the United States &c - Feb 7, 1792
                North Carolina No. 993. By an Act for the relief of the Officers and Soldiers of the Continental Line, in consideration of the bravery and zeal of Samuel Skutchens, granted unto William Tuton, assignee of said Scutchens, a tract of land containing 640 acres in Davidson County on Mulherins Creek and on Caney Fork adjoining James Gloster's tract. Surveyed for William Tuton Nov 10, 1788 by James Mulherin, D.S. in consequence of a Military Warrant No. 1898. Located Nov 5, 1788. May 18, 1789.

Page   6 -   HANNAH PORTER - Territory of the United States &c - Feb 7, 1792

This indenture made 14 Dec 1791 between John Lucas of Davidson County of one part and Hannah Porter of same place of the other part. John Lucas conveyed unto Hannah Porter a tract of land containing 40 acres in Davidson County on the west side of Whites Creek adjoining Widow Lucas' line south of a small creek. Jan Term 1792.

Page   7 -   SAMUEL KERR - Territory of the United States &c - Feb 7, 1792
                This indenture made 8 Feb 1791 between Joseph Kerr of Rowan County, State of North Carolina of one part and Samuel Kerr of same place of the other part. Joseph Kerr conveyed unto Samuel Kerr a tract of land containing 640 acres in Mero District on the north side of Cumberland River in Davidson County on the head branches of Gibsons Creek and Buchanan's Spring branch adjoining James Scott's line and John Buchanan's corner. Wit: Nat. Braly, Robert Weakley, Arthur Henry and James Kerr. Jan Term 1792.

Page   7 -   SAMUEL WEAKLEY - Territory of the United States &c - Feb 7, 1792
                This indenture made 7 Oct 1791 between William Cathey of Rowan County, State of North Carolina of one part and Samuel Weakley of Davidson COunty of the other part. William Cathey conveyed unto Samuel Weakley a tract of land containing 213 acres in Davidson County on the north branches of the east fork of Stones River adjoining Richard Cathey's corner. Said land was granted to the said William Cathey by the State of North Carolina by virtue of a Military Warrant granted under the heirs of William Sarrett, deceased, for 640 acres the above being the south end of said tract of 640 acres. Wit: Robert Weakley. Jan Term 1792.

Page   8 -   ANDREW EWING - Territory of the United States &c - Feb 8, 1792
                This indenture made 10 Jan 1792 between Samuel Barton of Davidson COunty of one part and Andrew Ewing of same place of the other part. Samuel Barton conveyed unto Andrew Ewing a tract of land containing 100 acres in Davidson County on the waters of Browns Creek adjoining said Barton's Preemption whereon he now lives. Jan term 1792.

Page 8 - ROBERT CAROTHERS - Territory of the United States &c - Feb 8, 1792

This indenture made 5 Jan 1791 between Robert Irwin of Mecklenburgh County, North Carolina of one part and Robert Carothers of same place of the other part. Robert Irwin conveyed unto Robert Carothers a tract of land containing 320 acres in Davidson County on the south side of Cumberland River and waters of Little Harpeth adjoining James Leiper's line. Said survey and held by patent granted to the said Robert Irwin dated 13 Nov 1790. Wit: John Neely, David Johnston and Ezekiel Carothers. Jan term 1792.

Page 9 - DAVID ALLISON - Territory of the United States &c - Feb 8, 1792

This indenture made 9 Nov 1791 between Joshua Thomas of Davidson County of one part and David Allison of same place of the other part. Joshua Thomas conveyed unto David Allison a tract of land containing 640 acres in Davidson County on the north side of Cumberland River about two miles from Nashville. Wit: Andrew Jackson and Bennett Searcy. Jan Term 1792.

Page 9 - THOMAS MOLLOY - Territory of the United States &c - Feb 8, 1792

This indenture made 4 Aug 1791 between Eden Lewis and Chloe Lewis as to William Goodman, deceased, of Hertford County, North Carolina of one part and Thomas Molloy of Davidson County of the other part. Eden Lewis and Chloe Lewis conveyed unto Thomas Molloy a tract of land containing 640 acres in Davidson County on the Big Harpeth River. Said land being granted to the said Chloe Goodman, now Chloe Lewis, as heiress to William Goodman, by the State of North Carolina for his services as a soldier of the Continental Line, grant dated Mar 16, 1790 and No. 1285. Wit: Mat Brickett, John Gatling, Daniel Ross and Alias (blank). Jan Term 1792.

Page 10 - ROBERT WEAKLEY - Territory of the United States &c - Feb 8, 1792

This indenture made 29 June 1791 between James Cole Montflorence of Davidson County of one part and Robert Weakley of same place of other part. James Cole Montflorence conveyed unto Robert Weakley a tract of land containing 2000 acres in the Western District on the waters of Obion River on the north side adjoining Dugan's and Blount's corners, it being the south end of a tract of 2500 acres located by Robert Weakley joining Ephraim McLane's line . Said land being conveyed by the said Robert Weakley to the said James Cole Montflorence by deed dated 28 July 1790. Wit: Andrew Jackson and Andrew Cassellman. Jan Term 1792.

Page 10 - ROBERT ERWIN (IRWIN) - Territory of the United States &c - Feb 8, 1792

North Carolina No. 1175. By an Act for the relief of the Officers and Soldiers of the Continental Line, in consideration of the bravery and zeal of Fountain Jordan, a private in the said line, granted unto Robert Irwin, assignee of Fountain Jordan, a tract of land containing 640 acres in Davidson County on south side of Cumberland River and waters of Little Harpeth adjoining James Crockett's Preemption, James Leiper's corner and surveyed for said Robert Irwin Nov 6, 1789 by John Buchanan, D.S. in consequence of a Military Warrant No. 754. Located Nov 1, 1784. Nov 30, 1790.

Page 11 - LARDNER CLARKE - Territory of the United States &c - Feb 9, 1792

This indenture made 9 Jan 1792 between ·Thomas Hickman, late Sheriff of

239

Davidson County, lately part of North Carolina, of one part and Lardner Clarke, Esq. of same place of other part. Thomas Hickman conveyed unto Lardner Clark a tract of land containing 720 acres belonging to real estate of William Gubbins, deceased, as assignee of Elijah Robertson, assignee of Philemon Thomas and afterwards granted by the State of North Carolina to the said Gubbins by patent dated Nov 14, 1789 and No. 100. Jan Term 1792.

Page   11 - DAVID JOHNSTON - Territory of the United States &c - Feb 9, 1792
            This indenture made 13 Jan 1792 between Ephraim McLane of Davidson County of one part and David Johnston of Mecklenburg County, North Carolina of the other part. Ephraim McLane conveyed unto David Johnston a tract of land containing 700 acres on the waters of Duck River in the Middle District on the south side of Duck River. Jan term 1792.

Page   12 - ANDREW CASSELLMAN - Territory of the United States &c - Feb 9, 1792
            This indenture made 9 Jan 1792 between Lardner Clarke, Esq. of one part and Andrew Cassellman of the other part, both of Davidson County. Lardner Clarke conveyed unto Andrew Cassellman a tract of land containing 720 acres in Davidson County adjoining Thomas Finney's boundary and corner of William Gubbins' tract of 500 acres and William Lucas' boundary. Which said land was granted by the State of North Carolina to William Gubbins as assignee of Elijah Robertson, assignee of Philemon Thomas, ensign in the Commissioners Guard by patent dated Nov 14, 1789 and No. 100 and afterward conveyed to the said Lardner Clark by Thomas Hickman, High Sheriff of Davidson County by deed dated Jan 9, 1792. Jan term 1792.

Page   12 - JOHN BUCCHANAN - Territory of the United States &c - Feb 9, 1792
(2nd page)   North Carolina No. 377. We have given unto John Bucchanan, assignee of Joshua Lewis, a private in the said line, a tract of land containing 640 acres in Davidson County on Stones River adjoining Cornelius Ruddles' line. Dated 15 Sept 1787.

Page   13 - ROBERT WEAKLEY - Territory of the United States &c - Feb 9, 1792
            This indenture made 13 Oct 1791 between Samuel Graham of Rowan County, North Carolina of one part and Robert Weakley of Davidson County of the other part. Samuel Graham conveyed unto Robert Weakley a tract of land containing 1000 acres in Davidson County on the north side of Duck River adjoining q 2000 acre tract of said Weakley on the north on Caney Spring Creek. Said land being the west end of a tract of 2000 acres granted unto Samuel Graham by the State of North Carolina by patent No. 142 and dated July 10, 1788. Proven by oath of E. Patton Chambers. Jan Term 1792.

Page   13 - EZEKIEL NORRIS - Territory of the United States &c - Feb 9, 1792
            This indenture made 12 Nov 1791 between Jason Thompson of Davidson County of one part and Ezekiel Norris of Sumner County of the other party. Jason Thompson conveyed unto Ezekiel Norris a tract of land containing 640 acres in Davidson County on the waters of Mill Creek being the one half of the 640 acres granted to Jason Thompson, No. 212, being the upper half of said tract. Said land joining Adam Hope's corner and John Cockrill's boundary. Containing 320 acres. Test: Lardner Clarke and Anthony Crutcher. Jan Term 1792.

Page   14 -   MOSES OLDHAM - Territory of the United States &c - Feb 10, 1792

This indenture made 18 Aug 1791 between William Mabane of Orange County, State of North Carolina of one part and Moses Oldham of Caswell County, State of North Carolina of the other part. William Mabane conveyed unto Moses Oldham a tract of land containing 1028 3/4 acres in Davidson County on the west fork of Big Harpeth River it being No. 1 of Mabane's large grant beginning at the east corner of the original survey, and running to corner of No. 5. Test: Jesse Oldham and George Oldham.   Jan Term 1792.

Page   14 -   JOHN BUCHANAN - The territory of the United States &c - Feb 10, 1792

North Carolina No. 83. We have granted unto John Buchanan, Jnr. a tract of land containing 640 acres in Davidson County on Mill Creek. Dated 17 April 1786.

Page   15 -   ELIJAH HAMILTON - Territory of the United States &c - Feb 10, 1792

This indenture made 7 Dec 1791 between John Hannah of Tennessee County of one part and Elijah Hamilton of Davidson County of the other part. John Hannah conveyed unto Elijah Hamilton a tract of land containing 320 acres in Davidson County on the south side of Cumberland River and on the waters of Harpeth River being half of a preemption granted to Samuel Moore by virtue of a Warrant No. 361. Said land joining a tract belonging to James Robertson. Test: William Deloach and Robert Heaton.   Jan Term 1792.

Page   15 -   DANIEL ROWAN - Territory of the United States &c - Feb 10, 1792

This indenture made 11 Nov 1791 between Hugh Bell of Davidson County of one part and Daniel Rowan of same place of the other part. Hugh Bell conveyed unto Daniel Rowan a tract of land containing 125 acres in Davidson County on the south side of Cumberland River near the Stone Lick and joining the lands of John Kirkpatrick and Cockrill's line. Test: David McGavock and John Bosley. Jan Term 1792.

Page   16 -   ARGOLAS JETER - Territory of the United States &c - Feb 10, 1792

This indenture made 13 Sept 1791 between Elijah Gower of Davidson County of one part and Argolas Jeter of same place of the other part. Elijah Gower conveyed unto Argolas Jeter a tract of land containing 240 acres in Davidson County on the south side of Cumberland and between Indian Creek and Pond Creek. The said land being the said Elijah Gower's share or dividend of a tract of 640 acres granted to the said Elijah Gower, Elisha Gower and William Gower by patent dated 10 July 1788. Test: Edward Lucas and James Russell. Jan Term 1792.

Page   16 -   JOHN HANNAH - Territory of the United States &c - Feb 11, 1792

This indenture made 27 Dec 1791 between Elijah Hamilton of Davidson County of one part and John Hannah of Tennessee County of the other part. Elijah Hamilton conveyed unto John Hannah a tract of land containing 87½ acres in Davidson County on the west side of Whites Creek. Said land being part of a tract of land granted by the State of North Carolina to Joshua Howard, grant dated 7 Mar 1786 and No. 115. Jan Term 1792.

Page   17 - SAMUEL SHANNON - Territory of the United States &c - Feb 11, 1792
        This indenture made 10 Nov 1791 between Robert Nelson of Tennessee
County of one part and Sanuel Shannon of Davidson County of the other part. Robert
Nelson conveyed unto Samuel Shannon a tract of land containing 640 acres on the east side
of Big Harpeth on Nelsons Creek adjoining John Nelson's line. Test: William Shaw, James
Shaw and Turner Williams. Jan Term 1792.

Page   17 - JOHN McROREY - Territory of the United States &c - Feb 18, 1792
        North Carolina No. 655. By an Act for the relief of the Officers and
Soldiers of the Continental Line, in consideration of the bravery and zeal of David Brown,
a private in the said line, granted unto John McRory, assignee of the heirs of David Brown,
a tract of land containing 640 acres in Davidson County on the south waters of Big
Harpeth about two miles east of the big south road adjoining Thomas McRoryand Andrew
Carnahan's corners. Surveyed for said John McRory Aug 4, 1786 by John Buchanan, D.S. in
consequence of a Military Warrant No. 1267. Located May 1, 1786. Dec 8, 1788.

Page   17 - THOMAS McROREY - Territory of the United States &c - Feb 18, 1792
        North Carolina No. 733. By an Act for the relief of the Officers and
Soldiers of the Continental Line, in consideration of the bravery and zeal of Abraham
Reaby, a private in the said line, granted unto Thomas McRorey, assignee of the heirs of
Abraham Reaby, a tract of land containing 640 acres in Davidson County on the west side
of Stones River. Beginning at the mouth of the first creek above the Old Station, William
More's corner and Turnbull's line. Surveyed for Thomas McRorey Apr 1786. Dated July
10, 1788.

Page   18 - BENJAMIN REED - Territory of the United States &c - Feb 18, 1792
        North Carolina No. 120. By an Act for the relief of the Officers and
Soldiers of the Continental Line, in consideration of the bravery and zeal of Benjamin
Reed, a private in the said line, granted unto Benjamin Reed a tract of land containing 640
acres in Davidson County on the waters of Little Harpeth River. Surveyed for Benjamin
Reed Dec 20, 1784 by B. William Pollock, D.S. in consequence of a Military Warrant No.
130. Located Feb 17, 1784. Mar 7, 1786.

Page   18 - THOMAS COTTON - Territory of the United States &c - Feb 18, 1792
        North Carolina No. 246. By an Act for the relief of the Officers and
Soldiers of the Continental Line, in consideration of the bravery and zeal of James Smith,
a private in the said line, granted unto Thomas Cotton, assignee of said James Smith, a
tract of land containing 640 acres in Davidson County on the south side of Cumberland and
waters of Stones River adjoining a survey of Thomas Cotton. Surveyed for Thomas Cotton
Apr 22, 1785 by John Buchanan, D.S. in consequence of a Military Warrant No. 723.
Located Aug 5, 1784. Mar 7, 1786.

Page   18 - WILLIAM STUART - Territory of the United States &c - Apr 2, 1792
        North Carolina No. 1364. By an Act for the relief of the Officers and
Soldiers of the Continental Line, in consideration of the bravery and zeal of Corbyn
Weymouth, a private in the said line, granted unto William Stuart, of said Weymouth, a
tract of land containing 360 acres in Davidson County including a Service Right of 20 acres

20 acres belonging to William Stuart on the north side of Cumberland River on the lower side of Whites Creek adjoining Peter Sides western and Amos Heaton's boundaries and a conditional line with Thomas Molloy. Surveyed for William Stuart Sept 30, 1785 by Thomas Molloy, D.S. in consequence of a Military Warrant No. 485. Located Aug 2, 1784. Nov 16, 1790.

Page   19 -   MARTIN ARMSTRONG & ANTHONY CRUTCHER - Territory of the United
                States &c - Apr 2, 1792
                North Carolina No. 427. We have given and granted unto Martin Armstrong
and Anthony Crutcher, assignees of John Ford, a lieutenant in the Continental Line, a tract
of land containing 460 acres in Davidson County on Thompsons Creek on the south side of
Cumberland River. Dated 15 Sept 1787. Signed by Richard Caswell.

Page   19 -   LARDNER CLARK - Territory of the United States &c - Apr 2, 1792
                This indenture made 10 July 1790 between James Cole Montflorence of town
of Nashville and District of Mero and Lardner Clark of the other part. James Cole
Montflorence conveyed unto Lardner Clark a tract of land containing 1560 acres in Sumner
County and District of mero on Thompsons Creek. Said land being part of the land granted
by the State to John Ford for his services in the Continental Line. 27 July 1790.

Page   19 -   THOMAS WILLIAMSON - Territory of the United States &c - Apr 4, 1792
                I, Benjamin Jostling of Davidson County am bound unto Thomas Williamson in
the sum of $1000.00 to be paid to said Williamson or heirs or executors &c , I bind myself
and my heirs, executors and every of them jointly dated 18 Nov 1791. Sold unto Thomas
Williamson 640 acres of land on Stones River and located on the waters of the east fork of
Stones River adjoining Col. Isaac Shelby's corner, located 11 Nov 1789 and held by a
Military Warrant No. 2324. Test: Lardner Clarke and Betsey Clarke. 3 Apr 1792.

Page   20 -   THOMAS WILLIAMSON - Territory of the United States &c - Apr 4, 1792
                I, Benjamin Josling of Davidson County am bound unto Thomas Williamson
of same place in the sum of $4000.00 to be paid to said Thomas Williamson of his attorney
&c. I do bind myself this 18 Nov 1791. The obligation is such that Benjamin Josling has
sold unto Thomas Williamson an entry survey of land on the waters of the east fork of
Stones River containing 640 acres adjoining Col. Isaac Shelby's north corner. Test: David
McGavock, Alex. Ewing and Lardner Clark. 3 Apr 1792.

Page   20 -   JOSEPH MEARS - Territory of the United States &c - Apr 25, 1792
                This indenture made 20 Apr 1791 between Robert Nelson of Tennessee
County of one part and Joseph Mears of Montgomery County, State of Virginia of the
other part. Robert Nelson conveyed unto Joseph Mears a tract of land containing 440
acres in Davidson County on the head of Nelsons Creek east branch of Big Harpeth
adjoining Col. John Nelson's claim. Apr Term 1792.

Page   21 -   RICHARD HARRISON - Territory of the United States &c - Apr 25, 1792
                This indenture made 11 Apr 1792 between James Bosley of Davidson County of one
part and Richard Harrison of same place of the other part. James Bosley conveyed unto
Richard Harrison a tract of land containing 100 acres in Davidson County on the south side
of Cumberland River near the Stone Lick adjoining Samuel Deason's first boundary and
Levi Hord's line. Signed by James B. Bosley. Apr Term 1792.

Page 21 - THOMAS EDMONDSON - Territory of the United States &c - Apr 26, 1792

This indenture made (date blank) 1791 between Isaac Thomas of Davidson County of one part and Thomas Edmondson of same place of the other part. Isaac Thomas conveyed unto Thomas Edmondson a tract of land containing 224 acres in Davidson County on the east fork of Mill Creek adjoining James McCutchen's corner, John Buchanan's boundary, and Robert Gilkey's boundary. Which land was granted to the said Isaac Thomas by the State of North Carolina in (blank) of the Military Service of Joshua Prewitt by patent dated 26 Nov 1789 and No. 1084. Apr Term 1792.

Page 22 - SALLIE BOYD - Territory of the United States &c - Apr 26, 1792

I, John Boyd, Sr. of Davidson County, for love and affection that I have for my daughter Sallie Boyd, do give to said Sallie and her heirs forever one negro girl, Poll, with the increase of said negro girl, one bed and furniture, one side saddle, two heifers and one steer, yearling all of which I do give my daughter Sally and her heirs forever, also one lot in the town of Nashville, No. 54. It is a Deed of Gift that if the said Sally should die leaving no legiti mate heir in and that case the property herein before mentioned shall go to her sister Nancy together with the increase of said negro girl, Poll, or in case both Sally and Nancy should die leaving no legitimate heir of their body begotten then and in that case the above property before mentioned shall go to the survivors of their brothers then living to be equally divided. This 4 Nov 1791. Test: Simon Sugg, Lewis Ford and John Rains. Apr Term 1792.

Page 22 - ADAM BRAVARD HUDSON - Territory of the United States &c - Apr 26, 1792

This indenture made 3 Oct 1791 between Benjamin Hudson of Worchester County, State of Maryland of one part and Adam Bravard Hudson of same place, farmer, of the other part witnesseth that a certain William Ross of Pitt County, State of North Carolina, had granted unto him a tract of land, No. 330, by patent dated 28 July 1787, for 640 acres of land by said grant and the said William Ross by deed duly executed and recorded in Newburn North Carolina, bearing date 14 Aug 1787, did convey unto Benjamin Hudson all that tract of land, No. 330, containing 640 acres of land in Davidson County on the ridge between Red River and Station Camp Creek. Test: John Rice and Joel Rice. Apr Term 1792.

Page 23 - JOHN BOYD - Territory of the United States &c - Apr 26, 1792

This indenture made 10 Apr 1792 between James Robertson of Davidson County of one part and John Boyd of same place of the other part. James Robertson conveyed unto John Boyd one half lot of land in the town of Nashville and known as Lot No. 9, formerly granted by Samuel Barton, Thomas Molloy and James Shaw, directors and trustees of the town of Nashville, dated 19 July 1784. Test: John Rice Jones, William Tate and John Boyd, Jr. Apr term 1792.

Page 23 - JAMES ESPEY - Territory of the United States &c - Apr 26, 1792

This indenture made 11 Apr 1792 between John Kirkpatrick of Davidson County of one part and James Espey of same place of the other part. John Kirkpatrick conveyed unto James Espey a tract of land containing 113 acres in Davidson County on the north side of Cumberland River. Which land is part of two tracts that was granted to Ephraim

McLane by patent dated 8 Oct 1787. The other granted to Green Hill dated 7 Mar 1786. Apr Term 1792.

Page   24 - DANIEL ROWAN - Territory of the United States &c - Apr 27, 1792

This indenture made 27 Feb 1792 between James Bosley of Davidson County of one part and Daniel Rowan of same place of the other part. James Bosley conveyed unto Daniel Rowan a tract of land in Davidson County , lately purchased by Daniel Rowan from Hugh Bell adjoining John Low's land. Containing 53½ acres. Test: William Rowan and Anne Rowan. Apr Term 1792.

Page   24 - SAMUEL BUCHANAN - Territory of the United States &c - Apr 27, 1792

This indenture made 4 Apr 1792 between John Tucker of Davidson County of one part and Samuel Buchanan of same place of the other part. John Tucker conveyed unto Samuel Buchanan a tract of land containing 240 acres in Davidson County on the south side of Cumberland River, the waters of Mill Creek adjoining John Tucker's Preemption, Cockrill's line. Which land is part of Preemption granted to John Tucker by patent dated 17 Apr 1786 and No. 54. Test: John Kirkpatrick and John Harlin. Apr Term 1792.

Page   25 - WILLIAM ROWAN - Territory of the United States &c - Apr 27, 1792

This indenture made 25 Feb 1792 between James Bosley and James Hoggatt, both of Davidson County of one part and William Rowan of same place of the other part. James Bosley and James Hoggatt conveyed unto William Rowan a tract of land in Davidson County on the south side of Cumberland River adjoining said river, also lands of William Thomas, Beal Bosley, Samuel Deason and John Lowe. Containing 222 acres. Test: Daniel Rowan and John Collins. Apr Term 1792.

Page   25 - JOSEPH BARTON - Territory of the United States &c - Apr 28, 1792

We, Samuel Barton, Thomas Molloy, James Shaw, Joel Rice and David Hay, directors and trustees of the town of Nashville, conveyed unto Joseph Barton the Lot No. 154 in town of Nashville. Apr Term 1792.

Page   26 - STERLING CLACK ROBERTSON - Territory of the United States &c -
          Apr 28, 1792

This indenture made 16 Mar 1792 between George Augustus Suggs of Davidson County, District of Mero, of one part and Sterling Clack Robertson of same place of the other part. George Augustus Suggs conveyed unto Sterling Clack Robertson a tract of land in Davidson County on the south side of Cumberland River and on the head waters of the first creek above Stones Lick Creek on the east side of Stones River. Containing 640 acres, which said tract of land the said George Augustus Suggs became entitled by a grant from the State of North Carolina and by virtue of a Military Warrant No. 2703. Test: Bennett Searcy, Seth Lewis and George Selden. Apr Term 1792.

Page   26 - STERLING CLACK ROBERTSON - Territory of the United States &c -
          Apr 28, 1792

This indenture made 16 Mar 1792 between George Augustus Suggs of Davidson County of one part and Sterling Clack Robertson of same place of the other part. George Augustus Suggs conveyed unto Sterling Clack Robertson a tract of land in

245

Davidson County on the south side of Cumberland River and on the head waters of the first creek above Stones Lick Creek on the east side of Stones River, containing 640 acres, which said tract of land the said Suggs became entitled to by a grant issued from the State of North Carolina, and by virute of a Military Warrant No. 2766, adjoining Aquilla Sugg's survey Warrant No. 1510. Test: Bennett Searcy, Seth Lewis and George Selden. Apr Term 1792.

Page   27 - DAVID JOHNSTON - Territory of the United States &c - Apr 20, 1792
                This indenture made 5 Jan 1791 between Robert Irwin of Mecklenburg, State of North Carolina of one part and David Johnston of Caswell County, North Carolina of the other part. Robert Irwin conveyed unto David Johnston a tract of land containing 320 acres in Davidson County on the south side of Cumberland River and waters of Little Harpeth adjoining Robert Carothers' corner, Thomas Evans' north boundary, James Crockett's corner and James Leiper's corner. Which land by survey and held by a patent granted to the said Robert Irwin dated 30 Nov 1790. In witness whereof the said Robert Irwin and Mary Irwin, his wife, hath set their hands and seals the day and year above written. Test: Ezekiel Carothers, Robert Carothers and John Neely. Apr Term 1792.

Page   27 - JOHN BOYD, JR. - Territory of the United States &c - Apr 30, 1792
                I, John Boyd, Sr., Territory of the United States south of the Ohio, for love and affection that I bear to my oldest son John Boyd, Jr., I do give grant unto John Boyd, his heirs and signs forever, one lot in the town of Nashville, No. 3 and one negro boy child named Surma(?) and one feather bed and furniture. This my Deed of Gift, that if the said John should die leaving no heir then and in that case the property herein mentioned shall go to his two oldest brothers Harrison and Richard Boyd. Share and share alike. This 10 April 1792. Test: J. Childers and Thomas Crutcher. Apr Term 1792.

Page   28 - WILLIAM HOOPER - Territory of the United States &c - Apr 30, 1792
                This indenture made 9 Apr 1792 between Absolom Hooper of Davidson County of one part and William Hooper of same place of the other part. Absolom Hooper conveyed unto William Hooper a tract of land containing 85 acres in Davidson County on the east side of Whites Creek and north side of Cumberland River. Said 85 acres of land or whatever maybe included in the above boundaries, be it more or less being part of a Preemption of 640 acres of land, granted unto Benjamin Drake as assignee originally of James Hollis of the State of North Carolina. Test: Thomas Crutcher and Michael Glaves. Apr Term 1792.

Page   28 - DEED OF GIFT TO CHARLES ROBERTSON'S CHILDREN - Territory of the
                United States &c - Apr 30, 1792
                Green County, North Carolina. I, Elijah Robertson of Davidson County have sold and conveyed unto the children of Charles Robertson, which are as follows, Ann, James, Elizabeth, Christopher, Elijah and Mary. Two tracts of land each containing 640 acres on the waters of the Caney Fork, No. 818, beginning at a white oak and dogwood, northwest corner to his tract assignee to the heirs of Matthias Dunley also No. 814. Beginning at a poplar tree, northeast corner to his tract as assignee to the heirs of William Diggs, running thence north two hundred and twenty six poles to a stake, which lands I do warrant and defend from me and my heirs forever to the above named children

said Ann, James, Elizabeth, Christopher, Elijah and Mary. This 10 Jan 1789. Signed by Elijah Robertson. Apr Term 1792.

Page 28 - STEPHEN BARTON - Territory of the United States &c - May 1, 1792
We, Samuel Barton, Thomas Molloy, James Shaw, Joel Rice and David Hay, directors and trustees of the town of Nashville, Davidson County conveyed unto Stephen Barton the lot of land No. 110 in town of Nashville. This 6 Aug 1790. Apr Term 1792.

Page 29 - ELIJAH ROBERTSON - Territory of the United States &c - May 1, 1792
We, Samuel Barton, Thomas Molloy, James Shaw, Joel Rice and David Hay, directors and trustees of the town of Nashville, conveyed unto Elijah Robertson the lot of land No. 138 in town of Nashville. This 6 Aug 1790. Apr Term 1792.

Page 29 - ELIJAH ROBERTSON - Territory of the United States &c - May 1, 1792
We, Thomas Molloy, Samuel Barton, James Shaw, Joel Rice and David Hay, directors and trustees of the town of Nashville conveyed unto Elijah Robertson the lot of land No. 136 in town of Nashville. This 6 Aug 1790.

Page 29 - EDWIN HICKMAN - Territory of the United States &c - May 1, 1792
We, Samuel Barton, Thomas Molloy, James Shaw, Jorl rice and David Hay, directors and trustees of the town of Nashville conveyed unto Edwin Hickman the lot of land No. 144 in town of Nashville. This 6 Aug 1790. Apr Term 1792.

Page 30 - DAVID ALLISON - Territory of the United States &c - May 1, 1792
We, Samuel Barton, Thomas Molloy, James Shaw, Hoel Rice and David Hay, directors and trustees of the town of Nashville, conveyed unto David Allison the lot of land No. 112 in town of Nashville. This 6 Aug 1790. Apr Term 1792.

Page 30 - DAVID ALLISON - Territory of the United States &c - May 1, 1792
We, Samuel Barton, Thomas, James Shaw, Joel Rice and David Hay, directors and trustees of town of Nashville, conveyed unto David Allison a lot of land No. 106 in town of Nashville. This 6 Aug 1790. Apr Term 1792.

Page 30 - JOHN RAINS - Territory of the United States &c - May 2, 1792
We, Samuel Barton, Thomas Molloy, James Shaw, Joel Rice and David Hay directors and trustees of the town of Nashville, conveyed unto John Rains a lot of land No. 105 in town of Nashville, This 6 Aug 1790. Apr Term 1792.

Page 31 - GEORGE WALKER - Territory of the United States &c - May 2, 1792
We, Samuel Barton, Thomas Molloy, James Shaw, Joel Rice and David Hay, directors and trustees of town of Nashville, conveyed unto George Walker the lot of land No. 147 in Nashville. This 6 Aug 1790. Apr Term 1792.

Page 31 - GEORGE WALKER - Territory of the United States &c - May 2, 1792
We, Samuel Barton, Thomas MOlloy, James Shaw, Joel Rice and David Hay, directors and trustees of the town of Nashville, conveyed unto George Walker a lot of land No. 85 in Nashville, This 6 Aug 1790. Apr Term 1792.

Page   31 -   THOMAS OVERTON - Territory of the United States &c - May 2, 1792
We, Samuel Barton, Thomas Molloy, James Shaw, Joel Rice and David Hay, directors and trustees of the town of Nashville, conveyed unto Thomas Overton a lot of land No. 104 in Nashville. This 6 Aug 1790. Apr Term 1792.

Page   32 -   DANIEL JAMES - Territory of the United States &c - May 2, 1792
We, Samuel Barton, Thomas Molloy, James Shaw, Joel Rice and David Hay, directors and trustees of town of Nashville, conveyed unto Daniel James a lot of land No. 132 in Nashville. This 6 Aug 1790. Apr Term 1792.

Page   32 -   BENNETT SEARCY - Territory of the United States &c - May 2, 1792
We, Samuel Barton, Thomas Molloy, James Shaw, Joel Rice and David Hay, directors and trustees of town of Nashville, conveyed unto Bennett Searcy a lot of land No. 128 in town of Nashville. This 6 Aug 1790. Apr term 1792.

Page   32 -   ANTHONY HART - Territory of the United States &c - May 2, 1792
We, Samuel Barton, Thomas Molloy, James Shaw, Joel Rice and David Hay, directors and trustees of town of Nashville, conveyed unto Anthony Hart a lot of land No. 109 in Nashville. This 6 Aug 1790. Apr Term 1792.

Page   33 -   VALENTINE SEVIER - Territory of the United States &c - May 2, 1792
We, Samuel Barton, Thomas Molloy, James Shaw, Joel Rice and David Hay, directors and trustees of town of Nashville, conveyed unto Valentine Sevier the lot of land No. 102 in town of Nashville. This 6 Aug 1790. Apr Term 1792.

Page   33 -   JOHN HAGUE - Territory of the United States &c - May 2, 1792
We, Samuel Barton, Thomas Molloy, James Shaw, Joel Rice and David Hay, directors and trustees of town of Nashville, conveyed unto John Hague a lot of land No. 86 in town of Nashville. This 6 Aug 1790. Apr Term 1792.

Page   33 -   EDWARD WARE HAY - Territory of the United States &c - May 3, 1792
We, Samuel Barton, Thomas Molloy, James Shaw, Joel Rice and David Hay, directors and trustees of the town of Nashville, conveyed unto Edward Ware Hay a lot of land No. 114 in town of Nashville. This 6 Aug 1790. Apr Term 1792.

Page   34 -   EDWIN HICKMAN - Territory of the United States &c - May 3, 1792
We, Samuel Barton, Thomas Molloy, James Shaw, Joel Rice and David Hay, directors and trustees of the town of Nashvile, conveyed unto Edwin Hickman a lot of land No. 134 in town of Nashville. This 6 Aug 1790. Apr term 1792.

Page   34 -   ANTHONY HART - Territory of the United States &c - May 3, 1792
We, Samuel Barton, Thomas Molloy, James Shaw, Joel Rice and David Hay, directors and trustees of town of Nashville, conveyed unto Anthony Hay a lot of land No. 141. This 6 Aug 1790. Apr Term 1792.

Page   34 -   JAMES MULHERIN - Territory of the United States &c - May 3, 1792
We, Samuel Barton, Thomas Molloy, James Shaw, Joel Rice and David Hay,

248

directors and trustees of the town of Nashville, conveyed unto James Mulherin a lot of land No. 100 in town of Nashville. This 6 Aug 1790. Apr Term 1792.

Page   35 - JOSIAH LOVE - Territory of the United States &c - May 3, 1792
        We, Samuel Barton, Thomas Molloy, James Shaw, Joel Rice and David Hay, directors and trustees of the town of Nashville, conveyed unto Josiah Love a lot of land No. 145 in town of Nashville. This 6 Aug 1790. Apr Term 1792.

Page   35 - JOSIAH LOVE - Territory of the United States &c - May 3, 1792
        We, Samuel Barton, Thomas Molloy, James Shaw, Joel Rice and David Hay, directors and trustees of the town of Nashville, conveyed unto Josiah Love a lot of land No. 87 in town of Nashville. This 6 Aug 1790. Apr Term 1792.

Page   35 - JOSIAH LOVE - Territory of the United States &c - May 3, 1792
        We, Samuel Barton, Thomas Molloy, James Shaw, Joel Rice and David Hay, directors and trustees of the town of Nashville, conveyed unto Josiah Love a lot of land No. 140 in town of Nashville. This 6 Aug 1790. Apr term 1792.

Page   36 - JOSIAH LOVE - Territory of the United States &c - May 3, 1792
        We, Samuel Barton, Thomas Molloy, James Shaw, Joel Rice and David Hay, directors and trustees of the town of Nashville, conveyed unto Josiah Love a lot of land No. 123 in Nashville. This 6 Aug 1790. Apr Term 1792.

Page   36 - JOSIAH LOVE - Territory of the United States &c - May 3, 1792
        We, Samuel Barton, Thomas Molloy, James Shaw, Joel Rice and David Hay, directors and trustees of town of Nashville, conveyed unto Josiah Love a lot of land No. 108 in town of Nashville. This 6 Aug 1790. Apr Term 1792.

Page   36 - HOWEL TATUM - Territory of the United States &c - May 4, 1792
        We, Samuel Barton, Thomas Molloy, James Shaw, Joel Rice and David Hay, directors and trustees of the town of Nashville, conveyed unto Howel Tatum a lot of land No. 92 in town of Nashville. This 6 Aug 1790. Apr Term 1792.

Page   37 - DAVID ALLISON - Territory of the United States &c - May 4, 1792
        We, Samuel Barton, Thomas Molloy, James Shaw, Joel Rice and David Hay, directors and trustees of the town of Nashville, conveyed unto David Allison a lot of land No. 99 in Nashville. This 6 Aug 1790. Apr Term 1792.

Page   37 - DAVID ALLISON - Territory of the United States - May 4, 1792
        We, Samuel Barton, Thomas Molloy, James Shaw, Joel Rice and David Hay, directors and trustees of the town of Nashville, conveyed unto David Allison a lot of land No. 142 in Nashville. This 6 Aug 1790. Apr Term 1792.

Page   37 - GEORGE WALKER - Territory of the United States &c - May 4, 1792
        We, Samuel Barton, Thomas Molloy, James Shaw, Joel Rice and David Hay, directors and trustees of the town of Nashville, conveyed unto George Walker a lot of land No. 96. This 6 Aug 1790. Apr Term 1792.

Page   38 - BENNETT SEARCY - Territory of the United States &c - May 4, 1792
        We, Samuel Barton, Thomas Molloy, James Shaw, Joel Rice and David Hay, directors and trustees of the town of Nashville, conveyed unto Bennett Searcy a lot of land No. 107. This 6 Aug 1790. Apr Term 1792.

Page   38 - BOUNDARY OF DAVIDSON AND TENNESSEE COUNTIES
        Delivered into court April Term 1792. To wit, Pursuant to an Act of the General Assembly provided for the erection of Tennessee County, wherein Robert Weakley, George McWhirter and Robert Nelson were appointed Commissioners for running the division line between the Counties of Davidson and Tennessee. Beginning on the line of Sumner County on the dividing ridge between Cumberland River and the Red River and near the head of Mansos Creek and to the lower end of Major Cofield's Plantation. Dec 29, 1790.

Page   39 -THOMAS LETTER OF ATTORNEY TO JACKSON - Territory of the United
             States &c - May 4, 1792
        I, Isaac Thomas of District of Washington, appoint Andrew Jackson of the District of Mero, my lawful attorney for me and in my name to transact all business for me to make a conveyance to Thomas Edmonson a tract of land containing 274 acres, agreeable to a bond given by me the said Isaac Thomas to Thomas Blackamore and signed to the said Thomas Edmonson. This 17 Aug 1791. Test: Josiah Love. Apr Term 1792.

Page   39 - JAMES G. BREHON - Territory of the United States &c - May 15, 1792
        North Carolina No. 951. By an Act for the relief of the Officers and Soldiers of the Continental Line, in consideration of the bravery and zeal of Jacob Strain, a private in the said line, granted unto James G. Brehon, assignee of said Jacob Strain, a tract of land containing 640 acres in Davidson County on the waters of Mulherin Creek adjoining William Tuton's tract and John Brown's corner. Surveyed for said Brehon Nov 10, 1788 by James Mulherin, D.S. in consequence of a Military Warrant No. 3498. Located Nov 5, 1788. May 18, 1789.

Page   39 - JAMES G. BREHON - Territory of the United States &c - May 15, 1792
        North Carolina No. 950. By an Act for the relief of the Officers and Soldiers of the Continental Line, in consideration of the bravery and zeal of William Johnson, a private in the said line, granted unto James G. Brehon, assignee of said William Johnson, a tract of land containing 640 acres in Davidson County on the Caney Fork adjoining James Mulherin's tract. Surveyed for said Brehon Nov 10, 1788 by James Mulherin, D.S. in consequence of a Military Warrant No. 3388. Located Mar 5, 1788. May 18, 1789.

Page   40 - JAMES G. BREHON - Territory of the United States &c - May 16, 1792
        North Carolina No. 998. By an Act for the relief of the Officers and Soldiers of the Continental Line, in consideration of the bravery and zeal of Author Venters, a private in the said line, granted unto James Glocester Brehon, assignee of the heirs of said Venters, a tract of land containing 640 acres in Davidson County on the north side of Cumberland River beginning on the north side of Red River about five miles below the Old Station. Surveyed for said Brehon July 10, 1799 by William Crutcher, D.S. in

consequence of a Military Warrant No. 2890. Located June 5, 1788. May 18, 1789.

Page   40 -   JAMES G. BREHON - Territory of the United States &c - May 16, 1792
                North Carolina No. 1001. By an Act for the relief of the Officers and
Soldiers of the Continental Line, in consideration of the bravery and zeal of Demsey
Archer, a private in the said line, granted unto James G. Brehon, assignee of the heirs of
said Demsey Archer, a tract of land containing 640 acres in Sumner County on the waters
of Red Riverabout three miles from where William Thacker now lives. Surveyed for James
G. Brehon July 12, 1788 by William Crutcher, D.S. in consequence of a Military Warrant
No. 2899. Located June 5, 1788. May 18, 1789.

Page   40 -   JAMES G. BREHON - Territory of the United States &c - May 16, 1792
                North Carolina No. 999. By an Act for the relief of the Officers and
Soldiers of the Continental Line, in consideration of the bravery and zeal of Andrew
Skepton, a private in the said line, granted unto James Gloster Brehon a tract of land
containing 640 acres in Davidson County adjoining David Henry's Preemption. Surveyed
for said Brehon (date blank) by Anthony Foster, D.S. in consequence of a Military Warrant
No. 2882. Located Feb 6, 1786. May 18, 1789.

Page   41 -   JAMES G. BREHON - Territory of the United States &c - May 17, 1792
                North Carolina No. 1002. By an Act for the relief of the Officers and
Soldiers of the Continental Line, in consideration of the bravery and zeal of Jacob
Witherington, a private in the said line, granted unto James Gloster Brehon, assignee of
the heirs of Jacob Witherington, a tract of land containing 640 acres in Davidson County
on the waters of Red River on the trace from the Old Station to Sulphur Creek
Settlement. Sueveyed for James G. Brehon July 10, 1788 by William Crutcher, D.S. in
consequence of a Military Warrant No. 2892. Located June 5, 1788. May 18, 1789.

Page   41 -   JAMES G. BREHON - Territory of the United States &c - May 17, 1792
                North Carolina No. 1003. By an Act for the relief of the Officers and
Soldiers of the Continental Line, in consideration of the bravery and zeal of John Stone, a
private in the said line, granted unto James G. Brehon, assignee of the heirs of said John
Stone, a tract of land containing 640 acres in Davidson County on the north side of
Cumberland River on the waters of Sulphur Fork of Red River. Surveyed for James G.
Brehon Oct 10, 1788 by Anthony Foster, D.S. in consequence of a Military Warrant No.
2881. Located Oct 3, 1786. May 18, 1789.

Page   41 -   JAMES G. BREHON - Territory of the United States &c - May 17, 1792
                North Carolina No. 935. By an Act for the relief of the Officers and
Soldiers of the Continental Line, in consideration of the bravery and zeal of Thomas
Joyner, a lieutenant in the said line, granted unto James G. Brehon, assignee of said
Thomas Joyner, a tract of land containing 2560 acres in Davidson County on the south side
of Cumberland River about eight or nine miles above the Big Salt Lick on the said river
and surveyed for said James Gloster Brehon Feb 8, 1786 by Edwin Hickman, D.S. in
consequence of a Military Warrant No. 3551. Located Jan 23, 1786. May 18, 1789.

Page 42 - JAMES G. BREHON - Territory of the United States &c - May 17, 1792
          North Carolina No. 1004. By an Act for the relief of the Officers and
Soldiers of the Continental Line, in consideration of the bravery and zeal of Absalom
Turner, a private in the said line, granted unto James G. Brehon, assignee of the heirs of
Absalom Turner, a tract of land containing 640 acres in Davidson County adjoining James
Cole Montflorence on the dividing ridge between the head waters of the Sulphur Fork and
Gaspers Creek. Surveyed for James Gloster Brehon Dec 30, 1786 by Robert Ewing, D.S. in
consequence of a Military Warrant No. 2887. Located Sept 30, 1786. May 18, 1789.

Page 42 - JAMES G. BREHON - Territory of the United States &c - May 17, 1792
          North Carolina No. 992. By an Act for the relief of the Officers and
Soldiers of the Continental Line, in consideration of the bravery and zeal of Charles
Brown, a sergeant in the said line, granted unto James G. Brehon, assignee of the heirs of
Charles Brown, a tract of land containing 1000 acres in Davidson County on the north side
of Cumberland River on the waters of Red River about one mile west of the Old Station.
Surveyed for James Gloster Brehon July 12, 1788 by William Crutcher, D.S. in consequence
of a Military Warrant No. 3331. Located June 5, 1788. May 16, 1789.

Page 42 - THOMAS GLOSTER - Territory of the United States &c - May 17, 1792
          North Carolina No. 1016. By an Act for the relief of the Officers and
Soldiers of the Continental Line, in consideration of the bravery and zeal of Mallica Dan,
a private in the said line, granted unto Thomas Gloster, assignee of the heirs of Mallica
Dan, a tract of land containing 640 acres in Davidson County on the north side of
Cumberland River and on the south side of Red River including a remarkable Cave Spring
about three miles below the Old Station. Surveyed for Thomas Gloster by William
Crutcher, D.S. in consequence of a Military Warrant No. 3098. Located June 5, 1788.
May 18, 1789.

Page 43 - FREDERICK STUMP - Territory of the United States &c - June 4, 1792
          This indenture made 3 July 1791 between James Cole Montflorence of
Davidson County of one part and Frederick Stump of same place of the other part. James
Cole Montflorence conveyed unto Frederick Stump all that lot in the town of Nashville,
next the Courthouse Lot No. 8 of one acre opposite Mr. Deaderick's store. Wit: Johnston
O'Neal. 23 May 1792.

Page 43 - JOHN BARROW - Territory of the United States &c - June 4, 1792
          North Carolina No. 85. By an Act for the relief of the Officers and Soldiers
of the Continental Line, in consideration of the bravery and zeal of Samuel Moore, one of
the guards to the Commissioners, granted unto John Barrow, assignee of the said Samuel
Moore, a tract of land containing 320 acres in Davidson County on the north side of
Cumberland River. Surveyed for John Barrow July 10, 1785 by James Sanders, D.S. in
consequence of a Warrant No. 388. Entry Apr 4, 1784. July 10, 1788.

Page 43 - GEORGE A. SUGG - Territory of the United States &c - June 4, 1792
          North Carolina No. 989. By an Act for the relief of the Officers and
Soldiers of the Continental Line, in consideration of the bravery and zeal of Isaac Benford,
a private in the said line, granted unto George Augustus Sugg, assignee of the heirs of said

252

Isaac Benford, a tract of land containing 640 acres in Davidson County on the south side of Cumberland River on the headwaters of the west fork of the first creek above Stones Lick on the east side of Stones River. Surveyed for said Sugg May 14, 1788 by William Nash, D.S. in consequence of a Military Warrant No. 2703. Located Apr 2, 1788. May 10, 1789.

Page   44 -   GEORGE A. SUGG - Territory of the United States &c - June 4, 1792
          North Carolina No. 909. By an Act for the relief of the Officers and Soldiers of the Continental Line, in consideration of the bravery and zeal of Applewhite Sanders, a private in the said line, granted unto George Augustus Sugg, assignee of the heirs of said Sanders, a tract of land containing 640 acres in Davidson County on the headwaters of the first creek above Stones Lick Creek on the east side of Stones River. Surveyed for George A. Sugg Mar 11, 1788 by William Nash, D.S. in consequence of a Military Warrant No. 2766. Located Apr 3, 1788. May 18, 1789.

Page   44 -   BENJAMIN SHEPPARD - Territory of the United States &c - June 6, 1792
          North Carolina No. 366. By an Act for the relief of the Officers and Soldiers of the Continental Line, in consideration of the bravery and zeal of Frederick Pugh, a private in the said line, granted unto Benjamin Sheppard, assignee of the heirs of Frederick Pugh, a tract of land containing 640 acres in Davidson County on both sides of the east fork of Drakes Creek of Big Barren River adjoining a survey of 640 acres of said Sheppard, No. 2338. Surveyed for said Sheppard Feb 6, 1786 by Edwin Hickman, D.S. in consequence of a Military Warrant No. 2330. Located Feb 7, 1786. Sept 7, 1787.

Page   44 -   JESSEE COBB - Territory of the United States &c - June 6, 1792
          North Carolina No. 664. By an Act for the relief of the Officers and Soldiers of the Continental Line, in consideration of the bravery and zeal of Thomas Lain, a private in the said line, granted unto Jessee Cobb, assignee of said Lain, a tract of land containing 274 acres in Davidson County on Brush Creek adjoining Lewis' corner. Surveyed for said Cobb Mar 15, 1787 by Robert Nelson, D.S. in consequence of a Military Warrant No. 1261. Located July 8, 1786. Dec 8, 1787.

Page   45 -   BRADLEY GAMBREL - Territory of the United States &c - June 7, 1792
          North Carolina No. 1242. By an Act for the relief of the officers and Soldiers of the Continental Line, in consideration of the services of Martin Armstrong, surveyor, granted unto Bradley Gambrel, assignee of said Armstrong, a tract of land containing 64 acres in Davidson County on Mill Creek adjoining George Neville's Guard Right and John Buchanan's line, Thomas Hardiman's line, and James Menees' corner and also David G(illegible)'s line. Surveyed for said Gambrel Nov 23, 1789 by John Buchanan, D.S. in consequence of the said Service Right. Entered (no date given). Nov 16, 1790.

Page   45 -   BRADLEY GAMBREL - Territory of the United States &c - June 7, 1792
          North Carolina No. 1350. By an Act for the relief of the Officers and Soldiers of the Continental Line, in consideration of the bravery and zeal of George Granston, a private in the said line, granted unto Bradley Gambrel, assignee of the heirs of George Granston, a tract of land containing 640 acres in Davidson County on the waters of Bartons Creek adjoining Jacob Cassellman's corner. Surveyed for said Gambrel Nov 11,

1788. Nov 16, 1790.

Page   45 - SAMUEL BARTON - Territory of the United States &c - June 17, 1792
North Carolina No. 105. By an Act for the relief of the Officers and Soldiers of the Continental Line, in consideration of the services of Martin Armstrong, surveyor, granted unto Samuel Barton, assignee of said Armstrong, a tract of land containing 100 acres in Davidson County on the headwaters of Hays Creek adjoining Dr. Fergus' south boundary line, being William Madries' north east corner. Surveyed for Samuel Barton Feb 1, 1791 by John Buchanan, D.S. in consequence of the Service Right of said Armstrong. Entered June 9, 1789. The ___ day of Dec 1791.

Page   46 - SAMPSON WILLIAMS - Territory of the United States &c - July 17, 1792
This indenture made 28 Apr 1792 between Thomas Thompson of Davidson County of one part and Sampson Williams of same place of the other part. Thomas Thompson conveyed unto Sampson Williams a tract of land containing 170 acres in Davidson County on waters of Browns Creek adjoining Johnsthan Drake's corner and Jason Thompson's tract of land and Thomas Thompson's land. Said land being part of said Thompson's Preemption by patent dated 10 July 1788. Test: John Overton. July Term 1792.

Page   46 - SHERROD BARROW - Territory of the United States &c - July 17, 1792
North Carolina No. 1372. By an Act for the relief of the Officers and Soldiers of the Continental Line, in consideration of the bravery and zeal of Charles Hensel, a private in the said line, granted unto Sherrod Barrow, assignee of the heirs of said Hensel, a tract of land containing 640 acres in Davidson County on the south side of Cumberland River and on the waters of the Big Harpeth adjoining Col. Hardy Murfree's Military Claim of 5760 acres. Apr 20, 1791.

Page   47 - PHILIP SHUTE - Territory of the United States &c - July 17, 1792
This indenture made 31 May 1792 between Peter Turney of Sumner County of one part and Phillip Shute of Davidson County of the other part. Peter Turney conveyed unto Philip Shute a tract of land containing 540 acres in Davidson County on the south side of Cumberland River adjoining Isaac Johnson's line, a conditional line between said Turney and Mark Robertson and also a line between Turney and George Freeland. Which land is part of a Preemption of 640 acres granted to said Turney by the State of North Carolina by patent dated Apr 17, 1786 and No. 65. Test: Andrew Ewing and Isaac Roberts. July Term 1792.

Page   47 - HENRY BARROW - Territory of the United States &c - July 17, 1792
North Carolina No. 1373. By an Act for the relief of the Officers and Soldiers of the Continental Line, in consideration of the bravery and zeal of John Pursley, a private in the said line, granted unto Henry Barrow, assignee of the heirs of John Pursley, a tract of land containing 640 acres in Davidson County on the south side of Cumberland River adjoining Clement Hall's Military Claim of 3840 acres. Dated Apr 20, 1791.

Page   48 - SIMON SUGG - Territory of the United States &c - July 17, 1792
This indenture made 20 June 1791 between George A. Sugg of Davidson

County of one part and Simon Sugg of same place of the other part. George A. Sugg conveyed unto Simon Sugg three tract of land containing 640 acres each on the headwaters of the Marrow Bone adjoining a tract of Frederick Fisher's tract of 640 acres. The other tract adjoining Frederick Fisher's tract. The whole containing 1920 acres of land, including the house and improvements, I mean to live on, on the headwaters of Marrow Bone and located and surveyed by Anthony Foster. Test: William Sugg and David Shaffer. July Term 1792.

Page   48 -   JACOB ROCHEL - Territory of the United States &c - July 17, 1792
            North Carolina No. 226.   By an Act for the relief of the Officers and Soldiers of the Continental Line, in consideration of the bravery and zeal of Josiah Rochel, a private in the said line, granted unto Jacob Rochel an heir of Josiah Rochel, a tract of land containing 640 acres in Davidson County between Red River and Sulphur Fork adjoining Sergeant Renold's line and John Reynold's line. Surveyed for said Jacob Rochel Sept 24, 1784 by James Sanders, D.S. in consequence of a Military Warrant No. 727. Located Sept 7, 1784. Mar 9, 1786.

Page   49 -   MATHEW TALBOT - Territory of the United States &c - July 18, 1792
            This indenture made 6 May 1792 between Eleaser Hamilton of Davidson County of one part and Mathew Talbot of same place of the other part. Eleaser Hamilton conveyed unto Mathew Talbot a tract of land containing 65 acres in Davidson County on both sides of Whites Creek, the north side of Cumberland River adjoining Robert Weakley's corner and Elijah Hamilton's corner. (One spelling Eleazer Hamilton). Test: Thomas Talbot, alias. July Term 1792.

Page   49 -   WILLIAM WICUFF - Territory of the United States &c - July 18, 1792
            This indenture made 18 May 1791 between Lardner Clarke, Esq. of town of Nashville, Davidson County of one part and William Wicuff, Jnr. of the same place, merchant, of the other part.   Lardner Clarke conveyed unto William Wicuff all that valuable plantation and tract of land in Davidson County including the forks of Mill Creek on the south side of Cumberland River and above the town of Nashville adjoining Ebenezer Titus' corner and John Shehon's corner, containing 600 acres of land, being part of that Preemption of 640 acres granted by the State of North Carolina to the said Lardner Clarke as assignee of John Wilson. Said tract belonging unto the said William Wicuff, Jr.'s heirs and assigns forever. May Term 1792.

Page   50 -   WILLIAM WICUFF - Territory of the United States &c - July 18, 1792
            This indenture made 18 May 1791 between Lardner Clark, Esq. of town of Nashville, Davidson County of one part and William Wicuff of same place of the other part. Lardner Clark conveyed unto William Wicuff all that tract of land in Davidson County on the west fork of Mill Creek, containing 96 acres. Adjoining said Clark's Preemption as assignee of Jos. Wilson and John Foreman's cornerand Peter Catron's line. Test: Ho. Tatum and James C. Montflorence. July Term 1792.

Page   50 -   WILLIAM HAY - Territory of the United States &c - July 21, 1792
            This indenture made 24 May 1792 between Samuel Barton of Davidson County of one part and William Hay of same place of the other part. Samuel Barton conveyed

unto William Hay a tract of land containing 100 acres in Davidson County on the waters of Browns Creek adjoining Barton's Preemption whereon said Barton now lives, and Andrew Ewing's corner. Test: Andrew Ewing and Samuel McCutchen. July Term 1792.

Page   51 -   PETER BACOTE - Territory of the United States &c - July 21, 1792
            North Carolina No. 46. By an Act for the relief of the officers and Soldiers of the Continental Line, in consideration of the bravery and zeal of Peter Bacote, a captain in the said line, granted unto said peter Bacote a tract of land containing 3840 acres in Davidson County on the north side of Duck River. Beginning on the bank of a pond supposed to be where the river formerly ran and about five or six miles above the mouth of said river Elijah Moore's corner. Surveyed for said Peter Bacote Aug 12, 1785 by Henry Rutherford, D.S. in consequence of a Military Warrant No. 265. Located May 9, 1785. Mar 14, 1786.

Page   51 -   HARDY MURFREE - Territory of the United States &c - July 21, 1792
            This indenture made 21 Jan 1791 between Elisha Hunt of Southampton County, State of Virginia, of the one part and Hardy Murfree of Hertford County, North Carolina, of the other part. Elisha Hunt conveyed unto Hardy Murfree a tract of land containing 640 acres on the head of the Lonf Fork of Sycamore Creek and headwaters of Whites Creek on Buffalo River. Said land being granted to the said Elisha Hunt for his services as a soldier in the Continental Line of State of North Carolina, grant dated Mar 14, 1786, No. 141. Test: William Figures and John Crier and alias. July Term 1792.

Page   52 -   JOHN OVERTON & BENNETT SEARCY - Territory of the United States &c - July 23, 1792
            This indenture made 10 July 1792 between Sampson Williams, Sheriff of Davidson County of one part and John Overton and bennett Searcy of Davidson County of the other part. Whereas a certain Frederick Fisher of Davidson County files a bill of injunction against a certain Samuel Buchanan on a judgment that the said Buchanan obtained against said Fisher for the sum of 16 £ and 16 shillings at Nov Term 1791. Said Sheriff levied upon the goods and chattels of said Frederick Fisher and 640 acres in Davidson County on the headwaters of the dry fork of Whites Creek. Which said land was entered by virtue of a Military Warrant issued by the State of North Carolina and entered 18 Sept 1790 in the name of Frederick Fisher, page 367, which said land was conveyed unto John Overton and Bennett Searcy. July Term 1792.

Page   53 -   THOMAS SHANNON - Territory of the Unites States &c - July 23, 1792
            This indenture made 10 July 1792 between John Crow of Montgomery County, State of Virginia of one part and Thomas Shannon of same place of the other part. John Crow conveyed unto Thomas Shannon a tract of land containing 320 acres in Davidson County on the fork of Whites Creek. Land being part of a tract of 640 acres granted unto said John Crow by patent. Signed by John Crow, L.S. by Samuel Shannon, his attorney in fact. This 15 Sept 1791. Proven by John Mears. July Term 1792.

Page   54 -   GEORGE PIRTLE - Territory of the United States &c - July 23, 1792
            This indenture made 10 July 1792 between John Whitesell of Sumner County, District of Mero of one part and George Pirtle of Davidson County of other part. John

Whitesell conveyed unto George Pirtle a tract of land containing 640 acres in Davidson County being a Military Claim surveyed for said John Whitesell, assignee of the heirs of William Cane, in Davidson County on both sides of Smith's Fork a branch of Caney Fork. July Term 1792.

Page   54 -   CHLOE GOODMAN - Territory of the United States &c - July 23, 1792
North Carolina No. 1885. By an Act for the relief of the Officers and Soldiers of the Continental Line, in consideration of the bravery and zeal of William Goodman, a private in the said line, granted unto Chloe Goodman, heiress of the said William Goodman, a tract of land containing 640 acres in Davidson County on Big Harpeth River adjoining Thomas Molloy and George Neville's corner. Surveyed for Chloe Goodman Sept 11, 1785 by Thomas Molloy, D.S. in consequence of a Military Warrant No. 706. Located Aug 2, 1784. Nov 16, 1790.

Page   55 -   DAVID SHELBY - Territory of the United States &c - July 24, 1792
This indenture made 14 Feb 1792 between Robert Nelson of Tennessee County of one part and David Shelby of Sumner County of the other part. Robert Nelson conveyed unto David Shelby a tract of land containing 640 acres on the east side of Harper and north side of Nelsons Creek on the north of land that said Nelson sold John Edmondson. Test: Robert Weakley. July Term 1792.

Page   55 -   JOHN JOHNSTON - Territory of the United States &c - July 5, 1792
This indenture made 5 Feb 1791 between Minos Cannon of Guilford County, State of North Carolina of one part and John Johnston of Davidson COunty of the other part. Minos Cannon conveyed unto John Johnston a tract of land containing 200 acres in Davidson County on the waters of the east fork of Mill Creek near the bridge joining the waters west side of the Old Hurricane. Test: Oliver Williams, William Armstrong and John Johnston. July Term 1792.

Page   56 -   SIMON SUGG - Territory of the United States &c - July 25, 1792
I, George A. Sugg of Davidson County sold unto Simon Sugg of same place all that part of the lot known by No. 24 in town of Nashville on Cumberland River which was deeded by James Robertson to John Sappington and from the said Sappington to the said George A. Sugg, which part joins Lot No. 25. This 15 Dec 1791. Test: William Sugg and David Shaffer. July Term 1792.

Page   56 -   THOMAS MOLLOY - Territory of the United States &c - July 25, 1792
This indenture made 25 Aug 1791 between John Armstrong and William Poindexter, executors of Thomas Evans, late of Surry County, State of North Carolina of one part and Thomas Molloy of the territory of the United States south of the Ohio, of the other part. John Armstrong and William Poindexter conveyed unto Thomas Molloy a tract of land containing 768 acres in Davidson County on the waters of Big Harpeth River adjoining John Cockrill's Preemption and Thomas Spencer's corner and James Crockett's line. Said land being part of a tract of 3840 acres granted by the State of North Carolina to Thomas Evans for his services as a captain in the Continental Line, grant dated Sept 15, 1787 and No. 503. Test: John Gatling and John Terry. July Term 1792.

Page   57 -   THOMAS HICKMAN - Territory of the United States &c - July 25, 1792
                This indenture made 10 July 1791 between James Hoggatt of Davidson
County of one part and Thomas Hickman of same place of the other part. James Hoggatt
conveyed unto Thomas Hickman a tract of land containing 70 acres in Davidson County on
the north side of Cumberland River and on Sulphur Creek and adjoining the lands lately sold
by James Hoggatt to Thomas Hickman and Ezekiel Smith's entry. Said land being the full
contents of a patent by the State of North Carolina to the said James Hoggatt the 30Nov
1790. Test: Absolom Hooper and Robert Weakley. July Term 1792.

Page   57 -   CHARLES PARKER - Territory of the United States &c - July 25, 1792
                This indenture made 6 July 1791 between Absolom Hooper of Davidson
County of the one part and Charles Parker of same place of the other part.   Absolom
Hooper conveyed unto Charles Parker a tract of land containing 118 acres in Davidson
County on the east fork of Whites Creek on the north side of Cumberland River adjoining a
corner of a 640 acre Preemption of Benjamin Drake, assignee originally of James Hollis by
the State of North Carolina, and to a corner of land whereon George Cook now lives. Test:
Ennis Hooper and Joseph Hooper. July Term 1792.

Page   58 -   WILLIAM WALTON - Territory of the United States &c - July 25, 1792
                This indenture made the __ of July 1792 between Sampson Williams, Sheriff
of Davidson County, of one part and William Walton of same place of the other part.
Sampson Williams was directed to sell 200 acres of land being part of a tract containing
500 acres, which late he recovered against Ransom Savage for the sum of 20£ before John
Davidson, Esq.one of the Justices of the said Davidson County, also the sum of 19 shillings
and 3 pence cost of the suit. Said Williams conveyed unto William Walton, a tract of 200
acres in Davidson County on the north side of Cumberland on a small fork of Kaspers
Creek called Lillegible) Fork adjoining Simon Kuykendall's boundary. Sold 27 Feb 1790.
July Term 1792.

Page   59 -   WILLIAM WICUFF - Territory of the United States &c - July 26, 1792
                This indenture made 18 May 1791 between Lardner Clark, Esq. of the town of
Nashville of one part and William Wicuff, Jr. of same place of the other part. Lardner
Clark conveyed unto William Wicuff, Jr. a tract of land containing 320 acres in Davidson
County on the forks of Mill Creek of the south side of Cumberland River adjoining the
Preemption granted to said Lardner Clark as assignee of James Wilson and Peter Catron's
boundary. Test: Howell Tatum and James Cole Montflorence. May Term 1792.

Page   59 -   DAVID EARHART - Territory of the United States &c - July 26, 1792
                This indenture made 9 July 1792 between Absolom Hooper of Davidson
County of one part and David Earhart of same place of the other part. Absolom Hooper
conveyed unto David Earhart a tract of land containing 48 acres in Davidson County on the
waters of east fork of Whites Creek on the north side of Cumberland River. Beginning on
Hooper's line of the tract whereon he now lives. Said land being the southeast corner of a
Preemption of 640 acres granted to Benjamin Drake, Senior, assignee of originally of James
Hollis by the State of North Carolina. Test: John Tremble and Ennis Hooper. July Term
1792.

Page   60 -   THOMAS COTTON - Territory of the United States &c - July 26, 1792

This indenture made 1 Aug 1787 between Benjamin Reed of Hertford County, North Carolina of one part and Thomas Cotton, Jur. of same place of the other part. Benjamin Reed conveyed unto Thomas Cotton, Jun. a tract of land containing 640 acres in Davidson County on the waters of Little Harpeth River. Which land was granted unto Benjamin Reed as a soldier in the North Carolina Continental service, by grant dated Mar 7, 1786, No. 120. Test: H. Murfree, George Swope and John Gatling. July Term 1792.

Page   60 -   HENRY RUTHERFORD - Territory of the United States &c - July 26, 1792

North Carolina No. 7. By an Act for the relief of the Officers and Soldiers of the Continental Line, in consideration of the services of Col. Martin Armstrong, surveyor, granted unto Henry Rutherford, assignee of said Armstrong, a tract of land containing 320 acres in Davidson County on Sycamore Creek at the place where the lower path crosses said creek joining a survey of 1645 acres on the lower side. Surveyed for Henry Rutherford Feb 9, 1786 by R. Weakley, D.S. in consequence of a Service Right. Located Nov 2, 1785. Oct 8, 1787.

Page   61 -   JOHN CUMMINS - Territory of the United States &c - July 26, 1792

This indenture made 11 Jan 1792 between William Wicuff, Junior of Monmouth County, State of New Jersey of the one part and John Cummins of Sumner County of the other part. William Wicuff, Jun. conveyed unto John Cummins a tract of land containing 600 acres in Davidson County on Mill Creek, being the same conveyed by Lardner Clark, Esq. to the said William Wicuff by deed dated 8 May 1791 in the forks of Mill Creek, being also part of the tract commonly called Wilson's Preemption granted to Lardner Clark, Esq. by grant dated Apr 16, 1786, also one other tract of land joining the above containing 96 acres granted to said Lardner Clark by the State of North Carolina by grant dated Oct 8, 1787 and conveyed by said Lardner Clark to said William Wicuff by deed dated May 18, 1791. Test: John Deaderick and Bennett Searcy. May Term 1792

Page   61 -   FREDERICK STUMP - Territory of the United States &c - July 26, 1792

This indenture made 2 Apr 1792 between Frederick Stump, Jr. of Tennessee County of one part and Frederick Stump. Senior, of Davidson County of the other part. Frederick Stump, Jr. conveyed unto Frederick Stump, Sen. a tract of land containing 640 acres in Davidson County on Whites Creek adjoining Frederick Stump, Senior's line. Said land being granted to the said Frederick Stump. Junior, by the State of North Carolina as heirs of Jacob Stump, deceased. Grant dated Nov 17, 1790, No. 301. Test: Thomas Molloy and Martha Molloy. July Term 1792.

Page   62 -   JAMES ROBERTSON - Territory of the United States &c - July 26, 1792

This indenture made 20 June 1792 between Sampson Williams of Davidson County of one part and James Robertson of same place of the other part. Sampson Williams conveyed unto James Robertson a tract of land containing 2000 acres, being part of a tract of 2560 acres the property of Thomas Clark. Said land being a judgment against said Thomas Clark. Land being on on the south side of Cumberland River opposite the upper end of the first island above the mouth of Red River, Letia Archer's corner. James Robertson bought said land 30 Sept 1789. Sampson Williams was Sheriff of Davidson County. July Term 1792.

Page   62 -   ELISHA HUNT - Territory of the United States &c - July 27, 1792
                North Carolina No. 141. By an Act for the relief of the Officers and
Soldiers of the COntinental Line, in consideration of the bravery and zeal of Elisha Hunt, a
private in the said line, granted unto said Elisha Hunt a tract of land containing 640 acres
in Davidson County on the head of the Long Fork of Sycamore Creek and head waters of
Whites Creek. Surveyed for Elisha Hunt Mar 10, 1785 by Henry Rutherford, D.S. in
consequence of a Military Warrant No. 117. Located Dec 6, 1784. Mar 14, 1786.

Page   63 -   THOMAS MOLLOY - Territory of the United States &c - July 27, 1792
                This indenture made 4 Apr 1792 between William Walton of Sumner County
of the one part and Thomas Molloy of Davidson County of the other part. William Walton
conveyed unto Thomas Molloy a tract of land containing 274 acres in Davidson County
about three miles from Nashville on the waters of Richland Creek adjoining the Preemption
of Francis Hodge and also John Cockrill's line, Peter Turney's line. Said land being granted
to Richard Flow(illegible) by the State of North Carolina for his services as a soldier in the
Continental line, grant dated Feb 16, 1786 and No. 9. Test: Jessee Glasgow, Henry Glisson
and Daniel Ross. July Term 1792.

Page   63 -   WILLIAM WALTON - Territory of the United States &c - July 27, 1792
                This indenture made this ___ Jan 1792 between Simon Kuykendall of Sumner
County of one part and William Walton of Davidson County of the other part. Simon
Kuykendall conveyed unto William Walton a tract of land containing 46½ acres in Davidson
County on the south side of Manskers Creek. Test: Jesse Glasgow and James McDaniel.
July Term 1792.

Page   64 -   MATHEW TALBOT - Territory of the United States &c - July 27, 1792
                This indenture made 18 May 1792 between John Marney and James Russell of
Davidson County of the one part and Mathew Talbot of the other part. Said Marney and
Russell conveyed unto Mathew Talbot a tract of land containing 255 acres in Davidson
County on both sides of Whites Creek, the north side of Cumberland adjoining Thomas
James' line and on the banks of Heatons Creek. Test: J. Childers, Pleasant Lockett and
William DeLoach. July Term 1792.

Page   64 -   JOHN MOTHERAL - Territory of the United States &c - July 27, 1792
                North Carolina No. 1225. By an Act for the relief of the Officers and
Soldiers of the Continental Line, in consideration of the bravery and zeal of Shadrach
Roberts, a private in the said line, granted unto John Motheral, assignee of said Shadrach
Roberts, a tract of land containing 228 acres in Sumner County on the north side of
Cumberland River adjoining the lower corner of Gideon Lamb's tract of 6171 acres.
Surveyed for said John Motheral July 5, 1790 by James Mulherin, D.S. in consequence of a
Military Warrant No. 1826. Located Mar 9, 1790. Nov 16, 1790.

Page   65 -   DANIEL ROSS - Territory of the United States &c - July 28, 1792
                This indenture made 10 July 1791 between Thomas Molloy of Davidson
County of one part and Daniel Ross of the other part. Thomas Molloy conveyed unto
Daniel Ross a tract of land containing 86 acres in Davidson County on Whites Creek near
the mouth thereof and joining Robert Weakley's line, James Hamilton's boundary, Mark

Brown Sappington's line. Said land being part of a tract of 640 acres granted by the State of North Carolina to said Thomas Molloy, grant dated Aug 11, 1789 and No. 1043 and also part of a tract of 200 acres granted by said State to Robert Nelson and by him to said Thomas Molloy. Test: Andrew Ewing and John Sappington. July Term 1792.

Page   65 - WILLIAM WICUFF TO HOWEL TATUM - Letter   of   Attorney   &c   -
            July 28, 1792
            I, William Wicuff of Monmouth County, State of New Jersey, appoint Howel Tatum of Davidson County, District of Mero, my lawful attorney for me in my name to transact all my business in the District of Mero, between Lardner Clark and muself. This 23 Apr 1791. Test: John Curtis. May Term 1792.

Page   66 - WILLIAM WICUFF TO HOWEL TATUM - A Letter of Attorney -
            July 28, 1792
            I, William Wicuff, Junior of the County of Monmouth, State of New Jersey appoint Howel Tatum of Davidson County my true and lawful attorney for me and in my name to make and execute a deed of conveyance unto John Cummins for 640 acres of land on Mill Creek in Davidson County and being part of that tract known by the name of Wilson's Preemption also to convey in my name either by deed unto Dr. James White of of Davidson County for 274 acres of land including Russell Gower's houses on the south side of Cumberland River. This 23 Apr 1791. Test: John Curtis. May Term 1792.

Page   66 - AQUILLA SUGG - Territory of the United States &c - July 30, 1792
            North Carolina No. 890. By an Act for the relief of the Officers and Soldiers of the Continental Line, in consideration of the bravery and zeal of Patrick Martin, a sergeant in the said line, granted unto Aquilla Sugg, assignee of the heirs of Patrick Martin, a tract of land containing 1000 acres in Davidson County on both sides of the main east fork of Stones River adjoining Reed's corner. Surveyed for Aquilla Sugg Mar 21, 1788 by William Nash in consequence of a Military Warrant No. 1824. Located Mar 1, 1786. Jan 17, 1789.

Page   66 - AQUILLA SUGG - Territory of the United States &c - July 30, 1792
            North Carolina No. 907. By an Act for the relief of the Officers and Soldiers of the Continental Line, in consideration of the bravery and zeal of Johnston Cherry, a private in the said line, granted unto Aquilla Sugg, assignee of the heirs of Johnston Cherry, a tract of land containing 640 acres in Davidson County on the second creek above Stuarts Creek on the east side of Stones River adjoining a corner of George Augustus Sugg's Warrant No. 2768. Surveyed for Aquilla Sugg Mar 20, 1788 by William Nash, D.S. in consequence of a Military Warrant No. 2446. Located May 25, 1786. Jan 17, 1789.

Page   67 - AQUILLA SUGG - Territory of the United States &c - July 30, 1792
            North Carolina No. 933. By an Act for the relief of the Officers and Soldiers of the Continental Line, in consideration of the bravery and zeal of Mathew Pollard, a private in the said line, granted unto Aquilla Sugg, assignee of the heirs of Mathew Pollard, a tract of land containing 640 acres in Davidson County on the waters of the first creek above Stones Lick Creek on the east side of Stones River. Surveyed for

Aquilla Sugg May 10, 1788 by William Nash, D.S. in consequence of a Military Warrant No. 1510. Located Apr 3, 1788. May 18, 1789.

Page   67 -   AQUILLA SUGG - Territory of the United States &c - July 30, 1792
            North Carolina No. 934.   By an Act for the relief of the Officers and Soldiers of the Continental Line, in consideration of the bravery and zeal of Solomon Parker, a private in the said line, granted unto Aquilla Sugg, assignee of Solomon Parker, a tract of land containing 640 acres in Davidson County on the second creek above Stuarts Creek on the east side of Stones River adjoining George A. Suggs on the lower side. Surveyed for Aquillla Sugg May 15, 1788 by William Nash, D.S. in consequence of a Military Warrant No. 2214. Located Apr 5, 1788. May 18, 1789.

Page   67 -   AQUILLA SUGG - Territory of the United States &c - July 30, 1792
            North Carolina No. 887.   By an Act for the relief of the Officers and Soldiers of the Continental Line, in consideration of the bravery and zeal of Rice Price, a private of the said line, granted unto Aquilla Sugg, assignee of the heirs of Rice Price, a tract of land containing 640 acres in Davidson County on the first creek above Stones Lick Creek on the east side of Stones River adjoining George Augustus Sugg's corner of a survey of 640 acres, Warrant No. 2236.   Surveyed for Aquila Sugg Mar 20, 1788 by William Nash, D.S. in consequence of a Military Warrant No. 2218. Located May 25, 1786. Jan 17, 1789.

Page   68 -   AQUILLA SUGG - Territory of the United States &c - July 30, 1792
            North Carolina No. 920.   By an Act for the relief of the Officers and Soldiers of the Continental Line, in consideration of the bravery and zeal of Joshua Fowler, a private in the said line, granted unto Aquilla Sugg, assignee of the heirs of Joshua Fowler, a tract of land containing 640 acres in Davidson County on the south side of Cumberland River and on the waters of the first creek above Stones Lick on the east fork of Stones River adjoining Hambleton's corner.   Surveyed for said Sugg (date not listed) by William Nash. D.S. in consequence of a Military Warrant No. 1503.   Located Apr 2, 1788. May 18, 1789.

Page   68 -   AQUILLA SUGG - Territory of the United States &c - July 30, 1792
            North Carolina No. 927.   By an Act for the relief of the Officers and Soldiers of the Continental Line, in consideration of the bravery and zeal of JesseDavis, a private in the said line, granted unto Aquilla Sugg, assignee of the heirs of Jesse Davis, a tract of land containing 640 acres in Davidson County on the east side of the main fork of Stones River adjoining John Read's corner of a survey of 640 acres.   Surveyed for Aquilla Sugg May 10, 1788 by William Nash. D.S. in consequence of a Military Warrant No. 2800. Located Apr 5, 1788. May 18, 1789.

Page   68 -   AQUILLA SUGG - Territory of the United States &c - July 30, 1792
            North Carolina No. 988.   By an Act for the relief of the Officers and Soldiers of the Continental Line, in consideration of the bravery and zeal of Job. Sanders, a private in the said line, granted unto Aquilla Sugg, assignee of the heirs of Job. Sanders, a tract of 640 acres in Davidson County on the headwaters of the west fork of the first creek above Stones Lick Creek on the east side of Stones River adjoining George Suggof the mouth of his survey Warrant No. 2766. Surveyed for said Sugg May 15, 1788 by William

Nash, D.S. in consequence of a Military Warrant No. 1511. Located Apr 3, 1788. May 18, 1789.

Page   69 -   AQUILLA SUGG - Territory of the United States &c - July 30, 1792
North Carolina No. 919. By an Act for the relief of Officers and Soldiers of the Continental Line, in consideration of the bravery and zeal of Joshua Fowler, a private in the said line, granted unto Aquilla Sugg, assignee of the heirs of Joshua Fowler, a tract of land containing 640 acres in Davidson County on the south side of Cumberland River on the east side of Stones River and on the first creek above Stones Lick Creek adjoining another survey of said Sugg and William Nash's survey with Logue's line. Surveyed for Aquilla Sugg Mar 18, 1788 by William Nash in consequence of a Military Warrant No. 2416. Located May 25, 1786. May 18, 1789.

Page   69 -   AQUILLA SUGG - Territory of the United States &c - July 30, 1792
North Carolina No. 918. By an Act for the relief of the Officers and Soldiers of the Continental Line, in consideration of the bravery and zeal of John Blackwell, a private in the said line, granted unto Aquilla Sugg, assignee of the heirs of John Blackwell, a tract of land containing 640 acres in Davidson County on the east side of Stones River on the first creek above Stuarts Creek beginning three or four miles from Stones River. Surveyed for Aquilla Sugg Jan 10, 1788 by William Nash, D.S. in consequence of a Military Warrant No. 1505. Located Apr 5, 1788. May 18, 1789.

Page   69 -   AQUILLA SUGG - Territory of the United States &c - July 31, 1792
North Carolina No. 891. By an Act for the relief of the Officers and Soldiers of the Continental Line, in consideration of the bravery and zeal of Peter Lancers, a private in the said line, granted unto Aquilla Sugg, assignee of the heirs of Peter Lancer, a tract of land containing 640 acres in Davidson County on the west side of the main fork of Stones River adjoining a survey of John Read's 640 acres, Warrant No. 1547. Surveyed for Aquilla Sugg (no date given) by William Nash, D.S. in consequence of a Military Warrant No. 3424 (?). Located Mar 1, 1786. Jan 13, 1789.

Page   70 -   WILLIAM PARR - Territory of the United States &c - Jan 31, 1792
North Carolina No. 117. By an Act for the relief of the Officers and Soldiers of the Ontinental Line, in consideration of the bravery and zeal of William Parr, a private in the said line, granted unto William Parr a tract of land containing 274 acres in Davidson County on the north side of Cumberland River on the first branch below the mouth of Red River. Surveyed for William Parr Jan 25, 1785 by Thomas Molloy, D.S. in consequence of a Military Warrant No. 992. Located Oct 7, 1784. Mar 7, 1786.

Page   70 -   MICHAEL GLAVES - Territory of the United States &c - July 31, 1792
North Carolina No. 297. For 10 lbs per 100 acres paid by Michael Glaves was granted a tract of land containing 640 acres in Davidson County on the south side of Cumberland River about a mile and a half below Jones' improvement. Surveyed for said Glaves Sept 10, 1789 by Henry Bradford, D.S. in consequence of a Warrant No. 563. Entry Aug 3, 1784. Nov 17, 1789.

Page   70 -   THOMAS MOLLOY - Territory of the United States &c - July 31, 1792

North Carolina No. 304. For 10 lbs per 100 acres paid by Thomas Molloy was granted a tract of land containing 640 acres in Davidson County on the bank ofCumberland River, Elijah, Elisha and William Gower's corner and Russell Gower's corner. Surveyed for Thomas Molloy Apr 3, 1789 by himself in consequence of a Warrant No. 537. Entered July 17, 1784. Nov 17, 1790.

Page   71 -   THOMAS MOLLOY - Territory of the United States &c - July 31, 1792

North Carolina No. 1293. By an Act for the relief of the Officers and Soldiers of the Continental Line, in consideration of the bravery and zeal of Jennings Brown, a private in the said line, granted unto Thomas Molloy, assignee of Jennings Brown, a tract of land containing 228 acres in Davidson County on the north side of Cumberland Riverat two miles above Marrow Bone Creek adjoining Martin Armstrong's corner. Surveyed for said Thomas Molloy by himself Oct 18, 1786 in consequence of a Military Warrant No. 1690. Located May 22, 1786. 16 of __ 1790.

Page   71 -   FREDERICK STUMP - Territory of the United States &c - July 31, 1792

North Carolina No. 301. For 10 lbs per 100 acres paid by Frederick Stump was granted a tract of land containing 640 acres in Davidson County on Whites Creek adjoining Frederick Stump's line. Surveyed for Frederick Stump July 13, 1784 by James Sanders, D.S. agreeable to a Warrant No. 138. Entered Jan 16, 1784. Nov 17, 1790.

Page   71 -   JACOB BLOUNT - Territory of the United States &c - Aug 1, 1792

North Carolina No. 304. For 10 lbs per 100 acres paid by Jacob Blount was granted a tract of land containing 5000 acres in the Western District on the south side of Big Hatcha adjoining a corner of John Estes' survey No. 2145. Surveyed for said Jacob Blount Nov 11, 1786 by Isaac Roberts, D.S. in consequence of a Warrant No. 1253. Dated June 24, 1784. Apr 25, 1789.

Page   72 -   ROBINSON MUMFORD - Territory of the United States &c - Aug 1, 1792

North Carolina No. 306. For 10 lbs per 100 acres paid by Robinson Mumford was granted a tract of land containing 5000 acres in the Western District on the waters of Big Hatcha River on the north side adjoining a corner of Robinson Mumford's entry No. 1256. Surveyed for Robinson Mumford Nov 13, 1786 by Isaac Roberts, D.S. in consequence of a Warrant No. 2098. Dated Jan 20, 1785. Apr 25, 1789.

Page   72 -   ROBINSON MUMFORD - Territory of the United States &c - Aug 1, 1792

North Carolina No. 302. For 10 lbs per 100 acres paid by Robinson Mumford was granted a tract of land containing 5000 acres in the Western District on the east side of the Mississippi River adjoining a corner of Jas. Porterfield's entry No. 491. Surveyed for Robinson Mumford Oct 5, 1786 by Isaac Roberts, D.S. in consequence of a Warrant No. 1257. Dated June 24, 1784. Apr 25, 1789.

Page   72 -   ROBINSON MUMFORD - Territory of the United States &c - Aug 1, 1792

North Carolina No. 300. For 10 lbs per 100 acres paid by Robinson Mumford was granted a tract of land containing 5000 acres in the Western District on the south side of Big Hatcha adjoining Jacob Blount's corner of entry No. 1253. Surveyed for said

Robinson Mumford Nov 12, 1786 by Isaac Roberts, D.S. in consequence of a Warrant No. 1256. Dated June 24, 1784. Apr 25, 1785.

Page   73 - JOHN EATON - Territory of the United States &c - Aug 1, 1792
         North Carolina No. 1070. By an Act for the relief if the Officers and Soldiers of the Continental Line, in consideration of the bravery and zeal of Seth Spear, a private on the said line, granted unto John Eaton, assignee of Seth Spear, a tract of land containing 640 acres in Davidson County on the north side of Cumberland Riveron the waters of Persons Creek on the waters of Red River adjoining Johnathan Drake's corner and Renden Blount's line. Surveyed for John Eaton June 23, 1786 by Robert Weakley, D.S. in consequence of a Military Warrant No. 2499. Located Apr 28, 1786. Nov 14, 1789.

Page   73 - THOMAS PASTURES - Territory of the United States &c - Aug 1, 1792
         North Carolina 501. By an Act for the relief of the Officers and Soldiers of the Continental Line, in consideration of the bravery and zeal of Thomas Pastures, a lieutenant in the said line, granted unto Thomas Pastures a tract of land containing 2560 acres in Davidson County on the east side of Big Harpeth River adjoining Alexander Nelson's corner. Surveyed for Thomas Pastures 16 Jan 1786 by Robert Nelson, D.S. in consequence of a Military Warrant No. 299. Located 28 Aug 1784. Sept 15, 1787.

Page   73 - HOWEL TATUM - Territory of the United States &c - Aug 1, 1792
         North Carolina No. 1422. By an Act for the relief of the Officers and Soldiers of the Continental Line, in consideration of the bravery and zeal of Francis Newham, granted unto said Tatum a tract of land containing 640 acres in Davidson County on the north side of Cumberland River on Marrow Bone Creek adjoining George A. Sugg's corner. Surveyed for Howel Tatum May 13, 1791 by George Walker in consequence of a Warrant No. 3681. Located May 11, 1791. Nov 20, 1791.

Page   74 - CHARLES GILMORE - Territory of the United States &c - Aug 1, 1792
         North Carolina No. 1075. By an Act for the relief of the Officers and Soldiers of the Continental Line, in consideration of the bravery and zeal of Jacob Watson, a private in the said line, granted unto Charles Gilmore, assignee of Jacob Watson, a tract of land containing 640 acres in Davidson County on the north side of Cumberland River on the south side of Sycamore Creek adjoining a ridge George Frazer's corner. Surveyed for Charles Gilmore Sept 7, 1789 by Robert Weakley in consequence of a Military Warrant No. 3231. Located Sept 7, 1789. Nov 14, 1789.

Page   74 - CHARLES GILMORE - Territory of the United States &c - Aug 3, 1792
         North Carolina No. 535. By an Act for the relief of the Officers and Soldiers of the Continental Line, in consideration of the bravery and zeal of Robert Sherrod, a private in the said line, granted unto Charles Gilmore, assignee of the heirs of Robert Sherrod, a tract of land containing 640 acres in Davidson County on the north side of Cumberland River near the road that leads from Nashville to Red River on the first branch of Sycamore Creek, that said road crosses adjoining Readen Blount's corner. Surveyed for Charles Gilmore Aug 10, 1786 by Robert Weakley, D.S. in consequence of a Military Warrant No. 1979. Located May 12, 1786. Sept 15, 1787.

Page   74 - CHARLES GILMORE - Territory of the United States &c - Aug 3, 1792

North Carolina No. 476. By an Act for the relief of the Officers and Soldiers of the Continental Line, in consideration of the bravery and zeal of Mathew Dawson, a private in the said line, granted unto Charles Gilmore, assignee of Mathew Dawson, a tract of land containing 640 acres in Davidson County joining the east boundary of a military survey, north west 141, beginning on Spring Creek. Surveyed for Charles Gilmore July 15, 1786 by Joseph Brock, D.S. in consequence of a Military Warrant No. 3269. Located May 15, ___. Sept 15, 1789.

Page   75 - CHARLES GILMORE - Territory of the United States &c - Aug 3, 1792

North Carolina No. 728. By an Act for the relief of the officers and Soldiers of the Continental Line, in consideration of the bravery and zeal of Authur Pollock, a private in the said line, granted unto Charles Gilmore, assignee of Authur Pollock, a tract of land containing 640 acres in Davidson County on the Cumberland River on the north waters of Sycamore Creek adjoining a survey of Robert Weakley, includes Turnbull's horse stamp, and Elijah Robertson's corner, and Mark Noble's corner, also Josiah Ramsey's line, to John Nichol's corner. Surveyed for Charles Gilmore Oct 17, 1786 by Robert Weakley, D.S. in consequence of a Military Warrant No. 3503. Located May 15, 1786. July 11, 1788.

Page   75 - CHARLES GILMORE - Territory of the United States &c - Aug 4, 1792

North Carolina No. 536. By an Act for the relief of the Officers and Soldiers of the Continental Line, in consideration of the bravery and zeal of Francis Buman, a private in the said line, granted unto Charles Gilmore, assignee of the heirs of said Francis Buman, a tract of land containing 640 acres in Davidson County on the north side of Cumberland River on the headwaters of Little Brush Creek that runs into the Sulphur Fork. Surveyed for Charles Gilmore Aug 10, 1786 by Robert Weakley, D.S. in consequence of a Military Warrant No. 1987. Located May 12, 1786. Sept 15, 1787.

Page   75 - CHARLES GILMORE - Territory of the United States &c - Aug 4, 1792

North Carolina No. 610. By an Act for the relief of the Officers and Soldiers of the Continental Line, in consideration of the bravery and zeal of Robert Hagar, a private in the said line, granted unto Charles Gilmore, assignee of the heirs of Robert Hagar, a tract of land containing 640 acres in Davidson County on the waters of Stones Creek adjoining Col. Murfree's survey 1168 acres. Which land was surveyed for Charles Gilmore May 17, 1786 by Joseph Brock, D.S. in consequence of a Military Warrant No. 2659. Located 15 May 1786. Sept 15, 1787.

Page   76 - CHARLES GILMORE - Territory of the United States &c - Aug 6, 1792

North Carolina No. 1096. By an Act for the relief of the Officers and Soldiers of the Continental Line, in consideration of the bravery and zeal of Hampton Bowden, a private in the said line, granted unto Charles Gilmore, assignee of Hampton Bowden, a tract of land containing 640 acres in Davidson County on the north side of Cumberland River on both sides of the Long Fork of Sycamore Creek adjoining David Edwards' corner. Surveyed for Charles Gilmore Sept 8, 1789 by Robert Weakley, D.S. in consequence of a Military Warrant No. 3418. Located Jan 16, 1789. Nov 26, 1789.

Page   76 -   CHARLES GILMORE - Territory of the United States &c - Aug 6, 1792

North Carolina No. 1092. By an Act for the relief of the Officers and Soldiers of the Continental Line, in consideration of the bravery and zeal of George Manshare, a private in the said line, granted unto Charles Gilmore, assignee of George Manshare, a tract of land containing 640 acres in Davidson County on the north side of Cumberland River on the north branches of Sycamore Creek adjoining a survey of Robert Weakley on the west, which includes Turnbull's horse stamp, also Anthony Hart's line. Surveyed for Charles Gilmore Aug 17, 1786 by Robert Weakley, D.S. in consequence of a Military Warrant No. 3514. Located May 15, 1786. Nov 26, 1789.

Page   76 -   JOSEPH MONTFORT - Territory of the United States &c - Aug 9, 1792

North Carolina No. 74. By an Act for the relief of the Officers and Soldiers of the Continental Line, in consideration of the bravery and zeal of Joseph Montfort, a captain in the said line, granted unto Joseph Montfort a tract of land containing 3840 acres in Davidson County on the main east fork of Stones River. Surveyed for Joseph Montfort July 12, 1785 by Robert Hays in consequence of a Military Warrant No. 340. Located June 29, 1784. Mar 10, 1786.

Page   77 -   WILLIAM MUIR - Territory of the United States &c - Aug 9, 1792

This indenture made 31 Mar 1791 between Joseph Montfort of Halifax County, State of North Carolina of one part and William Muir of same place of the other part. Joseph Montfort conveyed unto William Muir a tract of land containing 3840 acres in Davidson County on Stones River. Said land being all that tract of land granted by State of North Carolina to the said Joseph Montfort for his services as captain in the Continental Line, by deed dated 14 Mar 1786. Test: James Tatum and Archibald Jett and alias. 7 Aug 1792.

Page   77 -   ROBERT WEAKLEY - Territory of the United States &c - Aug 10, 1792

North Carolina No. 114. By an Act for the relief of the Officers and Soldiers of the Continental Line, in consideration of the services of Martin Armstrong, surveyor, granted unto Robert Weakley, assignee of said Armstrong, a tract of land containing 38 acres in Davidson County on the north waters of Little Harpeth adjoining Thomas Molloy's tract of 2500 on the east and also James Dean's corner and Abraham Jones' corner. Surveyed for Robert Weakley by himself Mar 21, 1791. Located Mar 10, 1791. Dec 16, 1791.

Page   78 -   GEORGE McWHIRTER - Territory of the United States &c - Sept 3, 1792

North Carolina No. 306. For 10 lbs per 100 acres paid by George McWhirter was granted a tract of land containing 640 acres in Davidson County beginning on the Cumberland River, one quarter of a mile above the mouth of Marrow Bone Creek. Surveyed for George McWhirter Mar 10, 1789 by Thomas Molloy, D.S. agreeable to a Warrant No. 455. Entered May 20, 1784. Nov 17, 1790.

Page   78 -   PETER RHEM - Territory of the United States &c - Sept 10, 1792

North Carolina No. 1052. By an Act for the relief of the Officers and Soldiers of the Continental Line, in consideration of the bravery and zeal of Peter Rhem, a private in the said line, granted unto Peter Rhem a tract of land containing 428 acres in

Davidson County on the south side of Cumberland River about one mile from the same and on the first large creek below Red River by same called Budds Creek adjoining Thomas Davis's boundary. Surveyed for said Peter Rhem Nov 18, 1785 by Thomas Molloy, D.S. in consequence of a Military Warrant No. 528. Located July 2, 1784. Nov 14, 1789.

Page   78 -   THOMAS HARDIMAN - Territory of the United States &c - Nov 19, 1792
              North Carolina No. 112.   By an Act for the relief of the Officers and Soldiers of the Continental Line, in consideration of the services of Johnathan Drake, a sergeant in the Commissioners guard, granted unto Thomas Hardiman, assignee of said Drake, a tract of land containing 640 acres in Davidson County on the south side of Cumberland River on the Little Harpeth adjoining Samuel McCutchen's Preemption and Daniel Dunam's west boundary. Surveyed for Thomas Hardiman Dec 10, 1789 by Jas. Mulherin, D.S. in consequence of a Warrant No. 367. Dated Mar 23, 1784. Dec 20, 1791.

Page   79 -   JOHN CHILDERS - Territory of the United States &c - Nov 19, 1792
              North Carolina No. 377.   For 10 lbs per 100 acres paid by John Childers was granted a tract of land containing 2000 acres in the Western District on the third creek above the mouth of Duck River adjoining said Childers' entry No. 1511. Surveyed for John Childers Feb 23, 1791 by Isaac Roberts, D.S. in consequence of a warrant from the secretary's office 1512. Dated Feb 20, 1784.

Page   79 -   JOHN CHILDERS - Territory of the United States &c - Nov 19, 1792
              North Carolina No. 374.   For 10 lbs per 100 acres paid by John Childers was granted a tract of land containing 5000 acres in the Western District on the south side of Tennessee, beginning at the mouth of the third creek above the mouth of Duck river. Surveyed for John Childers Feb 22, 1791 by Isaac Roberts, D.S. in consequence of a Warrant No. 1511. Dated Feb 20, 1784. Dec 20, 1791.

Page   79 -   JOHN CHILDERS - Territory of the United States &c - Nov 19, 1792
              North Carolina No. 376.   For 10 lbs per 100 acres paid by John Childers was granted a tract of land containing 5000 acres in the Western District on the south side of Tennessee River, beginning below the mouth of the fourth creek above the mouth of Duck River. Surveyed for John Childers Feb 22, 1791 by Isaac Roberts, D.S. in consequence of a Warrant No. 1510. Dated Feb 2, 1784. Dec 20, 1791.

Page   80 -   JAMES MENESS - Territory of the United States &c - Nov 19, 1792
              North Carolina No. 298.   For 10 lbs per 100 acres paid by James Meness was granted a tract of land containing 640 acres in Davidson County on the west side of Mill Creek adjoining Thomas Hardiman's line. Surveyed for James Meness June 9, 1788 agreeable to a Warrant No. 78. Located Jan 12, 1784. Nov 17, 1790.

Page   80 -   JAMES MENESS - Territory of the United States &c - Nov 19, 1792
              North Carolina No. 101.   By an Act for the relief of the Officers and Soldiers of the Continental Line, in consideration of the services of James Meness, one of the Commissioners Guard, was granted a tract of land containing 320 acres in Davidson County on the west side of Mill Creek. Surveyed for James Meness June 9, 1788 by John Buchanan, D.S. agreeable to a Warrant No. 418. Nov 16, 1790.

Page   80 -   DANIEL CHAMBERS - Territory of the United States &c - Nov 20, 1792
North Carolina No. 305. For 10 lbs per 100 acres paid by Daniel Chambers was granted a tract of land containing 640 acres in Davidson County on the south fork of Whites Creek adjoining William Logan's Preemption and Daniel Frazers' boundary. Surveyed for Daniel Chambers Sept 17, 1789 by Sampson Williams, D.S. agreeable to a Warrant No. 558. Entered July 28, 1784. Nov 19, 1792.

Page   81 -   ALEXANDER REED - Territory of the United States &c - Nov 20, 1792
North Carolina No. 1143. By an Act for the relief of the Officers and Soldiers of the Continental Line, in consideration of the bravery and zeal of Thomas Jimmison, a private in the said line, granted unto Alexander Reed, assignee of Thomas Jimmison, a tract of land containing 228 acres in Sumner County on the north side of Cumberland River on Drakes Creek joining the west boundary of William Montgomery's Preemption. Surveyed for Alexander Reed Nov 24, 1787 by Daniel James, D.S. in consequence of a Military Warrant No. 875. Located Aug 9, 1785. Nov 14, 1789.

Page   81 -   JAMES BOSLEY - Territory of the United States &c - Nov 20, 1792
North Carolina No. 2. For 141 lbs paid by James Bosley, directing the sale of the Salt Lick and Springs in Mero District, granted unto James Bosley a tract of land containing 640 acres in Davidson County including Dentons Lick begining on a line formerly run by the Commissioners about the said Lick, and on the bank of Cumberland River. Surveyed for James Bosley Dec 22, 1790 by Anthony Foster, D.S. inconsequence said Act of General Assembly at Fayetteville (NC) Dec 22, 1789. Dated Dec 20, 1791.

Page   81 -   JAMES BOSLEY - Territory of the United States &c - Nov 20, 1792
North Carolina No. 112. By an Act for the relief of the Officers and Soldiers of the Continental Line, in consideration of the services of Martin Armstrong, surveyor, granted unto James Bosley, assignee of the said Armstrong, a tract of land containing 75 acres in Davidson County on the south side of Cumberland River adjoining John Bell's line. Surveyed for James Bosley Jan 31, 1791 by George Walker, D.S. in consequence of the Service Right of said Armstrong. Dec 20, 1791.

Page   82 -   GEORGE PIRTLE - Territory of the United States &c - Nov 21, 1792
North Carolina No. 310. For 10 lbs per 100 acres paid by George Pirtle was granted a tract of land containing 640 acres in Sumner County on the waters of Spencers Creek adjoining the Preemption of George Pirtle. Surveyed for said George Pirtle Mar 20, 1788 by John Buchanan, D.S. agreeable to a Warrant No. 798. Entered Feb 12, 1788. Nov 17, 1790.

Page   82 -   JOHN STERN SINGLETARY - Territory of the United States &c -
Nov 21, 1792
This indenture made 14 Apr 1792 between Robert Thompson of Davidson County of one part and John Stern Singletary of same place of the other part. Robert Thompson conveyed unto John Stern Singletary a tract of land containing 130 acres in Davidson County adjoining Robert Thompson's line, John Singletary's corner and said land being part of a tract of 640 acres granted to James Thompson, late deceased, in right of Preemption by patent dated Apr 17, 1786 and by heirship became the property of the said

269

Robert Thompson. Test: John Marney, Nehemiah Courtney and James Donnelly. Oct Term 1792.

Page   83 -   JAMES BRENAN - Territory of the United States &c - Nov 21, 1792
            This indenture made 27 Apr 1791 between Gabriel Vingsborough of Wilmington, County of New Hanover, State of North Carolina of one part and James Brenan of the town of Fayetteville, of Cumberland County, North Carolina of the other part. Gabriel Vingsborough conveyed unto James Brenan a tract of land containing 535 acres in Davidson County on the waters of Mill Creek adjoining Edward Cox's boundary and James Bosley's boundary. Test: Joshua Handly (also spelled Hadley) and J. Hurns.

Page   83 - GEORGE PIRTLE - Territory of the United States &c - Nov 21, 1792
            North Carolina No. 311. For 10 lbs per 100 acres paid by George Pirtle was granted a tract of land containing 640 acres in Sumner County on the waters of Spencers CreekDerngeth's (?) boundary. Surveyed for George Pirtle Mar 20, 1785 by John Buchanan, D.S. agreeable to a Warrant No. 683. Entered Feb 15, 1785. Nov 17, 1790.

Page   84 - JOHN WILLIAMSON - Territory of the United States &c - Nov 22, 1792
            North Carolina No. 531. We have granted unto John Williamson, assignee of John Haynes, a private in the Continental Line of this state, a tract of land containing 228 acres in Davidson County on the waters of Mill Creek adjoining John Rice's corner. Dated 15 Sept 1787.

Page   84 - SAMUEL MOSBEY - Territory of the United States &c - Nov 22, 1792
            North Carolina No. 106. By an Act for the relief of the Officers and Soldiers of the Continental Line, in consideration of the service of Samuel Mosbey, one of the Commissioners Guard, granted unto said Mosbey a tract of land containing 320 acres in Davidson County on the headwaters of Hays Creek a branch of Big Harpeth River adjoining Daniel Williams' corner. Surveyed for Samuel Mosbey Jan 29, 1790 by John Buchanan, D.S. in consequence of a Warrant No. 444. Entered May 12, 1784. Dec 20, 1791.

Page   84 - THOMAS DICKEY - Territory of the United States &c - Nov 22, 1792
            North Carolina No. 237. By an Act for the relief of the Officers and Soldiers of the Continental Line, in consideration of the bravery and zeal of Alex McDaniel, a corporal in the said line, granted unto Thomas Dickey, assignee of Jane Dickey, heiress of the said Alexander McDaniel, a tract of land containing 1000 acres in Davidson County on the waters of West Harpeth River adjoining Lieut. Robert Hays 2560 acre survey. Surveyed for Thomas Dickey May 2, 1785 by B. William Pollock, D.S. in consequence of a Military Warrant No. 1222. Located Jan 28, 1785. Mar 17, 1786.

Page   85 - JOSEPH KERR - Territory of the United States &c - Nov 23, 1792
            North Carolina No. 686. By an Act for the relief of the officers and Soldiers of the Continental Line, in consideration of the bravery and zeal of Francis Fox, a private in the said line, granted unto Joseph Kerr, assignee of the said Francis Fox, a tract of land containing 274 acres in Davidson County on a branch of Big Harpeth River, and on the west side of said river adjoining Donaldson's line. Surveyed for said Kerr (no date given) by John Donaldson, D.S. in consequence of a Military Warrant No. 498. Located May 2, 1785. Dec

8, 1787.

Page   85 -   JAMES LOCK - Territory of the United States &c - Nov 23, 1792
            North Carolina No. 723.   By an Act for the relief of the Officers and
Soldiers of the Continental Line, in consideration of the bravery and zeal of Jonathan
Zealott, a private in the said line, granted unto James Lock, assignee of Jonathan Zealott,
a tract of land containing 274 acres in Davidson County on the main Tennessee River
beginning just above where the Virginia Line strikes said river.   Surveyed for James Lock
Sept 20, 1787 by Isaac Roberts, D.S. in consequence of a Military Warrant No. 3234.
Located Sept 3, 1784.

Page   85 -   STOCKLEY DONALDSON - Territory of the United States &c - Nov 23, 1792
            North Carolina No. 959.   By an Act for the relief of the Officers and
Soldiers of the Continental Line, in consideration of the bravery and zeal of Haddin Hudger,
·a private in the said line, granted unto Stockley Donelson, assignee of the heirs of Haddin
Hudger, a tract of land containing 640 acres in Davidson County near the head of the first
creek that runs into Stones River above   Stones Creek adjoining John Howel's survey.
Surveyed for Stockley Donaldson Mar 22, 1788 by William Nash, D.S. in consequence of a
Military Warrant No. 1830. Located May 19, 1786.May 11, 1789.

Page   86 -   THOMAS DICKEY - Territory of the United States &c - Nov 23, 1792
            North Carolina No. 254.   By an Act for the relief of the Officers and
Soldiers of the Continental Line, in consideration of the bravery and zeal of Joseph Eller, a
private in the said line, granted unto Thomas Dickey, assignee of John Eller, heir of Joseph
Eller, a tract of land containing 640 acres in Davidson County on the waters of Stones
River adjoining Col. Martin Armstrong's corner.   Surveyed for Thomas Dickey (date not
listed) by Robert Hays, D.S. in consequence of a Military Warrant No. 1221.   Located Mar
9, 1785. Mar 7, 1786.

Page   86 -   MARTIN ARMSTRONG - Territory of the United States &c - Nov 24, 1792
            North Carolina No. 1.   By an Act for the relief of the Officers and Soldiers
of the Continental Line, in consideration of the services of Martin Armstrong, surveyor,
granted unto Martin Armstrong 3840 acres in Davidson County on both sides of Sugar
Creek.   Beginning at Captain Benjamin Carter's corner on the Officers and Soldiers south
boundary line.   Surveyed for Martin Armstrong Sept 10, 1785 by Robert Hays, D.S. in
consequence of a Service Right, entered Mar 28, 1784. Feb 16, 1786.

Page   86 -   ROBERT NELSON - Territory of the United States &c - Nov 24, 1792
            North Carolina No. 1448.   By an Act for the relief of the Officers and
Soldiers of the Continental Line, in consideration of the bravery and zeal of Samuel
Dawden, a private in the said line, granted unto Robert Nelson, assignee of Samuel Dawden,
a tract of land containing 640 acres in Davidson County on the east side of Big Harpeth on
a north branch of Nelsons Creek adjoining said Nelson's other claim of 640 acres.   Surveyed
for said Robert Nelson by himself May 30, 1791 in consequence of a Military Warrant No.
1286. Located Apr 13, 1791. Dec 20, 1791.

Page   87 -   DAVID SHELTON - Territory of the United States &c - Nov 30, 1792
North Carolina No. 1260. By an Act for the relief of the Officers and Soldiers of the Continental Line, in consideration of the bravery and zeal of William Long, a private in the said line, granted unto David Shelton, assignee of assignee of William Long, a tract of land containing 640 acres in Davidson County on the waters of Round Lick Creek. Surveyed for David Shelton Nov 14, 1789 by John Buchanan, D.S. in consequence of a Military Warrant No. 1002. Located Sept 19, 1785. Nov 16, 1790.

Page   87 -   PHILLIPS PHILLIPS - Territory of the United States &c - Nov 30, 1792
North Carolina No. 1076. By an Act for the relief of the Officers and Soldiers of the Continental Line, in consideration of the bravery and zeal of Peter Johnston, a private in the said line, granted unto Phillip Phillip, assignee of Peter Johnston, a tract of land containing 640 acres in Davidson County on the waters of Stones River and Mill Creek adjoining William Gowen's corner. Surveyed for Phillip Phillips Dec 4, 1788 by John Buchanan, D.S. in consequence of a Military Warrant No. 2192. Located Feb 25, 1786. Nov 26, 1789.

Page   87 -   PHILLIP PHILLIPS & MICHAEL CAMPBELL - Territory of the United States &c - Dec 1, 1792
North Carolina No. 1349. By an Act for the relief of the Officers and Soldiers of the Continental Line, in consideration of the bravery and zeal of Henry Bennett, a private in the said line, granted unto Philip Phillips and Michael Campbell, assignees of the heirs ofHenry Bennett, a tract of land containing 640 acres in Davidson County on the east side of Stones River joining William Nash's survey. Surveyed for said Phillips and Campbell July 30, 1790 by William Nash, D.S. in consequence of a Military Warrant No. 2837. Located July 6, 1790. Nov 16, 1790.

Page   88 -   PHILIP PHILLIPS & MICHAEL CAMPBELL - Territory of the United States Dec 3, 1892
North Carolina No. 1315. By an Act for the relief of the Officers and Soldiers of the Continental Line, in consideration of the bravery and zeal of James Grace, a private in the said line, granted unto Philip Phillips and Michael Campbell, assignees of the heirs of James Grace, a tract of land containing 640 acres in Tennessee County on the south side of Cumberland on the Middle Fork of Bartons Creek adjoining a survey of said Phillips and Campbell's No. 2188. Surveyed for said Phillips and Campbell July 28, 1790 by George Walker, D.S. in consequence of a Military Warrant No. 2124. Located July 25, 1790. Nov 16, 1790.

Page   88 -   JOHN ELLIOTT - Territory of the United States &c - Dec 3, 1792
North Carolina No. 1289. By an Act for the relief of the Officers and Soldiers of the Continental Line, in consideration of the bravery and zeal of John McVey, a private in the said line, granted unto John Elliott, assignee of the heirs of John McVey, a tract of land containing 640 acres in Davidson County on the west fork of Stones River. Beginning at the mouth of Overalls Creek on the west side of said creek. Surveyed for John Elliott Mar 18, 1786 by William Nash, D.S. in consequence of a Military Warrant No. 270. Located July 8, 1784. Nov 16, 1790.

Page 88 - JOHN ELLIOTT - Territory of the United States &c - Dec 3, 1792
North Carolina No. 1245. By an Act for the relief of the Officers and Soldiers of the Continental line, in consideration of the bravery and zeal of James Faulks, a private in the said line, granted unto John Elliott, assignee of James Faulks, a tract of land containing 640 acres in Davidson County on the west fork of Stones River and east side of said fork about four miles from the fork including a large spring. Surveyed for John Elliott May 19, 1786 by William Nash, D.S. in consequence of a Military Warrant No. 268. Located 8 July 1784. Nov 16, 1790.

Page 89 - THEODORUS MALLETT - Territory of the United States &c - Dec 4, 1792
This indenture made 3 Apr 1792 between William Gunn and Sally Gunn, his wife, of Davidson County of the one part and Theodorus Mallett of the other part. William Gunn and Sally Gunn conveyed unto Theodorus Mallett a tract of land 640 acres, granted to Elijah Robertson by virtue of a Military Warrant, granted unto Isaac Dunbar, No. 3307, in Sumner County on the waters of Caney Fork River, to his tract as assignee of the heirs of Robert Nixon. Test: Jesse Hood and William Hickman. 24 Nov 1792.

Page 89 - JASON THOMPSON - Territory of the United States &c - Dec 4, 1792
North Carolina No. 1464. By an Act for the relief of the Officers and Soldiers of the Continental Line, in consideration of the bravery and zeal of Joseph Branner, a private in the said line, granted unto Jason Thompson, assignee of said Joseph Branner, a tract of land containing 640 acres in Tennessee County south side of Cumberland River and on both sides of west fork of Jones Creek adjoining John Larkins's corner. Surveyed for Jason Thompson July 20, 1791 by John Dickson, D.S. in consequence of a Military Warrant No. 2348. Located Dec 21, 1792. Jan 4, 1792.

Page 90 - MICHAEL GLAVES - Territory of the United States &c - Dec 19, 1792
This indenture made 9 Jan 1792 between Daniel Chambers of Natchez District and province of West Florida of one part and Michael Glaves of Davidson County of the other part. Daniel Chambers conveyed unto Michael Glaves a tract of land containing 640 acres in Davidson County adjoining William Loggin's Preemption and Joseph Love's boundary and John Walker's boundary, and Stephen Ray's boundary. Land being a tract of land granted to the said Chambers a Preemption Right as assignee of Dennis Condry. Jan Term 1792.

Page 90 - MICHAEL GLAVES - Territory of the United States &c - Dec 19, 1792
This indenture made 9 Jan 1792 between Daniel Chambers of Natchez District, province of Florida of one part and Michael Glaves of Davidson County of the other part. Daniel Chambers conveyed unto Michael Glaves a tract of land containing 640 acres in Davidson County on the south side of Cumberland River in Jones Bent. Test: James Shaw. Jan term 1792.

LACKEY (LACKY): 112, 113, 191
LACY: 187, 220
LAMB: 260
LAMBERT: 189
LANCASTER: 180, 221
LANCERS: 263
LANDER: 148
LANE (LAIN): 101, 127, 163, 236, 253
LARKIN: 141, 273
LASSETER: 235
LATIMORE: 95, 137, 175
LATON: 80
LAWRENCE (LAURENCE): 91, 141, 142, 178, 193, 194
LAWREY: 147
LAWSON: 42, 43
LEATON: 14, 25
LEE (LEA): 191, 195
LEEPER (LEIPER): 39, 40, 114, 214, 230, 239, 246
LEFEVER: 208
LENEAR (LANIER, LENIER): 16, 17, 60. 61. 62. 65, 84, 86, 87, 93, 105, 106, 112, 119, 120, 135, 137, 180
LEWIS: 11, 59, 77, 119, 120, 122, 132, 183, 196, 223, 228, 239, 240, 245, 246, 253
LINSEY: 1, 2, 5, 6, 7, 8, 9, 11, 12, 19, 62, 76, 77, 82, 83, 84, 85, 87, 88, 89, 93, 139, 180
LINTON (LINTOR): 14, 22, 25, 103
LLEWALLEN: 5, 6
LOCK: 156, 228, 271
LOCKART: 34, 61, 179, 209
LOCKETT: 63, 260
LOGAN: 36, 63, 67, 182, 184, 203, 269
LOGGINS: 36, 52, 63, 76, 83, 85, 87, 158, 159, 161, 181, 193, 194, 234, 235, 273
LOGUE: 183, 191, 263
LOMAX: 89
LONG: 94, 156, 215, 272
LONGMIER: 144, 231
LOOMAS: 64
LOONEY: 6, 191, 196, 197, 214
LOPP: 152
LOVE: 97, 136, 138, 158, 169, 180, 194, 221, 236, 249, 250, 273
LOVING: 111, 196
LOWE (LOW): 245
LUCAS (LUCUS): 7, 8, 17, 84, 117, 138, 139, 159, 163, 195, 196, 203, 209, 231, 238, 240, 241
LYLES: 135
LYNN: 77, 178, 179
LYTLE: 3, 10, 78

MABANE: 14, 65, 66, 86, 217, 241
MACER: 146
MACKEY: 20, 22, 26
MADDRY: 194
MADLIN: 152
MADRIE (MADRY): 132, 254
MAGRAY: 10
MALLETT (MALETT): 179, 194, 273
MALLOBEY: 26
MAN: 60, 70
MANIFEE (MANIFFEE): 26, 40, 56, 57, 112, 163, 164, 215, 236

MANION: 51
MANSHARE: 267
MANSKER: 49, 55, 57, 64, 68, 131, 144, 145, 187, 206, 207
MARLEY: 38, 81, 82
MARLIN: 204
MARNEY: 61, 62, 86, 106, 129, 136, 179, 223, 224, 230, 260, 270
MARR (MARS): 43, 66, 72, 143, 188
MARSHALL (MARSHAL): 35, 36, 39, 40, 44, 46, 123, 126, 143, 146
MARSHAM: 170, 224
MARSONE: 155, 156
MARTIN: 2, 3, 7, 8, 10, 17, 20, 21, 22, 25, 26, 32, 55, 63, 70, 74, 76, 82, 89, 100, 107, 108, 118, 121, 127, 140, 154, 161, 165, 173, 220, 261
MASON: 71, 233
MASSEY: 68
MASTEN: 179
MATHEWS: 73, 94
MATLOCK: 181
MAULDIN (MAULDON): 6, 73, 98, 115, 216
MAXELL (MAXEL): 32, 58, 77, 131, 143, 159, 166, 188
MAXEY (MAXY): 44, 48, 106, 166
MAXWELL: 58, 155
MAY (MAYE): 18, 89
MAYFIELD: 24, 39, 46, 47, 181, 183, 207, 230
MAYORE: 143
MEANS (MEAN): 35, 37
MEARS: 157, 219, 243, 256
MECKLIN (MECLIN): 4, 194
MEELIN: 38, 233
MENESS (MENESSE, MENEES): 10, 119, 203, 220, 237, 253, 268
MERCHANT: 23, 61, 62, 86
MESSICK: 80, 81
MIDDLETON: 209
MILLER: 107, 145, 146, 197
MILLIFORD: 78
MILLS: 33, 154, 189
MILNER: 128
MITCHELL (MITCHEL): 32, 52, 75, 111, 140, 149, 161, 179, 186, 193, 194, 235, 237
MOLLOY (MOLLOW): 1, 2, 3, 4, 5, 6, 7, 8, 9, 10, 11, 12, 13, 15, 16, 17, 19, 20, 23, 30, 32, 33, 36, 38, 44, 45, 48, 49, 54, 62, 67, 80, 82, 84, 85, 86, 89, 90, 91, 92, 98, 104, 106, 109, 110, 111, 128, 139, 140, 141, 143, 144, 149, 154, 155, 156, 157, 158, 159, 163, 164, 166, 167, 168, 181, 182, 188, 192, 193, 199, 200, 204, 207, 208, 209, 214, 216, 217, 218, 220, 222, 225, 230, 239, 243, 244, 245, 247, 248, 249, 250, 257, 259, 260, 261, 263, 264, 267, 268
MONHOUSE: 42
MONTFLORENCE: 42, 43, 44, 82, 86, 95, 97, 105, 126, 127, 129, 133, 136, 137, 140, 158, 161, 168, 169, 170, 175, 176, 177, 178, 181, 192, 193, 221, 222, 224, 237, 239, 243, 252, 255, 258
MONTFORT: 106, 107, 267
MONTGOMERY: 62, 74, 75, 85, 131, 162, 205, 269
MOORE (MORE, MOOR): 11, 12, 16, 23, 30, 46, 47, 51, 53, 60, 64, 71, 73, 93, 96, 101, 130, 152, 161, 163, 165, 168,

279

www.ingramcontent.com/pod-product-compliance
Lightning Source LLC
Chambersburg PA
CBHW021854020426
42334CB00013B/331

* 9 7 8 0 8 9 3 0 8 4 6 1 5 *